Photography Off the Scale

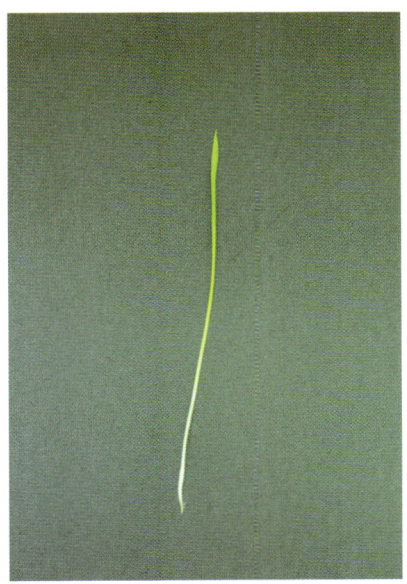

Technicities

Series Editors: John Armitage, Ryan Bishop and Joanne Roberts, Winchester School of Art, University of Southampton

The philosophy of technicities: exploring how technology mediates art, frames design and augments the mediated collective perception of everyday life. Technicities will publish the latest philosophical thinking about our increasingly immaterial technocultural conditions, with a unique focus on the context of art, design and media.

Editorial Advisory Board

Benjamin Bratton, Cheryl Buckley, Sean Cubitt, Clive Dilnot, Jin Huimin, Arthur Kroker, Geert Lovink, Scott McQuire, Gunalan Nadarajan, Elin O'Hara Slavick, Li Shqiao, Geoffrey Winthrop-Young

Published

Lyotard and the Inhuman Condition: Reflections on Nihilism, Information and Art
Ashley Woodward
Critical Luxury Studies: Art, Design, Media
Edited by John Armitage and Joanne Roberts
Cold War Legacies: Systems, Theory, Aesthetics
Edited by John Beck and Ryan Bishop
Fashion and Materialism
Ulrich Lehmann
Queering Digital India: Activisms, Identities, Subjectivities
Edited by Rohit K. Dasgupta and Debanuj DasGupta
Zero Degree Seeing: Barthes/Burgin and Political Aesthetics
Edited by Ryan Bishop and Sunil Manghani
Rhythm and Critique: Technics, Modalities, Practices
Edited by Paola Crespi and Sunil Manghani
Photography Off the Scale: Technologies and Theories of the Mass Image
Edited by Tomáš Dvořák and Jussi Parikka

www.edinburghuniversitypress.com/series/TECH

Photography Off the Scale

Technologies and Theories of the Mass Image

Edited by Tomáš Dvořák and Jussi Parikka

EDINBURGH
University Press

Edinburgh University Press is one of the leading university presses in the UK. We publish academic books and journals in our selected subject areas across the humanities and social sciences, combining cutting-edge scholarship with high editorial and production values to produce academic works of lasting importance. For more information visit our website: edinburghuniversitypress.com

© editorial matter and organisation Tomáš Dvořák and Jussi Parikka, 2021
© the chapters their several authors, 2021

Edinburgh University Press Ltd
The Tun – Holyrood Road, 12(2f) Jackson's Entry, Edinburgh EH8 8PJ

Designed and typeset in Sabon
by Biblichor Ltd, and
printed and bound in Malta by Melita Press

A CIP record for this book is available from the British Library

ISBN 978 1 4744 7881 6 (hardback)
ISBN 978 1 4744 7884 7 (webready PDF)
ISBN 978 1 4744 7882 3 (paperback)
ISBN 978 1 4744 7883 0 (epub)

The right of Tomáš Dvořák and Jussi Parikka to be identified as the Editor of this work has been asserted in accordance with the Copyright, Designs and Patents Act 1988, and the Copyright and Related Rights Regulations 2003 (SI No. 2498).

Contents

Acknowledgements vii
Series Editors' Preface viii
Notes on Contributors ix

1 Introduction: On the Scale, Quantity and Measure of Images
   Jussi Parikka and Tomáš Dvořák 1

I SCALE, MEASURE, EXPERIENCE

2 Mass Image, Anthropocene Image, Image Commons
   Sean Cubitt 25

3 Beyond Human Measure: Eccentric Metrics in Visual Culture
   Tomáš Dvořák 41

4 Living with the Excessive Scale of Contemporary Photography
   Andrew Fisher 61

5 Feeling Photos: Photography, Picture Language and Mood Capture
   Michelle Henning 77

6 Online Weak and Poor Images: On Contemporary Feminist Visual Politics
   Tereza Stejskalová 97

II METAPICTURES AND REMEDIATIONS

7 Photography's Mise en Abyme: Metapictures of Scale in Repurposed Slide Libraries
   Annebella Pollen 113

8 The Failed Photographs of Photography: On the Analogue and Slow Photography Movement
   Michal Šimůnek 140

9 Strangely Unique: Pictorial Aesthetics in the Age of Image Abundance
   Josef Ledvina 158

III MODELS, SCANS AND AI

10 On Seeing Where There's Nothing to See: Practices of Light beyond Photography
    Jussi Parikka 185

11 Planetary Diagrams: Towards an Autographic Theory of Climate Emergency
    Lukáš Likavčan and Paul Heinicker 211

12 Undigital Photography: Image-Making beyond Computation and AI
    Joanna Zylinska 231

13 Coda: Photography in the Age of Massification
    A Correspondence between Joan Fontcuberta and Geoffrey Batchen 253

Names Index 289
Subject Index 293

Acknowledgements

This book was kickstarted at the Film and TV School of the Academy of Performing Arts (FAMU) in Prague and supported by the Czech Science Foundation project Operational Images and Visual Culture: Media Archaeological Investigations (19-26865X). In addition to the institutional support from FAMU, the Czech Science Foundation, and Winchester School of Art at University of Southampton (Jussi Parikka's other institutional affiliation), we are thankful to the many people – colleagues, friends and others – who supported this project with conversations, ideas and suggestions. Thanks go, on behalf of us both as co-editors of the project (and in no particular order), to Ryan Bishop, Sean Cubitt, Pasi Väliaho, Mihaela Brebenel, Carol Macdonald, Michelle Henning, Sunil Manghani, Ed D'Souza, Jane Birkin, Abelardo Gil-Fournier, Simone Venturini, Silvie Demartini, Martin Charvát and Veronika Jirsová.

We also want to thank, together, the Operational Images project team as well as the editors of the Technicities series. We owe a thank you to the Edinburgh University Press staff for their diligence and support in getting this book out and into the world. It has been a pleasure. And we also specifically want to thank Elise Hunchuck for her work and expertise in fine-tuning our language and our arguments. A further thank you to Fiona Screen for the copy editing.

Series Editors' Preface

TECHNOLOGICAL TRANSFORMATION has profound and frequently unforeseen influences on art, design and media. At times technology emancipates art and enriches the quality of design. Occasionally it causes acute individual and collective problems of mediated perception. Time after time technological change accomplishes both simultaneously. This new book series explores and reflects philosophically on what new and emerging *technicities* do to our everyday lives and increasingly immaterial technocultural conditions. Moving beyond traditional conceptions of the philosophy of technology and of techne, the series presents new philosophical thinking on how technology constantly alters the essential conditions of beauty, invention and communication. From novel understandings of the world of technicity to new interpretations of aesthetic value, graphics and information, Technicities focuses on the relationships between critical theory and representation, the arts, broadcasting, print, technological geneaologies/histories, material culture and digital technologies and our philosophical views of the world of art, design and media.

The series foregrounds contemporary work in art, design, and media whilst remaining inclusive, both in terms of philosophical perspectives on technology and interdisciplinary contributions. For a philosophy of technicities is crucial to extant debates over the artistic, inventive, and informational aspects of technology. The books in the Technicities series concentrate on present-day and evolving technological advances but visual, design-led and mass mediated questions are emphasised to further our knowledge of their often-combined means of digital transformation.

The editors of Technicities welcome proposals for monographs and well-considered edited collections that establish new paths of investigation.

John Armitage, Ryan Bishop and Joanne Roberts

Notes on Contributors

Geoffrey Batchen is Professor of History of Art at the University of Oxford. Batchen's work as a teacher, writer and curator focuses on the history of photography. Besides his interest in the historiography of the medium, Batchen has helped to pioneer the study of vernacular photographs. His books include *Burning with Desire: The Conception of Photography* (1997, and in Spanish, Korean, Japanese, Slovenian, Chinese, Italian and Ukrainian); *Each Wild Idea: Writing, Photography, History* (2001, and in Chinese); *Forget Me Not: Photography and Remembrance* (2004); *William Henry Fox Talbot* (2008); *What of Shoes?: Van Gogh and Art History* (2009, in German and English); *Suspending Time: Life, Photography, Death* (2010, in Japanese and English); *Repetition och Skillnad* (in Swedish, 2011); *Emanations: The Art of the Cameraless Photograph* (2016); *Obraz a diseminace* (in Czech, 2016); *More Wild Ideas* (in Chinese, 2017); and *Apparitions: Photography and Dissemination* (2018). He has also edited *Photography Degree Zero: Reflections on Roland Barthes's* Camera Lucida (2009) and co-edited *Picturing Atrocity: Photography in Crisis* (2012). His exhibitions have been seen in Brazil, Netherlands, United Kingdom, United States, Japan, Germany, Iceland, Australia and New Zealand.

Sean Cubitt is Professor of Screen Studies at the University of Melbourne. His publications include *The Cinema Effect*, *Ecomedia*, *The Practice of Light: Genealogies of Visual Media*, *Finite Media: Environmental Implications of Digital Technology* and *Anecdotal Evidence: Ecocritique from Hollywood to the Mass Image*. Series editor for Leonardo Books at MIT Press, his current research is on political aesthetics, media art history, ecocriticism and practices of truth.

Tomáš Dvořák is Assistant Professor in the Department of Photography at FAMU in Prague. He studied philosophy, art history, media studies and sociology at Charles University in Prague and The Graduate Center, City University of New York. His research focuses on philosophy and history of media, and philosophy and history of science, and the interrelations between these fields, especially media archaeology of science and knowledge. He has authored or co-authored a number of books in Czech: *Epistemology of (New) Media* (NAMU 2018), *Photography, Sculpture, Object* (NAMU 2017), *Temporality of (New) Media* (NAMU 2016), *Contemporary Approaches in Historical Epistemology* (Filosofia 2013), *Chapters from the History and Theory of Media* (AVU 2010), and *Waste Management: Texts, Images and Sounds of Recent History* (Filosofia 2009).

Andrew Fisher is a research fellow in the Department of Photography at FAMU in Prague, and Principle Investigator of the Prague-based collaborative research project 'Scale, Measure and Proportion in Contemporary Visual Cultures'. He is founding editor of the peer-reviewed journal *Philosophy of Photography* (2010–present) and, between 2008 and 2019, was Lecturer in the Department of Visual Cultures at Goldsmiths, University of London. One of his major research interests is the significance of different conceptions of scale for historical and contemporary forms of photography. This has resulted in a series of publications including: 'Imaginative Variation: Photographic Scale and Photographic Horizons', in *Too Big to Scale*, Florian Dombois and Julie Harboe (eds), Zurich Hochschule der Künste, Scheidegger & Spiess Verlag, Zürich, 2017; 'On the Scales of Photographic Abstraction', in *Photographies* Vol. 9, No. 2, Summer 2016; and 'Photographic Scale', in *On the Verge of Photography: Imaging Beyond Representation*, Daniel Rubinstein, Johnny Golding and Andrew Fisher (eds), Birmingham, ARTicle Press Birmingham City University, 2013.

Joan Fontcuberta is a renowned conceptual photographer, as well as being a writer, editor, curator and teacher, who has played a significant role in achieving international recognition for the history of Spanish photography. Fontcuberta graduated in Communication at the Autonomous University of Barcelona in 1977. After working in advertising, he taught at the Faculty of Fine Arts at the University of Barcelona from 1979 to 1986. He was one of the founders of *Photovision* magazine, which was originally launched in 1980 and became a major publication in the field of European photography. From 1993 to 2010 he was Professor of Communication Studies at the University Pompeu Fabra in Barcelona. Among the most representative institutions where his work has been exhibited are: MACBA (Barcelona), Museo Nacional Centro de Arte Reina Sofía (Madrid), CCCB (Barcelona), MNAC (Barcelona), Zabriskie Gallery (New York), the Science Museum (London), The Art Institute (Chicago), MoMA (New York), and the Maison Européene de la Photographie (Paris). In 1994 he was ordained Knight of the Order of Arts and Letters by the French Ministry of Culture. In 2011 he won the National Essay Prize in Spain and in 2013 obtained the prestigious Hasselblad Photography Award.

Paul Heinicker is a design researcher, investigating critical and speculative design concepts with a focus on the culture and politics of diagrams and data visualisations. He is a research associate at the Interaction Design Lab at the University of Applied Sciences in Potsdam and PhD student at the University of Potsdam at the Institute for Media and Art. He received an MA in Design from FH;P in 2015 and participated in post-graduate programs at Malmö University and Strelka Institute for Media, Architecture and Design in Moscow.

Michelle Henning is Professor in Media and Photography at the University of Liverpool. She has written numerous essays on photography, new media, museums and exhibitions and cultural history. Her book *Photography: The Unfettered Image* was published by Routledge in 2018. She is also the editor of *Museum Media* (Blackwell 2015) and author of *Museums, Media and Cultural Theory* (Open University Press 2006). Her background is in art, art history and cultural studies. She has combined academic research with her work as an artist/designer since 1991, designing record covers for PJ Harvey among others. Her current writing addresses both historical and contemporary photographic media and is concerned with the relationship between technology, materiality and aesthetic and sensory experience. In 2018–19 she was awarded an AHRC Leadership Fellowship to research in the 1920s and 1930s archives of the photographic company Ilford Limited. She is currently turning that research into a book, and writing on 'affective realism' in digital photography.

Josef Ledvina is Assistant Professor at the Film and TV School of the Academy of Performing Arts in Prague (FAMU) and editor-in-chief of Prague-based art magazine *Art+Antiques*. He studied art history and history at Charles University, Prague. He is the author of several book chapters and articles in Czech scientific journals and regularly contributes to Czech art magazines as an art critic. His lecturing focuses on the history of twentieth-century art and photography. His research currently focuses on general questions of critical evaluation and aesthetic experience in visual arts.

Lukáš Likavčan is a researcher and theorist, writing on philosophy of technology and political ecology. He teaches at the Center for Audio-visual Studies, FAMU in Prague, and Strelka Institute for Media,

Architecture and Design, Moscow. Likavčan is a member of Display – Association for Research and Collective Practice, Prague, and the author of *Introduction to Comparative Planetology* (Strelka Press, 2019).

Jussi Parikka is Professor of Technological Culture and Aesthetics at University of Southampton and Visiting Professor at FAMU, Prague where he leads the project Operational Images and Visual Culture (2019–23, funded by the Czech Science Foundation). He is the author of several books on media and digital culture, alongside work on media archaeology. Books include *Digital Contagions* (2007, 2nd edn 2016), *Insect Media* (2010), *What is Media Archaeology* (2012) and *A Geology of Media* (2015). He is the co-editor of books such as *Media Archaeology: Approaches, Applications, and Implications* (2010, with Erkki Huhtamo) and *Writing and Unwriting (Media) Art History: Erkki Kurenniemi in 2048* (2015, with Joasia Krysa). In addition, he was a co-editor of *Across and Beyond: A Transmediale Reader on Postdigital Practices, Concepts, and Institutions* (2016).

Annebella Pollen is Reader in History of Art and Design at University of Brighton, UK. Her research interests include histories of popular image cultures, especially in relation to mass photographic practice. She has published on photographic abundance in her books *Mass Photography: Collective Histories of Everyday Life* (2015) and *Photography Reframed: New Visions in Contemporary Photographic Culture* (2018, co-edited with Ben Burbridge), as well as in numerous scholarly essays. Her other books include a 2015 study of a utopian interwar youth movement, *The Kindred of the Kibbo Kift: Intellectual Barbarians*, and the forthcoming *Art without Frontiers*, a commissioned history of the British Council's art collection and its use in eight decades of global cultural relations.

Michal Šimůnek is affiliated with the Film and TV School of Academy of Performing Arts in Prague. Educated in media studies and sociology, his research and lecturing focus on the theory and history of photography, media, visual culture and consumer culture. His current research interests include vernacular photography, creative misuse of technology, and photographic communities of consumption. He is the author of several book chapters and articles in Czech scientific journals and is also the translator of Geoffrey Batchen's *Photography and Dissemination: Towards a New History for Photography* (NAMU, 2016) and Jussi Parikka's *What is Media Archaeology?* (NAMU, forthcoming).

Tereza Stejskalová is Assistant Professor at the Film and TV School of the Academy of Performing Arts in Prague and curator at tranzit.cz. Her recent endeavours include a long-term research on the cultural diplomacy and internationalism of Czechoslovakia in collaboration with Zbyněk Baladrán. She is the editor of *Filmmakers of the World, Unite! Forgotten Internationalism, Czechoslovak Film and the Third World* (Prague: tranzit, 2017) and co-editor of *Navigation edition* (tranzit.cz). Her research interests include feminist and postcolonial perspectives on Eastern European contemporary art.

Joanna Zylinska is a writer, lecturer, artist, curator and – according to the ImageNet Roulette's algorithm – a 'mediatrix'. She works as Professor of New Media and Communications at Goldsmiths, University of London. The author of a number of books, including *The End of Man: A Feminist Counterapocalypse* (University of Minnesota Press, 2018) and *Nonhuman Photography* (MIT Press, 2017), she is also involved in experimental and collaborative publishing projects such as *Photomediations* (Open Humanities Press, 2016). Her art practice involves playing with different kinds of image-based media.

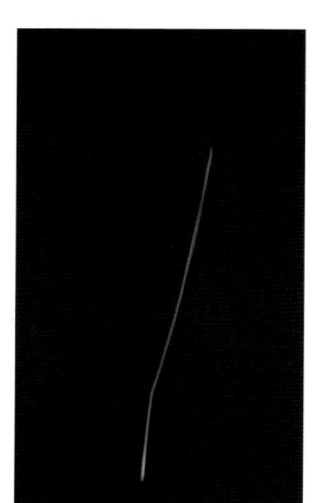

1 Introduction: On the Scale, Quantity and Measure of Images

Jussi Parikka and Tomáš Dvořák

At Which Scale?

AS THE WEATHER and climate seem increasingly off their hinges, so, too, do our images of the world. With the frequency of so-called 'extreme weather events' increasing, forms of representation have had to come up with commensurately complex ways of dealing with this new reality that does not easily take the form of an image. Weather and climate models and simulations operate only due to the extensive computational capacities that enable the emergence of visualisations of predictable and increasingly unpredictable events. The imaging capacities that have been handed down since the nineteenth century – data visualisation, graphical information systems such as maps of different statistical quantities, as well as photographs and especially scientific photography – have had to try to keep up with this mass of information, extensive both in scope and impact.

While weather and the climate may be acute reference points and metaphors to discuss how computational culture and big data have transformed forms of photographic discourse as part of visual culture, leading into discussions of data visualisation, cultural analytics by computational means, and the sheer storage capacity for the organisation of images as datasets that throw our usual coordinates for *what is a photograph* off the scale, this also works the other way round – at least as far as the popular discourse about images goes.

Figure 1.1 (next page) Erik Kessels: *24 Hrs in Photos*, installation, 2014, courtesy of Eric Kessels/Kessels Kramer. Figure 1.1 Erik Kessels: *24 Hrs in Photos*, installation, 2014, courtesy of Eric Kessels/Kessels Kramer.

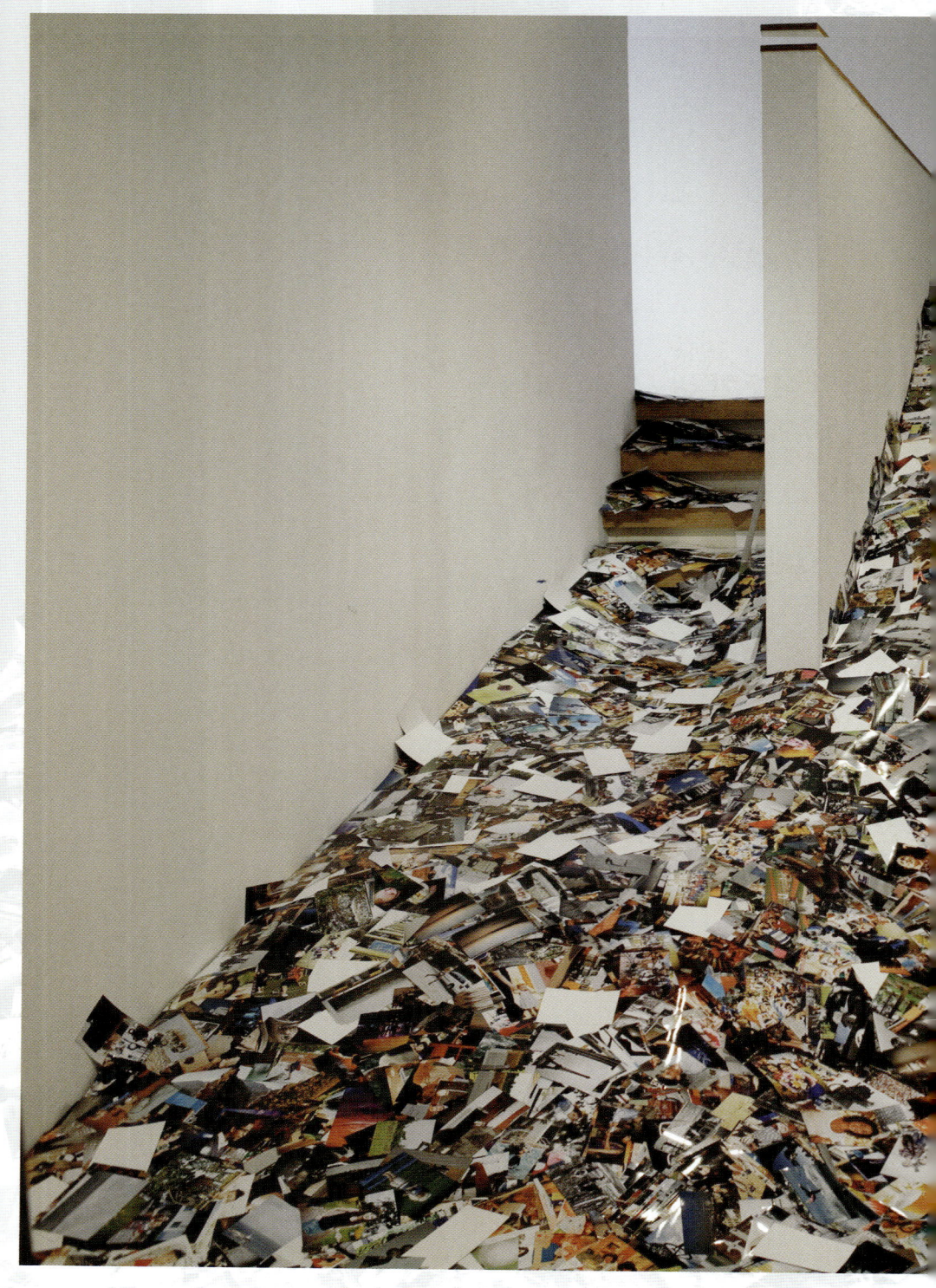

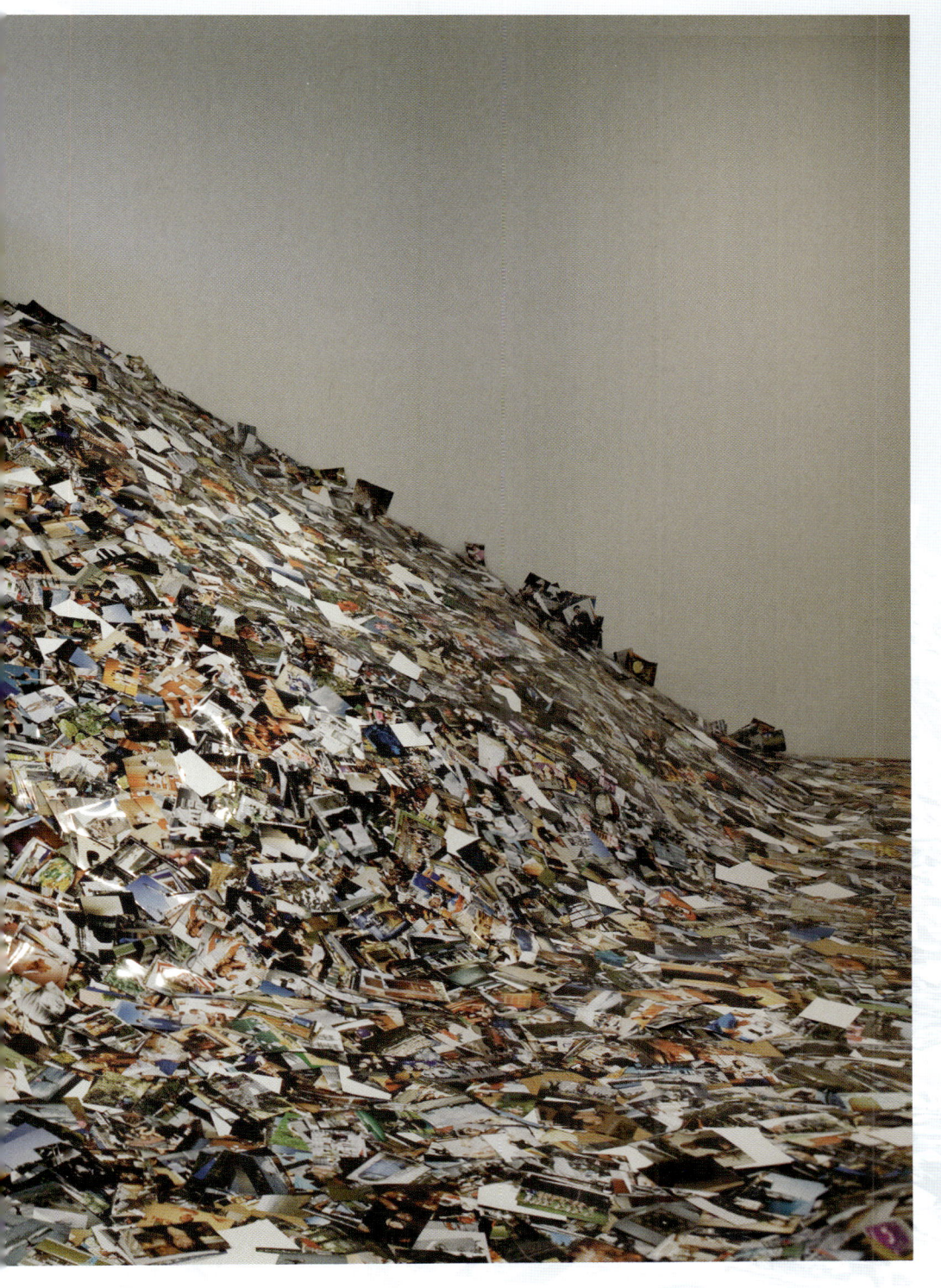

Indeed, a sense of the catastrophic has crept into how we speak, think and write of photographs in digital culture. The current state of photographic production is often characterised in the apocalyptic terms of a deluge or avalanche, an explosion or eruption, a tsunami or storm. Each of these terms evokes the impression of an unmanageable and unstoppable cascade of images that exceeds any traditional notion of photographic aggregates of series, collections, archives or databases, and their catastrophic overtones indicate a moment in which photographs cease to act as mediators between us and the world, instead making it opaque and obscure. In his installation, *24 Hrs in Photos*, Erik Kessels visualised the feeling of drowning in images by filling a room with the hundreds of thousands of printed images uploaded to online image-sharing sites during one day (Figure 1.1). The promise of total visibility and transparency, whether joyfully embraced or worryingly defied, opens a horizon of blindness, just as looking directly into too much light means we see nothing at all. This horizon of blindness relates to the often perceived quantity of images in cultures of big data: to see an image is by necessity to consider it as part of an extensive dataset or a database.

Despite an increase in methodological attempts to deal with images as data (with computational means such as cultural analytics, for example), and given that the photographic and visual spheres are seen anew and differently through such quantities, the visual and the photographic are not simply resolvable by the calculation of quantities alone. Instead, this book sets out to address and explain why and how questions of scale and its related concepts of measure and quantity are central to contemporary photographic and visual culture. While a conversation about photographic scale in network culture (see, for example, Fisher 2012) has been slowly emerging over the last decade, we aim to offer a strong set of conceptual coordinates and thematic anchors that address the two questions that bind this volume together: first, in what ways are questions of the contemporary technical media culture of photography understood through discussions of scale and quantity; and, second, how does this discussion include issues of politics, subjectivity, gender and technological practice as part of its repertoire in ways that shift the terms of aesthetic discourse into a firm dialogue with broader developments in media and cultural theory?

Could it be that scale is not only a useful entry point to photographic theory and history, but that photography also offers its own contribution to the broader questions of the humanities concerning scale and measure? In many ways, photography already included the possibility of representation and transformation across multiple scales. It also included the possibility of combining varied, dynamic perspectives, for as Andrew Fisher (2012: 323) points out: 'a basic function of all forms of photography is also to register the ostensible spatial and temporal state of things, to fix these together at a certain scale and according to a combination of prefigured and anticipated scales.' Indeed, scales are constantly made and remade, differentiated but also synthesised, in a combinatorial fashion.

In this introduction, we offer a first set of suggestions as to why the question of scale is important, how the insights in this book aim to address it, and where the connections to the broader field of the investigation of digital visual culture are to be located. Our opening chapter is followed by texts that will offer methodological, thematic and critical angles on how to discuss contemporary visual culture of mass quantity and scale. At a time when big science has become normalised as business as usual in terms of dealing with the interdisciplinary scale of complexity of the contemporary world (see Fukushima 2018), with billions of pictures snapped daily, quintillion bytes of data transmitted daily or terabytes after terabytes of data stored in various archives and datasets, we must also assess what the terms of these discussions are. What kind of entity is one billion photos? What kind of perceiver does it presuppose? Do such vertiginous quantifications imply something about the changing nature of photography, and, if so, in what sense? What happens to images when the displays are turned off? Are we producing streams of redundant images just to train machines to see?

These are not merely technical questions. They are also part of how we design our research frameworks, where questions of scale are incorporated into how we formulate our objects of reference (see Lobato 2018) to ensure they are treated dynamically – as they should be. Thus, in our book, scale becomes less a reference to things big or small, many or less, but rather a dynamic of qualification, of positioning, and of valorisation that is part and parcel of such material practices and discourses of quantity and measure.

Photographic Blind Spots

We often assume an abundance of objects when it comes to our contemporary culture of data and images – such as in the rhetoric of an overwhelming quantity of digital data – and see this as part of the current technical condition. But what we assume here also sits as part of a longer-term characterisation of the impact of media vis-à-vis our capacities to interpret and experience the world. The sense of the overwhelming becomes expressed both in vocabularies of experience and in the meticulous search for management and order that one subsequently finds in information systems such as libraries.

The history of information overload, which can be traced back to complaints about the abundance of manuscripts in antiquity and the acceleration of book production after the introduction of printing in the fifteenth century (Blair 2010), teaches us that the experience of overload is tightly connected with the enthusiastic drive to accumulate, collect, memorise, share and make accessible. The experience of information overload was limited to a privileged elite before the nineteenth century when the industrial-scale production of texts and images began to inundate most of the Western population. However, the gradual impact of schemes on how to deal with collections through metadata, knowledge about knowledge, and the quantities of so-called cultural objects through qualitative evaluation persisted as the important link where experience and information infrastructures met – and are continually meeting – every time we dealt with search queries, access, organisation of data, and the excavation of items from a mass that is itself otherwise beyond our cognitive capacities to comprehend. Or as Sean Cubitt (2014: 7) puts it, '[e]numeration is a pledge against disorder', where counting and calculation assure us of an ordered presence when faced with a multitude: the promise of measure underpins many of our epistemological coordinates since modern technical media, and the quantified world of discrete units comes to rule our cultural sphere and experience too.

While valorisation of the unique has persisted in aesthetic discourse since the nineteenth century, new technical media such as photography came along with the promise of the multiple. Since its early days, photography has been praised for its ability to reproduce an image in large numbers. More precisely, certain photographic techniques were championed for their reproducibility, portability and accessibility, as David Brewster's comparison of the Daguerreotype with Talbot's paper-based negative process makes clear:

> The great and unquestionable superiority of the Calotype pictures . . . is their power of multiplication. One Daguerreotype cannot be copied from another, and the person whose portrait is desired must sit for every copy that he wishes. When a pleasing picture is obtained, another of the same character cannot be produced. In the Calotype, on the contrary, we can take any number of pictures, within reasonable limits, from a negative; and a whole circle of friends can procure, for a mere trifle, a copy of a successful and pleasing portrait. (Brewster 1843: 333)

The 'reasonable limits' were breached, step by step: through the perfection and simplification of the photographic process; the proliferation of inexpensive, easy-to-use cameras; the delegation of specific sections of the process to professional services. It was the gradual automation of all aspects of taking and making photographs. Indeed, the sense of automated mass imagining and its promise of objective images 'uncontaminated by interpretation' (Daston and Galison 2010: 139) that characterised early scientific photography already in the nineteenth century finds an echo in more recent discourses about objectivity by numbers and validity through data.

But such images, mass-produced and seemingly automated, come with politics attached. Walter Benjamin's (2008/1936) notes about reproducibility demonstrate the link between reproducibility, aesthetics, and capitalist modes of quantification and production. One could indeed go as far as to claim that the forms of abstraction and exchange that emerge in technical media since the early nineteenth century – if not earlier – and the contemporary capitalist money form are in close resonance, or as Cubitt (2014: 7) puts it: 'both are mediations'. Peter Szendy devoted his latest book and an exhibition at Jeu de Paume (*The Supermarket of Images*, 2020) to the economic aspects of the life of images – their circulation, exchangeability, storage and management – or, what might be called 'the double iconomic equivalence', where 'not only is currency made in the image of the image, but the image, in turn, is made in the image of money' (Szendy 2019: 7). These questions gain urgency precisely due to the current over-production of images.

Even if the multiple and questions of reproduction were already features of early photographic discourse through a recognition of the technicity of the medium, it is not clear that photographic scholarship has ever been able to fully address the issue of the mass image. Let us consider, for example, two recurring touchstones of theory from the early 1980s, the period when digital imaging started to become increasingly discussed: Roland Barthes's *Camera Lucida* and Vilém Flusser's *Towards a Philosophy of Photography*. The two books are vastly different in both their approach and aim and can be seen, at best, as complementary: Barthes has much to say about the way we look at photographs and Flusser about the way we make them. However, if we focus on what they each avoid to address rather than on what they claim, both books reveal a shared blind spot – a blind spot which can be attributed to their (rather unorthodox) phenomenological inclinations and their particular rhetoric in how they address photographs.

The analysis of photography and our experience of photographic images in *Camera Lucida* proceeds through a detailed discussion of several images (Figure 1.2). Twenty-five are reproduced, while one of them, the child portrait of Barthes's mother and uncle in the Winter Garden, is not reproduced in the book, and another one, Daniel Boudinet's polaroid from 1979 (which is the only colour reproduction, though not mentioned in the text itself), is included as a frontispiece – and is

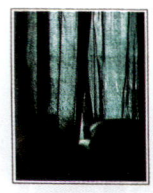 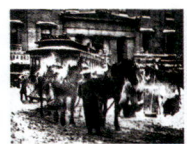 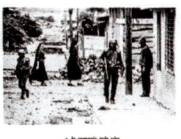 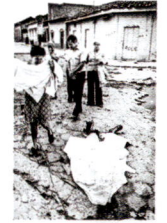 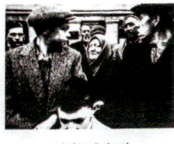
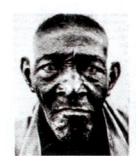 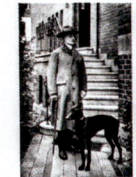 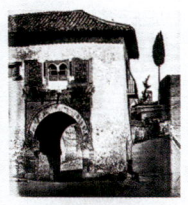 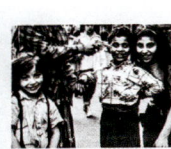
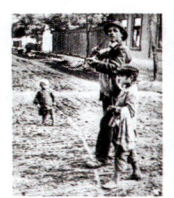 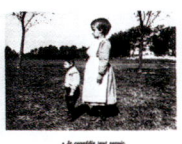 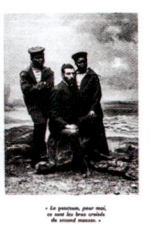 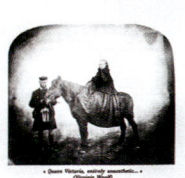
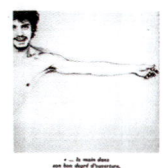 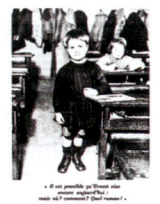 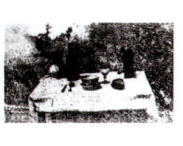
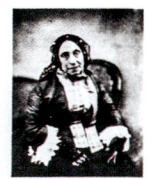 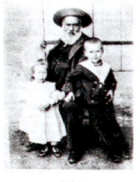 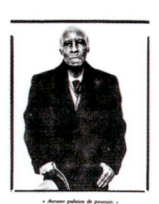 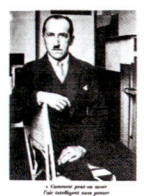 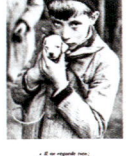

surprisingly omitted in many later editions. If we look at the images Barthes chose en masse, almost as if they were assembled on a contact sheet and so most likely in a different perspective from the one which the author intended, we notice that they have something in common: they all picture faces, human figures or groups of human figures. A few do so indirectly: the Boudinet polaroid shows a bedside with pillows and curtains; there is the *Dinner Table* by Niépce, mistakenly labelled as 'the first photograph' and probably included for that very reason; and the house in Alhambra by Charles Clifford, with a tiny, dwarfed figure sitting next to it that Barthes labels with the caption: 'I want to live here . . .' Even these three unpeopled images are filled with the traces of human presence: the table is laid out for diners, someone just got up from the bed, the house asks to be inhabited.

Barthes's preference for human subjects becomes even clearer when he discusses images that do not affect or interest him in any way: 'There are moments when I detest Photographs: what have I to do with Atget's old tree trunks . . . ?' (Barthes 1981: 16). Here we may recall Walter Benjamin's comments on the emptiness of Atget's photographs, of the images of a city devoid of humans, of deserted streets, of empty corners, the margins and recesses of the cityscape. Within that same discussion in his *Little History of Photography*, Benjamin pronounces that 'to do without people is for photography the most impossible of renunciations' (Benjamin 2005: 519) – a renunciation that seems truly impossible for Barthes but, as we see, is now increasingly a topic for nonhuman photography (Zylinska 2017).

Another, even more revealing example is found in Barthes's comment on Edgerton's strobe photography, images that reveal things human eyes could never see:

> For fifty years, Harold D. Edgerton has photographed the explosion of a drop of milk, to the millionth of a second (little need to admit that this kind of photography neither touches nor even interests me: I am too much of a phenomenologist to like anything but appearances to my own measure). (Barthes 1981: 33)

Camera Lucida circumscribes a certain field within the photographic realm that is to the scale of a particular human observer. In our context, it also raises the question of what measures are left out, which measures are important, and how measures are themselves an entry point to what photographic theory could be.

In many ways, Flusser takes a different strategy when approaching images but reveals another blind spot, which for our purposes is a useful

Figure I.2 *Camera Lucida* illustrations. Photograph by Tomáš Dvořák/Zuzana Lazarová.

cue. Flusser does not discuss individual images, but rather suggests to draw a line between categories of informative and redundant photographs. He selects a handful of meaningful pictures from the vast universe of images:

> In the following, no account will be taken of redundant photographs since the phrase 'taking photographs' will be limited to the production of informative images. As a result, it is true, the taking of snapshots will largely fall outside the scope of this analysis. (Flusser 2000: 26)

The strategy seems, at first, smart: focus on quality rather than quantity, select exclusive and valuable specimens rather than stereotypical banalities. In other words, define a measure, standard or parameter of what a (good) photograph is. In the mathematical theory of communication that Flusser draws on, the redundant is something conventional, predictable, repeatable and repeated. In the case of photography, the redundant is typically image clichés from birthday photographs to sunsets. In the logic of his apparatus theory, it is not only important that friends or tourists take the same or very similar pictures but that they travel and organise birthday parties to take such pictures in the first place.

The realm of the redundant, ordinary or vernacular has also been traditionally excluded and downplayed by curatorial and historiographical approaches. In terms of numbers, however, it constitutes the vast majority of photographs ever made and to be made. It deserves to be taken seriously and rid of the prevalent depreciation and prejudice. Geoffrey Batchen called vernaculars 'photography's *parergon*, the part of its history that has been pushed to the margins (or beyond them to oblivion)' (Batchen 2000: 262) and stimulated a whole range of scholarly studies (see, for example, Zuromskis 2013; Pollen 2016; Campt et al. 2020) that are beginning to fill this gap in photography's history. Thus, instrumental and vernacular modes of photography exemplify measures that have certainly shaped what photography theory could be but also what it might become.

The Image as Quantity

Is it possible to argue that contemporary discourses about the mass image and the excluded parergon are now even more so the entry point to understanding practices of digital images, from snapshots to machine vision? We find it useful to consider what, besides pictures, are incorporated in photographs; namely, infrastructures, operations, apparatuses, and the aesthetic questions of measures and scales. Our contemporary networked and data-intensive phase of image production adds a further infrastructural layer to earlier questions about reproduction and the multiple. Online image-sharing platforms not only enable and stimulate image production and circulation but also make it possible to 'see' the gigantic proportions of the picture universe while this seeing is, itself, instrumental to the functioning of the current platform capitalist economy (Srnicek 2016). The metaphors of overflow are often supported by staggering statistics, accompanied by vast numbers that tend to grow at an ever-increasing pace: 'Around sixty billion photographs are taken every year,' estimated Julian Stallabrass (1996: 13). However, Joan Fontcuberta updated those figures more recently: '800 million images are uploaded to Snapchat every day, together with 350 million to Facebook and 80 million to Instagram' (quoted in Batchen and Fontcuberta's chapter in this volume). When Josh Lovejoy presented Google Clips, a hands-free AI-powered camera which automatically recognised and captured moments without human intervention, he emphasised the overwhelming amount of images that seem to break away from human vision: 'This year, people will take about a trillion photos, and for many of us, that means a digital photo gallery filled with images that we won't actually look at' (Lovejoy 2018). This does not, however, remove the possibility that 'your pictures are looking at you', as Trevor Paglen (2016) argues in the context of machine vision and the primacy of machine-readable digital images, where issues of data and visibility conflate at the centre of recent and ongoing discussions about facial recognition and urban spheres of surveillance.

What these vertiginous figures – or at least, the rhetoric that mobilises such figures – indicate is that ours is an age of image excess; they denote a situation of liminality when a normative order has been exceeded. Excess often evokes negative associations like abundance and waste, matter out of place, pathological and epidemic. Some of this discourse carries with it troubling gender connotations (see Henning's chapter in this collection), while some of it is based on unchecked disciplinary bias. It is, after all, claimed that the arts and humanities have not considered quantitative imaging, image analysis software, and subsequent expert practices with the same epistemological focus and intensity as the sciences (Elkins 2011). In astronomical proportions, photographs become inflated, trivial, redundant and contaminated; they cannot be measured by traditional standards and norms. In other words, the excessive photograph is not a photograph any more in the sense that the photograph had become a stabilised object of reference during the history of photographic theory: it has become a different kind of image – or perhaps even a different kind of entity. And it is these questions of quantity, data and scale that are the crucial coordinates required to map this transition. For some, this causes anxiety (images exceed the human capacity of interpretation); for others, it presents a case of the new normal (photographs are simply data, and as such, part of the modus operandi of contemporary digital culture).

In either case, data visualisation is often pitched as one response to reformulating data as experiential, but also a new form of visual expression although, as one can point out, it dates back at least to the nineteenth century, with an even longer history in statistics (Beniger and Robyn 1978). Diagrams and graphs might not be part of the history of photography, but they are part of the media archaeology of visual expression of mathematical measures in ways that came later to intersect with photography, for example, through photogrammetry. However, perhaps it is only through data visualisations that the quantity of images can become represented as visual statistics. It is thus essential to note that questions of scale and quantity, as they are posed to photographic practice and theory, are also shared in many of the critical data visualisations. As Richard Wright (2008: 79) explains:

> One of the fundamental properties of software is that once it is being executed it takes place on such a fine temporal and symbolic scale and across such a vast range of quantities of data that it has an intrinsically different materiality than that with which we are able to deal with unaided. Visualization is one of the few techniques available for overcoming this distance.

Such arguments concerning the centrality of software and data for our sense of the visual then trigger multiple parallel histories and tracks of investigation for photography in addition to merely the photographic: histories of information systems, data management, and practices of graphs, diagrams and charts (see Cubitt 2017). Or even more provocatively, as John May (2019: 50) argues, current digital and electronic images are not related to the history of photography so much as they are part of the lineage of electrical engineering, telegraphy, television, military intelligence and experimental physiology. According to his reasoning, photography, when understood through its chemical base, is merely an obsolete remainder of a reference that misses the major transformation as to imaging in contemporary contexts of digital data.

The availability of large datasets and the focus on data as a (cultural) resource has also triggered a range of methodological suggestions, especially in Digital Humanities. Dealing with quantities by way of digital tools has produced suggestions such as 'distant reading' (Moretti 2013) and other computational methods. Perhaps closest to the field of photography and visual culture remains cultural analytics, mainly promoted by Lev Manovich, as one of the most prominently discussed techno-methodological frameworks of the past ten to fifteen years. Cultural analytics is premised as a visual analytical method to engage with large datasets, moving beyond what is argued to be the traditional humanities focus on 'small data', or even canons (Manovich 2016). Hence, cultural analytics as a form of 'science of culture' is suggested both as a way to deal with the vastness of large data (instead of restricted interpretational methods) and as a new way to understand the vernacular visual culture, as Manovich argues (2016): 'Tens or hundreds of millions of posts, photos, or other items are not uncommon. Since the great majority of user-generated content is created by regular people rather than by professionals, social computing studies the non-professional, vernacular culture by default.' Photographs, whether from historical archives or from contemporary platforms such as Instagram,[1] are then no longer merely visual objects so much as quantified input for data visualisation and pattern recognition.

Cultural analytics positions its approach not only in terms of existing datasets and units of description (cf. Birkin, forthcoming) but also in terms of how digital objects incorporate and reveal other scales: the images as counted units (one to many); but also what the image contains as multiple dimensions. To paraphrase Manovich, it is not merely a matter of counting existing units, but being able to (somewhat) forensically investigate images at a multitude of scales. Hence it calls for importing some methods from machine vision and computer science to the arts and humanities:

> In the fields of computer media analysis and computer vision, computer scientists use algorithms to extract thousands of features from every image, a video, a tweet, an email, and so on. So, while, for example, Vincent van Gogh only created about 900 paintings, these paintings can be described according to thousands of separate dimensions. Similarly, we can describe everybody living in a city according to millions of separate dimensions by extracting all kinds of characteristics from their social media activity. For another example, consider our own project *On Broadway* where we represent Broadway in Manhattan with 40 million data points and images using messages, images and check-ins shared along this street on Twitter, Instagram, and Foursquare, as well as taxi ride data and the U.S. Census indicators for the surrounding areas. (Manovich 2016: 14)

Wide data expresses potentials in 'very large and potentially endless numbers of variables describing a set of cases' (Manovich 2016: 14). The digital image, whether photographic or other, is itself already always a quantity that can shift across scales of description, analysis and comparison in ways that puts measure into focus, and in novel ways. The image then contains a multitude of scales of potential interpretation that redefine what counts as a photograph in the age of the quantified, calculated image that was, in the first place, a sensorially sampled bit of light transformed into discrete signals. If photographs have been fundamental in the quantification of cultural reality since their origins in the nineteenth century, current electronic and digital images have opened up any image as a multitude of scales of reference, zooming in and out, across pixel space and its multitude of combinatorial possibilities.

However, such methodological suggestions do not resolve the complex ecology of aesthetic and epistemological concerns about the constitutive conditions of scale and quantity. In other words, we are interested in how such a mass mobilisation of photographs and images as data relates to questions of infrastructure as well as the material loop between methodologies of visualisation of large datasets as part of the restructuring of, for example, urban patterns. Is there enough range, then, to question how these methods work, instead of mobilising them as computational solutions to fundamentally social, political and aesthetic concerns (see also Drucker and Bishop 2019)? This book's chapters provide responses to these issues.

The Structure of the Book

This introduction works to set the scene for the in-depth and detailed analyses that follow. The book is written by a wide range of authors with different disciplinary backgrounds but the same brief and task: to engage with the mass image and its variations in cultural and media discourse of photography and visual culture to provide us with a set of coordinates as to how images scale, and what measures we need to take to understand this.

The five chapters in the first section, 'Scale, Measure, Experience', link epistemologies and rhetoric of measure with the embodied and political realities of experience. How are the operations of measured normalisation and photographic scale related to embodied forms of socio-political realities in contemporary visuality? How are archaeologies and genealogies of photographic practice informative of insightful analysis of the current data-driven mass-image culture? What is the formative function of a visual aesthetic that builds on notions of scale but also embeds questions of scale as an approach into the online circulation of images?

This section responds to the seemingly incommensurable question raised by Sean Cubitt in his text; while images seem meaningful to many of the people taking, looking or uploading them, the 'images themselves are insignificant', functioning as mere data points in databases and big data analytics. Cubitt builds on the history of photography towards an analysis of the non-representational operations of images now in the context of contemporary powers of data-driven image practices. Tomáš Dvořák's chapter continues this line of thought by offering a more detailed genealogy of the history of photography. Seen through issues of scale and measure, he asks how this history is entangled with questions of aesthetics such as scales of the sublime. Moving in and out of specific genres such as scientific photography, Dvořák presents these themes as one way to narrate the implications of the gigantic and the immeasurable as they sometimes attach to practices such as astronomy – for example, the black hole imaging project of 2019 – but also as ways to re-narrate the media archaeology of photography. In his chapter, 'Living with the Excessive Scale of Contemporary Photography', Andrew Fisher renews the discussion about aesthetics and philosophy of photography in the contemporary context. In dialogue with the writings of Jean-Luc Nancy, Fisher develops an elegant argument about the qualitative impact that comes from vast amounts of photographic images; from the mere registering of the plentifulness of images, there is a much more fundamental question of aesthetics and subjectivity at play that articulates 'asymmetrical, heterogeneous and variable modes of being in relation to others'. Here, as Fisher makes clear, such a question is not merely tied to the rigid division of analogue versus digital photography. Fisher takes Nancy's philosophical discussion even further, making connections to themes that Cubitt raised earlier, of the possibility of thinking photography beyond the human subject of the click to 'include all sorts of functions, machines, distributed forms and artificial intelligences . . . which have the ability to inaugurate a photographic event'.

Michelle Henning's chapter maintains the politics of the subject in a different way, offering additional nuance by way of discussions of gender. 'Feeling Photos: Photography, Picture Language and Mood Capture' links the book's discussion to the twentieth-century development of a universal language with references to Edward Steichen and Otto Neurath, the inventor of Isotype. According to Henning, in 'the mid-twentieth century, it became commonplace to argue that photography is the one "language" able to transcend national and cultural boundaries, matched only by the presumed universality of human facial expressions'. This pronouncement leads into a discussion of the contemporary online culture of emojis as part of this innovative genealogy of photographic emotion leading to mood capture. More than merely noting this genealogy and its ties to photographic discourse, Henning brings into play a necessary specification as to the gendered discourse of photography of the mass image often branded as kitsch and how this reads in relation to the current politics of emotions. Consequently, the vocabularies of a 'flood of information', tsunami, deluge, and so on, come with the historical baggage of being heavily gendered through the political history of the masses depicted as both feminine and passive, where emotional capitalism relies considerably on the strategic mobilisation of discourses of authenticity and affective investment.

Henning's detailed discussion offers a platform for Tereza Stejskalová's chapter, 'Online Weak and Poor Images: On Contemporary Feminist Visual Politics', which examines US Democratic Party politician Alexandra Ocasio-Cortez's public image (including her Instagram feed) in relation to theoretical discourses ranging from Hito Steyerl to Lauren Berlant. The generation of empathy relates both to the often unacknowledged labour of emotional expression and sharing as well as to the collective politics of empowerment. Stejskalová connects these multiple registers to current debates about images and empathy, from experimental VR (such as Hyphen-Labs) to the politics of online images. Here, questions of gender and women of colour are crucial reference points for Stejskalová as she carves out one response to the question of capitalist contexts of social production and reproduction: activist histories of feminism can be storehouses, leveraged for the political use of social media.

In the second section, 'Metapictures and Remediations', articulations of different practices and their discursive repetitions problematise clear divisions between the analogue and the digital, investigating both historical and institutional circumstances of what scale has meant in different contexts. A key concept that the section mobilises is the metapicture, defined by W. J T. Mitchell as a picture that also reveal things about a picture: metapictures embody a self-referential quality that triggers a metalevel discursive opportunity to consider what and where, when and how pictures operate: 'Any picture that is used to reflect on the nature of pictures is a metapicture' (Mitchell 1994: 56). As such, one can already see metapictures as being at the centre of questions of scale and measure as they conceptually enable the understanding of scalar shifts and repositioning of pictures and photographs in visual culture.

Annebella's Pollen's chapter, 'Photography's Mise en Abyme', discusses the repurposing of slide libraries as metapictorial devices, where a core infrastructure that has sustained art history – slide libraries – is approached from the point of view of the metapicture. Mentioning theoretical entry points from writings by other contributors to this volume including Andrew Fisher, Michelle Henning, Geoffrey Batchen and Joan Fontcuberta, Pollen's take on the post-photographic context includes not only a discussion of recent photographic art such as that of Erik Kessels and Oriol Vilanova but also calls attention to slide libraries as original sites of collection and accumulation, where the quantity of images turned into qualitative techniques of image analysis. Pollen's chapter thus shows how such seemingly obsolete 'media infrastructures' of education and interpretation harbour fascinating points about quantity in ways also expressed in conceptual art.

A different sense of the obsolete is negotiated in 'The Failed Photographs of Photography: On the Analogue and Slow Photography Movement'. Here, Michal Šimůnek addresses the Lomography movement as a seeming resistance to the abundance of digital images that contemporary scholarship often addresses. The chapter's discussion of counter-practices of photography opens to what at first appears to differ from the digital and yet, is completely embedded in digital platforms and digitally enabled practices. Šimůnek mobilises Marc Lenot, Ernst van Alphen and Vilém Flusser's theoretical work – among others – in order to understand the hybrid status of such practices, all the while focusing on Lomography. A position of against the mainstream is not, however, one easily resolved. What come to the fore are various contradictions and frictions that characterise the apparently singular in the context of the mass image. Questions of the unique and the generic are maintained, albeit in a different fashion, in Josef Ledvina's chapter, 'Strangely Unique: Pictorial Aesthetics in the Age of Image Abundance'. The chapter draws a link from the earlier, assumed period of image scarcity to the current proliferation of the image in and across digital platforms, from issues of scale that hone in on the image at the level of its pixels and glitches to the question of the copy and its identity. Ledvina's discussion draws from philosophical aesthetics and art history, from László Moholy-Nagy's *Telephone Pictures* to contemporary digital images, including the artistic practice of Penelope Umbrico. While Goodman's *Languages of Art* offers one point of reflection, Ledvina moves to a provocative but much-needed proposition: even in the age of seemingly freely multiplying images every single image inscription can be addressed as a unique instance, begging for a more careful methodological and conceptual consideration.

One of our book's aims, addressed explicitly in the third section, 'Models, Scans and AI', is to elaborate the transformation of photography in the context of technologies of automation and artificial intelligence, including the new kinds of mechanisms of imaging that emerge in systems such as autonomous vehicles. In cases such as those discussed, it becomes clear that photography becomes a historical reference point, whereas the actual imaging processes are closer to genealogies of calculation. While our book steers clear from structuring our arguments around the assumed change that comes about with the switch from analogue to digital, or old media to new media, it is important to track the post-optical, post-lenticular landscapes that define practices of visuality in computational culture. In such cases, issues of infrastructures of imaging become a central way to look at the multiscalar operations of visuality and digital images.

Jussi Parikka's chapter examines autonomous vehicles and technologies, such as lidar, as forms of nonhuman photography, as coined by Joanna Zylinska (2017). Parikka contends that such technologies of light pulsing have a history that reaches back to the nineteenth-century emergence of the controlled light pulse. Used as a form of measurement and the foundation of radar technologies, these light pulses have become a non-visual way of mapping urban and non-urban landscapes, as demonstrated by the work of ScanLAB and in Liam Young's experimental video, *Where the City Can't See*. The text engages with the multiple and complex scales of infrastructural arrangements that build upon the city as an ecology of light and sensing that is itself the target of new post-lenticular practices, demonstrated by ScanLAB's *Post-lenticular Landscapes* and *Dream Life of Driverless Cars*.

Lukáš Likavčan and Paul Heinicker continue the dialogue about scale through a consideration of Earth imagining in the context of climate emergency. Likavčan and Heinicker propose that we are not dealing with traditional data-driven images but, instead, autographic visualisations (building upon the work of Dietmar Offenhuber), where the Earth becomes legible as a forensic trace, from tree rings to ice-core samples, from inscriptions to other patterns. This legibility represents a positioning of the planetary surface as 'a photographic inscription of human and nonhuman processes'. Exploring such inscriptions through the visual art of Susan Schuppli and the forensic work of Eyal Weizman, Likavčan and Heinicker propose that the Earth is no longer merely a visual image, but a material evidential trace of its own dynamics.

In 'Undigital Photography: Image-Making beyond Computation and AI', Joanna Zylinska contends that questions of scale in digital culture are not merely about quantity, but are more about the changing ontology of photographic practice. Zylinska's chapter offers essential insight into how traditional subject positions of photography seem to be taken over by the machine. This does not, however, lead to simplistic nonhuman futurism. Instead, she evaluates the contexts of AI in relation to, for example, human labour. With references to contemporary photographic discourse and practices related to AI and machine vision, such as that of Trevor Paglen, Zylinska outlines a case for the undigital photographic image. Besides referring to the digital post-processing of images, undigital photography becomes a conceptual tool for 'rethinking our current frameworks and modes of understanding image-making as developed in both media theory and visual culture'. In Zylinska's case, this also includes *View from a Window*, her photographic project which engages with Amazon Mechanical Turk labour operations. As the other side of

AI, it is itself undigital 'in the sense that, even though it uses digital technology to perform at least partially digital tasks, simulating the work of machines in its quiet efficiency, it also ruptures the seamless narrative and visualisation of the machine world'.

Through our investigation of photography off the scale, we were led to the fundamental task of studying what scales, models, theories and concepts we are employing in the first place. It is only fitting, therefore, that our book concludes with a discussion between photographer Joan Fontcuberta and theorist and historian Geoffrey Batchen. Moving from post-digital photography to the mass image and contemporary photographic art, their conversation provides us with a snapshot of theory–practice dialogues deeply relevant to current photographic discourse, rounding up many of the core themes of the book. As Batchen declares in the interview: 'The death of photography has been declared so many times that I regard such declarations as signs of life, as an inevitable marker of the rise of yet another photographic phoenix from the ashes of its predecessor.' This echoes our contention too: investigating scale, quantity and measure is a methodological way to approach not just a shift in *how many* images there are – stored or circulating, seen or unseen – but *how* images operate in cultural practices and their infrastructures.

Note

1. For a sample of projects working on photography, see the Cultural Analytics Lab website at <http://lab.culturalanalytics.info>

References

Barthes, Roland (1981), *Camera Lucida: Reflections on Photography*. New York: Hill and Wang.

Batchen, Geoffrey (2000), 'Vernacular Photographies', *History of Photography*, 24(3): 262–71.

Beniger, James R., and Dorothy L. Robyn (1978), 'Quantitative Graphics in Statistics: A Brief History', *The American Statistician*, 32(1): 1–11.

Benjamin, Walter (2005), 'Little History of Photography', in Walter Benjamin, *Selected Writings, Volume 2, Part 2, 1931–1934*, Michael W. Jennings, Howard Eiland and Gary Smith (eds), Cambridge, MA, and London: The Belknap Press of Harvard University Press, pp. 507–30.

Birkin, Jane (forthcoming), *Archive, Photography and the Language of Administration*. Amsterdam University Press.

Blair, Ann (2010), *Too Much to Know: Managing Scholarly Information before the Modern Age*. New Haven and London: Yale University Press.

Brewster, David (1843), 'Photogenic Drawing, or Drawing by the Agency of Light', *The Edinburgh Review*, 76(154): 309–44 (published anonymously).

Campt, Tina, Marianne Hirsch, Gil Hochberg and Brian Wallis (eds) (2020), *Imagining Everyday Life: Engagements with Vernacular Photography*. Göttingen: Steidl.

Cubitt, Sean (2014), *The Practice of Light: A Genealogy of Visual Technologies from Prints to Pixels*. Cambridge, MA: The MIT Press.

Cubitt, Sean (2017), 'Processing'. Available at: <https://www.fotomuseum.ch/en/explore/still-searching/series/29898_processing> (last accessed 8 July 2020).

Daston, Lorrain, and Peter Galison (2010), *Objectivity*. New York: Zone Books.

Drucker, Johanna, and Claire Bishop (2019), 'A Conversation on Digital Art History', in Matthew K. Gold and Lauren F. Klein (eds), *Debates in Digital Humanities 2019*. Minneapolis: University of Minnesota Press, pp. 321–34.

Elkins, James (2011), 'Visual Practices across the University: A Report', in Oliver Grau with Thomas Veigl (eds), *Imagery in the 21st Century*. Cambridge, MA: The MIT Press, pp. 149–73.

Fisher, Andrew (2012), 'Photographic Scale', *Philosophy of Photography*, 3(2): 310–29.

Flusser, Vilém (2000), *Towards a Philosophy of Photography*. London: Reaktion Books.

Fukushima, Masato (2018), 'Scaling', in Celia Lury et al. (eds), *Routledge Handbook of Interdisciplinary Research Methods*. London and New York: Routledge, pp. 343–6.

Lobato, Ramon (2018) 'Rescaling', in Celia Lury et al. (eds), *Routledge Handbook of Interdisciplinary Research Methods*. London and New York: Routledge, pp. 68–70.

Lovejoy, Josh (2018), 'The UX of AI'. Available at: <https://design.google/library/ux-ai> (last accessed 8 July 2020).

Manovich, Lev (2016), 'The Science of Culture? Social Computing, Digital Humanities and Cultural Analytics', *Journal of Cultural Analytics*, May 23, 2016. Available at: <https://culturalanalytics.org/article/11060> (last accessed 8 July 2020).

May, John (2019), *Signal, Image, Architecture*. New York: Columbia Books on Architecture and the City.

Mitchell, W. J. T. (1994), *Picture Theory: Essays on Verbal and Visual Representation*. Chicago and London: University of Chicago Press.

Moretti, Franco (2013) *Distant Reading*. London: Verso.

Paglen, Trevor (2016), 'Invisible Images (Your Pictures Are Looking at You)', *The New Inquiry*, 8 December 2016. Available at: <https://thenewinquiry.com/invisible-images-your-pictures-are-looking-at-you> (last accessed 8 July 2020)

Pollen, Annebella (2016), *Mass Photography: Collective Histories of Everyday Life*. London: I. B. Tauris.

Srnicek, Nick (2016), *Platform Capitalism*. Cambridge: Polity.

Stallabrass, Julian (1996), *Gargantua: Manufactured Mass Culture*. London and New York: Verso.

Szendy, Peter (2019), *The Supermarket of the Visible: Toward a General Economy of Images*. New York: Fordham University Press.

Wright, Richard (2008), 'Data Visualization', in Matthew Fuller (ed.), *Software Studies: A Lexicon*. Cambridge, MA: The MIT Press, pp. 78–87.

Zuromskis, Catherine (2013), *Snapshot Photography: The Lives of Images*. Cambridge, MA: The MIT Press.

Zylinska, Joanna (2017), *Nonhuman Photography*. Cambridge, MA: The MIT Press.

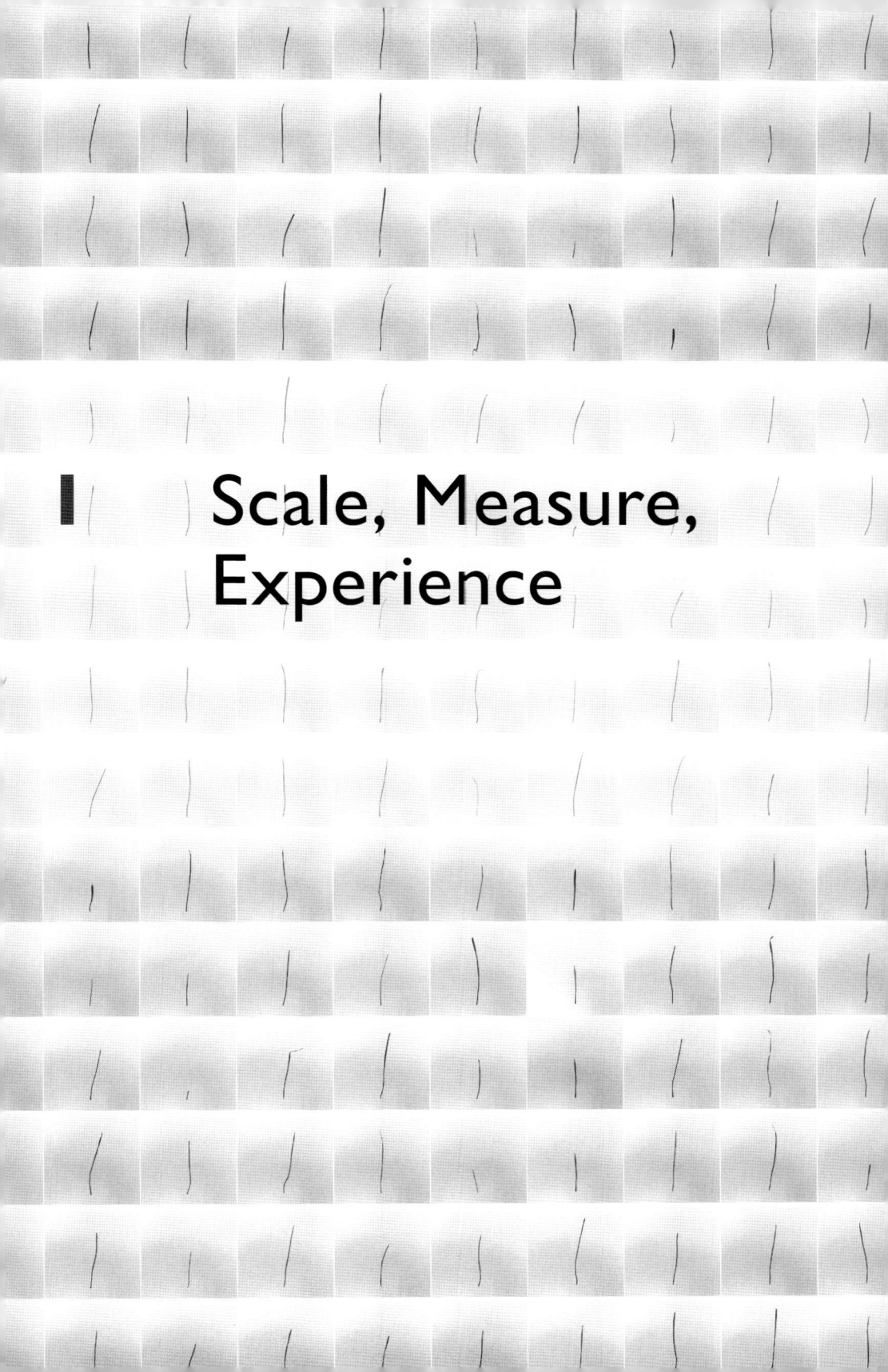

I Scale, Measure, Experience

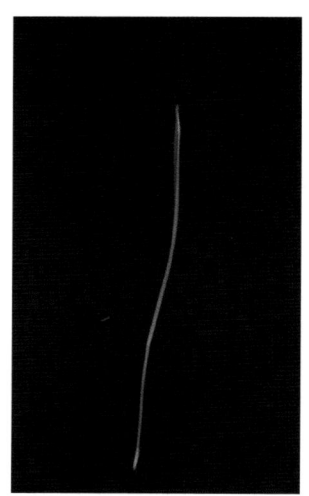

2 Mass Image, Anthropocene Image, Image Commons

Sean Cubitt

The Mass Image Hypothesis

LET US START where I would like to end, with the mass image: not the image of apocalypse but the apocalypse of images, as Jean Baudrillard might say. Absurdly, given the immense proliferation of images, the mass image is, strictly speaking, invisible (Mackenzie and Munster 2019). It is a name for the huge aggregation of images and their metadata amassed in the vast corporate databases of Google – YouTube – Facebook – Instagram – WhatsApp – Twitter – Vine – IAC – Vimeo – Tinder and in repositories of medical and scientific imaging, by CCTV, with its supports of facial recognition and biometrics collected not only by police forces but at airports and shopping malls, and in rather different ways and under severe financial constraints in cultural archives. To exist, an image must be discoverable, and for that it must be incorporated in a database. We retrieve some few images for care and attention – the care *of* attention characteristic of cultural archives – but there are limits. At a conservative estimate, in 2018 over thirty million images were uploaded to Twitter, fifty-two million to Instagram, and 350 million to Facebook – daily. If everyone on Earth dedicated eight hours a day, they could not possibly look at all of them with any kind of seriousness.

In many respects, even though they retain significance for their uploaders and their immediate circle, the images themselves are insignificant. From the perspective of the database, the image is not only meaningless (the machine does not recognise semantic or affective values), it exists only as a point of transit for what databases really treasure – relations. Relational databases like these are more interested in metadata – geolocation, personal identifiers, device identifiers, date stamps, facial recognition, distances and dimensions recorded by autofocus functions, upload addresses and the kinds of measurement prized by astronomical and meteorological databases. Commercially operated databases combine such data with data from searches and likes, swipes, shares, tags and other interactions, to construe from the *relations between* images a mass image of the world in constantly evolving organisational diagrams that only machines can read.

Run an image search for any popular tourist spot. If it isn't already tagged by the user or their device, algorithms associate uploaded GPS data with data from Google Maps and Street View to fill in information on cameras' orientations; temporal data provides a fourth dimension. The mass image of your site appears. It is an aggregate portrait tending towards a total image, especially of popular sites like Times Square, or the Charles Bridge, extending in time (during spring; at dawn; in 1945). Your search results will include links to video content, whose moving-image and audio elements also become components of the account the machine can now give itself of the place. Google is busy training artificial intelligences to recognise the world they depend on but which their status as representational media excludes them from. On the one hand, the mass image aspires to become the most ecological image possible: complete, formed of intricate webs of connections, and permanently evolving. On the other, it is already the most environmentalising of images, in the sense that it constructs a total image of the world so complex and complete that it excludes the world it depicts, turning it into pure context, pure environment, that which environs what is truly valued. The mass image inscribes the world as data.

At its first level, the one we can at least glimpse if not really see, the mass image undertakes to compose a total photographic and videographic image of the world. At a second level, this image is invisible. The individual images we see arrayed in the archetypal modernist grid are only an epiphenomenon of the mass image, whose actuality is constant processing in topologies we might vaguely intuit, and whose properties we could derive from the algorithms if they were public, but which even then we would not be able to see in action because the mass image is only truly perceptible to the machines that house it. What you saw in an image search yesterday will not repeat tomorrow, and you will get a different result from me, because the display responds to your data history and its position in the evolving global environment of searches, clicks and links. The display page of an image search is itself a representation, not of Times Square or the Charles Bridge but of the activity of the database collating the images and the behaviours of its viewers. It looks like a wall of pictures but is in fact a data visualisation.

Archaeology of the Mass Image

To understand how this might constitute an apocalypse of images, let me try a very short history of photography. The earliest photographs concentrate the duration of exposure into a single artefact, the plate, in this way imitating drawing, a temporal practice that results in an immobile object which, however, because it was made over time and of time invites us to spend time contemplating it. Long-exposure glass plate photography represented time, not only by recording and making endure, but, as Benjamin wrote, by producing 'the inconspicuous spot where in the immediacy of that long-forgotten moment, the future nests so eloquently' (Benjamin 1999: 510). To look into one of those early photos is to recognise, curled within it, the viewer's present, as potential and as an obligation to honour that lost moment: there is a continuum between the sitter and the viewer. Here re-presentation, while never denying the existence of the sitter, focuses on what connects the sitter and the viewer: the continuity of history that relates one to the other. The photographic snapshot invented in the mass take-up of the Box Brownie created a rift in time by tearing the stilled instant out of the continuum; both the continuum of sitter and viewer and the ecological continuum of time. The snapshot's capture of reflected light fails to unify image, appearance and being (in the way drawings could aspire to). And yet, snapshots have a saving grace, deriving from their exile from the continuum: they are negatives not only in the technical sense of the physical intermediary between exposure and print, but because they negate what they represent – the unhappiness of the world that confronts them as referent. What we look at and prize in a snapshot is not the truth of the moment but its non-identity: the capacity of the moment to be otherwise than it is.

The movies came almost immediately to repair both trauma and non-identity by adding another image and another and another in emulation of the flow of time that the snapshot had interrupted. They created a new art whose raw material was time. Scanned and interlaced video introduced time into the individual frame, and overcame the ending problem that dogged cinema, replacing the interruption that structured films as narrative units with unending broadcast flow. Today, however, there is a new cure for the trauma of images: the mass image construed in relational databases. In place of the temporal arts of film – montage, mobility, under- and over-cranking and all – the mass image agglutinates every image, still and moving, into a single vast, inter-connected artifice. The mass image heals the rift by negating the negation of the real, so losing the capacity to picture the world as otherwise than it is. The mass image is relentlessly positive, and therefore incapable of change. Thus in its way the mass image fulfils Fox Talbot's claim to allow reality to write itself in the photograph. In place of perpetual change, establishing networks connecting each item to any other is a more complete, more complex emulation of the planetary ecology than film or broadcast flow could ever provide.

At the same time, the mass image not only negates the world as potential but the image too. The mass image is no longer interested in the image *as* image, that is, as artefact in and of time, nor even in the tragic seriality of the moving image, whose striving for impossible completion so accurately sums up the alienation of humanity from nature. The mass database collects images not for themselves but as instances of behaviours and the distributions that behaviours form. Potential as the presence of futurity is annihilated in the simulation of the world accomplished in the mass image, which no longer distinguishes between real and probabilistic.

The ubiquity of exchange value has its equivalent in the equivalence of all nodes and all relations in a database. Not only is every image exchangeable for any other, as is clear from the unique results of every given image search, but the various forms of relation between images are allocated numerical values to render the relations machine-readable. These numerical relations distinguish the database from the ecologies, social or physical, that it still tries not only to replicate (as total image) but to displace (the represented world-as-data is analysable as messy reality is not). The total image of the world risks not only emulating the futureless world of waste and debt, and not only healing the rift in time by ending time altogether, but of making it appear that the world is truly accounted for in this architecture without potential, where action can no longer occur, and no future other than the present can emerge. As Flusser (2013: 57) says, only slightly over-stating the case, '[t]he aim of networked dialogues is not the production of new information but feedback.'

The ecology (in the singular), which includes the natural, technological and human worlds, is not the same as the internal ecology of a database. This is so because, firstly, the planetary ecology, dependent on lunar cycles and sunshine and bathed in cosmic radiation, is borderless, but there is a definitive outside-of – an outside that defines – the database, which creates and is defined by its externalities and environments. Secondly, the planetary ecology has no goal, while the goal of proprietary databases is profit. The planetary ecology has an eschatology, the database has a teleology. The teleology of the mass image is no longer human, because the profit that it calculates is entirely financial and no longer anchored in even residual lip-service to the welfare of humanity or planet; and because the viewer for whom, phenomenologically, the mass image exists, is no longer human but mechanical. The apocalypse of images in database logic heals the rift in time by constructing a timeless, homeostatic universe which – and this is its tragedy – is also the model of the ecology seized on by deep ecology and other environmentalist movements. Such cybernetic models of ecology posit stasis as the only alternative to disaster.

Jennifer Gabrys calls the social effect of this 'Programmable Earth': 'Programmability, the programming of Earth, yields processes for making new environments not necessarily as extensions of humans, but rather as new configurations or "techno-geographies" that concretize across technologies, people, practices, and nonhuman entities' (Gabrys 2016: 4). Her analysis not only suggests that the dynamic structuring typical of the database economy is the pinnacle, to date, of the logistics of empire, but also makes a critical distinction between environments as techno-geographies and as extensions of humans. Those early photographs still presumed an individual human viewer. Photography and cinematography in their use as scientific instruments moved towards a collective subject, Science, the assembled 'One who knows'. But with the mass image, the phenomenological centrality of the human, individual or collective, in technical media, reformulates the decay of individualism, not into a new social formation like science, but into a distributed cloud of behaviours. Perhaps nothing demonstrates this phenomenological crisis more than the ubiquitous selfie, a photo we capture so repeatedly precisely because the self is in crisis, an action vainly attempting to anchor its presence as present in the moment of its dissolution.

The Anthropocene Image

The eternal present of homeostatic systems, among which we must now count the mass image, is the enemy of history which, as Dipesh Chakrabarty (2009) has argued, is now indistinguishable from natural history. The mass image, however, does not exclude the Anthropocene but attempts to assimilate it. To understand this attempt we have to look at the genesis and practice of data visualisation so crucial to contemporary understanding of climate change.

Though it has a precursor in maps (Harley 2001; Kitchin et al. 2017), data visualisation can be traced back to the late eighteenth century, when William Playfair's *Statistical Breviary* (Wainer and Spence 2005) introduced the use of pie charts, bar charts and line diagrams and standardised the use of the horizontal t-axis to include time in spatial representation. Like earlier map-makers, Playfair assembled information garnered from various sources, reconciled them to his satisfaction, and produced a visual account. This first stage involved turning already existing narratives and numerical tables into graphical form by an act of abstraction.

The second phase arrived with the design of instruments tailored to the production of new data in forms ready for abstraction, specifically instruments that not only tracked vectors, like a compass, but that returned numerical accounts of the phenomena they observed, like thermometers and seismometers. In the third stage, networks of standardised measuring instruments provided large, and eventually huge, quantities of usable readings (Adams 2003; Edwards 2010), processing so as to make them amenable to the abstracting processes of data visualisation.

One of the instruments tailored for this informational processing was the photographic camera. The advent of CCD and CMOS chips brought the principle of sampling into photography. Each discrete pixel on the chip reacted to incoming photons by averaging their wavelength and frequency to produce a single value for the pixel over the duration of exposure, expressed as charge. Digitising the charge (and the addresses of the pixels it was associated with) produced an account of the light reaching the whole chip in an array typically arranged in the same order as the receiving pixels, thus delivering an image. But as anyone who has used photographic software knows, there are many other ways of reading image files through histograms and other visualisation tools. Digital images are in this sense visualisations, specific orderings of data in a form perceptible to humans. They become truly *data* visualisations when the recording instrument not only administers light but also the metadata associated with the exposure (time-stamp and location for example, corresponding to the address already associated with a particular colour and luminance value for individual pixels). The mass image completes the final step in processing the data produced from photons and their spatio-temporal placing when it organises all images in its purview under a single topological regime. Structured not only by the unit-counting of discrete devices and the assimilation of time (starting with date stamps, rising to the ability to sort vast numbers of images by date), this topology also conforms the relations between images to the commodity form.

The mass image is in this sense an already functioning post-human hybrid of work and labour performed by natural human and technical agencies. But it is also structured in an ascending hierarchy of enclosure, the production of units, and the conversion of units into tradable entities. The isolated unit is subsumed into relational topologies where its individual characteristics are of diminishing value, but only because they can be treated as counters in an exchange whose capacity to produce value is greater than that of the units traded. The depth of this organisation of what once was given but is now captured, stored and processed for profit can be seen in the cultural ubiquity of grids, from interfaces to street maps, and their functional universality in workplace media.

It is no longer a question of conforming, or attempting to conform, human perception to the media, because human perception is no longer central to the media's functioning. Reduced to their behaviours, humans need only perceive in order to respond, and their responses have no agency because they are raw materials for processing as data commodities. This has its positive side: the individualism that plagued Western civilisation from Luther to Freud is overcome by a simultaneous dissolution of the self and the compulsory collection of its fragments into supra-individual formations that are no longer exclusively human. Becoming human is an unfinished project. We are in the middle of a sea change in its history. Since we are no longer senders and receivers, it is clear that all of us are channels, although not entirely returned to the primal state in which we were all media. Channels are after all communicative rather than mediating: they connect pre-existing senders and receivers, but in this instance the sender and the receiver are the same: the enclosed feedback loop of a cyborg communication system. Our dreams of identity are symptoms of our estrangement from this cycle which nevertheless subsumes us under its own dream of totality.

Individual photographic images are still shaped by an older system, centred on the camera body imitative of the human eye socket and lenses designed to reproduce 'perspective as symbolic form'. That system persists in promoting the idea that the sovereign individual (historically denoted by the gender-presumptive 'Man') is the focal point and fixed centre of the universe. The new network system has no centre, its dynamic topology has no fixity, and it has no focus because it is not primarily visual (or in any humanly recognisable sense perceptual). At the interface between these two systems, the human that disappears is only the 'data subject' articulated by the European Union's General Data Protection Regulation (GDPR), already necessarily performing its commodifying and biopolitical tasks in the mass image. The human as data is wholly subsumed, but the human as code, and therefore performative, also persists as the ghost of work in a world of labour.

The human code is performative, then, but in great measure only for the network. Its value lies in being an intermediary between the network (which in its quest for universality must exclude what environs it) and the planetary ecology it externalises. It is because humans still have bodies and senses that they can act as intermediaries. At the same time, because they are both embodied and networked, emblematised in the mass image as the mismatch between perspective and diagram, humans in the wealthy sectors of the world – those closest to and most integrated in networks – are suffering an epidemic of mental illness. Torn between (physical and therefore ecological) *body* and (photographic and data-oriented, app-mediated) *body-image*, the contemporary human condition is that of the schiz once proposed by post-structuralism as the panacea for bourgeois individualism. Yet this dividual condition is indeed the grounds for a more generative, post-digital, post-network collectivity. As intermediary between ecology and technology, the human mass is no longer an aggregate of individuals, a single population acting as an efficient agent in the market model of economists like von Mises (1998), but an affective storm, whose capabilities are unexplored and dangerous.

So, too, may prove to be the forces of technology, notably of artificial intelligences at work analysing the behaviours collected in the mass image. In the *Grundrisse*, Marx (1973: 690–711) describes technologies as 'dead labour', the aggregation into concrete form of all the skills and knowledge gathered by our forerunners, owned and enslaved in the form of 'fixed capital'. Where traditional cultures respect and converse with their ancestors, we keep ours locked in black boxes. Liberating computers (Nelson 1974) is an admirable strategy towards freedom of all humans ('Even the dead will not be safe', as Benjamin [2003: 391] wrote, if fascism triumphed); but the risk of auto-orienting AIs is that the ancestors, after their centuries of isolation and indentured labour, may be mad. The same may be the case, we are beginning to understand, with the symptoms of the Anthropocene, a savage return of repressed nature. All three phyla – human, technical and natural – are potentially on the brink of catastrophic breakdown, although it is the technical sphere that seems to be triumphant in the ubiquity of programming and its embedding not only in machinery (my computer does not play certain files, not because it doesn't want to but because Apple doesn't want it to) but in, for example, the audit culture that everybody hates and few people escape or rebel against. Affective irrationality is, however, only the obverse of techno-rationality; and mental illness is not a solution because it hurts. Politically, in the day-to-day conduct of public affairs, the Anthropocene features only as a terrain for antagonism between the credibility of science and neo-populist table-thumping. As with radicals discovering that they needed to defend the FBI against Trump, environmentalists rally to the cause of science, even though science's credibility and politically progressive credentials are by no means assured. On the negative side, science rested on a set of protocols designed to produce certainty but which have moved towards the production of probabilities and the uncertainty principle. More self-reflexive but more prone to self-doubt, science no longer claims to know but to ascertain likelihood. Science no longer lays claim to Truth as it did in its triumphal era from Newton to Humboldt. On the positive side, science's planet-spanning networks have undone an older faith in the reliability of witnessing, of the self-evident, of the eye-witness, of the testimony of my own senses when weighed in the scales against the witnessing of others, human and nonhuman. Dr Johnson could not refute Berkeley today by kicking a stone. The value of this photograph of a departed friend does not prove that the mass image doesn't exist, and vice versa.[1]

Bereft of universality, truth fails. It cannot form the basis of politics in its second sense – the pursuit of happiness for all of us – because even science admits that no truth is universal. The suspiciously coherent rage of demagogues may truthfully encapsulate the wrath of electorates but cannot articulate the differences within them, since it is bound to the logic of representation. The mass image can claim universality but only by environmentalising the ecology, including much of what we cling to in our residual and ecologically embedded bodies. Its truth as representation rests on this curtailed universality, and so is not truth if by truth is meant a statement that both names and enacts what is the case. The central problem, especially as expressed in photography and the mass image, is that the modes of truth they appear to claim rest on either the identity of the image with the object-world it names, or the self-identity of the image. In the first case, no flat, rectangular image *is* the world it pictures; in the second, both the gap between represented and representation, and the distinction between the image as image and the image as print or screen display, demonstrate that there is not even a self-identity (the image, qua object in the world, does not contain in itself the reason why it is so and not otherwise). Images are inherently non-identical, and to that extent cannot be bearers of truth. The unique capacity of photographic images, however, is to picture not what is the case but the potential of the represented to become other than it was, since that has already happened in the moment when the scene in front of the lens became an image, that is, something utterly different. Photographs do not image the world as it is but in the moment of its becoming otherwise. They show the world as it might or could or should have been or be or become. Photographs are subjunctive.

Or perhaps photographs *were* subjunctive, and retain the power of the subjunctive as a residue of their older role that distinguished them from drawing. Drawing produced a complete and self-sufficient work: photographs, as tears in the continuum, were insufficient, until the mass image constructed a framework for producing a total image of the world, an image which by definition is complete and certainly aims to be self-sufficient, specifically in the sense of no longer requiring the world to complement it. Without that congruence and its inconsistency, the mass image can no longer reveal the non-identity and therefore the potential of the world to be otherwise. This could not have come at a worse time. The subjunctive is the precise mode we need for a humanity defined by its massed behaviours and a nature in crisis. It is the one mode that can embrace the pure act of giving that erases itself in the moment of the gift, and the great chain of giving that modulates and evolves whatever passes along it. Can it be possible that the subjunctive retains its utopian power when we consider the mass image as the activity of ancestral labour made concrete in its apparatus?

The Image Commons

When humans donate their work to a system that abstracts it in the form of data, property and exchange value, they act exactly as their ancestors did. Their free gift of knowledge, skill and creativity was concretised in the dead labour of machinery. So, too, is our living work concretised in the vast accumulations of the mass image. As we have seen, this must be understood as an enclosure of free creativity, and a result of the real subsumption of consumption, but it is also accumulation in the economic sense of investment in land, machinery and money itself, from which capital expects to derive profit. Investment implies both accumulation and the extraction of profit. In theory, corporations invest in human capital and expect to accumulate and exploit it. In practice, they invest as little as possible, demanding that other agents, formerly the state, now the individual, invest in themselves so that capital can exploit them. The importance of the mass image is that it represents a novel way to accumulate human capital in a form that can be exploited, like technology, without paying wages. The problem is the risk of over-accumulation.

There appears to be a generalised belief that the accumulation in the digital industries, especially among the FAANG companies (Facebook, Apple, Amazon, Netflix and Google), is infinite; that there will never come a moment when the accumulation of capital and its reinvestment fails to find new consumers. There is a degree of truth in this belief. The systems of image capital are premised on a feedback loop whose major channel is human behaviours and which can be constantly monitored to track evolving desires and meet these with evolving products. This solution succeeds earlier ones – continuing enclosure of new sources of physical or informational wealth (primitive accumulation seen as a permanent resort of capital since Rosa Luxemburg's 1913 analysis [Luxemburg 1951], moving fixed capital to new territories and the creation of new markets). Each of those, however, eventually comes up against the limits of growth, marked in our instance by the finite resources of the planet characterised most distinctively by the Anthropocene. Culturally we are caught between faith in infinite continuation of the present regime of accumulation and fear of its sudden and catastrophic demise as a result of external factors. But these factors only appear external because they have been environmentalised, excluded as externalities from the internal working of a total system that recognises nothing beyond itself.

This contradiction, rather than the contradiction between over-accumulation and under-consumption that instigated the debt crisis of 2007, sets the new terms for a new crisis. We have grown used to the idea that capital never lets a good crisis go to waste: that there are always factions within capital that make a profit from disaster. We also have a historical record that tells us that economic crises have a tendency to favour despotism. The exceptions have been aspects of Keynesianism and welfarism, state infrastructural investment providing employment to enable new consumption and state investment in social well-being to create new consumption and new opportunities for capital to contract for state business. There is every reason to ask why the oppressed have not similarly made the most of crises.

For historical reasons – basically the privatisation of telecoms in the Reagan–Thatcher era just before the internet and mobile communication booms – the state has little traction in the infrastructure or regulation of digital networks. In the period since the welfarist epoch in the wake of the Second World War, the historical trend has been towards state capture (Hellman et al. 2000), to the point that even the most powerful political factions are constrained to deliver the requirements of corporate and other capital – so bitterly clear in the incapacity of states to rein in the fossil fuel industries. Yet it is also the case that states act as a major buffer between their populations and the worst predations of capital (du Gay 2005). Regulation is correctly seen as the operation of power, but in many instances it is also the site of operations of resistance, assaulted by capital as 'bureaucracy' and 'red tape' opposed to the untrammelled working of the profit motive. This resistance has emerged historically as noise in the technical system, both environmental noise from beyond the system and system-generated noise, deriving from insufficiently disciplined uploaders and the internal frictions of operating protocols and the hardware they run on. Since the system reduces significance to a minimum in order to prioritise pure exchange, meaning functions as noise and vice versa: noise is meaningful. Where desire cannot be directly expressed but only assimilated indirectly in the form of behaviours, it operates as meaningful noise; and we should take technically generated and ecological noise as the expression of the excluded and unassimilated desires of natural and technical phyla.

Affective images – images designed to shock, images of excess – do not work in this way. They provide a reward for the beleaguered self in the form of feedback rather than new information, and reinforce the illusion that meaning is generated by and for a self rather than in a channel operating within a total system. If instead we take affect as the condition of primal mediation, then its mobilisation as meaningful noise, that is to say, desire, matches far better the new condition of distributed behaviours. Thus on the one hand humans become more intensely organised as channels and intermediaries through their dissolution into behaviours optimised for data mining, but on the other, beyond the behavioural schiz they become less exclusively human, approaching more and more the condition of ancestors and, as affect, the condition of nature.

It is time to reverse Stallman's motto, 'Free as in speech, not free as in beer'. Today free speech is not the right of free citizens that proves they are free, but compulsory and unpaid participation in generating content (Dean 2005). Nor does Stuart Brand's slogan 'Information wants to be free' foot the bill, not because information wants to be shared or has no volition of its own but because, as information, it has already lost the freedom of the gift. Instead, we could be forgiven for arguing, the visual wants to be free as in free beer: without cost, and prone to evoke jollity and mayhem rather than efficiency or, least likely, equilibrium.

The atomisation of the self has also shown that there is no single happiness that binds us: if there is to be a 'we', then not a single one can be left behind. If there is to be a 'we' adequate to the intermediary status of humans, it must be inclusive, and therefore bring to an end the political exclusion of ecology and technology, domains that are governed without a role in their own governing. The primordial soup of mediation is symmetrical: the same in every direction, forwards and backwards in time. Communication, with its structural division of sender, channel and receiver, introduced time as the condition of the message and its interruptions. At root belonging to the indicative mood that separates the speaker from the spoken ('There is a tree'), communication has always been vulnerable to takeover by the imperative ('Let the tree exist'). In its seizure of distribution, network communication not only assumes the imperative as the formal mood of software design but arrests the forward trajectory of time implicit in the communicative model, producing not timeless symmetry but the eternity of perpetual feedback. Noise – glitches, breakdowns, crises of over-production, over-accumulation and, more recently, over-distribution – reintroduces history as the zone of conflict within and between material and informational levels of the network.

The greatest of these crises is ecological, and on it depends the specific operation of older culturally specific binaries (religious, ethnic, gendered). The eternity of distributed networks has taken to itself a second mood, adding to the imperative the conditional, which allows it to simulate the future as projection of present data. Given that simulation is predominantly a technique for protecting against risk, it is ironic that many simulations point towards catastrophe. Humans are caught between image regimes: on one side the Intergovernmental Panel on Climate Change (IPCC)'s infamous hockey stick diagram of vertiginously rising temperatures; on the other emblematic images of a polar bear on an ice floe, shattering glaciers, or roof-stranded citizens of Dhaka. Any photo or video short outdoors today bears evidence of air pollution. Sharing and liking only assimilates these futures into the planned regime of networks, governed now more by concerns for security (as in climate change security for the wealthy masked as anti-migrant and anti-poor security and the 'war on terror' [Werrell and Femia 2018]) than for the welfare of humans, planet or even the technological infrastructure of the system itself.

The great skill of revolution is to precipitate a crisis that the oppressor cannot benefit from but the oppressed can. One possibility is an image strike: to refuse to make, upload or interact with images. For that to work beyond the individualist ethics of a consumer boycott requires organisation on the scale of the industrial-era trades unions which, however, can always be criticised for adopting the same disciplinary structures as the factory discipline they aimed to end. More powerful are those movements which have aimed at new organisational principles and new tasks, like the shop stewards' movement at Lucas Aerospace in the UK in the 1970s that proposed to turn the factories over from arms to socially useful products (Salisbury 2019). Now, in the era of distribution, it is not only production but distribution that needs to be remade. Practices aimed at developing tactics and strategies that might precipitate the crisis for the planetary oppressed are everywhere. Their major characteristic is their claim to the commons, from collaborative art and social projects to the Peer-to-Peer movement, and their openness to a future which, unlike the conditional simulations of the network, is entirely subjunctive. The lesson of the mass image for this aesthetic politics is that the future need not and should not be planned; and that it can only emerge in a working (but not labouring) alliance of humans, nature and technology. Already necessarily exceeding the prison-house of networks and the limits of human chauvinism, the means of revolution must be as joyful as the end.

Coda

Labour in the mass image is everywhere freely given and everywhere in chains. It encompasses

1. the work of the planetary ecosystem and the labour of capturing the free gift of light and natural processes;
2. the work of uploaders and viewers, freely donated, and the labour of converting it into copyright-protected and exchangeable units; and
3. the work of ancestors to devise skills and knowledges, an unforced legacy purloined as forced labour in the form of machinery and constrained to convert the use value of units into exchange value.

In all three cases, natural, human and technical work initially forms a commons which is then enclosed and exploited in the interests of capital. The initial work involves sharing; the labour involves ownership: converting into units, commodifying, and reducing to exchange value. It is clear that the labour component of these three layers of activity is entirely unnecessary, inefficient and absurd, since its only effect is to add a price tag to free beer. The mass image is novel because it completes the circuit of enclosure, objectification and conversion to exchange value. In the mass image, the real subsumption of consumption completes the cycle by converting viewing from playful reprocessing into labour. This happens in two phases. First, consumption becomes purposeful, a trait exploited by the excessive efficiency of search engines, which always deliver what you look for. The purpose of search engines is to provide gratification, in much the same way that classical cinema does: creating a desire in Shot A to see something, then magically providing it in Shot B. Gratification becomes self-fulfilling when we associate searching and finding as a single moment. Second, purposes become readable in the form of clicks, links and likes, and so become tradable data. Desires and gratifications, now identical, can form new objects, whose organisation into larger aggregations in database topologies provides the end-user – no longer the viewer but the database itself – with an image of gratified desire on which to build new self-enclosed micro-circuits of aspiration and fulfilment whose efficiency can be instantly read off from the next set of viewer behaviours. The result of this system is stasis, as such imitating homeostatic models of the free market and environmentalism with their belief that, if only aberrant agents like states and humans stopped interfering, the system would be perfectly self-equilibrating. Work is time, labour is eternity.

Unifying the collectivity of the three phyla in strength and hope at the crossroads of resistance, desire and meaning, the name of the commons is beauty.

Note

1. This does not prove that truth is relative, only that (phenomenologically) it appears differently to different observers. However, if truth is not manifest in itself but only in appearance, then it is no longer singular and self-sufficient, and therefore is not Truth as it was defined in the classical scientific era.

References

Adams, Robin D. (2003), 'International Seismology', in William H. K. Lee, Paul Jennings, Carl Kisslinger and Hiroo Kanamori (eds), *International Handbook of Earthquake & Engineering Seismology Part 1*. Amsterdam: Elsevier, pp. 29–37.

Benjamin, Walter (1999), 'Little History of Photography' (Edmund Jephcott and Kingsley Shorter, trans.), in *Selected Writings, Vol 2, Part 2, 1931–1934*, Michael W. Jennings, Howard Eiland and Gary Smith (eds), Cambridge, MA: Belknap Press-Harvard University Press, pp. 507–30.

Benjamin, Walter (2003), 'On the Concept of History' in *Selected Writings, vol. 4, 1938–1940*. Ed Howard Eiland and Michael W. Jennings, Cambridge MA: Bellknap Press/Harvard University Press, pp. 389–400.

Chakrabarty, Dipesh (2009), 'The Climate of History: Four Theses', *Critical Inquiry*, 35(2): 197–222.

Dean, Jodi (2005), 'Communicative Capitalism: Circulation and the Foreclosure of Politics', *Cultural Politics*, 1(1): 51–74.

du Gay, Paul (2005), *The Values of Bureaucracy*. Oxford: Oxford University Press.

Edwards, Paul N. (2010). *A Vast Machine: Computer Models, Climate Data, and the Politics of Global Warming*. Cambridge, MA: MIT Press.

Flusser, Vilém (2013), *Post-History* (Rodrigo Maltez Novaes, trans.; Siegfried Zielinski, ed.). Minneapolis: Univocal.

Gabrys, Jennifer (2016), *Program Earth: Environmental Sensing Technology and the Making of a Computational Planet*. Minneapolis: University of Minnesota Press.

Harley, John Brian (2001), *The New Nature of Maps: Essays in the History of Cartography* (Paul Laxton ed., Introduction by John H. Andrews). Baltimore: Johns Hopkins University Press.

Hellman, Joel S., Geraint Jones and Daniel Kaufmann (2000), '*Seize the State, Seize the Day*': *State Capture, Corruption, and Influence in Transition*. Policy Research Working Paper 2444, September. Washington, DC: The World Bank.

Kitchin, Rob, Tracey P. Lauriault and Matthew H. Wilson (eds) (2017), *Understanding Spatial Media*. London: Sage.

Luxemburg, Rosa (1951). *The Accumulation of Capital* (Agnes Schwarzschild, trans). London: Routledge & Kegan Paul.

Mackenzie, Adrian, and Anna Munster (2019), 'Platform Seeing: Image Ensembles and the Invisualities', *Theory Culture and Society*, 36(5): 3–22.

Marx, Karl (1973), *Grundrisse: Foundations of the Critique of Political Economy (Rough Draft)*. London: Pelican Books.

Nelson, Theodore H. ('Ted') (1974), *Computer Lib-Dream Machines*. Self-published.

Salisbury, Brian (2019), 'Story of the Lucas Plan'. Available at: <https://lucasplan.org.uk-story-of-the-lucas-plan> (last accessed 19 January 2020).

von Mises, Ludwig [1949] (1998), *Human Action: A Treatise on Economics* (Bettina Bien Greaves, ed.). Auburn, AL: Ludwig Von Mises Institute.

Wainer, Howard, and Ian Spence (2005), *Playfair's Commercial and Political Atlas and Statistical Breviary*. New York: Cambridge University Press.

Werrell, Caitlin E., and Francesco Femia (2018), 'Climate change raises conflict concerns'. *The UNESCO Courier* 2018–2. Available at: <https://en.unesco.org-courier-2018-2-climate-change-raises-conflict-concerns> (last accessed 8 July 2020).

World Meteorological Organization (2019), *WMO Statement on the state of the global climate in 2018*. Geneva: World Meteorological Organization. Available at: <https://library.wmo.int-index.php?lvl=notice-display&id=20799#.XJ9Wtuv7Q6h> (last accessed 19 January 2020).

3 Beyond Human Measure: Eccentric Metrics in Visual Culture

Tomáš Dvořák

> What was too small for the eye to detect was read by the aggregates; what was too large, by the units. (Emerson 2009: 23)

RAFAEL LOZANO-HEMMER'S project *Zero Noon* from 2013 is a digital clock that uses hundreds of different reference systems to 'tell time': it displays numbers of various occurrences on a clock dial, starting each day at noon. The clock aligns and compares the counts of, for example, the heartbeat of an average human being, quads of solar energy that hit the Earth, spam emails received, plastic bags used, deportations that have taken place in the US, Google website visits, tonnes of tortillas eaten in Mexico, UFOs spotted in Canada, suicides committed worldwide, numbers of financial transactions in Brazil, or the number of animal species that become extinct per day. The work is based on internet-refreshed statistics that come from government, financial and academic institutions, NGOs or media and reveal the immense scope of quantification of various natural, social, cultural, economic and other processes produced and released in nearly real-time. By gathering and synchronising them on one display, or several coordinated displays, Lozano-Hemmer makes these measurements commensurable: the viewer can switch from one metric to another with the push of a button, comparing them according to their own pace. 'The application of quantitative methods of thought to the study of nature had its first manifestation in the regular measurement of time' (Mumford 1934: 12); by remediating the clock dial with data from mobile apps, self-tracking devices, GPS trackers, scientific instruments and statistical offices, *Zero Noon* manages to link the current quantification rush with aged and sedimented practices of taking the measure of things in order to understand and control them (Figures 3.1 to 3.3).

The following chapter will address encounters with similar kinds of metrics, ones we experience on a daily basis. Quantified descriptions and self-descriptions seem to reveal something about us and the world we inhabit, yet we know that they are not simple representations of some pre-existing reality, but rather, generative methods that construct that world and, most importantly, specify our position in it through measuring, scoring, ranking and scaling. I will be not so much concerned with the reliability of similar data or with the broader issues surrounding the information economy, but primarily with the problem of confronting oneself with these figures. How do observers of *Zero Noon* relate to the numbers they see, browse through, and correlate? Can we understand metricisation as a process that contributes to 'the invention and projection of a global cognitive mapping, on a social as well as a spatial scale' that Fredric Jameson (1991: 54) proposed over thirty years ago? Or does it instead partake in a visual and discursive regime that is inherently decentring, 'that disorients under the banner of orientation' (Kurgan 2013: 26)? In other words, are the numbers and patterns created from them an unacceptable and distorting reduction of our lives or are they

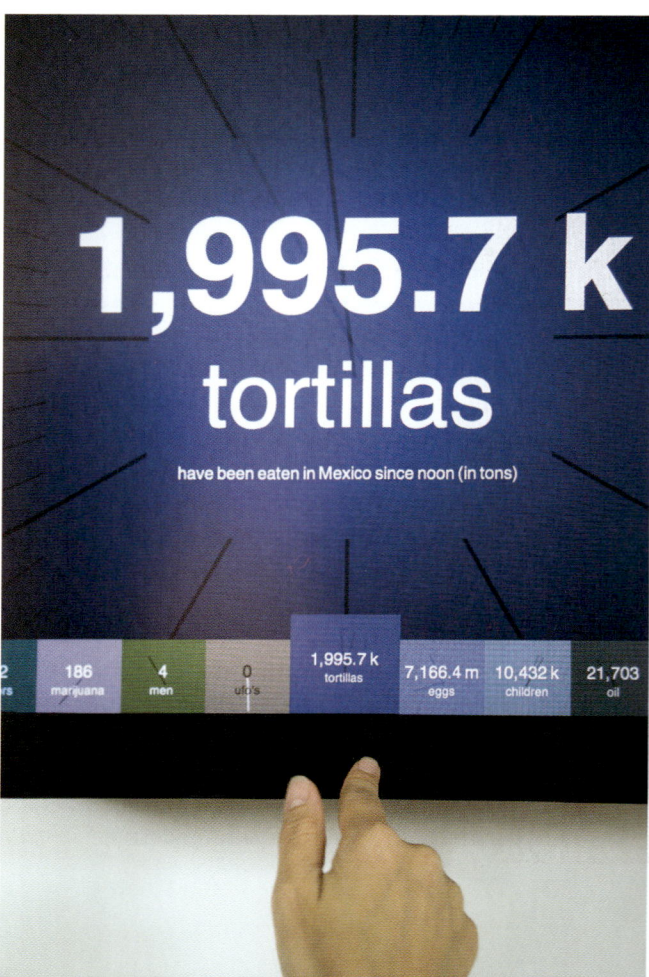

Figures 3.1, 3.2 and 3.3
Rafael Lozano-Hemmer:
Zero Noon, 2013.
Photograph by
Antimodular Research.

the essential, and perhaps the only, tool of achieving greater awareness of complex matters in the contemporary world?

The Epoch of the Gigantic

This book is concerned with numbers of images – large and growing numbers of images, to be precise. The number of pictures taken or uploaded per second would be an apt addition to *Zero Noon*'s metrics: the count seems so excessive that it suggests some kind of phase transition, a change in the state or character of what was once known as photography. The staggering statistics and metaphors of exponential growth imply a transformation, a leap through which the quantity of images becomes their new quality.

Interestingly enough, the origin of this figure of thought historically coincides with the emergence of photography itself, specifically with the developments in chemistry around 1800, a crucial field for the establishment

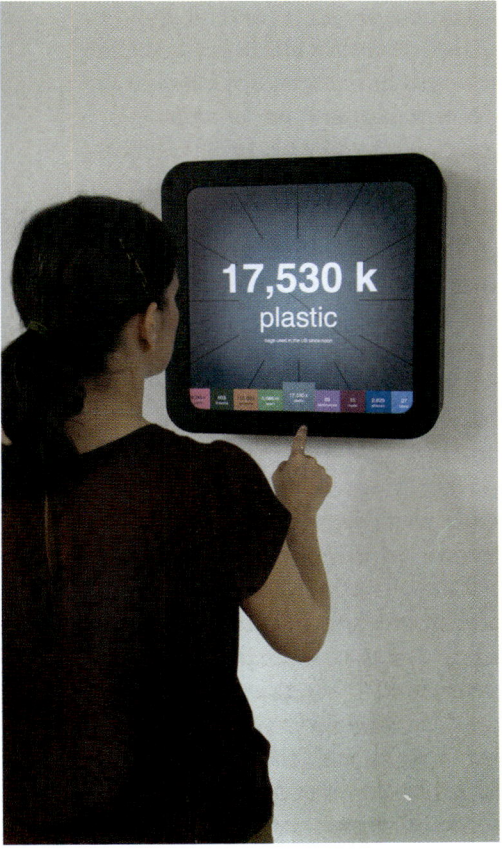
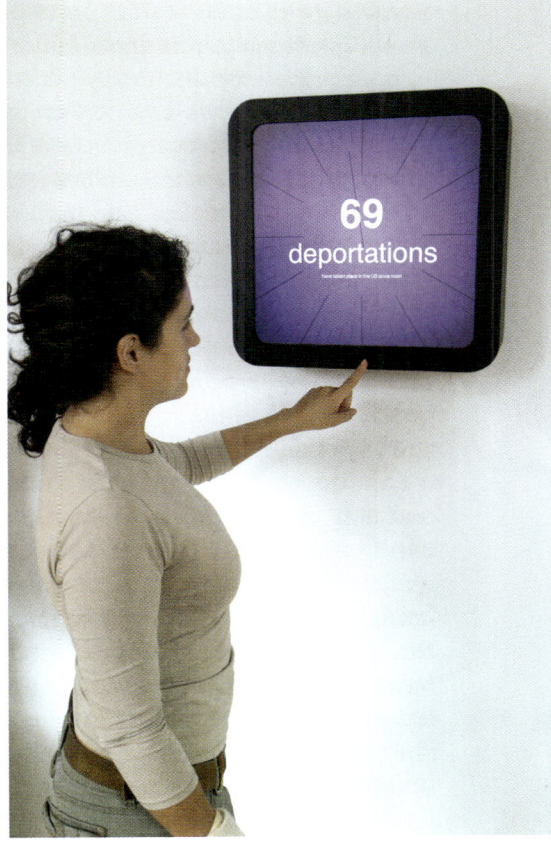

of our medium. Although the 'law of transformation' by which quantitative change becomes qualitative change is best known from Marxism – as formulated in Marx's *Capital* and Engels's *Anti-Dühring* – and from the later vulgar versions of dialectical materialism – especially the twentieth-century Soviet pataphysics of Michurin and Lysenko – the idea was first conceived by Hegel in his *Science of Logic* (its two volumes were published in 1812 and 1816; the revised edition in 1832).

Hegel introduces three stages of the determination of being: 'quality' is the determinacy that is identical with being and is immediate; 'quantity' is indifferent and external to it. A house remains a house, whether it is bigger or smaller; red remains red, whether it is brighter or darker. The third stage is 'measure': the unity of quality and quantity, 'qualitative quantity', in which the being attains its complete determinacy. All things have their measure or magnitude as they are determined both qualitatively and quantitatively, and although the quantity is to some degree indifferent to them, it has its limits. Hegel illustrates this point by the classical philosophical paradoxes of 'the bald' and 'the heap':

> The question was put: does the plucking of one hair from someone's head or from a horse's tail produce baldness, or does a heap cease to be a heap if one grain is removed? The expected answer can safely be conceded, for the removal amounts to a merely quantitative difference, and an insignificant one at that. And so one hair is removed, one grain, and this is repeated with only one hair and one grain being removed each time the answer is conceded. At last the qualitative alteration is revealed: the head or the tail is bald; the heap has vanished. In conceding the answer, it was not only the repetition that was each time forgotten, but also that the individually insignificant quantities (like the individually insignificant disbursements from a patrimony) *add up*, and the sum constitutes the qualitative whole, so that at the end this whole has vanished: the head is bald, the purse is empty. (Hegel 2010: 290)

These examples show that the quantitative is not wholly arbitrary or external and cannot be divorced from the qualitative since the alteration, which at first appears to be only quantitative, suddenly changes into a qualitative one. There is a certain critical or tipping point that interrupts the gradual change and induces an irruption of another state, a leap, just as the alterations of water temperature don't just make it colder or warmer but at some point cause it to pass into solid or gaseous states. In the section on measure, Hegel refers to contemporary developments in chemistry (oriented at the time towards determining qualitative differences between elements through numerical classifications) and converts its concepts into categories of logic. The category of measure is, however, applicable beyond the realms of natural science or logic:

> In *moral matters*, inasmuch as they are treated in the sphere of being, there occurs the same transition of the quantitative into the qualitative; different qualities appear to be based on a difference in magnitude. It is by a more and less that the measure of frivolous delinquence is overstepped and something entirely different comes irresistibly the scene, namely crime which makes right into wrong and virtue into vice. – Thus states, too, acquire through their quantitative difference, other things being assumed equal, a different qualitative character. The laws and the constitution of a state alter in character whenever its territory and the number of its citizens expand. A state has its own measure of magnitude and, if this measure is trespassed, it irresistibly disintegrates internally under the same constitution which, when with just different proportions, was the source of its good fortune and strength. (Hegel 2010: 322–3)

For Hegel, both nature and society are discrete, made of different orders of magnitude or scale domains. Although quantitative dimensions seem to unroll continuously in abstract universality and we can measure, for example, physical length from nanometres to parsecs, the world behaves differently in various regions of the scale, according to its measure.

Martin Heidegger picked up on this point in his seminal lecture 'The Age of the World Picture' from the mid-1930s, a critical analysis of the metaphysical foundations of modernity through the interrelated processes of science becoming research, humans becoming subjects and the world becoming a picture. In the modern age, the human subject became the measure of all things by calculating, planning and moulding the world to its disposal. Techniques and processes of quantification and calculation that made the world representable expanded to the point at which the 'gigantic' made its appearance. The gigantic is not the endlessly extended emptiness of the purely quantitative, says Heidegger, it is 'rather that through which the quantitative becomes a special quality and thus a remarkable kind of greatness' (Heidegger 1977: 135). It manifests itself in the very large and simultaneously in the very small; for example, in the numbers of atomic physics, in the annihilation of great distances by modern modes of transportation, or in the bringing of remote worlds close to us daily, by way of photography or radio.

> But as soon as the gigantic in planning and calculating and adjusting and making secure shifts over out of the quantitative and becomes a special quality, then what is gigantic, and what can seemingly always be calculated

completely, becomes, precisely through this, incalculable. (Heidegger 1977: 135)

Quantifying and calculating become excessive when reaching scales beyond human measure. Although we can still take measure of extreme phenomena in certain ways, they become unrepresentable in the traditional sense; an invisible shadow is cast around the well-structured world. 'By means of this shadow the modern world extends itself out into a space withdrawn from representation' (Heidegger 1977: 136). Heidegger understands modern technology as a way of seeing – a structured perception of things as extended, calculable, measurable and controllable, 'the pattern of generally calculable explainability, by which everything draws nearer to everything else equally and becomes completely alien to itself' (Heidegger 1999: 92). The gigantic is not only a figure of extreme proportions; it is also a name for the shift in which the technologies of world-picture-making develop into something unimaginable. Our ethics, aesthetics and epistemology, whose basic principles were formulated in previous centuries under conditions of low population density, shorter life span, smaller states and seemingly unlimited access to resources, face the problem of the gigantic:

> The Anthropocene is itself an emergent 'scale effect'. That is, at a certain, indeterminate threshold, numerous human actions, insignificant in themselves (heating a house, clearing trees, flying between the continents, forest management) come together to form a new, imponderable physical event, altering the basic ecological cycles of the planet. (Clark 2015: 72)

Universal Equivalent

The effects of systematic foregathering on visual culture were analysed in André Malraux's incisive study *The Imaginary Museum* from 1947. The rise of museums in the late eighteenth and nineteenth centuries imposes a wholly new attitude on spectators: as works of art are brought together, they are measured and valued against one another and simultaneously divorced from their original contexts. 'For they have tended to estrange the works they bring together from their original functions and to transform even portraits into "pictures"' (Malraux 1974: 14). In a museum (or a dealer's shop), the portrait's model is suppressed, and the image is determined instead by the name of its maker; 'Rembrandts' and 'Titians' become kinds of brand names. Assembling large numbers of artworks in museums evokes the idea of a collection of all the world's artworks, further propagated by art reproductions. It is, first of all, photographic reproductions that disclose the universe of artworks in its entirety.

'Photography ... seemed destined merely to perpetuate established values. But actually an ever greater range of works is being reproduced, in ever greater numbers, while the technical conditions of reproduction are influencing the choice of works selected' (Malraux 1974: 17).

Photographic reproductions extend the realm of available artworks from masterpieces to less significant works, thus transforming the very understanding of what a masterpiece is and substituting contemplation for an intellectualised attitude of pitting works of art against each other.

Such an effect is not limited, however, to reproductions of artworks. As early as 1859, Oliver Wendell Holmes published his praise of the stereoscope and in its final paragraphs outlined the future development of photography. In a confusing mixture of allusions to Aristotelian physics and ancient atomists' theory of vision, Holmes understands photographs as forms divorced from matter; thin membranes that peel off objects to be fixed by the camera:

> There is only one Coliseum or Pantheon; but how many millions of potential negatives have they shed, – representatives of billions of pictures, – since they were erected! Matter in large masses must always be fixed and dear; form is cheap and transportable. We have got the fruit of creation now, and need not trouble ourselves with the core. Every conceivable object of Nature and Art will soon scale off its surface for us. (Holmes 1980: 60)

Holmes envisions the formation of public and private stereographic collections that would house and preserve these billions of images and calls for 'a comprehensive system of exchanges' to facilitate their use. He compares photographs to bank notes; money is his main metaphor for the stereoscope's dematerialised forms. In his 1981 essay 'The Traffic in Photographs', Allan Sekula suggests that Holmes's description of photography is analogous to the capitalist exchange process, in which exchange values are detached from the use values of commodities, and concludes that:

> For Holmes, photographs stand as the 'universal equivalent', capable of denoting the quantitative exchangeability of all sights. Just as money is the universal gauge of exchange value, uniting all the world goods in a single system of transactions, so photographs are imagined to reduce all sights to relations of formal equivalence. (Sekula 1934: 99)

We may extend Sekula's analogy even further, beyond the parallelism of photography and bourgeois political economy. Thinkers like Weber, Simmel and Sombart have recognised that an economic system is determined by socially evolved calculative practices (of accounting and bookkeeping), and the rational economic mentality emerges within the larger and deeper tendency of mathematisation and parameterisation of nature and society. It has been common in writings on photography to stress its reliance on the laws of optics and chemistry, thus furnishing the belief in the mathematical and objective truth of the camera. The behaviour of light and the nature of photochemical reactions, however, do not imply any necessary form of representation – the photographic image is not natural or neutral in any way but instead governed by a set of discursive and graphic conventions. Photography, an industrial product of modern science as research, capitalises on modern society's 'trust in numbers' (Porter 1995) and its cultural techniques of quantification that translate our confusing and complex world into the standardised language of numbers. It is part of a broader set of technologies of representing and governing, including official statistics of modern states, the expansion of markets and capitalist economies, the introduction of unified systems of measurements and calibrated scientific instruments, or standardisation in industry and trade.

A number of authors have commented on these elective affinities, switching from Holmes's optimistic outlook to a more critical assessment. Susan Sontag is a case in point: 'Crushed hopes, youth antics, colonial wars, and winter sports are alike – are equalised by the camera. Taking photographs has set up a chronic voyeuristic relation to the world which levels the meaning of all events' (Sontag 1977: 11). 'Photography' or the 'camera' is often treated in these writings as taken for granted, thus prolonging the faith in its scientific neutrality. It is not, in fact, photography as such that has this effect but rather the techniques, practices and conventions that constitute photography as we know it. Holmes already hinted at the fact that the making of photographs needs to be standardised first:

> To render comparison of similar objects, or of any that we may wish to see side by side, easy, there should be a stereographic *metre* or fixed standard of focal length for the camera lens, to furnish by its multiples or fractions, if necessary, the scale of distances, and the standard of power in the stereoscope lens. In this way the eye can make the most rapid and exact comparisons. (Holmes 1980: 60)

To make things commensurable and to stabilise and standardise phenomena, we need techniques of measurement and standardisation, which first have to be standardised themselves. Before stating that photographs reduce all sights to relations of formal equivalence or that they level meaning of all events, we have to ask how and why photography has become this universal gauge in the first place. Looking at professional or pre-automatic photographic gear and materials, one quickly realises how essential measuring is to photography. The camera is covered with numbers, for the amount of light reaching the film or image sensor must be tamed by aperture size and shutter speed. Focal length is a measure of the convergence or divergence of light in the optical system; photographic processing involves measuring the density and contrast and close control of temperature, agitation or time. Any photograph is the result of a complex series of measurements, often embodied into standards and norms to facilitate the process. Even though in most contemporary devices the computing is done automatically and without our knowledge, it does not preclude the fact that every pretty picture emerges out of sedimented practices of measuring, scaling, grading and calibrating.

Disproportion of Vision

'Astronomical' figures originated, not surprisingly, in astronomy. Although measuring the universe has always dealt with large numbers, it was only during the seventeenth century that the proportions – the number of stars, their distance from the Earth and the size of the universe – expanded truly off the scale and beyond human imagination. The de-centring of the universe resulted in eccentric figures. In the pre-modern, ancient and medieval world, the reach of the human senses corresponded with the limits of the universe and human beings were understood to be naturally endowed with the capacity to experience and know their surrounding world. The human sensorium was believed to be made to the measure of the world, compatible with it and in proportion to it. Hans Blumenberg speaks of traditional astronomy's 'postulate of visibility', which 'corresponds to the assumptions of an anthropology in which man and cosmos are seen as coordinated in such a way that no essential incongruence can be assumed between man's organic equipment and the constituents of reality' (Blumenberg 1987: 629).

The Copernican Revolution and the discoveries of the telescope and microscope have significantly undermined this postulate and led to the divorce of the human senses from reality (or, more precisely, a redefining of what reality is) while substituting incommensurability and immeasurability for the symmetrical construction of the finite universe and man's central position in it.

> The breakdown of the postulate of visibility – understood in the widest sense – is brought to a point by a kind of reversal: The visible world is not only a tiny section of physical reality, but is also, qualitatively, the mere foreground of this reality, its insignificant surface, on which the outcome of processes and forces is only symptomatically displayed. Visibility is

itself an eccentric configuration, the accidental convergence of heterogeneous sequences of physical events. (Blumenberg 1987: 642–3)

The new optics of the seventeenth century exposed the immensity of nature and opened up other scales, inaccessible to human beings directly. In the process of making the previously unseen visible by means of optical instruments, the meaning of vision and sensory perception was redefined and denaturalised. The telescope does not just make new things visible; it demonstrates the difference between the visible and the invisible and reconstructs eye vision and telescopic vision as distinct regimes of visibility, where the theory of the instrument is informed by the theory of the eye, and vice versa. All observation is made conditional, dependent on its medium and surrounded by new realms of the imperceptible: telescopic vision simultaneously generates an anaesthetic field. 'We may understand this as the birth of a certain idea of science, positioned in the awkward space between sensory evidence and abstraction' (Vogl 2007: 22).

A similar abyss can be found at the other extreme, the microcosm. Blaise Pascal famously described humans' humiliating position between the two infinities of science in his fragment on 'Man's Disproportion', where he finds us situated between the extremities of the miniature and the gigantic, between the vastness of the firmament and the most delicate things known:

> Limited as we are in every respect, this condition of holding the midpoint between two extremes is apparent in all our faculties. Our senses perceive nothing extreme. Too much noise deafens us; too much light dazzles, too great a distance or proximity hinders our view. A great length or great brevity obscures the discourse; too much truth confounds us . . . We feel neither extreme heat nor extreme cold. Qualities in excess are harmful to us and cannot be perceived: we no longer feel but suffer them . . . In short, extremes are for us as though they did not exist, nor we for them. They escape us, or we them. (Pascal 2004: 61)

The incommensurability of the human perceptual mesocosm with the molecular and cosmic dimensions of nature gave rise to the new aesthetic concept of the sublime. The new postulate of invisibility also became a recurrent topos in philosophy; it often surfaces as the invisible shadow of technological breakthroughs in the visualisation of new layers of reality. But we may also encounter various attempts at reconciling the proportions of the human sensorium to the world.

Gotthold Ephraim Lessing wrote his short but remarkable fragment, 'That More than Five Senses are Possible for Human Beings', at the very close of his life, most likely in 1780. In several paragraphs, he outlines a conception of human development from simple forms to complex and advanced ones: human sensory apparatus is not fixed once and for all but evolves towards greater refinement and complexity. Our present stage of five senses was achieved through the combinatorics of individual ones: the soul 'will first have had each of these senses singly, then all ten combinations of two, all ten combinations of three, and all five combinations of four before it acquired all five together' (Lessing 2005: 180). The present combination is not, however, the final stage of development: senses determine the limits of the soul's representations, they are their order and measure and the way the soul is conjoined with matter – the senses are themselves material. Matter, however, is not monolithic; it contains homogeneous elements or masses that correspond to particular senses. Because we know that there are more than five homogeneous matters (although we cannot know for sure how many there are in the world altogether), we can assume that more senses are possible:

> Thus, just as the sense of sight corresponds to the homogeneous mass through which bodies attain a condition of visibility (i.e. light), so also is it certain that particular senses can and will correspond, e.g., to electrical matter or magnetic matter, senses through which we shall immediately recognize whether bodies are in an electrical or magnetic state. We can at present attain this knowledge only by conducting experiments. (Lessing 2005: 181)

Lessing illustrates his thesis with the classic motive of sensory impairment: if we lacked vision, for example, we would not be able to form any conception of it. After gaining sight, a 'whole new world will suddenly emerge for us, full of the most splendid phenomena' (Lessing 2005: 182). In the same way, we are aware (thanks to scientific research) of the existence of electrical or magnetic powers, but we cannot perceive them because we haven't developed special senses for them yet. Human perception is dependent upon a psychophysical constitution, which is not invariable.

Of course, Lessing does not speak in terms of purely biological evolution; his system is 'the oldest of all philosophical systems', the system of the soul's pre-existence and of metempsychosis. The idea of a process in which an immortal soul migrates into new complex beings was very popular in Lessing's time; aside from a rich tradition of metempsychosis speculation, he was most likely inspired by Charles Bonnet's theory of palingenesis.

Bonnet was one of the first authors to use the term evolution, although in a different manner to how we understand it from the nineteenth century on. His Leibnizian approach to evolution was marked by a belief in preformation, according to which every living being encapsulates in itself a primordial seed, an unchanging miniature replica of itself that is activated at fertilisation and develops into new identical organisms. At the creation of Earth, all future generations of living beings were embodied in these primordial germs, and the breeding of new creatures is essentially the production of an endless series of copies of a given species. Preformationism excludes change or variation in the later evolutionary sense. It is not, however, an entirely static system. In his *Philosophical Palingenesis* of 1769, Bonnet delineates an image of catastrophic revolutions that radically alter living conditions on Earth and lead to new rebirths. The physical bodies of organisms are destroyed during these periodical catastrophes, but their germs survive and are born again into new worlds. These new worlds bring about different living conditions from the preceding ones, which is the reason why organisms acquire new forms corresponding to these new environments. 'I conceive that the germs of all organized beings were originally constructed or calculated with a determinate correlation with the diverse revolutions which our globe was to undergo,' says Bonnet (cited in Lovejoy 1936: 285). Catastrophic revolutions are predetermined, just like the forms of the living, and they allow organisms to evolve towards greater biological complexity and higher spiritual perfection.

Translating the Scales

One consequence of the abandonment of the geocentric universe was a radical enlargement of the cosmos, by orders of magnitude. If the Earth orbits the Sun, how could constellations of stars look the same from all points along the orbit? This would be possible only if the stars were so far away that, from their perspective, the trajectory of the earth is negligible, a mere single dot. Around 1600, distances of the fixed stars were guessed at thousands of earth radii, while around 1700 the distance of the nearest stars was estimated to be billions of the same units.

> [T]he distance to the nearest fixed stars in terrestrial radii, let alone in miles, was awkward to express and almost impossible to comprehend. In the Middle Ages the then almost incomprehensible distance to the fixed stars, 20,000 e.r., had been illustrated by the calculation of how many years Adam would still have to walk, at a rate of 25 miles per day, to reach the fixed stars, had he started his journey on the day he was created. Now a new illustration was needed. Huygens's cannon ball, traveling at 600 ft/sec. was adequate for distance within the solar system, but it would take 691,600 years to reach a fixed star which he had calculated to be 27,664

times as far away as the Sun. Such a time span, was, however, difficult to comprehend. (Van Helden 1985: 159)

The newly discovered magnitudes exceeded not only human experience or the traditional Christian time frame of a few thousands of years; they were impossible to imagine, and so a number of rhetorical devices were invented in an effort to translate them into comprehensible scales. Huygens switched from distances to the time needed for a swift cannon ball to traverse such a distance. Another common simile was that of a falling body. Before geology, deep time was discovered as an equivalent of extreme distances. Jean de La Bruyère is an illustrative case in point since his writings addressed courtly society rather than astronomers. In his explanation, the speed of an orbiting moon is 'five thousand six hundred times faster than a race-horse running twelve miles an hour', the course of Saturn is 'above fifty-four hundred millions of miles in circumference; so that a race-horse, if supposed to run thirty miles an hour, must be twenty thousand five hundred and forty-eight years in going this round'. The distance between Sun and Earth is illustrated by a falling millstone: if it comes down 'with all swiftness imaginable, and even swifter than the heaviest bodies descend', it will take 114 years to fall down. This distance, if compared to that of the other stars, 'is so inconsiderable, that comparison is an improper term when mentioning such distances; for, indeed, what proportion is there between anything that can be measured, whatever its extent may be, and that which is beyond all mensuration?' (La Bruyère 1885: 480–2)

The question is whether and how we can translate that which is beyond all mensuration into our quotidian earthbound world of limited faculties; whether and how we can place the gigantic into some sort of comprehensible perspective; and whether and how we can see phenomena whose existence is hidden to an observer with field of vision limited by the humanly meaningful coordinates of locale or lifetime. 'After months of record temperatures, scientists say Greenland's ice sheet experienced its biggest melt of the summer on Thursday, losing 11 billion tons of surface ice to the ocean – equivalent to 4.4 million Olympic swimming pools' (Tutton 2019).

It may be due to the limits of my own imagination, but I have to confess that the comparison doesn't help me at all. I somehow understand it is a huge amount and an irregular and alarming event; however, I am not able to picture millions of Olympic swimming pools any better than billions of tonnes of ice. We encounter similar conversions almost daily, whenever there is some excessive, out-of-place occurrence. We usually understand them as 'records'. There is a close connection between the meaning of the word 'record' as an item of information that is put down

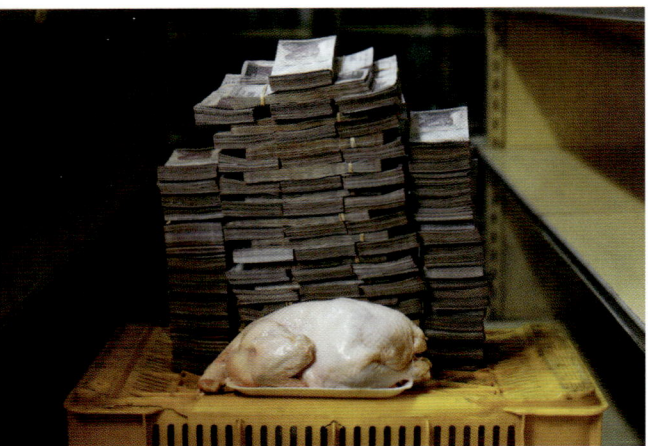

Figure 3.4 A 2.4-kg chicken is pictured next to 14,600,000 bolivars, its price and the equivalent of 2.22 USD, at a mini-market in the low-income neighborhood of Catia in Caracas, Venezuela, 16 August 2018. Globe Media/Reuters/Garcia Rawlins.

Figure 3.5 A kilogram of carrots is pictured next to 3,000,000 bolivars, its price and the equivalent of 0.46 USD, at a mini-market in the low-income neighborhood of Catia in Caracas, Venezuela, 16 August 2018. Globe Media/Reuters/Garcia Rawlins.

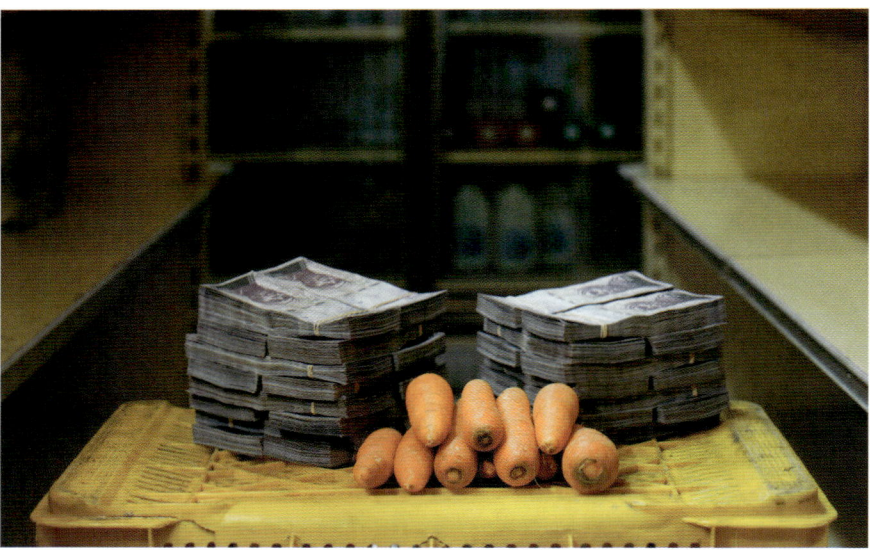

in some physical medium (as when we write down daily temperatures in a table to preserve them and make available for comparison) and as the most extreme value or achievement. Recording produces records, comparisons and ranking. In 2017, FC Barcelona sold the Brazilian footballer Neymar to Paris Saint-Germain. He became the most expensive player to date, worth 222 million euros. The press and social media were immediately filled with nonsensical conversions and comparisons that were meant to put the exceptional transfer fee into some kind of perspective, asking typically what one can buy for the price of one Neymar: three Boeing 737–700 passenger planes; enough spaghetti to cover Barcelona; 792,000,000 Freddo chocolate bars; the entire GDP of Tuvalu or 0.001% of the US national debt (BBC 2017). Eccentric figures can be measured only by other eccentric figures. It almost seems as if they should have their own category of numerals: before the Hindu-Arabic notation, the Egyptian hieroglyph for 1,000,000 or 'many' was expressed by a man with his arms stretched toward heaven in amazement.

An inflated value – one that is higher than it should be or than is reasonable – asks to be turned into a quotidian, commonplace measure in order to be comprehended at all. Price inflation, namely hyperinflation, has created its own photographic trope, juxtaposing images of everyday food and household items with piles of near-worthless banknotes. One recent example is the Venezuelan currency the bolivar, which hit 1,698,488% inflation in 2018. At the time, a 2.4-kilogram chicken cost 14,600,000 bolivars, a toilet roll 2,600,000 bolivars, a bunch of carrots 3,000,000 bolivars (BBC 2018) (Figures 3.4 to 3.6).

The photographs visualise the disproportion between a conventional, expected price, where money is believed to have some 'real' value or

Figure 3.6 A roll of toilet paper is pictured next to 2,600,000 bolivars, its price and the equivalent of 0.40 USD, at a mini-market in the ow-income neighborhood of Catia in Caracas, Venezuela, 16 August 2018. Globe Media/Reuters/Garcia Rawlins.

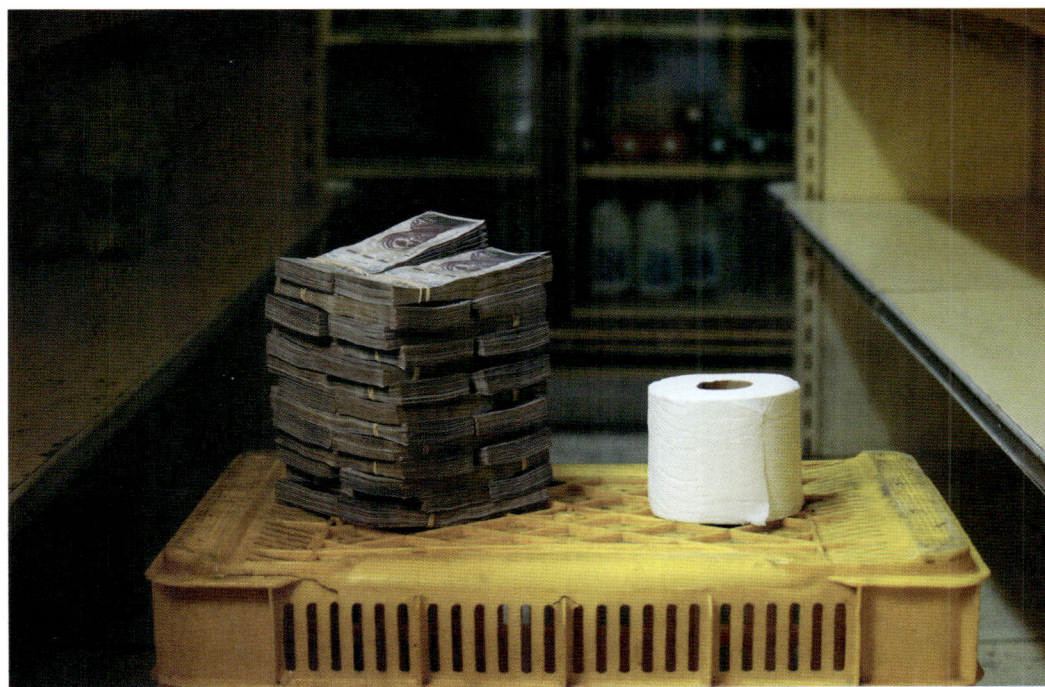

'substance', and the hyperinflated medium of money, which ceases to be the measure of anything but its own deterioration. The everyday products provide scale, like a human next to a pyramid, a matchbox next to an unfamiliar object. The abstract universality of homogeneous units is confronted with traditional vague and representational measures, such as were typically derived from human limbs and labour. The standard procedure of valuation is reversed: it is not the amount of money that determines the price of a commodity, but the commodity that determines the value of money instead. If the images pictured only the piles of banknotes, they would most likely evoke wealth and abundance, yet when compared with the 'standard' of a chicken, toilet roll or a bunch of carrots, they collapse into a nonsensical number. Of course, the images here are framed by a particular narrative, and we are used to similar illustrative pictures at least since the wheelbarrow money of the Weimar Republic. With a different kind of explanation, we could be looking at so-called singular goods such as unique and expensive chickens or carrots. In our contemporary era of fiat money where there is no capacity to measure its value against an external standard, such as gold, its purchasing power is determined by statistical indexes.

Photographs constitute spaces of equivalence and commensurability: 'What in reality is discrete, images join' (Sontag 1977: 175). This does not, however, necessarily imply that the meaning of all objects and events is levelled and universally equivalent, rather simply that the conditions for comparing things are established, especially when photographs circulate within large administrative and political systems of standardisation. It is the coming together necessary for any comparison and commensurability: images join realities as their *tertium comparationis*. They create relations between apples and pears through a common metric by defining their standards of appearance.

Transcending the Scales

One of the specific, puzzling, and often overlooked characteristics of photography is the way it relates to – and redefines – the relationship between the visible and the invisible. We often find passing comments on this power of the camera, typically in the context of discussions of microscopic and telescopic imagery:

> [P]hotography from being merely another way of procuring or making images of things already seen by our eyes, has become a means to ocular awareness of things that our eyes can never see directly. It has become the necessary tool for all visual comparison of things that are not side by side, and for all visual knowledge of the literally unseeable. (Ivins 1969: 134)

The fact that through photographs we can bring both the observable and unobservable in front of our eyes and place them side by side seems like a trivial statement. I would argue, however, that it has serious implications for our understanding of photography and technical images in general. In most traditional scholarship, we encounter a more or less implicit demarcation line between photographs that picture things that can be seen by a naked eye (at least potentially – the photographer can mediate views of remote or inaccessible scenes that could nevertheless be seen) and that picture the so-called 'invisible', delegated typically to the realm of 'scientific photography'. A number of books and exhibitions explored this phenomenon, often making the demarcation clear in their titles and opening statements. Take as an example Jon Darius's book *Beyond Vision*, which defines scientific photography as that which provides information inaccessible to the human eye: 'On all scales from the submicroscopic to the cosmic, photography has the ability to expand our limited vision, revealing invisible radiations, fleeting events, vanishingly faint images, remote realms of space and ocean which the naked eye cannot capture' (Darius 1984: 5).

Circumscribing photography of the invisible into the realm of scientific photography is rather unfortunate because it implies that a non-scientific photograph is basically a reproduction of the appearance of objects, a mirror reflection of reality, identified with human vision. This is clearly not the case as no photograph is adequate to our unaided visual impressions. We could develop a whole range of case-specific and heterogeneous categories of in/visibility, un/seeability, un/observability, in/accessibility, un/noticeability that would characterise the peculiar relationships of photographs to human vision and bypass the simplified dichotomy of the visible and invisible. The dichotomy feeds on the history of the disproportion of vision, outlined above, and also resurfaces in many contemporary accounts of nonhuman visual systems. The differences between the human and the technological and between the visible and the invisible do not match, but rather overlap in complex and evolving forms. The assumed distinction between the visible and the invisible needs to be replaced with studying the ways of generating the eccentric configurations of visibilities simultaneously with anaesthetic fields of invisibility: 'The entire history of images can thus be told as an effort to *visually transcend* the trivial contrasts between the *visible* and the *invisible*' (Didi-Huberman 2008: 133).

This history is not about what particular instruments and images reveal but rather about the multiplication and conjunction of images, their coming together and laying side by side. This history is less concerned with the relationship between the image and its referent than with the relationship between images themselves, since images en masse constitute new kinds of referents, paradoxical entities that are simultaneously real and constructed. Photographic aggregates transcend the here and now – the 'unique existence in a particular place' (Benjamin 2006: 103) – much like statistical regularities that cannot be attributed to individuals. It is not only particular objects or events that become commensurable through photographs but, more importantly, the various scales of reality, from the subatomic to the galactic, that can meet side by side.

Oliver Wendell Holmes continues his above-quoted discussion of rendering comparison of similar objects through photography with a prophetic paragraph:

> The next European war will send us stereographs of battles. It is asserted that a bursting shell can be photographed. The time is perhaps at hand when a flash of light, as sudden and brief as that of the lightning which shows a whirling wheel standing stock still, shall preserve the very instant of the shock of contact of the mighty armies that are even now gathering. The lightning from heaven does actually photograph natural objects on the bodies of those it has just blasted, – so we are told by many witnesses. The lightning of flashing sabres and bayonets may be forced to stereotype itself in a stillness as complete as that of the tumbling tide of Niagara as we see it self-pictured. (Holmes 1980: 61)

From mirrors with memory or drawing by light, Holmes turns to a very different register of metaphors, where photography becomes a discharge of enormous force and energy, lightning, a tumbling waterfall, a clash of armies in a battle. Such a massive image was soon to be realised in the Great War, the seminal catastrophe later called the First World War: not only did it picture battles, but it became part of warfare itself as the first occasion of aerial photography being strategically deployed as part of intelligence-based military operations. It required industrial production of thousands or rather millions of photographs pasted together and continuously updated: '20 workers might produce as many as 1,500 prints in an hour, working 16-hour shifts', notes Allan Sekula in his essay on instrumental images. He also points out the experience of cognitive dissonance inherent in seeing human figures in these images:

> [T]he human presence is peculiarly marked in these photographs. This markedness derives from a conflict between scale and desire; the human figure has to be searched out, dragged out, of the image. The anonymity of combatants and civilians teeters on the edge of invisibility. (Sekula 1984: 45)

In the First World War, the gigantic became reality. It is an event that can be best described by horrifying and astonishing figures and, simultaneously, from the perspective of its participants, as something utterly absurd and meaningless. In the First World War, human existence came closest to being a mere number. In his 1975 essay on the 'twentieth century as war', Jan Patočka urges us to rethink war not as an exceptional event – an unpleasant but necessary pause from the perspective of peace – but rather as that very perspective from which we need to interpret our present:

> WWI was a turning point in the history of the twentieth century and decided its whole character. It demonstrated that it necessarily takes a war to transform the world into a laboratory which would actualize energies accumulated over billions of years. It thus amounted to a definitive breakthrough in the way of understanding being. a breakthrough which began in the seventeenth century with the emergence of mechanistic natural sciences. It removed all those conventions that had lain in the path of this release of force and reevaluated all values in the name of force. (Patočka 1976: 119)

Our visual culture needs to be interpreted from this perspective as well: the mass image as a means for releasing accumulated force.

References

BBC (2017), 'What Can I Buy for the Price of One Neymar?', *BBC News*, 2 August 2017. Available at: <https://www.bbc.com-news-world-40806702> (last accessed 2 September 2019).

BBC (2018), 'Venezuelan Bolivar – What Can It Buy You?', *BBC News*, 20 August 2018. Available at: <https://www.bbc.com-news-world-latin-america-45246409> (last accessed 2 September 2019).

Benjamin, Walter (2006), 'The Work of Art in the Age of Its Technological Reproducibility: Second Version', in Walter Benjamin, *Selected Writings, Vol. 3, 1935–1938*, Cambridge, MA, and London: The Belknap Press of Harvard University Press, pp. 101–33.

Blumenberg, Hans (1987), *The Genesis of the Copernican World*. Cambridge, MA: The MIT Press.

Clark, Timothy (2015), *Ecocriticism on the Edge: The Anthropocene as a Threshold Concept*. London: Bloomsbury Academic.

Darius, Jon (1984), *Beyond Vision*. Oxford: Oxford University Press.

Didi-Huberman, Georges (2008), *Images in Spite of All: Four Photographs from Auschwitz*. Chicago: The University of Chicago Press.

Emerson, Ralph Waldo (2009), *Swedenborg: Introducing the Mystic*. London: The Swedenborg Society.

Hegel, Georg Wilhelm Friedrich (2010), *The Science of Logic*. Cambridge: Cambridge University Press.

Heidegger, Martin (1977), *The Question Concerning Technology and Other Essays*. New York and London: Garland Publishing.

Heidegger, Martin (1999), *Contributions to Philosophy (From Enowning)*. Bloomington: Indiana University Press.

Holmes, Oliver Wendell (1980), 'The Stereoscope and the Stereograph', in Beaumont Newhall (ed.), *Photography: Essays & Images*. New York: the Museum of Modern Art, pp. 53–61.

Ivins, William M. (1969), *Prints and Visual Communication*. Cambridge, MA: The MIT Press.

Jameson, Fredric (1991), *Postmodernism, or, The Cultural Logic of Late Capitalism*. Durham, NC: Duke University Press.

Kurgan, Laura (2013), *Close Up at a Distance: Mapping, Technology, and Politics*. New York: Zone Books.

La Bruyère, Jean de (1885), *The 'Characters'*. London: John C. Nimmo.

Lessing, Gotthold Ephraim (2005), *Philosophical and Theological Writings*. Cambridge: Cambridge University Press.

Lovejoy, Arthur O. (1936), *The Great Chain of Being: A Study of the History of an Idea*. Cambridge, MA: Harvard University Press.

Malraux, André (1974), *The Voices of Silence*. St Albans: Paladin.

Mumford, Lewis (1934), *Technics and Civilization*. New York: Harcourt, Brace and Company.

Pascal, Blaise (2004), *Pensées*. Indianapolis: Hackett Publishing Company.

Patočka, Jan (1976), 'Wars of the 20th Century and the 20th Century as War', *Telos*, No. 30, Winter, pp. 116–26.

Porter, Theodore M. (1995), *Trust in Numbers: The Pursuit of Objectivity in Science and Public Life*. Princeton: Princeton University Press.

Sekula, Allan (1984), *Photography against the Grain: Essays and Photo Works 1973–1983*. Halifax: The Press of the Nova Scotia College of Art and Design.

Sontag, Susan (1977), *On Photography*. New York: Farrar, Straus and Giroux.

Tutton, Mark (2019), 'Greenland's Ice Sheet Just Lost 11 Billion Tons of Ice – In One Day', *CNN International*, 16 August 2019. Available at: <https://edition.cnn.com-2019-08-02-world-greenland-ice-sheet-11-billion-intl-index.html> (last accessed 2 September 2019).

Van Helden, Albert (1985), *Measuring the Universe: Cosmic Dimensions from Aristarchus to Halley*. Chicago: The University of Chicago Press.

Vogl, Joseph (2007), 'Becoming-Media: Galileo's Telescope', *Grey Room*, No. 29, Fall 2007, pp. 14–25.

4 Living with the Excessive Scale of Contemporary Photography

Andrew Fisher

QUESTIONS OF SCALE permeate contemporary photography. To take up a photographically enabled device or to encounter a photographic image today is to be confronted with unprecedented and unavoidable facts of scale, processes of scaling and conditions of scalability (Fisher 2013). The most obvious (and most often noted) aspect of this situation is the enormous and ever increasing number of photographs now created and circulated on a daily basis (see Stallabrass 1996; Bratton 2016; Meeker 2019). This expansive and difficult-to-grasp horizon of large number frames every photographic image – as well as each act of imaging – in ways that are not yet really understood, despite the frequency with which they are remarked upon (Cohnen 2008; Hand 2012; Dombois and Harboe 2017). A vast de- and re-scaling of photography has transformed the ways in which photographic images continue to graft individual concerns onto global processes and, vice versa, how photography insinuates large-scale economic and political interests into individual lives (Steyerl 2011; Zylinska 2017). More than ever before, photographic images act as uncertain points of convergence between different possibilities and problems of scale (Fisher 2017). Coming to terms with the gigantic scale of contemporary photography will, accordingly, entail understanding what it means to say that the photographic image takes form as a constellation of scaled relations.

This chapter sets out to pursue this task through readings of two essays by Jean-Luc Nancy: 'Nous Autres' (We Others) and 'Human Excess' (Nancy 2000, 2005). The continuing promise of the photographic image – to render the world sensible and thus shareable – has been thrown into disarray by the exponential rescaling of photography. Considered alongside each other, these essays suggest a framework within which to conceptualise and to evaluate this situation. Key, here, will be a suggestion that Nancy makes in 'Nous Autres' to the effect that photography makes manifest our strangeness to ourselves and that it does so by articulating asymmetrical, heterogeneous and variable modes of being in relation to others. He writes:

> Each 'subject' in the photo refers tacitly, obstinately, to all the others, to this prodigious universe of photos in(to) which we all take ourselves and one another, at some time or another, this colossal and labyrinthine phototheque in whose depths there stalks – like a Minotaur – the monster, the monstration, and the prodigious image of our strangeness. (Nancy 2005: 106)

Note the scaled language of this passage, which is pivotal to Nancy's essay. Firstly, it is into a 'prodigious universe of photos' that we are '*all*' swept at some time or other (intertwined temporal and spatial modes of scaling applied to the mass of humanity). Then there's the second characterisation of photography, as such, and by allusion to Greek myth, as, 'this colossal and labyrinthine phototheque . . . in whose depths there stalks' an 'image of our strangeness'. This strangeness, itself, takes on the scale of 'the universe of photos' insofar as it, too, is 'prodigious'.

This is part of an overall theoretical picture in which being with others is ontologically primordial – fundamental to being human and, as such, for Nancy, to Being itself – and central to his philosophy (see Nancy 1991). Elaboration of what this means is the core concern of *Being Singular Plural*, the English edition of the book in which 'Human Excess' is published. Elsewhere in the book Nancy writes: 'That which exists, whatever this might be, coexists because it exists. The co-implication of existing . . . is the sharing of the world' (Nancy 2000: 29). In this light, at the risk of being reductive, one can remark upon the way in which the title *Being Singular Plural* announces Nancy's insistence that Being, as such, does not precede coexistence but, rather, emerges in and through being with others. Thus: 'Coexistence does not happen to existence; it is not added to it, and one cannot subtract it out: it is existence' (Nancy 2000: 187). As far as humanity is concerned, this incorporates an originary moment of alienation.

> Man began with the strangeness of his own humanity. Or with the humanity of his own strangeness. Through this strangeness he presented himself: he presented it, or figured it to himself. Such was the self-knowledge of man, that his presence was that of a stranger, monstrously similar. (Nancy 1996: 69)[1]

What is significant to note is that Nancy suggests that one's relation to others passes in a similar manner through that array of technical operations, historical practices and cultural formations that we gather together under the name of photography and conventionally condense into discussion of photographic images. To say this is to read against the grain of much scholarship on Nancy's writings about art and visual culture, which concentrates itself on his sustained analyses of the aesthetic category of the image (see Nancy 2005; Lechte 2012; Heppell 2016).[2] What may be different and distinctive about the theoretical characterisation of photography in 'Nous Autres' has received surprisingly little, if any, comment (see Giunta and Janus 2016). The inherently scaled character of this essay's notion of photography has, to date, gone completely unremarked.

'Nous Autres' unfolds as a densely wrought articulation of the large scale of photography figured through the small scale of a problematic and generalised existential standpoint. Nancy places at the heart of photography its capacity to articulate relations and this takes the form of an encounter with 'our strangeness to ourselves' as we navigate a 'colossal and labyrinthine phototheque'. The linkage between this and 'Human Excess' to be made here follows an intuition, namely, that photography's recent de- and rescaling threatens to dissolve this defining moment of alienation. What happens, one might ask, when the 'colossal and labyrinthine phototheque' mutates to appear yet more colossal and more labyrinthine with every passing moment? What happens to the colossal as a limit figure of perception and the labyrinth as a concern for orientation when the operations of a greater and greater percentage of images become ambivalent with regard to humans (are never apprehended by anybody who might get lost in their appearances) (see Derrida 1987; Mason 2013). What happens when every swollen statistic generated emphasises the sense in which, whatever has become of photography, the figures of the labyrinth and the colossal no longer seem adequate to it, appear restrictive where they used to imply the unbounded?

'Human Excess' calls into question the modes of excess and incalculability that are supposed to lie at the heart of demands for measure and proportion and that inform critical discourses of dismeasure and disproportion. It reorients relationships between these poles and questions the notion of the human as a measure of both the known and of that which exceeds knowledge. Read as an extension of 'Nous Autres', it also calls into question the assumption that the scaled character of contemporary photography can be resolved with any appeal to the human as its ultimate measure. But, rather than rendering the human obsolete or irrelevant to an understanding of contemporary photography, I argue that this challenges one to reconceive the way in which the figure of the human is presumed to have secured understanding of photography in its previous guises and how it operates in the contemporary photographic milieu.

The notion that photographic images take form in and as a constellation of scaled relations emerges, here, as a promising basis upon which to address this situation.

Photographic Constellations of Scale

If one wants to understand the ways in which photographic images help us to construct the fractious and heterogeneous visual world of the present it is, I argue, imperative to understand the constellations of scale met in and through these images. But what does this mean? A clue arises from the fact that the relations of scale in question here are multiple, complex and often vehemently contested. They matter. In the face of such vehemence, it is important to keep this multiplicity and this complexity in the foreground of analysis. Consider, for example, the individuals and technologies, political interests and geographies compounded in visualisations of migration across the Mediterranean in recent years. How is scale a specific issue for photography here?

It was encountered at simultaneously intimate and world-spanning registers in photographs showing the diminutive body of Aylan Kurdi washed onto a beach on Kos in 2015: a set of images that circulated globally to affect millions and produce moral outrage on a huge scale but that had little or no lasting political effect (Vis and Goriunova 2015). Here one is confronted by tragically compounded questions of scale that play over the surface of the image and that haunt its public form, not least because of the manner in which the images in question ended up reinforcing what appears to be an inescapable antinomy of photographic ethics.[3]

By contrast, consider the lack of images and of global outrage – but the centrality of distributed imaging devices – in the story of a packed migrant boat registered by surveillance agencies but left to drift across the Mediterranean in 2011; what became known as the 'left-to-die' boat (Heller and Pezzani 2014). This vessel's occupants were rendered visible from the skies while holding up mobile devices to photograph the potential rescuers hovering above them in a helicopter. The resulting situation did not end in their rescue nor did it produce a definitive image, but it was saturated with photographic concerns and possibilities. As Ariella Azoulay has shown, the visual characteristics of events like this might be highly attenuated, because on the face of it they produce no pictures, but they are no less 'photographic' for this fact (Azoulay 2008).

The point here is that attention to photography's role in these connected but contrasting examples shows it to be structured by multi-layered and simultaneous operations of scale, such as those measuring out the spaces and times of an image's making and reception, of embodied comportment towards particular places and events, of applied technical processes of scaling, mobilisations of mass emotion, determinations of social value and effects of unevenly distributed geo-political power. These very different senses of scale, scaling and scalability – pictorial, technical, phenomenological, social, geographical and political – collide with each other in these photographic events and in the images they generate. If one brackets, for a moment at least, the always pressing concern for what such fraught images may show, then what is left over is the variety of intercalated scales that enable them, that they operate within and which are applied to them (Fisher 2013: 311). On these bases one can remark that, whether realised materially and seen widely, or not, a photographic image takes form as the more or less stable meeting point between otherwise divergent senses, expectations, practices and possibilities of scale.

The photographic event of the 'left-to-die' boat stresses one implication of this insight, precisely insofar as it produced no defining image and yet nonetheless exemplifies the operative technical, geographical and political processes of scale at work in all photographic events. The often bemoaned inability of even the most tragically affective and singular images, like those of Aylan Kurdi, to effect real social and political change signals the difficult-to-accept fact that, for all that they concentrate attention on what they represent, and for all that this is tragic, images such as these coalesce around powerful and invisible forms of abstraction that determine how they come to be seen and that shape how they can exert affect (see Fisher 2016). Such cases stand to teach us that bracketing the dominance of representation analytically to reveal the constellations of scale that structure contemporary photographs is not a formal and unmotivated exercise. Rather, it promises ways of understanding how the most fraught and difficult of our images come to operate in the ways they do.

At risk of repetition, one can remark that in such fraught photographic situations, as well as in less heavily burdened cases, to take up a photographically enabled device, to be photographed or to encounter a photographic image, places one at the centre of a constellation of different facts of scale, processes of scaling and conditions of scalability. This has no doubt always been true of photography in its various historical forms but it has only recently become obvious as a consequence of globalised networked digital imaging technologies. In this milieu, scale takes on novel spatial and temporal, technical and experiential meanings that combine to shape what a photographic image can be and what it might do. Further, to make or encounter photographic images in this context involves dealing with the legacy of photography's promise to set the world to measure and to grant things proportion. But it also entails the obverse insofar as it situates one in a visualised world that seems governed by dismeasure and disproportionality (see Steyerl 2011; Weizman 2012). Theoretical elucidation of this convoluted state of affairs promises to enable ways of reconceptualising the ethically and politically urgent questions of visualisation that delineate the present and to understand photography's vital role in its making.

Photography as a Scaled Relation to Others

In 'Nous Autres', Nancy sets out to theorise a mode of being in relation to others. He does this through analysis of what it means to utter three pronouns and related pronominal phrases: 'I', 'we' and 'we others'. Significantly, in doing this, he engages with photography as a suite of activities: the act of photographing; the act of being photographed; and the act of looking at photographs. He takes these photographic activities to be interrelated modes of enunciation that identify someone or some group in a way that operates as if saying 'I', 'we' and 'we others'. In drawing this parallel between acts of photography and linguistic utterances, Nancy effectively reconceives of photography as a mode of being-with-others (in contrast, for instance, to taking it as a secondary apparatus of identification that is antecedent to pre-existing relationships). Moreover, he thinks of photography as a way of being-with-others that teaches one about a defining estrangement shaping all claims to identity, a fundamental entanglement with others that also passes through the machineries of photographing, being photographed and looking at photographs. Apart from one other essay in which photography features centrally, 'Masked Imagination' (which in many ways reads as a compliment to 'Nous Autres'), I can think of no other point in Nancy's oeuvre at which machinic operations of visualisation are granted such a significant, ontologically inflected role (Nancy 2005).

Nancy's argument in 'Nous Autres' unfolds as follows. To say 'I' is to identify oneself, to stake a claim to being a subject while also distinguishing oneself abstractly in opposition to all of those others who can say and do the same. He writes: 'In a definitive way *I* constitutes a performative in the sense that linguists give to the *speech* act: the enunciation itself produces the truth of the statement. I am by saying "I am"' (Nancy 2005: 102). He turns to a telling example to fill this out: '*I* can emerge . . . like the snap of a camera shutter: by pressing down, the finger says I' (Nancy 2005: 101). This is an act of identification that rests on a paradox, namely, while in performing it one marks oneself out as being without substitute – 'it's me, I'm here!' – one also implicitly acknowledges that this grammatical form routinely substitutes anybody and everybody in one's place.

This enunciative possibility hinges not just on the release of a shutter per se but on the explicit act of someone photographing someone else. I press the shutter and, in the process of picturing another, enunciate my presence and identity but also my isolation from and exchangeability with anyone else who can do this. Given that 'we all take ourselves and one another' into the ubiquitous visual milieu opened up when we embody such acts, the implication is that photography operates at something like the same level (in parallel to but separate from) as that of the strictly linguistic possibility after which Nancy models it. While it shares a necessity for embodiment with performative linguistic utterances, the photographic possibility placed in question here is also materially machinic or apparatic.

While the click of the camera shutter might say 'I', the photographic situation thus inaugurated also produces a 'you'. Because being photographed is not passive but is an act in its own right, someone else comes on the scene to say 'I' in performing the act of being photographed. A series of asymmetries is thus produced. The 'you' that also says 'I' in performing the act of being photographed embodies a superimposed enunciation of identity. And the possibility that this other, so to speak, intercalated subject might then take up the camera and turn the tables stands open as an implicit aspect of the intersubjective relation thus inaugurated. Furthermore, acting in unison, these two might go on to compound the enunciations of their-selves in the act of viewing the resulting image together, sharing in its relationality albeit from asymmetrically articulated standpoints. Thus an expanding series of intertwined but distinct photographic acts accrue as compounded modes of enunciation that are layered over and anticipated by the first.

Yet more possibilities of enunciation relating to this initial series could and do, of course, spin off to encompass effectively everyone and everything in the field of photographic relations. The positions and relations staked out in this way actively constitute an intersubjective topography. With an impressive economy of means this theory of photographic relationality spirals out to characterise the enormity of photographic culture and promises purchase on how it is lived, namely, from the billions of different points of simultaneous and consequent action – whether realised, in process or *in potentia* – that make up the contemporary visual milieu. This theory of photographic relationality is not exhausted, obviously, by the bare act of laying claim to one's numerical identity with oneself. An account of other possible modes of relationality is required to flesh it out.

Nancy continues: 'It is a quite different matter when it comes to saying "we"' (Nancy 2005: 101). This differs from the notional self-coincidence involved in saying 'I' or 'you', as it lays claim to a shared identity which is yet to be realised. It is to solicit something or to make a demand on someone: 'Every time someone says "we" . . . he formulates a request for identification' (Nancy 2005: 102). A 'we' has to be filled out in time and space. It implies a lack of coincidence in contrast to that supposed to be met with in saying 'I'. 'We', Nancy claims, is a pronoun of generic identifications, and of appeals to identity that often *impose* a generalised identity upon those it sets out to encompass, by soliciting compliance or demanding submission.[4]

Nancy returns to these questions of relation and the linguistic forms through which they are articulated in repeated analyses, such as in the following discussion of the pronoun 'we' and the concept of society from *Being Singular Plural*:

> Society knows itself and sees itself as bared, exposed to this common excess [*démesure*]. At one and the same time, it sees itself as something quite evident and transparent, whose necessity eclipses that of every *ego sum*, and as an opacity that denies itself every subjective appropriation. At that moment when we clearly come [to stand] before ourselves, as the lone addresser(s) facing the lone addressee(s), we cannot truly say 'we'.
>
> But it is through this that we now have to attain to a knowledge of the 'we' – attain to a knowledge and/or praxis of the 'we'. (Nancy 2000: 75–6)

The exemplary status granted photography in 'Nous Autres' – that it holds out the possibility of different ways of articulating social being – secures for it a very interesting if not fully thematised role in Nancy's broader ontological framework. I take this to be something like the necessity that Nancy posits in this passage, namely, of having to come to terms with an unresolvable knowledge of that dismeasure or excess lying at the heart of societal relations and revealed at the point of their enactment. It is notable that Nancy's contrast between the grammatical possibilities of saying 'I' and 'we' is more starkly delineated in the version reworked for publication in *The Ground of the Image* in comparison to in its original form as an essay accompanying a photographic exhibition of the same title in 2003. In particular, in the earlier text, a point of indifference appears to shape the relation between the possibilities of saying 'we' and 'we others'.

> Whereas *I* produces or creates its own identity, *we* projects it or superposes it. *We others* admits the understanding that when the time comes, upon enquiry, this *we* could become another subject entirely. 'We others' jointly contains a presumption, based on no evidence to back its enunciation. Who pronounces this 'we others'? That is anything but clear. (Nancy 2003: 124)

The intervening years since 2003 have seen reality shaping itself socially and politically around a much starker take on the rhetorics of 'we-ness' than Nancy projects in either version of this essay.

Between the bare alienation of the utterance 'I' and the coercive expectations imposed by assertions of 'we', lies, for Nancy, another possibility of enunciation, namely, the 'we others' of the essay's title. The phrase remains untranslated in the version I read because it doesn't exist in English. It is a grammatical possibility of Spanish (the language of the essay's original publication) and French, which Nancy takes to introduce a space for identification – and thus of relation to others – that does not take the bare serial form of 'I'. Nor does it impose the norms he associates with the act of lining up under a 'we'. To say 'we others', here, is to introduce questions of asymmetry, heterogeneity and productive non-coincidence into one's way of enacting one's relations with others. It has to be negotiated and at least starts out without imposing a norm. Crucially, it is photography and not language that stands as his example for this possibility: 'An essential non-coincidence makes *us* other than *ourselves* . . . This non-coincidence passes through photography in an exemplary way' (Nancy 2005: 104). Here, to expand on photography's role in all of this:

> The secret of the photograph, . . . is its flight into the strange in the very midst of the familiar. The photo captures the familiar, and immediately, instantaneously, it strays into strangeness. . . . The photograph estranges, it estranges us. Between the subject of the click and the subject grasped, there is a coexistence without coincidence. (Nancy 2005: 106)

Recall that, for Nancy, 'Coexistence . . . is existence', i.e., a basic sharing of the world (Nancy 2000: 187). But, here, the serial form of alienated identity implicit in the expectation of coincidence with oneself as an 'I' is absent, and so is the coercive horizon of any imposed coincidence with others in a determinate 'we'. Photography, in its acts of enunciation and modes of relation, captures the character of subjectivity in a 'coexistence without coincidence' that passes through the three modes of operation made central by Nancy: taking, being taken, and sharing in the taking of one another into the world of photography. The operations of the apparatus thus delineated appear basic to the shared but indeterminate world he articulates: 'Such is the straying and secret *I am* of the photo. Thus it does not say, "I is an other"; rather, it proffers the wholly other "I am" whose text consists in "we others"' (Nancy 2005: 106). Recall, also, that the question of who *these* others are remains in principle open, though it is, at least temporarily, concrete.

Insofar as it articulates a theory of relationality, the idea of photography developed in 'Nous Autres' is not tied to any particular form or apparatus of photography ('analogue' as opposed to 'digital', for instance). Nor does the entity that operates the controls and inaugurates these relationships need to be an embodied or present human being. The 'subject of the click' (or whatever register of operation is entailed) has only to be able to set the process off. Nancy emphasises human-to-human relations here. But nothing in his analysis actually excludes the plethora of other possibilities of relation that combine to make up contemporary photography and that include all sorts of functions, machines, distributed forms and artificial intelligences – as well as, for that matter, bums acting in conjunction with trouser pockets – which have the ability to inaugurate a photographic event.

Before its recent expansion – remember that 'Nous Autres' was first published in 2003 – one finds Nancy reimagining photography, in scaled terms, as a massively convoluted milieu of actions and operations through which identity and intersubjectivity are articulated and within which they learn of their ownmost modes of estrangement. Estrangement in this scaled framework is not incidental and does not come after the fact. It is integral to selfhood, and photography is pivotal to the revelation of this. As photography functions by dint of scaled operations and possibilities, its modes of scale, scaling and scalability appear integral to the formation of selfhood and relations to others. How, then, to understand this scaled idea of photographic relationality in the context of the exponential de- and rescaling of photography that is such a striking feature of contemporary life?

Negotiations of Measure

In 'Human Excess' Nancy develops a critical analysis of measure and dismeasure in an era habituated to bloated statistical values and the accelerated production of truthful but hollow measurements: 'Ten billion people on earth' as a 'prospective demographic truth', on the one hand, and, on the other, the trivial generation of huge numerical abstractions which establish 'facts devoid of meaning but not of truth' (Nancy 2000: 177).

Measure, in Nancy's analysis, is defined as 'the name for a propriety of one Being to another, or to itself', i.e., the degree of proportion that can be established between them (Nancy 2000: 177). What determines a particular measure of one thing against another is convention. Think of Nancy's characterisation of photography as a 'colossal and labyrinthine phototheque', where the meaning of the untranslated French word 'phototheque' is photo-library or photographic archive. Whatever the level of rigour with which it may be applied, and however widespread its use may be, the system of order applied to the images contained by the phototheque is imposed by convention. But one might also want to illustrate the size of this archive *itself* by, for instance, describing how many times it contents would span the world if laid end to end, a familiar trope that doesn't tell one anything significant about the images contained. For Nancy this would be to produce 'facts devoid of meaning but not of truth, albeit infinitely impoverished truth'. And, crucially, he continues: 'Within this order excess is impossible' (Nancy 2000: 178). Whether in the name of imposed convention or impoverished truth, he goes on to write, acts of bringing something to measure are engagements emerging from specific historical, economic and social contexts that constitute what he projects as the worldliness of a world construed, insofar as part of it is set to measure. In this context, regardless of their trivial or tragic character: 'each time, these figures measure a responsibility' and, further, '. . . the proliferation of large numbers in our culture, our interests and our needs . . . also defines the exponential growth of such responsibility' (Nancy 2000: 178).

This sketch of a critically articulated theory of measure seems particularly resonant with regard to the situation of photography discussed at the beginning of this chapter, especially given the ways in which photography's massive and accelerating rescaling impacts on individuals, institutions and social groups across the board. As noted briefly in the chapter's introduction, the contemporary photographic image carries over a promise from earlier photographic forms, namely, that it might render a disorientating world sensible and proportionate and enable individuals as well as institutions to orient themselves within the conflicted milieu they are supposed to share. It is debatable whether photography was ever able to fulfil such promise. But while the promise to render things commensurable has expanded in scope along with photography, any widespread belief in photography's ability to make good on its promise seems only to have diminished. This often-remarked prospect reveals something important with regard to the meaning of scale in and for photography today. More than ever before, photographic images act as uncertain points of convergence between the large scale and the small scale and thus new relationships forged between, for instance, power and desire, individuals and social groups, bodies and institutions. Coming to terms with the gigantic scale of contemporary photography will entail understanding what it means to say that the photographic image is such a convergence of scales or, better, that the photographic image takes form through a constellation of scaled relations.

Nancy's critique in 'Human Excess' maps onto the scaled theorisation of photography developed in 'Nous Autres', at least to the extent that the massive horizon of number – both qualitatively and quantitively characteristic of contemporary photography – entails an intensified and very often noted demand to understand the forms of dismeasure and disproportionality it introduces into the world. This is, indeed, a powerful figure of exponential growth in responsibility as Nancy describes. It also echoes the responsibility one bears in the face of that 'common excess' that characterises social being and that Nancy writes of as demanding 'we attain to a knowledge of the "we"' as mentioned above (Nancy 2000: 75–6). Further, within this context, the individual image or photographic event and any individuals interpolated in and through them all too easily come to stand in relation to the photographic horizon of very large number, just as the single countable thing stands in relation to the statistical abstraction that, Nancy argues, marks out a true but hollow fact incapable of encountering the excessive in any real sense.

In this light, I read the notion of responsibility that Nancy articulates in 'Human Excess' in parallel to the topologies of photographic relation developed in 'Nous Autres'. Responsibility appears as a moral or ethical call for a meaningful response, insisting on an answer but ultimately coming without any kind of proscribed measure. In this, it is precisely what is placed in question in Nancy's analysis of the possibilities of enunciation: 'I', 'we' and, in particular, the non-normative and open-ended relation implied by 'we others'.

Further, Nancy writes:

> excess is its own propriety and forms the measure of an 'un-heard-of' measure. It measures itself, that is, it is engaged as a totality. In today's world, excess (*la démesure*) is not an excess (*un excès*), in the sense that it is indeterminate with relation to normative structures. (Nancy 2000: 179)

The expansive scale of contemporary photography is conventionally discussed using vocabulary – deluge, flood, overload, multiplicity, multitude – that presumes that some norm, boundary, convention or acceptable standard has been exceeded.[5] And very often such presumptions colour an understanding of the relationship between photography's exponential growth and whatever appropriately gargantuan measures might have to be projected in order to cope with it. Read in terms of contemporary photography, 'Human Excess' highlights the ways in which the vocabulary applied to such massive scale is often mired in the determinate concerns of one or other partial viewpoint (which come all too often, also, with a strong undertow of racism and sexism or other mode of prejudice). Reference to Nancy's observations on excess aids in critically reconceiving the dismeasure, disproportion and disarray induced by the massive growth of photography. Importantly, he articulates the sense in which no appeal to humanity, to the axiomatic scale of human embodiment or humanistic principle, would resolve this situation.

> This magnitude, which is its own 'excessive' measure or measured excess, also provides the scale of a total responsibility . . . Man as the measure of all things has taken on a new, excessive meaning: far removed from every relation to the human as some mediocre standard, and also far removed from its remnants, this meaning relates humans themselves to an immense responsibility. (Nancy 2000: 179)

His point is not that if we search hard enough we might find an as yet unarticulated axiom of human scale that will ground everything. Nor is it to make yet another in a long line of calls to order or measure.

> In a certain way, all calls to measure are in vain, since there is no excess that can be determined with relation to a given measure, norm, scale, or mean. Thus, the use and/or the norm that gives the measure must itself be invented. (Nancy 2000: 180)

Rather, 'Nous Autres' and 'Human Excess' dovetail at this point to produce an idea of the photographic that is scaled according to the vast numbers that frame and impinge on the possibilities of the mass of individual relations that comprise this sphere. And, as 'Nous Autres' suggests, the modes of enunciation through which this numerically enormous horizon is thrown into relief can be thought of in ways that dissolve the hollow discourse of dismeasure that obscures the difficult relationships and responsibilities figured by photographs. The questions of scale foregrounded by contemporary photography suggest different photographic topographies of relation, ones that start out at least by soliciting negotiations of their own measure of being with others and that do not determine in advance who or what those others may be.

Notes

1. The translator, Peggy Kamuf, carries over Nancy's heavily gendered language into the English. In the current context it stands out as a prime example of the critique of coercive claims to shared identity developed below on the basis of other writings by Nancy.
2. See, for instance, Chris Heppell's discussion of 'Nous Autres' and the photographic image in 'Uncanny Landscapes of Photography' in Carrie Giunta and Adrienne Janus (eds), *Nancy and Visual Culture*, pp. 206–11. An exemplary instance of Nancy's analysis of the category of the image is 'The Image–The Distinct' in *The Ground of the Image*, pp. 1–14. A study

that is heavily influenced by Nancy's theorisation of the image, and which examines the historical continuities and disjunctions between traditional and contemporary image forms is John Lechte's *Genealogy and Ontology of the Western Image and Its Digital Future* (2012).
3. Now-classic moments in the history of ethical debates about the inability of such images to effect change are heavily shaped by Susan Sontag's influential studies *On Photography* (1977) and *Regarding the Pain of Others* (2003). Judith Butler's 2009 book, *Frames of War*, offers a trenchant critical evaluation of Sontag's view that photography remains largely inadequate in the face of traumatic events. Other notable studies are: Susie Linfield's *The Cruel Radiance* (2010); Sharon Sliwinski's *Human Rights in Camera* (2011); Geoffrey Batchen et al.'s *Picturing Atrocity* (2012); Thomas Keenan and Tirdad Zolghadr's *The Human Snapshot* (2013); and Liam Kennedy and Caitlin Patrick's *The Violence of the Image* (2014).
4. Out of a depressingly wide swathe of relevant examples from contemporary political life, one might refer here to the vocabulary of the racist German anti-immigrant movement Pegida and the Alt-right politics and cynical language of the Alternative für Deutschland party with their aberrant claims in the name of '*wir Deutsche*' (we Germans). For a specific analysis of such coercive and dubious uses of the pronoun 'we' in this context, see Heinrich Detering's astute analysis of such claims to shared identity in his *Was heißt 'wir'? Zur Rhetorik der parlamentarischen Rechten* ('What does "we" mean here? On the rhetoric of the parliamentary right') of 2019, which presents trenchant critical analyses of a number of recent public speeches made by key figures in Pigeda and the AfD. At the time of writing, parallel and equally alarming rhetorical strategies and racist overtones continue to shape divisive debates about Brexit, immigration, the 'sovereignty' of British institutions and the maintenance or dissolution of the United Kingdom.
5. In Chapter 3 of this volume, Tomáš Dvořák articulates an intellectual history of the gigantic as a figure of measure in modernity and with a focus on shifting relations between ideas of quantity and quality, especially in Hegel's and Heidegger's accounts of measurement. These antecedents inform Nancy's short critical theorisation of measure, proportion and disproportion in 'Human Excess'. Dvořák's analysis focuses on the problematic relation between proportionality and disproportionality in anthropomorphic understandings of the world construed through visual media. Nancy's account of excess as 'its own propriety' speaks to this problematic, especially, as I argue, when figured through contemporary photography.

References

Azoulay, Ariella (2008), *The Civil Contract of Photography*, Rela Mazall and Ruvik Danieli (trans.). New York: Zone Books.

Batchen, Geoffrey, Mick Gidley, Nancy K. Miller and Jay Prosser (eds) (2012), *Picturing Atrocity: Photography in Crisis*. London: Reaktion Books.

Bratton, Benjamin H. (2016), *The Stack: On Software & Sovereignty*. Cambridge, MA: MIT Press.

Butler, Judith (2009), *Frames of War*. London and New York: Verso.

Cohnen, Thomas (2008), *Fotografischer Kosmos. Der Beitrag eines Mediums zur visuellen Ordnung der Welt*. Bielefeld: Transcript.

Derrida, Jacques (1987), 'The Colossal', in Geoff Bennington and Ian McLeod (trans.), *The Truth in Painting*. Chicago and London: University of Chicago Press, pp. 119–47.

Detering, Heinrich (2019), *Was heißt hier 'wir'? Zur Rhetorik der parlamentarischen Rechten*. Stuttgart: Reclam Verlag.

Dombois, Florian, and Julie Harboe (eds) (2017), *Too Big to Scale*. Zürich: Scheidegger & Spiess Verlag.

Fisher, Andrew, 'Photographic Scale' (2013), in Daniel Rubinstein, Johnny Golding and Andrew Fisher (eds), *On the Verge of Photography: Imaging Beyond Representation*. Birmingham: ARTicle Press, Birmingham City University.

Fisher, Andrew (2016), 'On the Scales of Photographic Abstraction', in *Photographies*, 9(2), special issue on Photography & Abstraction.

Fisher, Andrew (2017), 'Imaginative Variation: Photographic Scale and Photographic Horizons', in Florian Dombois and Julie Harboe (eds), *Too Big to Scale*. Zurich: Scheidegger & Spiess Verlag.

Giunta, Carrie, and Adrienne Janus (eds) (2016), *Nancy and Visual Culture*. Edinburgh: Edinburgh University Press.

Hand, Martin (2012), *Ubiquitous Photography*. Cambridge: Polity Press.

Heller, Charles, and Lorenzo Pezzani (2014), '"All They Did was Taking Pictures": Photography and the Violence of Borders', *Philosophy of Photography*, 5(2): 93–7.

Keenan, Thomas, and Tirdad Zolghadr (eds) (2013), *The Human Snapshot*. Berlin: Sternberg Press.

Kennedy, Liam, and Caitlin Patrick (2014), *The Violence of the Image: Photography and International Conflict*. London: I. B. Taurus.

Lechte, John (2012), *Genealogy and Ontology of the Western Image and Its Digital Future*. New York & London: Routledge.

Linfield, Susie (2010), *The Cruel Radiance: Photography and Political Violence*. Chicago and London: The Chicago University Press.

Mason, Peter (2013), *The Colossal: From Ancient Greece to Giacometti*. London: Reaktion Books.

Meeker, Mary (2019), 'Internet Trends 2019'. Available at: <https://www.bondcap.com-pdf-Internet-Trends-2019.pdf> (last accessed 18 July 2020) Nancy, Jean-Luc (1991), *The Inoperative Community*, Peter Connor (ed.), Peter Connor, Lisa Garbus, Michael Holland and Simona Sawhey (trans.). Minneapolis: Minnesota University Press.

Nancy, Jean-Luc (1996), *The Muses*, Werner Hacher & David E. Welbery (eds), Peggy Kamuf (trans.). Stanford: Stanford University Press.

Nancy, Jean-Luc (2000), *Being Singular Plural*, Robert D. Richardson and Anne E. O'Byrne (trans.). Stanford: Stanford University Press.

Nancy, Jean-Luc (2003), 'OURSELVES-OUROTHERS', in *NosOstros: Photo Espana 2003*, exhibition catalogue, La Fabrica Editorial (ed.), Victoria Hughes (trans.). Madrid: La Fabrica, pp. 123–5.

Nancy, Jean-Luc (2005), *The Ground of the Image*, Jeff Fort (trans.). New York: Fordham University Press.

Sliwinski, Sharon (2011), *Human Rights in Camera*. Chicago and London: Chicago University Press.

Sontag, Susan (1977), *On Photography*. London and New York: Penguin Books.

Sontag, Susan (2003), *Regarding the Pain of Others*. London and New York: Penguin Books.

Stallabrass, Julian (1996), *Gargantua: Manufactured Mass Culture*. London and New York: Verso.

Steyerl, Hito (2011), 'In Free Fall: A Thought Experiment', in Maria Hlavajova, Simon Sheikh and Jill Winder (eds), *On Horizons: A Critical Reader in Contemporary Art*. Utrecht & Rotterdam: BAK & Post Editions, pp. 168–90.

Vis, Farida. & Olga Goriunova (eds) (2015), *The Iconic Image on Social Media: A Rapid Research Response to the Death of Aylan Kurdi*. Available at: <http://visualsocialmedialab.org-projects-the-iconic-image-on-social-media> (last accessed 23 September 2019).

Weizman, Eyal (2012), 'Material Proportionality', in Marta Kuzma (ed.), *The State of Things: Verksted 14*. Oslo, pp. 138–61.

Zylinska, Joanna (2017), *Nonhuman Photography*. Cambridge, MA: MIT Press.

5 Feeling Photos: Photography, Picture Language and Mood Capture

Michelle Henning

IT HAS OFTEN been argued that social media photography is a type of speech. A number of writers have noted this, describing it as 'visible speech', as 'gregarious', as a speech made of grunts and nods and 'silent mutterings to the self' (Rubinstein 2005: 113–118; Lister 2014: 11–12; Crano 2019: 1132). This idea recalls an earlier moment – projects such as August Sander's book *The Face of our Time* (1929) which he described as 'basically a declaration of faith in photography as universal language' and Edward Steichen's much-discussed exhibition *The Family of Man* (1955), which Steichen saw as providing 'irrefutable proof that photography is a universal language, that it speaks to all people; that people are hungry for that kind of language' (Sander 1978: 677; Steichen 1958: 167). These proponents of the idea of photography as a universal language thought that documentary photography, in particular, communicated shared human feelings and emotions as well as facts about the world. Now that so many people are taking photographs and sending them back and forth to one another, or displaying them to a potentially vast (but in practice often very small) audience, photography appears not as a language, but as speech: conversational and at the same time a form of 'speaking into the air' with perhaps the hope, but not the expectation, of a response.[1] As Paul Frosh notes, social media photography is phatic, a 'hi', a 'how are you?', a type of enunciation that is not so much about its apparent content as about maintaining sociability, forging connection, keeping a channel open (Frosh 2012: 133). The idea of photography as language seemed to singularise it, setting it apart from other media (except, perhaps, film) but the idea of photography as speech envisages something more hybrid, inseparable from text, graphics and video. While the notion of photography as a universal language seemed to aggrandise it, the vision of photography as chit-chat seems to present it as something diminished in status, if not in scale.

Arguments that photography is language-like and that it is speech-like are both accompanied by a recognition that it has become a mass practice. Discussions about photography as conversational respond to the context of mass mobile phone use, and while *The Family of Man* dealt with documentary and reportage, not amateur practice, Steichen's approach was informed by his observation that photography had introduced picture-making on an unprecedented scale (Steichen 1958: 159). Photography was associated, very early on, with a certain affectlessness, a cold gaze, a machinic inability to distinguish the meaningless from the meaningful, which in turn seemed to give it a kind of indifference (Henning 2018: 121–2). However, both the early conception of photography as a universal language and the more recent analysis of (digital, networked) photography as chatter suggest that photography can absorb and transmit nuances of communication that are primarily expressive and emotional, despite its historical claim to objectivity. Both see photography, used on a mass scale, as a technical mediator of human sociability.

This chapter reflects on the currency of social media photography, within an environment that includes text and emoji, and on the critical response to this. Observations that photography is like language or speech are rarely neutral. If to conceive of photography as a universal language requires an optimistic assessment of the medium's importance, the conversational turn is associated with a trivialising and demeaning of photography linked to its popularisation. Photography theorists emphasise the simple and 'light' emotional character of digital photo-sharing. It is understood as all felt response and no rational, logical analysis. At the same time, there remain the traces of that view of photography's huge significance, insofar as the mass circulation of images is frequently treated as a disaster of epic proportions (a 'flood', a 'tsunami'), and the images themselves are identified as a principal means by which emotions and mood are made alarmingly contagious. In an echo of much older debates about images, social media photographs seem to be regarded as both deeply attractive and deeply dangerous.

Universal Language, Rationalisation and Emotional Capitalism

In the mid-twentieth century, it became commonplace to argue that photography was the one 'language' able to transcend national and cultural boundaries, matched only by the presumed universality of human facial expressions. As Steichen wrote, 'It is the only universal language we have, the only one requiring no translation' (Steichen 1958:

160). In such 'universal language' arguments, pre- and post-war internationalist ambitions – to communicate across nations in the service of world peace – are translated into universalist ones. *The Family of Man* relied on the notion that photographs are recognisable to all people: that everyone can easily, and without prior acculturation, identify objects depicted in a photograph (and this despite the fact that photographs rely on a tradition of perspectival representation developed in Europe). Steichen clearly believed that audiences throughout the world *identified* with the images in *The Family of Man*, dismissing the fact that the exhibition was adapted for the different political and cultural contexts of different countries. As Allan Sekula notes, one figure that repeatedly appears in the discourse about the universal language of photography is that of the 'bushman' or the uncivilised 'savage' to whom it will speak 'in civilizing tones'. Photography appears as both the advocate of a 'technologically derived egalitarianism' and the perfect colonial instrument, its images a means to seduce the colonised, while taking control of their grasp on reality (Sekula 1981: 17).

Proponents of photography as a universal language assumed that, to a very large extent, context does not matter and that the photograph stands alone, meaningful in itself. Even complex symbolic meanings are believed to be self-evident in a photograph: thus Sander could say that an image of an infant in a gas mask 'would express the whole brutal, inhuman spirit of the time in universally comprehensible form' (Sander 1978: 676).[2] The universal language discourse drew on the thinking behind other picture languages such as Isotype, the visual statistics method that was briefly promoted as an international language by its inventor, Otto Neurath, during the 1930s. Yet while Neurath insisted on the limitations of Isotype, seeing it as an 'auxiliary language' that had to be adapted for different contexts, and that could not communicate emotion or affective states, photography was simultaneously presented as a purveyor of objective facts and conveyor of fellow-feeling.[3] Sekula writes that the universal language claim linked together two contrasting ideas: first, that 'photography would seem to be a way of knowing the world directly'; second that 'photography would also seem to be a way of feeling the world directly' (Sekula 1981: 21).

Sander's *The Face of our Time*, and his larger *Citizens* project to which it belonged, is essentially an inventory. Indeed, the idea of photography as a language is closely tied to its use in the production of inventories, record systems and archives, which is to say that it is conceived in bureaucratic terms. Steichen wrote:

> As a result of a survey that was made there are said to be forty million homes in the United States that have at least one camera. In that light,

consider the potentialities and possibilities of this medium. That means there are at least forty million photographers, forty million potential historians. And there lies a responsibility: What to do about this? How to direct this? (Steichen 1958: 159)

These are odd questions to ask of a so-called language, if by language we understand a creative, expressive and collective means of communication. Faced with the rise of amateur photography, Steichen's concern was about the governance of the means of communication and of the public record. Indeed, it is no coincidence that the universal language argument was most powerfully put forward at the moment of the emergence and rise of the commercial picture libraries and photo agencies, in the mid-twentieth century. These organisations expand with the 'accelerated development' of photography in the 1920s and 1930s, turning photographs into standardised and bankable commodities (Frosh 2003; Tagg 2009: 15; Blaschke 2016: 11, 40). Sekula notes that the identification of photography 'with the dream language' went hand in hand with 'the establishment of global archives and repositories' rooted in 'an aggressive empiricism' and manifesting 'a compulsive desire for completeness' that was ultimately bureaucratic (Sekula 1983: 197). To make pictures language-like also seems to be to make them calculable, quantifiable – it is a rationalisation of both pictures and human feeling.

In other words, the claim that photography is a universal language takes the capacity of this technological medium to express and communicate emotion, and ties it to attempts to 'direct' and organise an archive or inventory. This appears at first glance as serving a dream of a unified humanity and of world peace, and, at second glance, as a kind of male fantasy: a fantasy in which capacities and behaviours historically attributed or delegated to women, such as the maintenance of sociable connections, the expression of collective feeling and the nuanced reading of emotional expression, are treated as raw material subjected to a process of rationalisation and systematisation.

This rationalisation of emotion is characteristic of the new emotional regime that Eva Illouz identifies as emerging between the 1930s and the 1970s in the United States, during which time, freedom and equality increased at the price of 'a vast process of rationalization of intimate relations' (Illouz 2007: 30). As Illouz says, rationalisation formalises and intellectualises everyday life, making emotions into 'measurable and calculable objects' through processes of commensuration (that is, making qualitative differences into quantifiable ones) and textualisation (that is, 'locking' emotions into texts or language). This process clearly benefits certain kinds of institutions and commercial entities, but, she argues, it also enables people to navigate social relationships in late modernity (Illouz 2007: 32, 71).

Linked to the development of service economies, this new regime transformed the divisions of private and public that were characteristic of an earlier stage of capitalism. Historically, as Sue Campbell argues, gender had provided the justification for the hierarchical distribution of emotions or sentiments and their expression, with the overt expression of the feminine 'tender emotions' (such as compassion, love and sadness) simultaneously encouraged as 'limiting virtues' and dismissed as sentimental and conservative (Campbell 1994: 56, 61–2). Anger, meanwhile, remained largely the prerogative of men. Crucially, Illouz argues that this gendered division of emotion changed with the rise of a therapeutic model organised around self-reflection, soft communication skills and 'emotional intelligence'. The new 'emotional capitalism', as Illouz defines it, prioritised empathy, compassion, cooperation and an orientation towards others, and yet was simultaneously organised towards strategic self-interest and maximisation of productivity and efficiency. According to Illouz's diagnosis, then, emotional capitalism has unravelled the gender identities and private–public opposition on which capitalism was originally based, with sentimentality and emotionality now spreading to the public and economic sphere (Illouz 2007). In the United States, she argues, the rationalisation of emotions happens in the name of feminism, and is closely connected to the post-war rise of a language of rights (Illouz 2007: 36–8).

The Family of Man, and the extensive academic discussion of it, shows how the notion of photography as a universal language, the humanist discourse of rights, and an almost kitsch sentimentalism are connected. It was born in the context of the post-war promotion of social equality and the extension of rights, and while they disagree on its political orientation, most writers on the exhibition recognise that it was shaped by the new rhetoric of human rights.[4] Though he recognised this, Roland Barthes's early critique argued that the exhibition undermined any sense of people as political agents through its trite sentimentalism. For, though Steichen favoured straight photography and new objectivity, the exhibition was peppered with sayings and quotations that Barthes viewed as platitudes – phrases such as 'the land is a mother that never dies'. Barthes also pointed out the 'purely tautological' nature of the exhibition's message: if birth and death are universals, as they evidently are, then nothing remains to be said about them. Stripped of their historicity and their difference, anything that is said is meaningless (Barthes 1973: 101). Barthes's discussion recalls critiques of kitsch, from Clement Greenberg's description of kitsch as inauthentic and formulaic, to Milan Kundera's characterisation of kitsch as tautological – the 'idiotic tautology' epitomised for Kundera by the communist slogan 'long live life' (Didi-Huberman 2012; Greenberg 1961; Kundera 1985: 249; Binckley 2000: 142).

Barthes's analysis succeeds in articulating a direct link between the universal language claim and this kitsch sentimentality, because he finds that the exhibition's attempt to make photographs transparent and language-like produces a literalism which places emotion at a distance even while the exhibition declares its 'feeling for feeling'.[5] This literalism, according to Barthes, is not able to 'disorganise' us, but merely to evoke the sensation of being moved: 'The literal photograph introduces us to the scandal of horror, not to horror itself' (Barthes 1973: 73). It is a second-hand experience, emotion at one remove; as Clement Greenberg says of kitsch, it is 'vicarious experience and faked sensations' (Greenberg 1961: 10). Yet, Barthes's 'contempt for pathos', as Georges Didi-Huberman describes it, marks one of the limits of this analysis. At the very moment when the gendering of emotions is reconfigured by a therapeutic culture which values emotionality, the critique of kitsch sentimentality depends on a contrast between political agency and pathos understood in terms of feminised passivity and inauthenticity.[6]

It is not evident that therapeutic culture is as emotionally 'androgynous' as Illouz argues (Illouz 2007: 37), since certain disparaged forms of emotional expression continue to be associated with women. If, in the past, women's emotions were dismissed as indiscriminate and uncontrolled, in therapeutic culture, those forms of emotional expression used by young women are denigrated as not 'real' or 'authentic' (Campbell 1994: 56, 61–2). In the context of therapeutic culture, the demand is not just to smile, but to smile as if you really *mean* it. Emotional labour, as Arlie Hochschild famously characterised it, is accompanied by an attempt to rout out phoniness, and the carriers of this responsibility are disproportionately women (Hochschild 2012: ix). In work contexts, authentic emotional expression becomes ever harder to achieve, since emotions are entangled with involuntary bodily responses: the rationalisation and instrumentalisation of emotion that Illouz describes militates against the experience of emotions as authentic, even while authenticity is raised up as a value.

Picture Languages, Sentiment Analysis and Mood Tracking

For Sam Binkley, the epitome of the 'idiotic tautology' is the smiley face:

> [I]ts basic form, two points over a semi circle against a yellow disk, calls out 'have a nice day' from T shirts and lapel pins in a language that is at

once the most fundamental, trivial and universal of languages – simple human love of joy. This 'idiotic tautology' is nonetheless captivating in its ability to elevate the unique charm of the commonplace to a value of universal significance. (Binkley 2000: 146)

The ubiquitous yellow smiley face both illustrates a feeling and tells us how to feel by proposing we mimic it. It promotes a universal humanism predicated on happiness, a shared joy in being happy. This message is ironically undercut in Paul Connors' photograph of the designer of the smiley face, Harvey Ball, at his desk, wearing a wonderfully dour expression (Ball was hurt by not having received recognition or royalties for his design, Fig. 5.1). The graphic designer was commissioned by a US insurance company in 1964 to produce a badge intended to be worn by workers. The corporate merger of the State Mutual Life Assurance Company of Worcester, Massachusetts, and Ohio's Guarantee Mutual Company had damaged staff morale, prompting an internal PR campaign. The badges accompanied new policies requiring staff to smile, and the icon proliferated along with the phrases 'have a happy day' or 'have a nice day'. That is to say, it expanded with the rise of emotional labour: a corporate service culture in which employees are expected to convey a certain happy and helpful persona to customers.

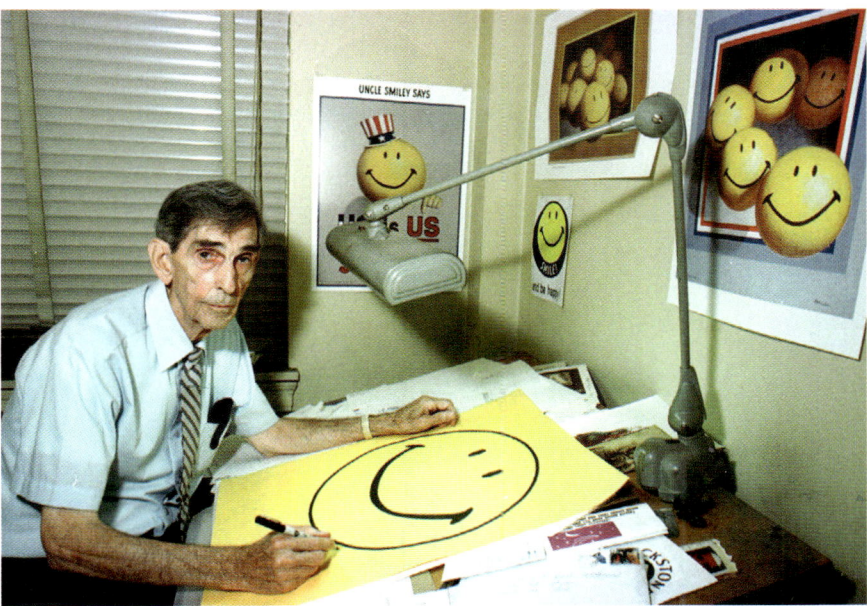

Figure 5.1 Smiley face creator Harvey Ball in his office, Worcester, Massachusetts, USA, 6 July 1998. Photograph by Paul Connors/AP/Shutterstock.

Though Ball did not make money from the spread of his design, others did, and the smiley face became subject to competing intellectual property and copyright claims. The symbol became a proprietorial means of expression. As such, it marks a turning point in the growing reification and objectification of emotions. In human encounters, expressing emotion is a combination of involuntary physical response (blushing, for example) and highly coded cultural gesture. The icon that stands in for an emotion disembodies it, simplifies it, fixes it and renders it uniform, while harnessing it to a market via trademark and copyright legislation. The smiley face as workplace badge represents a rationalisation of emotion and the triumph of kitsch sentimentality.

This is more explicit in emoji, originally invented in 1999 by Shigetaka Kurita, a designer for Japanese telecom carrier NTT DoCoMo ('emoji' is a Japanese term meaning picture-character or pictogram). Emoji followed the expansion of computer-mediated communication which required abrupt and abbreviated language, and the growing use of emoticons – little faces contrived out of punctuation marks. Unlike emoticons, emoji belongs specifically to the world of mobile media. It marks a shift from analogue graphic symbols (Isotype, the smiley face) to code, since the symbols are part of Unicode – the term is a condensing of 'universal code', a universal language system delegated to computers. Some writers have claimed of emoji that 'we are on the threshold of a universal symbolic language, where pictures replace words as the basic unit of communication'.[7] Like the modernist advocates of universal languages, they seem to be hoping for a pure system, unpolluted by local variation, ambiguity and the invasion of other systems and scripts. However, like Isotype, emoji has a great deal of cultural specificity, and bears the traces of its own cultural origins.[8] Like social media photographs, it works, not in isolation, but in league with moving and still images and text, part of an increasingly 'blended' writing system.

This picture language, emoji, is designed for the opposite purpose to Neurath's Isotype – to convey feeling, not facts. Emoji is distinguished from all earlier picture languages in being fully embedded in proprietorial, automated systems, accessible via keyboards and menus, and trackable as data. Emoji operates as a shortcut for the expression of feeling, since it is quicker to select an emoji than to type out words, especially on a mobile phone. Emoji symbols participate in the rationalisation of emotions, not only because emotions become objects to be 'observed' and 'manipulated', but because they are simplified, quantified, rendered commensurate (Illouz 2007: 33). They also positively encourage the expression of feeling: like kitsch, emoji stands for a certain commitment to feeling, a valuing of emotional communication, and a claim to the universality of certain sentiments. With emoji, as with kitsch, a need for immediacy favours a particular kind of imagery, with easy recognisability, a tendency to trigger sentiment quickly, and an ability to flatter the beholder.⁹

Emoji communications are typically phatic, used for sociable (rather than functional or business-like) purposes (Danesi 2016, 19).¹⁰ They originate in an attempt to capture and monetise the improvisational use of mobile media among young people, especially women, in Japan (Stark and Crawford 2015: 3). Traditionally, women bear the greater weight of the burden of sociability, holding families and social groups together, and emoji are currently more widely used by women than men. Ethnographic studies suggest that young women use emoji to lighten their tone, to create a sense of informality and playfulness, and some suggest that young Japanese men are less likely to use emoji than women because of their *kawaii* or cute associations.¹¹ Notwithstanding Illouz's argument that the rise of a culture of communication has rendered the gendered division of emotions less clear, in Japan these emphatic and explicitly emotional forms are viewed as largely feminine. Elsewhere, they are often dismissed as largely inauthentic, in line with a long history of forms of feminine communication being repeatedly denigrated as trivial, superficial and inauthentic (see Rakow 1988; Miller 2011).

As emoji have been adopted across social media platforms, the symbols have been subjected to proprietorial modifications which de-standardise and de-universalise the system in order to monetise it – so the emoji-style symbols used by Facebook, Instagram and other social media platforms are not unicode. William Davies describes their purpose on these platforms as 'emotional signalling' (Davies 2017: 34). For example, Facebook replaced its 'like' button with a range of six pop-up icons which have clearly defined or restricted meanings (unlike emoji). Additionally, the status update function offers users a 'feeling/activity' menu from which one can select from 200 emoji-like icons with precise meanings. These limited, pseudo-emojis offered to us on social media platforms are far more formulaic than actual emoji, intended to enable the platform to translate emotional responses into data. Luke Stark and Kate Crawford regard these icons as functioning to 'lure consumers to a platform, to extract data from them more efficiently, and to express a normative, consumerist and predominately cheery world-view' (Stark and Crawford 2015: 8; see also Stark 2018: 218). As Mark Andrejevic summarises, affect and emotion are increasingly recognised as 'decision-making drivers', and the valuable (sellable) data being captured is a 'trove' of 'affective response' (Andrejevic 2013: 31). Emoji-like symbols become a means to make desires, tastes, inclinations, moods and feelings – all things we might assume to be transient and difficult to articulate or quantify – into things that can be systematically classified. While gestures and behaviours can be used for mood tracking, and are registered on smartphones via sensors (such as accelerometers, gyroscopes and proximity sensors), the major ways in which emotional expression becomes analysable and quantifiable is via trackable elements such as hashtags and icons (Stark 2018: 216). Thus kitsch and *kawaii* become efficient means to trigger and track sentiment.[12]

This is a live mood-capture process that is not about recording so much as intervention, aiming not only to capture shifts in mood but to produce mood and emotional states: to manipulate users' emotions.[13] Online networks spread heightened feelings – such as outrage, fear and anger – but less noticeably, they also distribute more subtle or low-level 'ambient sentiments' such as boredom, detachment or emotional 'flatness'.[14] Emoji-style icons are often used as a means to gain instant feedback and for real-time tracking. In the context of social media, this allows changes in the flow or feed of images and text, on the basis of quick and even unconscious responses. Emoji-style icons facilitate 'instant, gut-fired, emotional, positive evaluations', as does the use of a touchscreen (Van Dijck 2013: 46). Simple icons such as the smiley face are effective enough for feeding back an emotional response, a good or bad experience, a good or bad mood. Indeed, we are constantly and increasingly asked to feed back, and not only online: Davies gives the example of a push button satisfaction rating system at the exit to a workplace, where attempts by employees to disrupt the system (pressing a button repeatedly, for example) still 'count' since they still contribute to metrics of overall workplace mood (Davies 2017: 41). A coffee machine has a screen which asks me to rate my experience using a star rating system; other feedback machines are located in toilets, in stores and at airports. Here, emotional labour takes on a new meaning as the felt responses of consumers, or users of a facility, impacts on the labour of cleaners, salespeople and airport staff (Figure 5.2).

The analytic techniques used on our data can quantify both spontaneous emotional outbursts and systematic performances of emotional states, but what is really being commodified and automated here is our sociability, our willingness to connect with one another using the technical means at our disposal. We feed emotional expressions into the system, not in dialogue with it, but with one another. Concepts like 'friendship', 'liking' and 'sharing' have shifted in meaning as technology and media corporations have adopted them to describe activities and connections between users, platforms and third parties. Affective relationships between humans have been appropriated and monetised. In social media, the objective of generating data is concealed beneath an allure of 'connectivity' and community, buried in a language of 'sharing' and caring (John 2013: 125; Van Dijck 2013; Chambers 2017: 29).

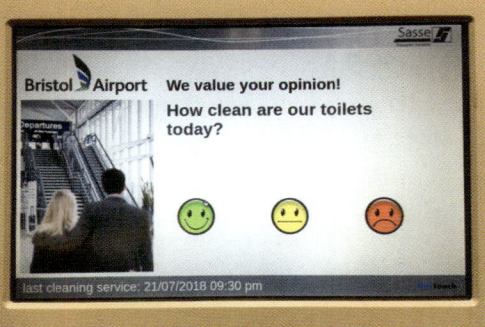 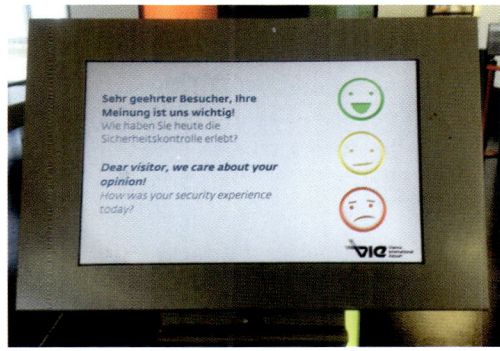

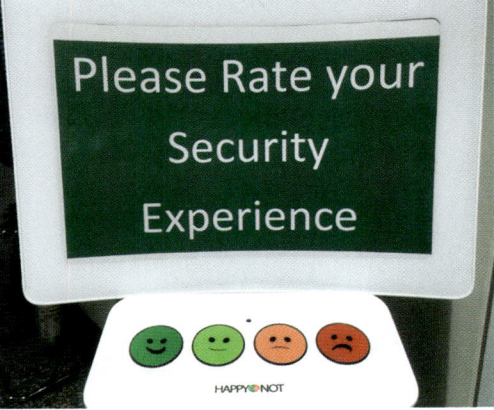 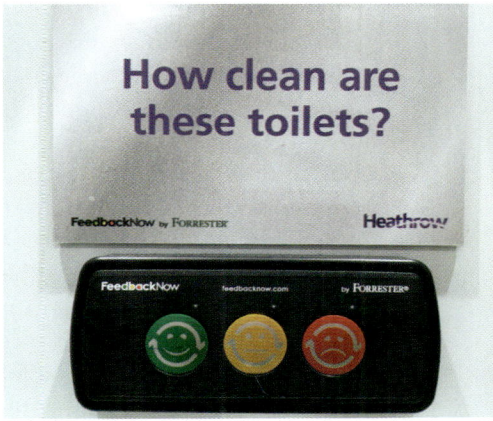

Figure 5.2 Customer feedback terminals. These performance measurement devices (in this case at various airports) made by companies such as the American market research company Forrester and the Finnish company HappyOrNot use various trademarked 'Smiley' devices to collect 'real-time' feedback data for immediate performance management. Photographs by Michelle Henning.

The Feedback Loop, Contagion and Flood

A click on a social media icon is not an expression of mood so much as what Paul Frosh calls the 'showing of sharedness': a gesture that is visible not just to the direct recipient but to others in the network (Frosh 2012). Like the service worker wearing a smiley badge, this involves an element of public performance, and it is this performed emotional expression and reaction that social media platforms depend upon. If photography in the mid-twentieth century aimed not only to capture essential human moods and collective feelings but to provoke certain feelings in the viewers of the photograph, contemporary social media takes this further, harnessing those feelings back into the circuit. The history of this feedback loop is the history of the algorithm, but it is also the history of the database, of market research, consumer behaviour research, psychometrics, sociological surveys, and focus groups. As early as 1985, Vilém Flusser anticipated the way in which such feedback loops do not merely respond to desires but produce them, in such a way that it begins to be the technology itself that is desiring. As the technical images and market research techniques become increasingly integrated, this feedback, according to Flusser:

> [E]nables the images to change, to become better and better, and more like the receivers want them to be; that is, the images become more and more like the receivers want them to be so that the receivers can become more and more like the images want them to be. (Flusser 2011: 55)

Flusser describes the self-perpetuating and growing feedback loop of media as centrally reliant on images. But it is also clearly reliant on language, both as audio recordings and as text. This raises the question of why images have become the central focus of critique, why images are attributed an ability to arouse feeling that has historically been attributed to literature, music and the other arts. One of the most curious aspects of this is that photography, long associated with an objective, affectless recording of the real, is now understood as almost exclusively affective and expressive. Yet, among the many reasons we might post images is one very traditional one – we post images to say: 'See, it's true, here is the evidence'. As studies of the family album in the 1980s and 1990s argued, popular image-making and viewing involves a lot of: 'Look! Here I am', or 'I was here', or 'Look at that!' (the photograph is deictic). In the sometimes heightened emotional and confrontational context of social media, one reason photographs and videos are widely shared is that they appear to be unemotional, objective confirmations of our existing prejudices. People with very different political perspectives will share the same or very similar video clips, each believing that the video shows evidence that proves their own understanding of events. Ironically, it is possible that one reason why certain images circulate so widely is not that they express a specific sentiment, but that they are ambiguous and this allows for the projection of any sentiment.

In the scenario envisaged both by social media platforms and by critics, images replace words because they are fun, light-hearted and simple, but also because they are primitive, shocking, sensual. The use of images is promoted by media and technology companies because they seem to promise total marketisation, facilitating the tracking of everyday social interactions and making it easier to transform these interactions into commercial exchange. Yet while algorithms can identify objects in photographs, their ability to analyse images in terms of emotion is very limited – not least because images don't 'express' emotion in any straightforward way.[15] Nevertheless, alongside emoji and emoji-like icons, photographs and video have become a powerful social currency. It is now received wisdom that sharing 'visual content' online will increase the number of clicks, retweets, and broaden and hasten the circulation of posts. Certainly, some kinds of images might circulate more effectively as part of a gathering mood, enhancing the possibility of the un-thought-through response and swift feedback. For these reasons, perhaps, photographic and video images are associated with the addictive and emotive character of contemporary media.

As images, both moving and still, photographic and graphic, circulate rapidly in this environment, they are described using familiar metaphors. The discourse of the flood, in particular, recurs alongside a common lament that there are just too many photographs, that the sheer volume of images is a kind of cultural crisis. Both Joanna Zylinska and Annebella Pollen have commented on the repeated references to a 'flood of information', a 'torrent' of images, a 'tsunami', a 'deluge', in journalistic and critical writing on our new image culture (Zylinska 2017: 170; Pollen 2019). Some of the best writing on new media indulges in such metaphors: Lister writes 'we are drowning in images'; Andrejevic postulates that we are 'a populace enjoined to rely on their emotions, their gut instinct, and their thoughtless thoughts, to anchor themselves in a flood of information' (Andrejevic 2013: 47; Lister 2014: 15).[16]

This discourse of the flood is also about the masses and about women. Klaus Theweleit's (1987) study of the diaries of German *Freikorps* soldiers showed how repeatedly fears and anxieties about women were expressed in terms of fear of floods, fear of being dissolved, of losing boundaries. Commenting on this and Gustave Le Bon's influential *The Crowd* (1895), Andreas Huyssen writes: 'The fear of the masses [was] . . . always also a fear of woman, a fear of nature out of control, a fear of the unconscious, of sexuality, of the loss of identity and stable ego boundaries . . .' (Huyssen 1986: 52). A fear of being overwhelmed, an anxiety relating to population, a notion of the mass as a threat to be harnessed or controlled, merges with fear of the inchoate, of the unformed or formless, of ambiguity and unboundedness. The vision of the feminised mass versus the masculine individual has historically permeated thinking about mass culture, about the mass media and the growing information society. Underpinning it is a politics of population which distinguishes between valuable and disposable lives (Murphy 2018: 145). Metaphors of glut and flooding are also used in the media and by right-wing politicians to talk about immigration, but at the same time crowds and 'the people' are appealed to as the justification for political action.[17] These different ways of describing the 'mass' – as a populace with a 'will' that must be obeyed, or as a flood – are two sides of the same coin. They suggest the fundamental ambiguity of the 'mass', a collective with no necessary shared cause or coherent identity, which can be summoned and invoked to claim legitimacy or arouse fear.

Emotional contagion is also largely associated with women and crowds through the concept of hysteria, and this term also recurs in the debates about social media images. Davies, for example, claims that:

> Contagions are in fact less a matter of verbal communication than of graphical and physical communication. When ideas are converted into images, and those images change the way we feel, then they start to travel through the crowd in the form of 'sentiments' passing from person to person. The role of brands and logos today, which manage to communicate an idea or mood without using words, is testimony to the power of visual icons in influencing behaviour. (Davies 2018: 13–14)

The choice of words related to flood and contagion is not just unfortunate but revealing of a position from which a 'problem' is identified. The terms of the debate recall Steichen's question 'How to direct this?', a question that can only be asked from the position of an individual who believes himself faced with the task of putting rational shape to disorderly, uncontrolled feelings and/or disorderly uncontrolled images (Steichen 1958: 159).

Like the figure of woman and of the mass, the image itself also seems dubious and enigmatic. W. J. T. Mitchell, in his book *What Do Pictures Want?* (2005), addresses the pervasive sense that images are both deeply attractive and deeply dangerous, that their inherent attractiveness ('eye-candy') is what makes them contagious and out of control. Mitchell points out that in psychoanalytic theories of spectatorship, woman *is* image. The threat that images pose is aligned with the threat of women (as castrated/castrator) and 'the power of pictures and of women is modeled on one another' (Mitchell 2005: 36). He characterises the iconoclastic aspects of contemporary culture as new manifestations of 'ancient superstitions about images', new forms whose 'deep structure remains the same'; this is 'a social structure grounded in the experience of otherness and especially in the collective representation of others as idolaters . . . the first law of iconoclasm is that the idolater is always someone else' (Mitchell 2005: 19). So, too, is the emotionally manipulated social media user, the other seduced by images.

The literal photograph is one response to this: literalness need not be a property of the individual photograph but a means of contextualising the image, marshalling it into sense, 'directing' it, rationalising it. This was the aim of the proponents of photography as universal language, and could be said to be the aim of social media platforms which render images dependent on captions or narration, and linked to one another by hashtags. Nevertheless, the speech-like aspect of social media photography also ties the pleasure in images to the pleasures of sociability, with the anticipation of a response and the enjoyment of looking, making and composing images keeping us 'posting' and 'sharing'. The sensual, attractive aspect of images becomes conflated with an emotional quality that belongs not to the photograph itself but to the interaction.

Conclusion

In a sense, the male fantasy of the domination of masculine rationality over feminine emotionality was also always a vision of technology as saviour. The universal language discourse was premised on a great deal of faith in technology. Technologically advanced warfare was represented in *The Family of Man* by a large backlit transparency of an atomic bomb explosion. Viewed in the United States, the atomic bomb could be read ambiguously, both as the ultimate symbol of 'man's inhumanity to man' and as its end point and the guarantor of a new world peace. Countering a faith in technology is the critical viewpoint which suggests that men have created a technology that is out of their control. Today this takes the form of an anxiety about 'machines that think' more rationally or logically than people, and as reason is outsourced to this apparatus, humans are conceived of as primarily emotional, feeling creatures. Theorists fret about being left 'out of the loop' as ever more images are produced to be seen only by machines, as machines communicate with one another, without ever translating it back to us, and as we seem to become mere feeling-fodder for an economy that trades in attention, experience, and raw emotion. They worry about the loss of individuality in the face of a mass of indifferent imagery. Photography is understood as a practice oriented purely to the expression of moods and feelings in the moment, all the better to harness us to this machinic circuit. The assumption of the image's primarily sentimental and seductive character – an assumption made both by cultural critics and by social media platforms – means that photographs are being reimagined as feeling images, even while that feeling is treated as something superficial, truncated and hackneyed. The response to the expansion of photography into a mass, daily practice is often to blame photographs for emotional contagion, to assert that through popularisation photographs have lost their cultural value, to treat the practices of taking and sharing photographs as akin to a devalued speech form – that of 'chattering' women. Thought to be too crude, too literal or too disposable to be 'authentic' emotional expression, the kinds of photographic images that circulate on social media are at the same time, and paradoxically, thought to be too emotional, too seductive, too contagious. Against this, I would argue that what is at stake here is not the degradation of photography through its reduction to simplified emotional expression, but the fact that photography is flourishing as part of the rich and complex practices of human sociability, even while it is being harnessed to manipulate and commodify those practices.

Notes

1. The term, and my understanding of it, comes from Peters (1999).
2. And yet, Steichen and Sander both made use of montage and sequencing to construct narratives that no individual photograph could convey.
3. Otto Neurath's Isotype (International System of Typographic Picture Education) originated in the 1920s as the Vienna Method of pictorial statistics, a pioneering attempt to make statistical information legible to non-expert and semi-literate audiences. During the 1930s, Neurath increasingly began to think of it as an auxiliary language, and to compare it to Esperanto and Basic English (Neurath 1936; Neurath 2010).
4. While Sekula argues that *The Family of Man* operated as a piece of cold war propaganda (Sekula 1981: 19), Georges Didi-Huberman reads it as a 'photographic response to the introduction, in the Nuremberg trials – which some of the images chosen by Steichen evoked – of the legal concept of the 'crime against humanity' (Didi-Huberman 2012: 15, my translation). Ariella Azoulay reads it as almost a visual embodiment of the United Nations' 1948 Universal Declaration of Human Rights, prescribing, rather than describing, the universality of rights (Azoulay 2013, 20). Tom Allbeson situates it in relation to UNESCO's promotional imagery, which, like the Declaration, was underpinned by the notion of one human 'family' which tended to occlude cultural difference (Allbeson 2015: 399).
5. The phrase is Binkley's (Binkley 2000: 142).
6. See Didi-Huberman for details of the gendering of this opposition in Barthes. He considers Barthes's analysis not only of *The Family of Man* but also of another exhibition *Shock Photos*, of Eisenstein's film *Battleship Potemkin*. He writes that Barthes's 'contempt for pathos in the political field is akin to the rejection of kitsch – the 'bad genre', the 'lack of taste' – in the aesthetic field' (Didi-Huberman 2012: 20, my translation).
7. Gn (2018), referring to claims made by Azuma (2012).
8. Isotype draws on the German language, with its tendency to aggregate words, while emoji arose easily in a culture used to mixed scripts – Japanese brings together the Chinese logographic script (*kanji*) with syllable scripts (*kana*), and does not use an alphabet as such. Neurath drew on existing precedents, such as cave paintings, Chinese writing, ancient Egyptian

wall-paintings and hieroglyphics, 'shinies' (scrapbook materials), and maps and diagrams. See Neurath (2010) *From Hieroglyphics to Isotype*. Kurita also drew on the resources surrounding him: from Chinese characters to manga, to street signs (see Negishi, 2014).

9. Unsurprisingly, therefore, emoji draw on aspects of *kawaii*, and share its broad aesthetic, deploying rounded, soft shapes and neutralising or sanitising any threatening or negative connotations. However, Joel Gn argues that emoji constitute a language of 'cuteness' that goes beyond the cultural specificity of *kawaii* (Gn 2018: np).

10. On the role of phatic communion in contemporary media see Frosh (2012: 133).

11. For example, see Sugiyama (2015). Usually translated as 'cute', *kawaii* can signify the small, the loveable and the pitiable, the whimsical, and that which rouses sympathy or is adorable. It is generally, though not exclusively, associated with femininity and with infantility. It has been critiqued for propagating submissive femininity and encouraging paedophilia, and has been linked to organisational and national 'soft power' (Macpherson and Bryant 2018: 42, 49).

12. On the role of hashtags in mediating sociability and in regulating, extending but also 'disintegrating' the self, see Frosh (2019: 93–113).

13. See Stark on the Facebook emotional contagion study (Stark 2018: 206). As Shoshana Zuboff argues, this is a trade not just in data but in human futures, behavioural 'prediction products' that are a derivative of data assets (Zuboff 2019).

14. The term 'ambient sentiment' is from Andrejevic, but I am also thinking of other writing on collective mood and banality here, such as Highmore (2017).

15. Nevertheless, while algorithms struggle with detecting sarcasm or irony and recognising metaphor in texts, facial recognition techniques are intended not just to recognise faces in images but also to distinguish and predict emotion, producing 'emotion metrics'. See Zuboff (2019).

16. Andrejevic's resort to such terminology is odd since elsewhere he recognises the potency of the metaphors used to describe the mass of images and data, noting that, '[i]t is telling that the advent of "big data" is figured as a force of nature: a wave, a flood, a gusher – a found resource that miners are tapping and harnessing' (Andrejevic 2013: 44).

17. A report published by the University of Oxford's Migration Observatory looked at the language used to describe migrants and migration in Britain's twenty national newspapers in the period 2010 to 2012. It found that terms such as flood, influx, and wave were regularly used (Migration Observatory 2013). On the contemporary mobilisation of the crowd, see Davies (2018), Chapter 1.

References

Allbeson, Tom (2015), 'Photographic Diplomacy in the Postwar World: UNESCO and the Conception of Photography as a Universal Language, 1946–1956,' *Modern Intellectual History*, 12(2): 383–415.

Andrejevic, Mark (2013), *Infoglut: How Too Much Information is Changing the Way We Think and Know*. London: Routledge.

Azoulay, Ariella (2013), 'The Family of Man: A Visual Universal Declaration of Human Rights', in Thomas Keenan and Tirdad Zolghadr (eds), *The Human Snapshot*. Berlin: Sternberg Press, pp. 19–48.

Barthes, Roland [1957] (1973), 'The Great Family of Man', in Roland Barthes, *Mythologies* (Annette Lavers, trans.). London: Paladin Books, pp. 100–2.

Barthes, Roland [1957] (1979), 'Shock Photos', in *The Eiffel Tower and Other Mythologies*. New York: Hill and Wang, pp. 71–3.

Binkley, Sam (2000), 'Kitsch as a Repetitive System: A Problem for the Theory of Taste Hierarchy', *Journal of Material Culture*, 5(2): 131–52.

Blaschke, Estelle (2016), *Banking on Images: The Bettmann Archive and Corbis*. Leipzig: Spector.

Campbell, Sue (1994), 'Being Dismissed: The Politics of Emotional Expression', *Hypatia*, 9(3): 46–65.

Chambers, Deborah (2017), 'Networked Intimacy: Algorithmic Friendship and Scalable Sociality', *European Journal of Communication*, 32(1): 26–36.

Crano, Ricky (2019), 'The Real Terror of Instagram: Death and Disindividuation in the Social Media Scopic Field', *Convergence*, 25(5–6): 1123–39.

Danesi, Marcel (2016), *The Semiotics of Emoji: The Rise of Visual Language in the Age of the Internet*. London: Bloomsbury Publishing.

Davies, William (2017), 'How Are We Now? Real-Time Mood-Monitoring as Valuation', *Journal of Cultural Economy*, 10(1): 34–48.

Davies, William (2018), *Nervous States: How Feeling Took Over the World*. London: Jonathan Cape.

Didi-Huberman, Georges (2012), 'Pathos et Praxis: Eisenstein contre Barthes', *Revue de l'association française de recherche sur l'histoire du cinéma*, 67: 8–23.

Flusser, Vilém [1985] (2011), *Into the Universe of Technical Images*. Minneapolis: University of Minnesota Press.

Frosh, Paul (2003), *The Image Factory: Consumer Culture, Photography and the Visual Content Industry*. London: Bloomsbury.

Frosh, Paul (2012), 'The Showing of Sharedness: Monstration, Media and Social Life', *Divinatio*, 35: 123–38.

Frosh, Paul (2019), *The Poetics of Digital Media*. Cambridge: Polity Press.

Gn, Joel (2018), 'Emoji as a "Language" of Cuteness', *First Monday*, September 2018. Available at: <https://firstmonday.org-ojs-index.php-fm-article-view-9396-7568> (last accessed 4 June 2019).

Greenberg, Clement [1939] (1961), 'Avant-Garde and Kitsch', in Clement Greenberg, *Art and Culture: Critical Essays*. Boston, MA: Beacon Press.
Henning, Michelle (2018), *Photography: The Unfettered Image*. London: Routledge.
Highmore, Ben (2017), *Cultural Feelings: Mood, Mediation and Cultural Politics*. London: Routledge.
Hochschild, Arlie Russell [1983] (2012), *The Managed Heart: Commercialization of Human Feeling*. Berkeley: University of California Press.
Huyssen, Andreas (1986), *After the Great Divide: Modernism, Mass Culture and Postmodernism*. London: Macmillan.
Illouz, Eva (2007), *Cold Intimacies: The Making of Emotional Capitalism*. London: Polity Press.
John, Nicholas A. (2013), 'The Social Logics of Sharing', *The Communication Review*, 16(3): 113–31.
Kundera, Milan (1985), *The Unbearable Lightness of Being*. London: Faber & Faber.
Lister, Martin, (2014), 'Overlooking, Rarely Looking and Not Looking', in Jonas Larsen and Mette Sandbye (eds), *Digital Snaps*. London: I. B. Tauris, pp. 1–24.
Macpherson, Iain, and Teri Jane Bryant (2018), 'Softening Power: Cuteness as Organizational Communication Strategy in Japan and the West', *Journal of International and Advanced Japanese Studies*, 10: 39–55.
Migration Observatory (2013), 'Migration in the News', 8 August 2013, report published by the University of Oxford's Migration Observatory. Available at: <https://migrationobservatory.ox.ac.uk-resources-reports-migration-in-the-news> (last accessed 4 June 2019).
Miller, Laura (2011), 'Subversive Script and Novel Graphs in Japanese Girls' Culture', *Language & Communication*, 31(1): 16–26.
Mitchell, W. J. T. (2005), *What Do Pictures Want?: The Lives and Loves of Images*. Chicago: University of Chicago Press.
Murphy, Michelle (2018), 'Against Population, Towards Afterlife', in Adele E. Clarke and Donna Haraway (eds), *Making Kin not Population: Reconceiving Generations*. Chicago: Prickly Paradigm Press, pp. 101–24.
Negishi, Mayumi (2014), 'Meet Shigetaka Kurita, the Father of Emoji,' *Wall Street Journal*, 26 March 2014. Available at: <https://blogs.wsj.com-japanrealtime-2014-03-26-meet-shigetaka-kurita-the-father-of-emoji> (last accessed 4 June 2019).
Neurath, Otto (1936), *International Picture Language: The First Rules of Isotype*. Psyche Miniatures, London: Kegan Paul.
Neurath, Otto (2010), *From Hieroglyphics to Isotype: A Visual Autobiography*. London: Hyphen Press.
Peters, John Durham (1999), *Speaking into the Air: A History of the Idea of Communication*. Chicago: University of Chicago Press.

Pollen, Annebella (2016), 'The Rising Tide of Photographs: Not Drowning but Waving', *Captures: Figures, Théories et Pratiques de l'Imaginaire*, 1(1). Available at: <revuecaptures.org-node-249> (last accessed 4 June 2019).

Rakow, Lana F. (1988) 'Women and the Telephone: The Gendering of a Communications Technology', in Cheris Kramarae (ed.), *Technology and Women's Voices: Keeping in Touch*. London: Routledge and Kegan Paul, pp. 207–29.

Rubinstein, Daniel (2005), 'Cellphone Photography: The Death of the Camera and the Arrival of Visible Speech', *Issues in Contemporary Culture and Aesthetics*, 2(1): 113–18.

Sander, August [1931] (1978), 'Photography as a Universal Language', Lecture Five of The Nature and Growth of Photography, German radio, 1931 (Anne Halley, trans.), in *Massachusetts Review*, 19(4): 674–5.

Sekula, Allan (1981), 'The Traffic in Photographs', *Art Journal*, 41(1): 15–25.

Sekula, Allan (1983), 'Photography between Labor and Capital', in Benjamin Buchloh and Robert Wilkie (eds), *Mining Photographs and Other Pictures, Photographs by Leslie Shedden*. Halifax: Press of the Nova Scotia College of Art and Design, pp. 193–268.

Stark, Luke (2018), 'Algorithmic Psychometrics and the Scalable Subject', *Social Studies of Science*, 48(2): 204–31.

Stark, Luke, and Kate Crawford (2015), 'The Conservatism of Emoji: Work, Affect, and Communication', *Social Media + Society*, 1(2): 1–11.

Steichen, Edward (1958), 'Photography: Witness and Recorder of Humanity', *The Wisconsin Magazine of History*, 41(3): 159–67.

Sugiyama, Satomi (2015), 'Kawaii meiru and Maroyaka neko: Mobile emoji for Relationship Maintenance and Aesthetic Expressions among Japanese Teens', *First Monday*, 20(10). Available at: <https://journals.uic.edu-ojs-index.php-fm-article-view-5826> (last accessed 21 September 2019).

Tagg, John (2009), 'The One-Eyed Man and the One-Armed Man: Camera, Culture, and the State', in John Tagg, *The Disciplinary Frame: Photographic Truths and the Capture of Meaning*. Minneapolis: University of Minnesota Press, pp. 1–49.

Theweleit, Klaus [1977] (1987), *Male Fantasies*, Vol. 1. Cambridge: Polity Press.

Van Dijck, José (2013), *The Culture of Connectivity: A Critical History of Social Media*. Oxford: Oxford University Press.

Zuboff, Shoshana (2019), *The Age of Surveillance Capitalism: The Fight for a Human Future at the New Frontier of Power*. London: Profile Books.

Zylinska, Joanna (2017), *Nonhuman Photography*. Cambridge, MA: MIT Press.

6 Online Weak and Poor Images: On Contemporary Feminist Visual Politics

Tereza Stejskalová

Bubble Vision Paradoxes

IN HER CONTRIBUTION to The Serpentine Galleries' *Marathon* in October 2017, Hito Steyerl discussed what she called the paradox of the 'bubble vision' created by immersive technologies, such as virtual reality technology or 360° videos (Steyerl 2017). In 'bubble vision', Steyerl notes, we are at the centre of an image from which we are simultaneously absent, as we do not see ourselves in it: we remain disembodied. The strange logic of the orb-based vision embracing an empty centre, that is, the subject, corresponds to the paradox of the two major challenges faced by the human species. In the so-called Anthropocene, the immensity of our power to influence the climate and other environmental processes is acknowledged while we threaten ourselves with our own extinction. Analogously, while we are able to develop sophisticated systems of AI, these systems simultaneously threaten to take our agency away from us. These two processes are not mutually exclusive: the profit-oriented development of technology and the Anthropocene are interlinked as capitalism is confronted with the limits of growth on a finite planet. If we treat bubble vision as a crystal ball, as Steyerl suggests, the future it predicts is one from which we are missing. Bubble vision, then, could be seen as a preparatory course to adapt humans to a humanless world.

As a metaphor, bubble vision invites us to consider the various complex social, economic and ecological repercussions of how the visual is implicated in the current technologised condition. It also hints at the ubiquity of digital images: their proliferation plays a significant role at the intersection of the Anthropocene and new technologies by setting the human subject aside. Sean Cubitt names this condition – the immense amount of images uploaded online all the time – as the 'mass image'. Instead of the immersive characteristics of digital images in which the subject becomes literally lost, here it is a humanly inconceivable quantity that marks the displacement of the human agent from the subjective centre of operations. This is due to the fact that the mass image, in its totality, is perceptible solely by the system of networked profit-driven digital platforms which host it (Cubitt 2017).

As a consequence, we find ourselves in a paradoxical situation, overwhelmed by both our power to influence and shape the planetary processes and the threat that technological development poses to us. Interestingly, Steyerl hints at the ways in which it is possible to resist by proposing that we use bubble vision as ammunition for resistance: she compares bubble vision to the crystal balls of the Harry Potter series, which were used less for prediction and more as weapons in battle, dropped by characters on the heads of their enemies. Is it possible to make use of online digital images in a way that presents any challenge to the mass-image, profit-driven networked platforms? For instance, can images on social platforms such as Instagram claim any oppositional agency?

In what follows, I would like to start with a particular example – US Congressional Representative of the Democratic Party Alexandra Ocasio-Cortez – as a point of departure to elaborate on feminist visual politics that makes a breakdown of technology (software or hardware) and human bodies its message and its medium. To do this, I will focus less on her political message and more on her strategies of visual communication; namely, her use of Instagram streaming. During a live session on 3 April 2019 at 10:00 p.m., Ocasio-Cortez (@ocasio-cortez2018) tried to assemble newly bought IKEA furniture while eating popcorn, drinking wine and discussing politics with her followers. As Ocasio-Cortez focused on activities other than talking to and with her followers, everything seemed unorchestrated and incidental. At the time, Ocasio-Cortez did not have internet installed at her apartment, and so her image occasionally turned blurry, the audio was far from perfect, the phone with which she was streaming was placed on the ground. Moreover, Ocasio-Cortez was clearly tired and unprepared: there were silences, unfinished sentences, awkward moments and unanswered questions like in any conversation with a fatigued person. Even if the casual character of the conversation drew one in, one might wonder why anyone would watch (what could be described by most) a failed performance of a politician at all. Of course, Instagram Live Videos vanish from the site – by default – after 24 hours and thus, afterwards, only selected moments and quotes from her video and image stream circulate online. As she is one of the most-watched American politicians (her presence on social platforms is watched and shared by millions of individuals as well as media outlets disrupting power hierarchies through more traditional communication channels), the 'fear of missing out' could, at least partially, account for the popularity of her Instagram streaming. In what follows, however, I will try to delve deeper in order to understand the power of encounter between Ocasio-Cortez and her mostly anonymous Instagram followers against the conditions of algorithmic manipulation, and explain why Ocasio-Cortez's amateurish Instagram stream should be considered as the realisation of Steyerl's 'bubble vision' used as munition. I will show how weak images and the vernacular worlds of algorithmic social media visuality contribute to the analysis of 'photography off the scale': it is a way in which the algorithmic, mass image can become a meaningful, political image.

Between Expertise and Incompetence

Let us first seek clarification in another contribution by Steyerl from almost ten years earlier. In her 2009 article 'In Defence of the Poor Image', the subversive potential of digital images is understood precisely in their 'poverty': they are low resolution and therefore accessible, easy to find and share. As by-products of global, digital networks, results of failed technologies and amateur production, poor images are defined not so much by what they depict as by their 'velocity, intensity, spread'. Instead of quality, quantity and speed are at stake. That is also why poor images are difficult to contain or control and why they often violate principles and values that govern the prevailing production and circulation of images in the contemporary media environment. They often refer to what is too weird, abject, degraded, dejected. Their political power is, however, ambivalent. Steyerl describes them as collaborative documents of shared affect and, as such, they can be used for emancipatory purposes but may, perhaps as easily, incite hatred. We should then understand them as potentially powerful tools that can be used in either an emancipatory or exploitative manner.

Importantly, as testaments to their own circulation, poor images refer less to their own content (their subject matter) and more to their own nature as a medium, underlining their own conditions of existence, that is, the increasingly machinic conditions of image production. What is more, poor images not only highlight network circumstances but 'mock the promise of digital technology' (Steyerl 2009). Through their glitches and blurs, they make visible the limitations of the networks of which they are the consequence, and they highlight the breaking points of machine and human interactions. Sean Cubitt notes how human bodies become mediators between the mass-image network and the physical world at the brink of collapse and subjectivities are torn between the virtual and physical realm (see Chapter 2 by Cubitt in this volume). Consequently, more and more people carry the burden of mental illness. The psychological toll of being increasingly connected to contemporary digital and networked media is also highlighted by Steyerl, who notes how bubble vision offers nothing but isolation (and narcissism) (Steyerl 2019). As the poor image is more transparent with regard to the conditions of its existence, it could be understood as one referring not only to the fragility of breakable machines but also the damage done to humans.

While the developers of the newest devices focus on hardware and computing power to make the devices as immersive and interactive as possible, the immersive and interactive qualities of poor images are of a different nature. These qualities depend precisely on the image being imperfect, amateur, compromised. It is, after all, these qualities that enable its distribution, appropriation and participation across a larger group of producers. Yet when we think of Ocasio-Cortez's video streaming, more is at stake. Involved is the power of what Boris Groys defines as 'weak image', a kind of representation which does not require any special skills, expertise or technology and can be made literally by anyone (Groys 2010). This notion is based on his understanding of the Avant-Garde as a movement involved in the radical deprofessionalisation of art-making, reducing art to the most simple and essential components, for example, Malevich's black square. What is essential is the power that Groys sees in this refusal of mastery and self-erasure, wherein he sees the reason for the Avant-Garde's universal success. These weak images are intimately related to what Groys calls 'everyday life', with which they share inconspicuousness, ordinariness, low visibility and endurance. The Polish feminist philosopher Ewa Majewska has noted how Groys's avant-garde lacks gender, class or race, and how it is strangely disembodied (Majewska 2016). The same critique can be applied to the vagueness of his notion of 'everyday life': if seen through a feminist perspective, as the sphere of social reproduction, it gains more specificity in terms of class and gender. Social reproduction can then be understood as the historically unacknowledged and systemically undervalued bulk of activities, behaviours, emotions and relationships involved in maintaining life usually undertaken by women (Fraser 2017: 21). If today 'everyday life begins to exhibit itself – to communicate itself as such – . . . through contemporary networks of communication' (Groys 2010), then digital images uploaded onto social networks are testaments and media of social reproduction, that is, how people, mentally or physically, sustain their own lives and the lives of others. Feminists understand capitalism as a system characterised by the contradiction between social production and reproduction (Fraser 2017: 22), which today we experience as a severe crisis in social reproduction, defined by inadequate public provision, reduced real wages, transfer of social reproduction work to insufficiently paid migrant workers, and so on (Fraser 2017: 34): this is what many of these digital images mediate. Today's true artist, understood here as a producer of poor and weak images, is one who understands well that she is not anyone special nor is she doing anything special but is, in principle, like any other social network user who makes manifest the (crisis of) emotions, relations and labour which sustain life itself.

Perhaps this is why we find poor images in the work of artists who appropriate images uploaded to social media as a means by which to critically comment on the crisis of social reproduction. In *Love Is The Message* (2016), for example, Arthur Jafa draws his images from multiple sources, with some images still wearing a Getty Images watermark, some coming from YouTube, and others still coming from various social media, in order to compile a lexicon capable of communicating the African-American experience that includes the killings of African-American men captured on mobile phones. Penny Lane's film *The Pain of Others* (2018) is composed entirely of amateur YouTube videos of women who by sharing their conditions, unrecognised by doctors, thus empower themselves; what they feel is real pain, and we are left wondering what the causes of that pain really are. This type of image production, however, is characterised by a tension between expertise and incompetence: knowledge and mastery, on the one hand; and amateurism, on the other.

This tension is explored by Majewska, who draws on Groys's concept of the weak image while trying to construct a feminist aesthetics coming from global peripheries and a sense of identity based on failure. Majewska discusses performances of vulnerability by the feminist artist Ewa Partum who, in her performance *Stupid Woman*, appeared naked as a frivolous 'party girl' likely to be abused while entirely in control as an artist (Majewska 2016). A similar combination of weakness, vulnerability and self-esteem also characterises Ocasio-Cortez, not only when she speaks about her own insecurities and fear in a self-assured manner, but even when she is ostensibly unconcerned about a bad internet connection and lack of technical equipment. Groys emphasises how weak images question and undermine the authority of images of mastery by pointing out their repressed ephemerality (Groys 2010) but Majewska is more politically grounded when she describes how Ewa Partum's performances work 'as a tool to destroy masculine hegemony, without ever presenting itself as authority or expertise' (Majewska 2016). In unspectacular resistance, there is political force and power, she argues, which can be used as an effective strategy for politicisation. She writes: 'It is in our weakness, not in our strength that we all meet as oppressed groups . . . It is therefore the weakness, not the strength that should be investigated as a possible beginning for universalising our struggles' (Majewska 2018). We all have a phone and an internet connection such that we can post low-quality images online and we are all exploited by Silicon Valley corporations. It is the weak and poor images that, in their poor quality, carry the potential to make visible the conditions of our communication and may thus constitute what Steyerl calls a 'visual bond' among the oppressed; an insight into existing social and economic relations that is able to organise individuals as politicised subjects. At the same time, of course, such images continue to be 'permeated by the most advanced commodification techniques' (Steyerl 2009). The artist of weak and poor images – the professional unprofessional – is the one who is not afraid to dwell in that space of ambivalence.

The Power of Affect

Ocasio-Cortez's Instagram live stream has been hailed as a breakthrough in the way politicians communicate with their potential electorate, and as such anticipating the future of politics. It has been described as evidence of how much technology impacts the portrayal, seizure and exercise of political power (Martínez 2019). It has been depicted as a sign that current politics have shifted and are now more and more about intimacy and authenticity (Perry 2018) or about the performance of honesty (Thompson 2019). While such strategies have already been employed for some time in popular culture and the entertainment industry, only recently have they entered the world of mainstream politics (Perry 2018; Cauterucci 2018). However, what exactly is that intimacy, authenticity or honesty that journalists speak about? What kind of performance is at stake? And, in what sense can we speak of bubble vision?

In virtual reality, we can become immersed in outside space without the consequences that could follow in real-life situations. VR enables observation that invokes a sense of realism, yet the immersive characteristics of Ocasio-Cortez's stream are defined by something other than reality-simulating technology. When Steyerl notes how poor image 'builds alliances as it travels', and how it 'creates new publics' (Steyerl 2009), it is a particular public that is at stake. When Ocasio-Cortez invites us to her private space, her own apartment, without the presence of any other mediator, the scene is both public and intimate: it takes place under the auspices of the market and has thousands of participants while at the same time the host's feelings and bodily states are discussed. Lauren Berlant's concept of 'intimate publics' is a place that strangers embrace because they expect to 'share a worldview and emotional knowledge that they have derived from a broadly common historical experience' (Berlant

2008: viii). There is a promise of belonging and emotional contact as well as confirmation, consolation and revelation that makes subjects willing to participate in such 'intimate publics'. It is a space that makes it possible to understand more clearly and critically one's situation and how to endure, resist or overcome it (Berlant 2008: viii).

Such emotional contact with Ocasio-Cortez also involves the 'performance' mentioned by Thompson, which describes the stance adopted by that particular kind of politician and which characterises her weak and poor images. Ocasio-Cortez manifests a total lack of regard for the amateur and imperfect visuality which blurs the distinction between consumer and producer. With nonchalance, she shows how her apartment has been only recently rented and has been left unfurnished so far; she repeatedly complains of failure, lack of time and fatigue. Such an openness towards and acceptance of failure, fatigue or weakness in both medium and message is not usually evidenced in communications by mainstream politicians. This does not only make her more relatable, as journalists claim (Cauterucci 2018), but could actually be said to do the job of 'intimate publics' which, as Berlant argues, 'legitimate qualities, ways of being, and entire lives that have otherwise been deemed puny or discarded. It creates situations where those qualities can appear as luminous' (Berlant 2008: 3). Thus, Ocasio-Cortez's Instagram streaming makes manifest the breakability of both the human body and technology as a point of departure for consciousness-raising, community building and, ultimately, for collective resistance: it features a human body interacting with machines while both the human and the machine are seen as failing or dysfunctional. Thus, in weak and poor images, what is really at stake is an alliance of machine and human, wherein it becomes difficult to differentiate the broken machine from the broken human.

Ocasio-Cortez's stream can be considered a twenty-first-century reinvention of Donna Haraway's cyborg, an example of what Sarah Sharma calls 'feminism of the broken machine' in which feminists literally learn from machines. Sharma analyses how the conservative political discourse points to feminists or non-compliant women in general, as 'machines which do not work well', which are, as a consequence, discarded and replaced by more smoothly functioning technology (most obviously sex-robots) (Sharma 2019). Sharma invites us to subversively affirm such perspective and follow its machinic logic. Referring to Marshall McLuhan and his understanding of the relationship between man and technology as mutually satisfactory sexual intercourse, she asks what happens when machines can no longer be relied upon to cooperate in that 'intercourse'. What can feminists learn from this? While Sharma is interested more in the shift in discourse than in particular political praxis, Ocasio-Cortez's stream might be an example of the latter inspired by the former. Unwilling to exit the situation she finds herself in, reluctant to be fixed, recharged, plugged back in, through her stream Ocasio-Cortez becomes a broken machine.

Clearly, communicating her fatigue and brokenness, the cyborg of intimate publics is engaged in intense emotional and affective labour: her emotions and affects are both exploited by the market and involved in generating social connections and their political possibilities. Berlant discusses the concept of intimate publics mainly in relation to popular literature for women readers in the nineteenth and twentieth centuries, yet we could also consider how social networks are involved in 'digital intimacy publics' (Dobson et al. 2019: 4–5). The social media platforms are 'training grounds in the development of platforms algorithms, protocols, and interfaces' (Dobson et al. 2019: xii) and a place where users' attention, time and affects are privatised; clearly, more is at stake. Recalling Groys, we have already seen how images on social networks are media of social reproduction. Kylie Jarrett, indebted to the work of Marxist feminists, considers our overall activity on social networks as following the contradictory logic of social reproduction activities, namely domestic labour. While our user activity is essential for corporations to generate surplus value, at the same time, it can involve something inalienable: what escapes it. The key is that social reproduction entails affective embodied activity (Jarrett 2017: 3–4). Our activity on social networks is both exploited and potentially emancipatory specifically because it involves affect[1] (Jarrett 2017: 117–18). At stake are affective acts such as liking other users' posts that contribute to user data but simultaneously can be constitutive of relations irreducible to exchange value. As Jarrett puts it: '[T]he Internet is a site for physical arousal, heightened emotions and the cultivation and maintenance of rich social relationships' (Jarrett 2017: 121). It is the affect that makes bubble vision a powerful weapon.

The tension between social reproduction and production takes different forms at different moments in the history of capitalist societies. Today, for many of us, it is most palpable in the digital realm. Here is where we can actually experience its 'dual character' (Federici 1975: 3–4; Jarrett 2017: 3), that is, how it simultaneously produces relationships to capital and our relationships to each other. It is a site of exploitation, but it is also where we can 'change the purpose of reproduction and work on our capacity for resistance and self-determination' (Stejskalová and Kleinhamplová 2015: 52). When Ocasio-Cortez cooks macaroni and cheese in an Instant Pot during another of her live streams on 9 November 2018, responding to questions and comments from her followers, be they personal or political, users are affectively and emotionally involved.

It is precisely those interactions involving emotional labour that are the most profitable, where expectations are disproportionately placed on women, who are more likely to like and comment on social sites (Cirucci 2018). When we watch on our screens the amateur images of a fatigued and slightly confused Ocasio-Cortez who, instead of resting, continues her work of political organising online; or when we watch her mention that she quit Facebook and will not use social media on weekends because it is detrimental to mental health (Isikoff and Klaidman 2019), the ambivalence between her embrace and refusal of social network sites is apparent. Of course, this kind of confusion is more than familiar to many users: through such ambivalences communicated by fatigue or confusion, the tension between exploitation and marketisation of relationships formed on social platforms and their potential, between production and reproduction, is felt quite distinctly. The bubble vision as poor and weak image emerges as a space where it is possible to collectively experience the tension which, in turn, constitutes its political potential.

Empathy Machines

The kinship of Ocasio-Cortez's Instagram stream and virtual reality is related to the fact that both can be understood as devices to generate empathy for (class, gender, race) difference. At least this is how virtual reality is generally understood. In Ocasio-Cortez's Instagram posts and live stream we experience racial and class identity by being invited to the space occupied by the body of a woman of colour from an immigrant background engaged in a specific way of speaking and writing that is conscious of differences. While we have shown that it is the affective and emotional experience that makes her video stream enticing and immersive (and also open to exploitation), this is also expressed in written and spoken language when Ocasio-Cortez speaks and writes about emotions as important guides in navigating alien spaces, such as when she writes about how as a woman of colour from a family of immigrants she felt intimidated entering the US Congress and how she was able to grow through such fear.[2] Her posts speak of the bodily experiences of the lives of oppressed subjects, and they make manifest self-awareness being born out of their physical realities.

Through her focus on embodied engagement and affective and emotional experience related to the experience of difference, Ocasio-Cortez can be described as a follower of women of colour feminism from the 1980s.[3] This is a tradition that Lisa Nakamura, a feminist theoretician of digital culture, finds uncannily related to virtual reality technologies (Nakamura 2018). Nakamura discusses how virtual reality's immersive and enticing characteristics are, for instance, used by corporations, namely Google, to allow its users to 'walk in other people's shoes'. In 'Exploring Race', a 60° virtual reality video format, Google invites users (presumably white) to immerse themselves in the traumatic experience of one of their employees – Dizzie, a woman of colour – in order to understand how Google is a safe space for everybody, including marginalised and oppressed subjects. Nakamura, however, makes clear that communication platforms are interwoven with systems of oppression: most technological devices are invented and designed by white, privileged men for white, privileged men (Nakamura).[4]

In response to this situation, Nakamura stresses the need for women of colour experts to appropriate the newest technology for their own goals. She gives the example of the Hyphen-Labs collective who combine their expertise in new technology and afro-futurist and feminist aesthetics. Their project, *NeuroSpeculative Afrofeminism*, aims to create an empathetic digital environment focusing on the experiences of black women: 'It makes you experience racial identity', Nakamura notes, 'by occupying some black space' (Nakamura 2018). Nevertheless, she laments the delay with which women of colour come to appropriate new technology. This is clearly not the case of Ocasio-Cortez, however, who, as a woman of colour, is among the few politicians who use social platforms in new, innovative ways, paving the path for others to follow. This is because bubble vision, composed of poor and weak images, involves a different strategy: the images do not require expert knowledge of the particular technology and instead question the very notion of expertise, as well as make visible the limits of access to that expertise. Their aim, in fact, is to express Ocasio-Cortez's status as an outsider – a woman of colour from an immigrant, working-class background with limited access to institutions of power – to the established political regime. This expression makes manifest and criticises, in both form and content, the unequal distribution of resources and privilege in American society. If virtual reality via advanced technology creates an inauthentic sense of realism without provoking any sense of social responsibility, the Instagram live stream as poor and weak image entices one to affectively experience a broken-down image as a representation of a reality that can be physically and mentally damaging, impacting more and more of us, and in which we are all implicated.

Perhaps never before have media technologies been so commodified and so interwoven with our intimate lives. As a result, private space has become an arena of uncompensated work, domination and surveillance. Feminist theoreticians speak about how the conditions that previously concerned only marginalised subjects such as women, people of colour and lgbtq+, now affect the majority of us (Nakamura 2018; Jarrett 2019: 105). Jarrett even defines the new paradigm of 'digital housewife' to underline how the conditions of our digital lives relate to the historical oppression of particular subjects (2017: 2). In the past, politicians have tried to master new media technologies in order to push for various kinds of causes and positions; those who were successful and who, like Ocasio-Cortez, were quick to learn how to make use of these new technologies for more effective communication with potential followers and voters, gained advantages over their rivals (Thompson 2019). It is worth noting that it is an activist, familiar with the history of feminism, who has emerged as the chief inventor of the political uses of social media in contemporary mainstream politics.

The lesson of Ocasio-Cortez, then, is that the history of resistance of the oppressed can play a significant role in finding ways to navigate the ambiguous landscape of online platforms. Her political intervention into the social media landscape in which poor and weak images of shared affect play a central role is informed by the history of such struggles, of weak resistance of artists and housewives, of women of colour feminism survival strategies: she is making them relevant again. Her visual politics, centred around the imperfect, flawed and breakable, creates the conditions for a shared affective experience of the fragility of our bodies, their social reproduction, and the ways in which the technologised condition is implicated. Immersed and enticed into the intimate space of another person, we participate in poor and weak images as imperfect machines become involved with imperfect bodies. As a result, we collectively experience the exhaustion of humans, machines and the environment. If bubble vision as virtual reality or 360° video anticipates the future of perfect technology and the humanless world, bubble vision as weak and poor image focuses on the damaged present as a call to arms for an alternative future. This is how photography off the scale, proliferating on social networks, finds its potential as a political force. We should understand that failure and weakness is a tool for politicisation; if we stop considering exhaustion – in any of its forms; technological, physical or mental – as something to overcome or fix, perhaps there is still hope for the exhausted world we occupy.

Notes

1. When defining affect, Jarrett relies on the concepts as put forth by Brian Massumi and Sara Ahmed. Jarrett understands affect as a sensory, bodily and, importantly, relational experience that refers to non-signifying processes which take place below the threshold of conscious awareness and meaning but are part of the social, cultural and psychological experience of subjects. Emotions, however, can be verbalised and consciously grasped (Jarrett 2017: 121–2).
2. Let's take, for example, the image from late January 2019, in which Ocasio-Cortez is leaning towards Ayanna Pressley, another woman of colour and

US Congressional Representative, who appears to whisper something in Ocasio-Cortez's ear. The image is chosen to signal a sense of alliance and sisterhood between women of colour in what is for them the unfamiliar and alien territory of the US Congress. The image is accompanied by the following text describing how Ocasio-Cortez struggled with the intimidating atmosphere of Congress: 'So yes, speaking up for the first time in this environment can be scary. Here's my trick: for a long time, I've used fear as a guiding light 💡 instead of a reason to turn off. Emotions are information and data too, and fear is telling us something. For me, fear isn't saying "go away", fear tells me "this is new, and it *could* be dangerous. There are stakes here." But I've very frequently interpreted fear as a growth cusp. Aside from some concrete fears, we often don't know what we're afraid of until we get there, and feel it. Fear tells us how to grow. Fear, like many discomforts, forces us to choose: 'Do I do this, or not?' Without fear, there is no courage. Without fear, we don't have the opportunity to prove ourselves in ways we never thought possible.' Ocasio-Cortez writes in her own words, yet her situation is described in a language that echoes the writing of women of colour feminists. Audre Lorde, the black lesbian poet, saw herself as a storyteller and a warrior; language was her weapon. Lester C. Olson observes how Lorde's speeches 'have an aphoristic, expansive quality resulting from her extensive use of metaphors, maxims, proverbs and stories' (Olson 1997: 49). Hers is an emotionally resonant language that mixes genres and codes, co-opting styles and weaving together the personal and the political. Like Ocasio-Cortez, Lorde appeals to the reader using polemical language: her arguments similarly centre around personal experience and research of emotions such as anger, guilt, fear. In *The Uses of Anger: Women Responding to Racism*, she speaks about anger as a legitimate response to racism and as a way towards social change and growth. Elsewhere, in *The Transformation of Silence into Language and Action*, she discusses the fear of visibility and the necessity to overcome it so that she could speak up in the context of her own fear of disease – in her case, breast cancer – that was a taboo topic at the time. As a result, Lorde's writing strikes one as situated and embodied, just like that of Ocasio-Cortez.
3. We can choose to understand Ocasio-Cortez's visual politics as part of a wave of activism (Black Lives Matter, #Metoo) or popular culture (Beyoncé) that makes this particular kind of feminist practice relevant again.
4. For instance, in the case of virtual reality, women are more likely to experience motion sickness than men because of how the design of virtual reality technology affects their specific hormonal and perception systems (boyd 2014).

References

Berlant, Lauren (2008), *The Female Complaint: The Unfinished Business of Sentimentality in American Culture*, Durham, NC and London: Duke University Press.

boyd, danah (2014), 'Is the Oculus Rift Sexist?', *Quartz*, 28 March 2014. Available at: <https://qz.com-192874-is-the-oculus-rift-designed-to-be-sexist> (last accessed 12 July 2019).

Cauterucci, Christina (2018), 'Instant Pot Politics', *Slate Magazine*, 20 November 2018. Available at: <https://slate.com-news-and-politics-2018-11-alexandria-ocasio-cortez-instagram-stories.html> (last accessed 12 July 2019).

Cirucci, Angela M. (2018), 'A New Women's Work: Digital Interactions, Gender, and Social Network Sites', *International Journal of Communication*, 12. Available at: <https://ijoc.org-index.php-ijoc-article-view-8348> (last accessed 11 July 2019).

Cubitt, Sean (2017), 'The Mass Image', *Fotomuseum*, 9 February 2017. Available at: <https://www.fotomuseum.ch-en-explore-still-searching-articles-30044-the-mass-image> (last accessed 26 September 2019).

Dobson, Amy Shields, Nicholas Carah, and Brady Robards (2019), 'Digital Intimate Publics and Social Media: Towards Theorising Public Lives on Private Platforms', in Amy Shields Dobson, Nicholas Carah and Brady Robards (eds), *Digital Intimate Publics and Social Media*, London: Palgrave Macmillan, pp. 3–29.

Federici, Silvia (1975), *Wages against Housework*. Bristol: Falling Wall Press.

Fraser, Nancy (2017), 'Crisis of Care? On the Social-Reproductive Contradictions of Contemporary Capitalism', in Tithi Bhattacharya (ed.), *Social Reproduction Theory. Remapping Class, Recentering Oppression*. London: Pluto Press, pp. 21–37.

Groys, Boris (2010), 'The Weak Universalism', *e-flux*, 15. Available at: <http://www.e-flux.com-journal-15-61294-the-weak-universalism> (last accessed 12 May 2019).

Isikoff, Michael, and Daniel Klaidman (2019), 'AOC Talks 2020 Election, Giving up Social Media and Why She Supports Rep. Omar', *Yahoo*, 19 April 2019. Available at: <https://www.youtube.com-watch?v=nbQBXcnbSgs> (last accessed 11 July 2019).

Jarrett, Kylie (2017), *Feminism, Labour and Digital Media: The Digital Housewife*. London: Routledge.

Jarrett, Kylie (2019), 'Through the Reproductive Lens: Labour and Struggle at the Intersection of Culture and Economy', in David Chandler and Christian Fuchs (eds), *Digital Objects, Digital Subjects: Interdisciplinary Perspectives on Capitalism, Labour and Politics in the Age of Big Data*. London: University of Westminster Press, pp. 103–16.

Lorde, Audre (2007), *Sister Outsider*, Berkeley: Crossing Press.

Majewska, Ewa (2016), 'Feminist Art of Failure, Ewa Partum and the Avant-garde of the Weak', *View: Theories and Practices of Visual Culture*, 16 January 2016.

Available at: <https://www.researchgate.net-publication-337223786-%27Feminist-Art-of-Failure-Ewa-Partum-and-the-Weak-Avant-Garde%27-in-Widok-Journal-for-visual-culture-2017> (last accessed 11 July 2019).

Majewska, Ewa (2018), 'The Weak Internationalism? Women's Protests in Poland and Internationally', *Art and Law*, 9 May 2018. Available at: <https://www.internationaleonline.org-research-politics-of-life-and-death-98-the-weak-internationalism-womens-protests-in-poland-and-internationally-art-and-law> (last accessed 12 May 2019).

Martínez, Antonio García (2019) 'How Alexandria Ocasio-Cortez Shapes a New Political Reality', *Wired*, 9 January 2019. Available at: <https://www.wired.com-story-how-alexandria-ocasio-cortez-shapes-new-political-reality> (last accessed 12 July 2019).

Moraga, Cherie, and Gloria Anzaldúa (1988), *This Bridge Called My Back*. New York: Kitchen Table: Women of Colour Press.

Nakamura, Lisa (2018), 'Call Out, Protest, Speak Back', *Transmediale*, 21 March 2018. Available at: <https://www.youtube.com-watch?v=DQ04m-mZfbTc> (last accessed 11 July 2019).

Olson, Lester C. (1997), 'On the Margins of Rhetoric: Audre Lorde Transforming Silence into Language and Action', *Quarterly Journal of Speech*, 83(1): 49–70.

Perry, David M. (2018), 'Alexandria Ocasio-Cortez has Mastered the Politics of Digital Intimacy', *Pacific Standard*, 30 November 2018. Available at: <https://psmag.com-social-justice-alexandria-ocasio-cortez-has-mastered-the-politics-of-digital-intimacy> (last accessed 12 July 2019).

Reilly, Claire (2019), 'Alexandria Ocasio-Cortez Says Democracy has a "Facebook problem"', *CNET*, 13 March 2019. Available at: <https://www.cnet.com-news-democracy-has-a-facebook-problem-says-alexandria-ocasio-cortez-aoc> (last accessed 11 July 2019).

Sharma, Sarah (2019), 'Feminism of the Broken Machine', *Studium Generale Rietveld Academie*, 14 May 2019. Available at: <https://www.youtube.com-watch?v=f0A1lydIUlA> (last accessed 11 July 2019).

Stejskalová, Tereza, and Barbora Kleinhamplová (2015), 'Emancipation through Care: Silvia Federici on Reproductive Work', in Tereza Stejskalová and Barbora Kleinhamplová (eds), *Who Is an Artist?*. Prague: Academy of Fine Arts, pp. 45–57.

Steyerl, Hito (2009), 'In Defense of the Poor Image', *e-flux*, 10. Available at: <https://www.e-flux.com-journal-10-61362-in-defense-of-the-poor-image> (last accessed 11 July 2019).

Steyerl, Hito (2017), 'Bubble Vision', *Serpentine Marathon*, 7 October 2017: Available at: <https://www.youtube.com-watch?v=boMbdtu2rLE> (last accessed 3 May 2019).

Thompson, Derek (2019), 'The Political Question of the Future: But Are They Real?', *The Atlantic*, 7 January 2019. Available at: <https://www.theatlantic.com-ideas-archive-2019-01-politicians-are-live-streaming-videos-instagram-579490> (last accessed 12 July 2019).

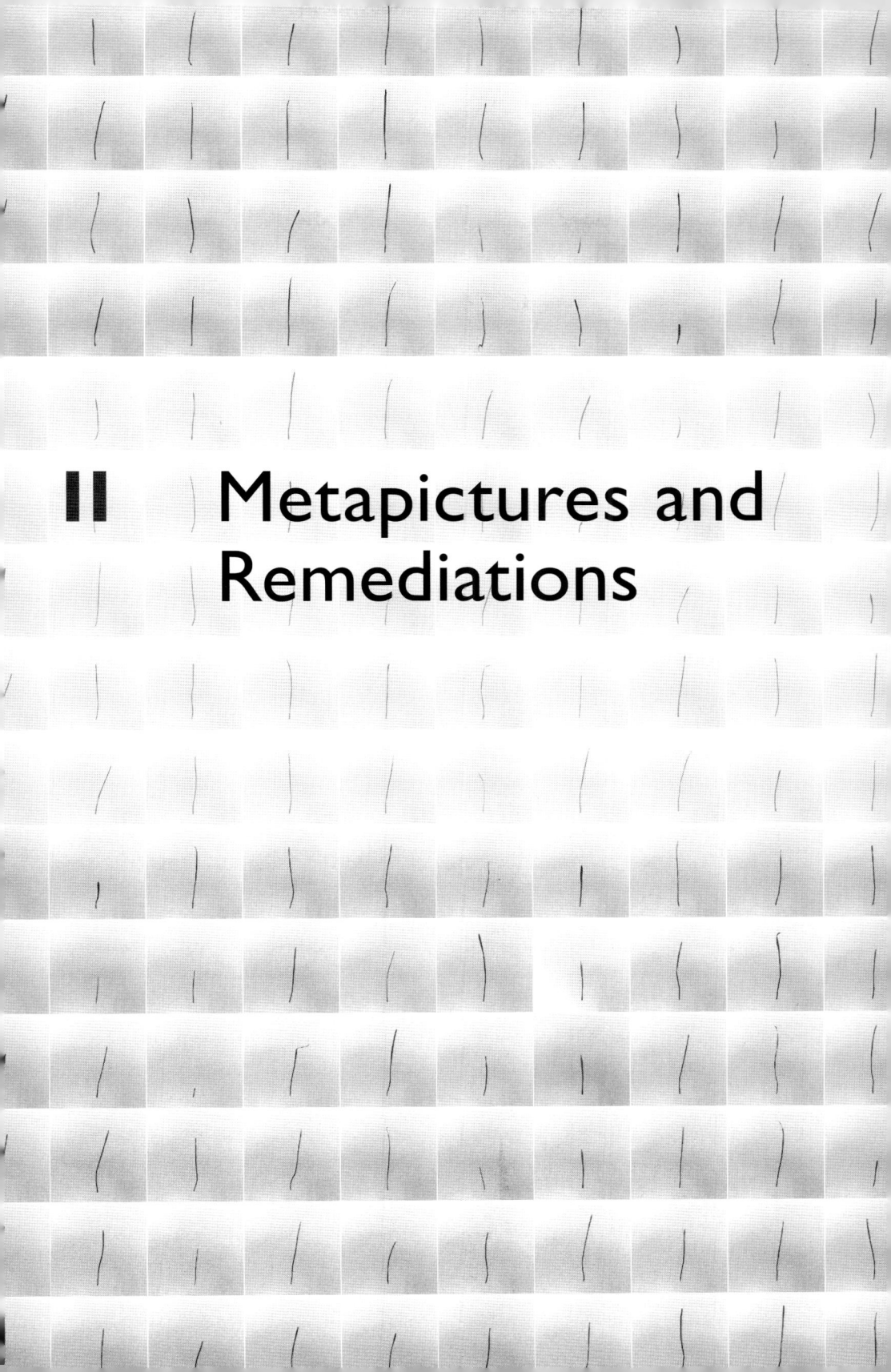

II Metapictures and Remediations

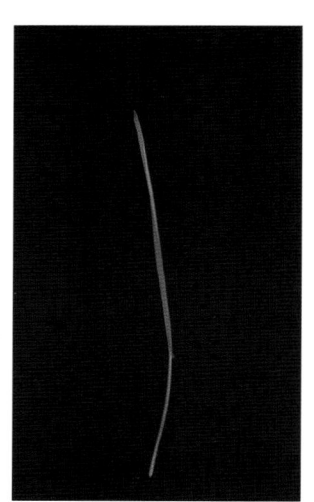

7 Photography's Mise en Abyme: Metapictures of Scale in Repurposed Slide Libraries

Annebella Pollen

LONG ABUNDANT, PHOTOGRAPHY's ubiquity and multiplicity has undoubtedly intensified in recent years. Photographs proliferate in the digital domain at an unprecedented scale, offering the partial realisation of many longstanding desires from a global encyclopaedic mapping of the visual world to a museum without walls. Photographic multitudes, however, also embody multifarious fears: of visual noise and mindless repetition, of metaphorical promiscuity and overpopulation. To engage with the apparently unmanageable excess of images is, it seems, to gaze into the abyss.

This chapter considers the photographic abyss through an examination of the visual and literary device of 'mise en abyme' and through W. J. T. Mitchell's concept of the metapicture, that is, self-referential images that 'might be capable of reflection on themselves, capable of providing a second-order discourse that tells us – or at least shows us – something about pictures' (Mitchell 1994: 38). Through an exploration of the recent work of contemporary artists who explore photographic enormity as their subject matter, particularly in relation to works that utilise obsolete photographic materials – in the form of 35mm slides from deaccessioned art history slide libraries – this chapter examines how such works and such materials employ and embody metapictorial strategies. In their oscillation between the tiny and singular and the massive and multiple, as reinterpreted by artists, the form and content of slide libraries necessarily expands and contracts to offer micro and macro views, confirming scale as a central photographic characteristic. As the works constitute images of images of images, I argue that they offer a productive metapictorial site for surveying desires and anxieties about image abundance and excess.

Size Matters

It has become a commonplace of twenty-first century discussions of photography to observe the form's enormously expanding quantities and to use this characteristic to communicate anxieties of a parallel scale (for summaries see Pollen 2015, 2016, 2018, 2020 and the Introduction to this volume). Amid apocalyptic claims, recent reflective publications have taken a more sober view, not least to put such claims into historical perspective. Philosopher of photography Andrew Fisher (2012), for example, has persuasively argued for scale as a central aspect of all photographic thinking, from minor to major. Visual communication scholars Robert Hariman and John Louis Lucaites (2016) propose, in order to shift the tone of the debate, that anxieties about photographic 'excess' should be positively repositioned as photographic 'abundance'. Photographic historian Michelle Henning (2018: 134) also argues that photography must always be considered in multiple, and not only because of our networked times. She notes, 'the singularity of an individual image was always a useful fiction', even in art history, which is based on reproductions of artworks, and in analogue forms, where still images were never properly still and never existed in isolation. With these touchstones in mind – that photographic expansion characterises current discussions of the form; that thinking about scale and multiplicity is essential to all thinking about photography; and that hierarchies and anxieties structure the debate – this chapter examines case studies of artistic practice that test how this thinking and doing plays out in empirical example.

The Art of Excess

As authors of recent surveys have observed, there is a tendency in contemporary practice for artists to work with photographic abundance as both medium and message. Robert Shore, for example, in *Post-Photography: The Artist with a Camera*, observed the tendency for photographers to 'conclude that the world-out-there is so hyper-documented there's no point taking your own pictures anymore'. He identified 'a leading post-photographic strategy' among artists who glean from the abundant resources of the online environment in the guise of curator and editor (Shore 2014: 7). Similarly, Joan Fontcuberta's exhibition and publication, *The Post-photographic Condition*, similarly noted a 'post-photographic readiness' among artists 'to make use of the overwhelming quantities of scale' made available by the expansion in photographic practice (2015: 40).

Figure 7.1 (next page) Oriol Vilanova: *To Be Precise*, 2015. Exhibition view: The Green Parrot, Barcelona. Photograph by Roberto Ruiz. Courtesy of the artist.

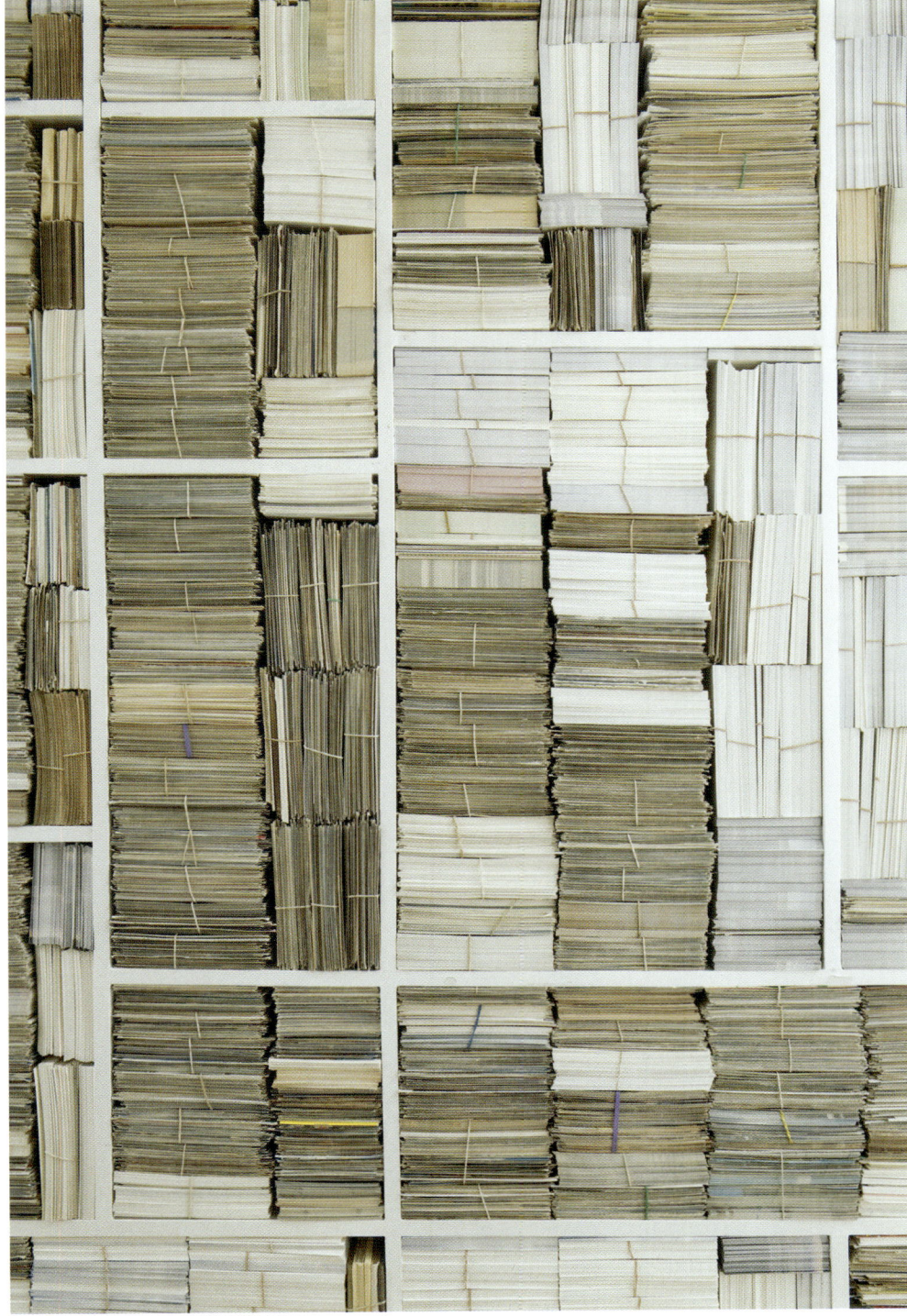

Examples of this self-referential tendency are numerous. Dutch artist and collector Erik Kessels, for example, has long worked with large-scale collections of so-called vernacular photographs. Size and quantity have been a key part of his practice, with his 2012 exhibition *Album Beauty*, for example, scaling up individual mid-century personal photographs of anonymous sitters to monumental wall-sized portraits to enable a shift in perspective and thus in status and value. Kessels's *24 Hrs in Photos*, shown since 2011 in a series of site-specific locations, also works with scale as its subject matter (see Figure 1.1 in this volume).

Approximately 950,000 photographs are printed from those uploaded to Flickr in a single day as a means of materialising the dizzying scale of photographic practice. Kessels's display strategy – piling the photographs high as if washed up flotsam and jetsam on the gallery floor – embodies the deluge metaphor in its suggestion of photographic excess, and indeed, Kessels regularly expresses sadness at digital photography's current proliferation. From a younger generation, Catalan artist Oriol Vilanova also uses mass found photographic material – in his case, picture postcards from flea markets – to make similar points about the superlative scale of the visual world (Figure 7.1). In gridded display formations and stacked and bundled piles, postcards with or without their images on show, demonstrate patterning and repetition, density and intensity. In both artists' exhibition strategies – wholly filling gallery walls and floors – immersive displays are designed to visualise the overpowering drama of scale; overwhelming visual effects speak of an overwhelming visual culture.

Art about Art History

A related body of artistic practice has adapted similar materials and display strategies using very particular materials: the 35mm slides recently deaccessioned from institutional library collections. Over the last decade or so, former slide libraries serving art history departments in higher education institutions across Europe and North America have been undertaking collection management exercises, from streamlining to entirely disposing of their pedagogical slides, now viewed as obsolete with the coming of commercial digital image collections and digital display mechanisms. Once the mainstay of art historical instruction and a central feature of art library collections, changes in technology – including the cessation of film stock, processing services and projection mechanisms – have led to widespread reconsiderations of slide libraries' utility (Parsons 2005; Caraffa 2011; Godfrey 2014a; Godfrey 2014b; Bouchard 2015; Schoen 2017).

The ramifications of these discussions have led to a range of different outcomes in practice, from digitisation of collections (for example, at the

Metropolitan Museum of Art), to a move from functional visual resource to archival special collection (at Manchester School of Art), from strategic 'weeding' (at Oxford University) to their complete disposal (at Ithaca College). A 1989 survey of slide collections in the UK identified that by far the largest collections of slides resided in higher education institutions (McKeown and Otter 1989; Stojković et al. 2015). A 2014 survey of 112 slide collections in Britain and North America revealed that more than 75% were no longer intact; the vast majority were undergoing culling, had been disseminated or had been put into storage (Visual Resources Association 2014).

Given that the discussions about reducing or disposing of collections were based in part on a dramatic reduction in usage by the art historians whose needs the collections were meant to serve, the question of what to do with unused slides showed the scale of the problem, not least as collections typically ranged in size from 80,000 to 550,000 slides (Visual Resources Association 2014). Indeed, slide libraries' expansive quantities were a key aspect of their form. Photographic historian Constanza Caraffa has argued that the accumulation of photographs has long characterised the discipline of art history; she quotes art historian Bernard Berenson on this point from the 1930s: 'Photographs! Photographs! In our work one can never have enough.' Similarly, art historian Erwin Panofsky is said to have claimed that he who has the most photographs wins (Caraffa 2011: 21). After enormities have been accumulated, but the institutions and their users no longer want them, where should they go? The answer has been, in many cases, to artists.

A 'Slide and Transitional Media Task Force' assembled by the international Visual Resources Association provided a 2014 overview of slide libraries' dissolution strategies. Nearly half (47%) the institutions surveyed had donated their slides to artists; this had resulted in the creation of artistic projects from the modes to the major (Visual Resources Association 2014). Ithaca's *Turn up the Transparency* project, for example, invited students and faculty to submit creative projects, which resulted in the creation of slide lampshades and jewellery. Visual Resources staff at Brown University explained that they distributed unwanted slides to artists as a means of avoiding 'the ignominy of disposal' (Bouchard 2015). The Metropolitan Museum of Modern Art in New York gave their entire collection to Materials for the Arts, a scrap store organised by the Department of Cultural Affairs to repurpose

Figure 7.2 (next pages) Philipp Goldbach: *Sturm/Iconoclasm*, 2013. 200,000 small-image format slides from the former archives of Cologne University's Institute of Art History, 900 cm x 1600 cm. Installation view: Museum Wiesbaden, Project Space, 2013. Photograph by Wolfgang Günzel, Offenbach. © DACS 2019.

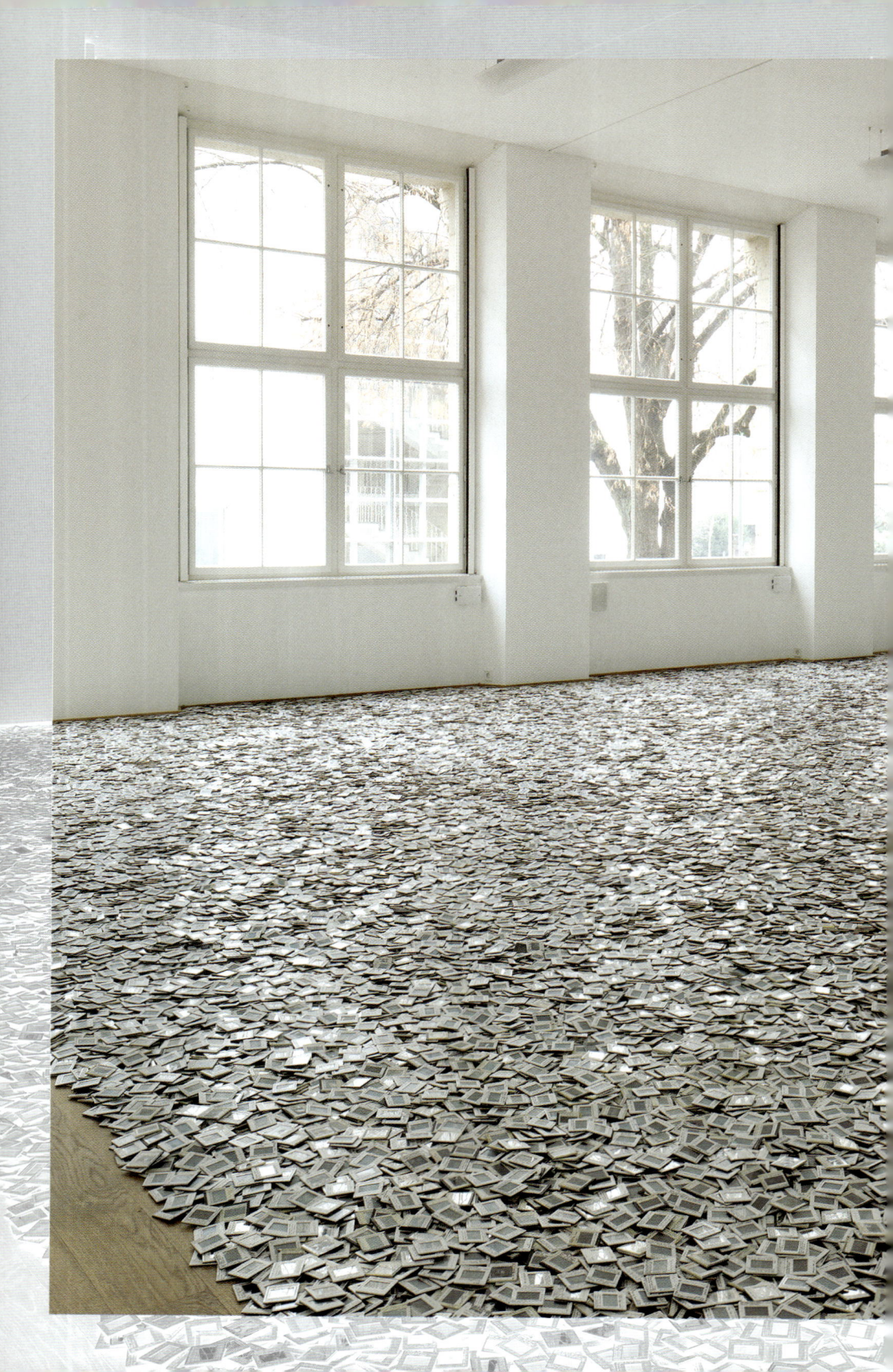

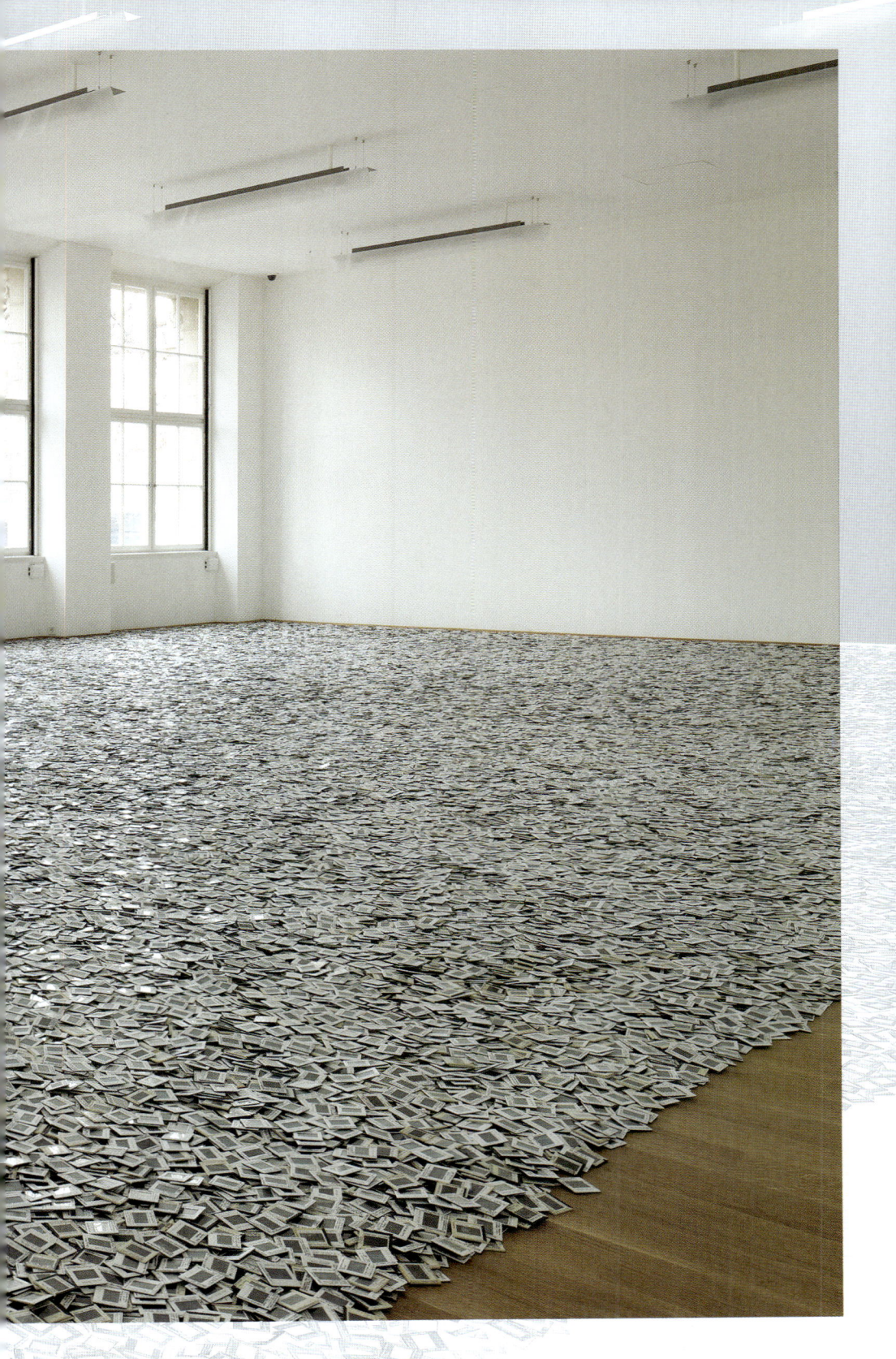

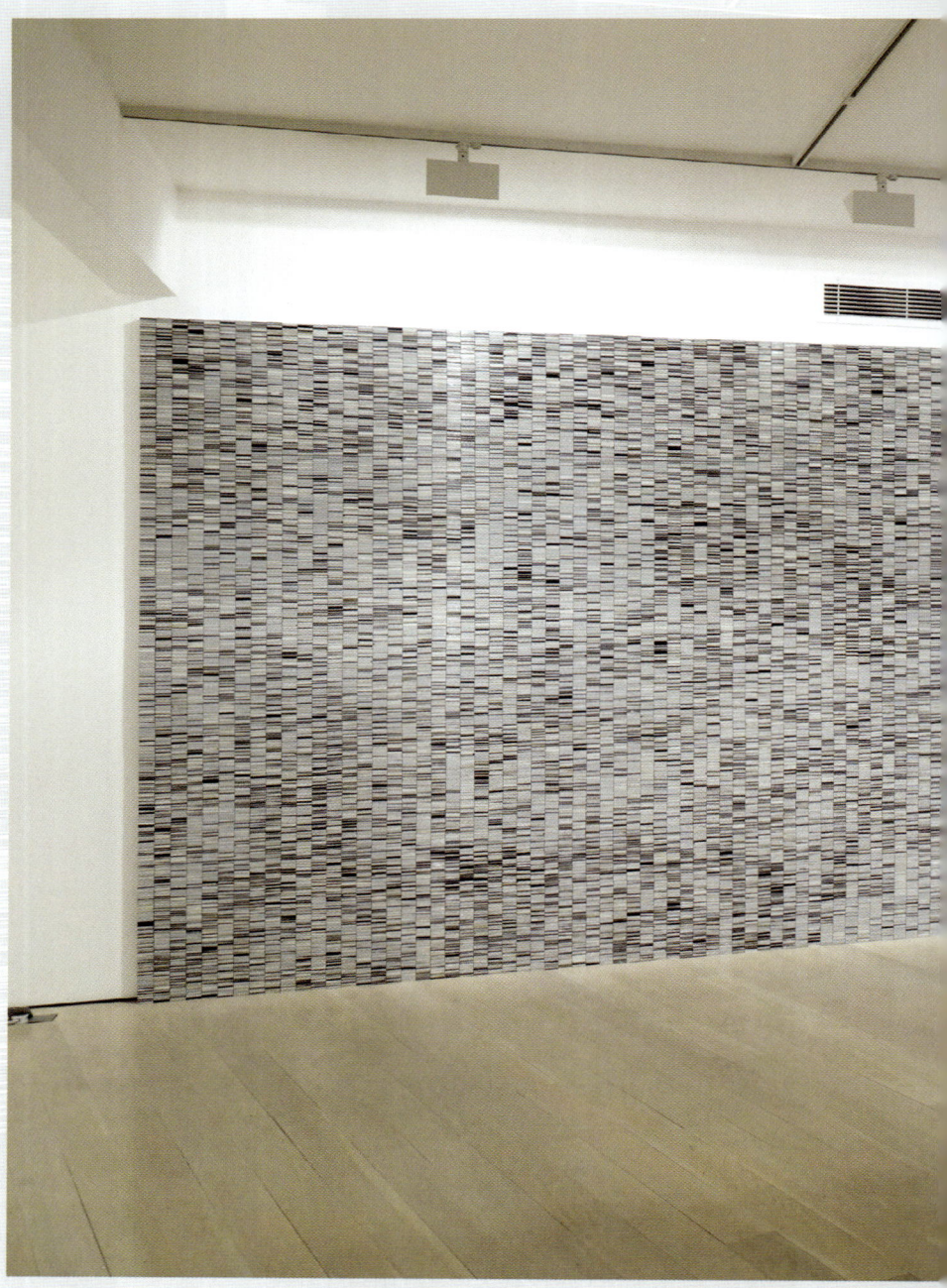

Figure 7.3 Philipp Goldbach: *Via Lucis*, 2015. 200,000 small-image format slides from the former archives of Cologne University's Institute of Art History, 270 cm x 800 cm. Installation view: Annely Juda Fine Art Gallery, London, 2016. Photograph by Philipp Goldbach. © DACS 2019.

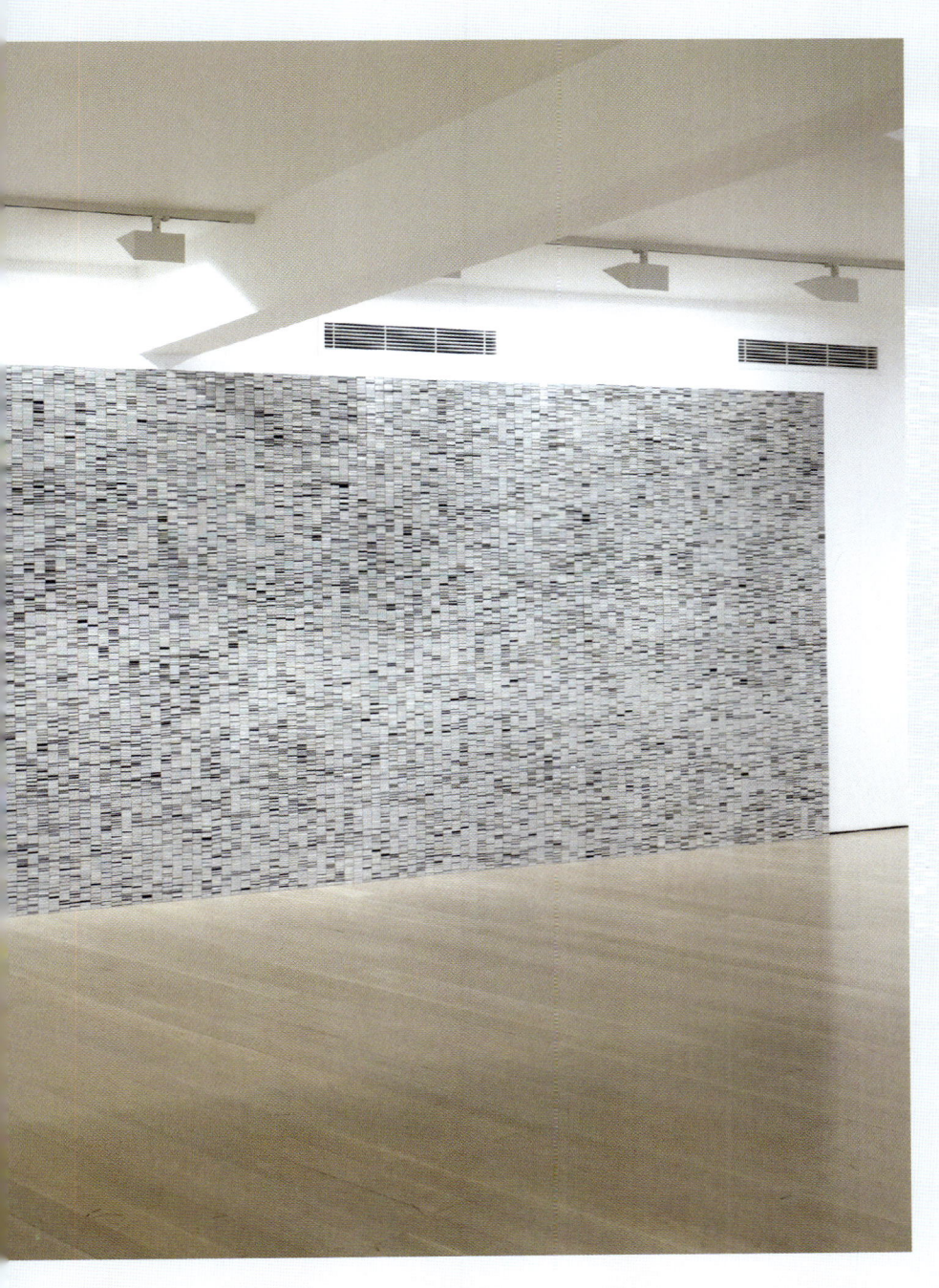

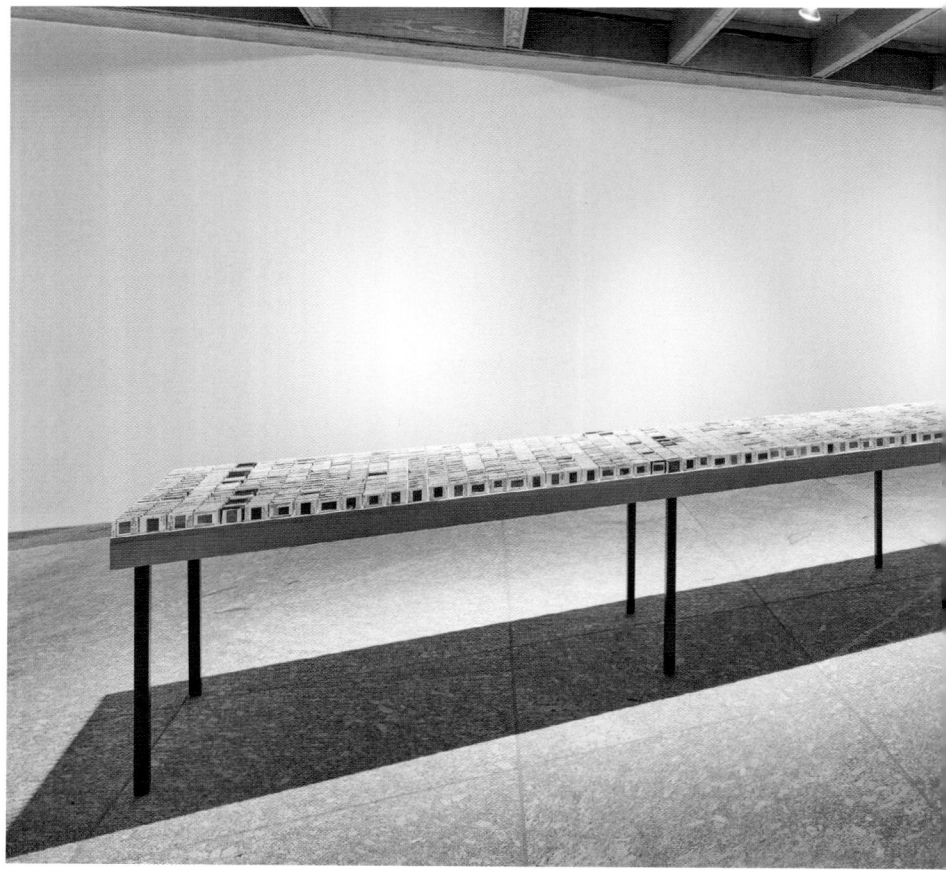

Figure 7.4 Philipp Goldbach: *Deaccession/Reaccession*, 2016. 15,000 small-image format slides from the archives of Bochum University's Institute of Art History, 1855 cm x 70 cm. Installation view: RUB art collections, 2016. Photograph by Paul Schöpfer, Cologne. © DACS 2019.

surplus items to arts organisations and schools (Barron 2017). These brief examples show a desire to keep the material out of landfill, and make the unwanted wanted, but also reveal the increasingly structured systems whereby artists acquire so-called found materials.

To link deaccessioned slide collections to debates about photographic scale, I will describe three substantial examples in further detail, each of which, I argue, demonstrates a metapictorial art practice that sheds light on photographic quantities. The first is the work of German artist Philipp Goldbach, who has used the 200,000 deaccessioned slides from the Institute of Art History, Cologne, in several different ways. In his 2013 installation *Sturm/Iconoclasm*, the entire collection was displayed, as if unceremonially dumped, across the floor of a whole gallery in Wiesbaden

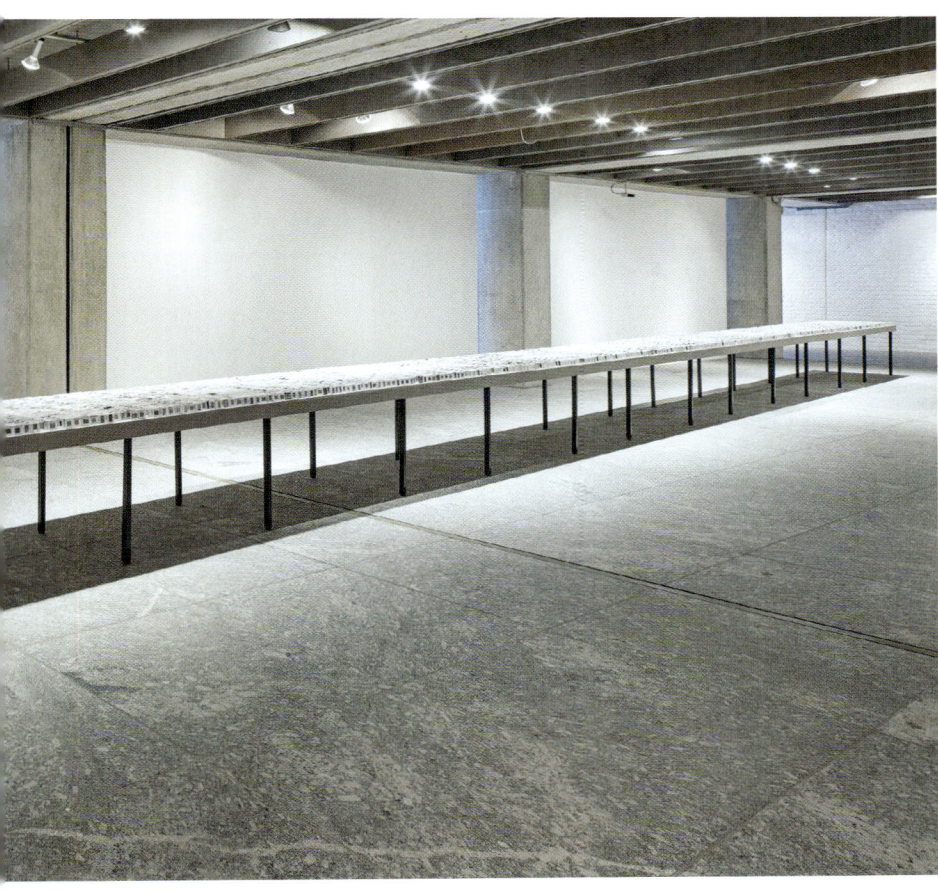

Museum (Figure 7.2). Taken at face value, *Sturm* suggests the fallen leaves of slides shaken from the tree of their institution after a period of dramatic turbulence; *Iconoclasm* seems to refer to their radical removal from storage and classification systems. Shaken down in this way, they become a floor-based sculpture, borrowing from the aesthetics of minimalism but utilising a form of maximalism in their overwhelming spread. Goldbach created *Via Lucis* in 2015 (Figure 7.3), using the same material, this time with only their black, grey or white edges visible in what the artist calls 'a kind of mural'. Stacked in a display of 2.7 by 8 metres, he explains, '[t]hey create a buzzing random pattern, almost like white noise on a TV screen, each slide adding a mark and collectively holding the imagery of art history in chaotic order' (Goldbach 2019). In 2016's *Deaccession/ Reaccession* (Figure 7.4), Goldbach reorganised slides disposed of by Ruhr University Bochum's Institute of Art History into a single horizontal densely packed table-based display. As the artist stated, this reflects on and makes visible 'the systematology of the archive' (Goldbach 2019).

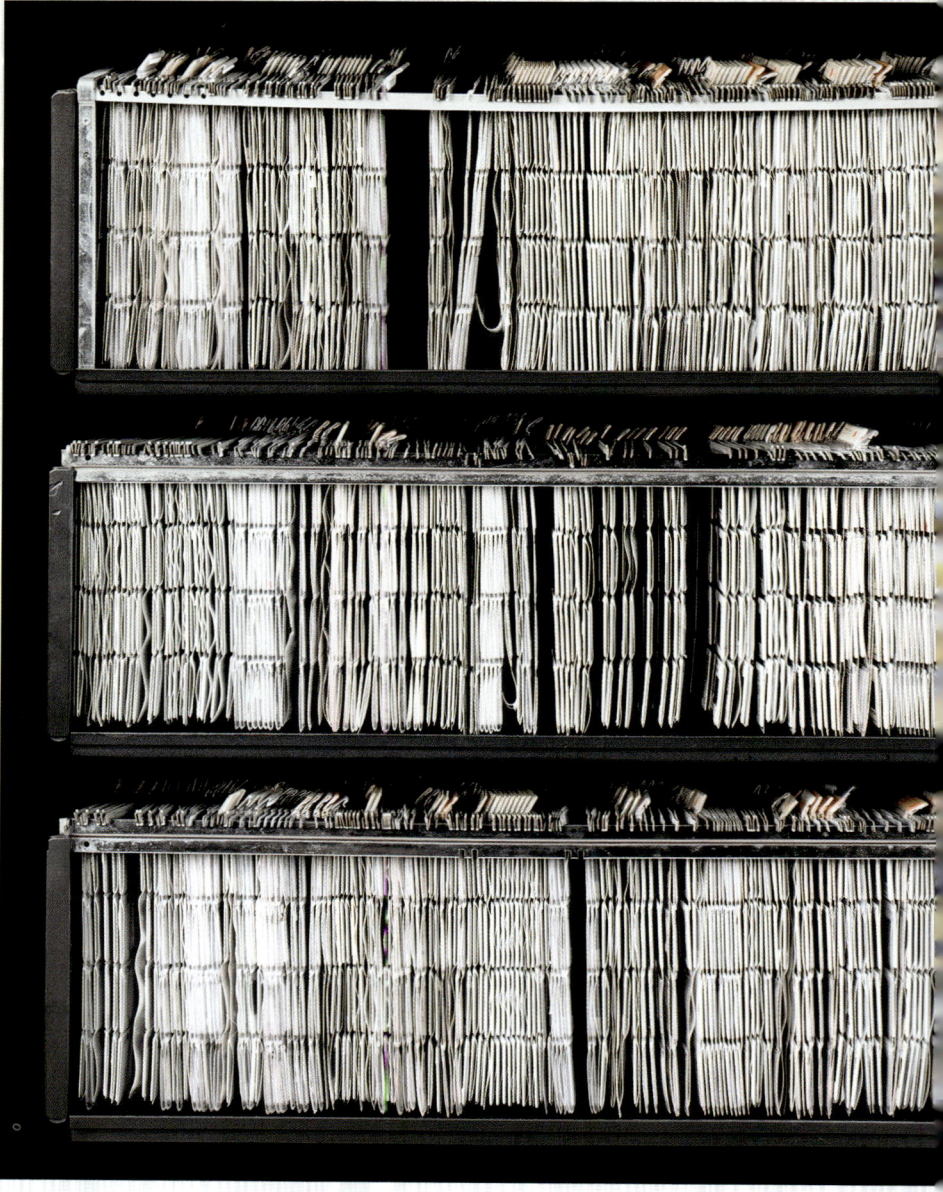

Figure 7.5 Susan Dobson: *Photographers A–Z*. C-print from digital file, 2018, 40 in x 65.5 in (101.6 cm x 166.6 cm). Courtesy of the artist.

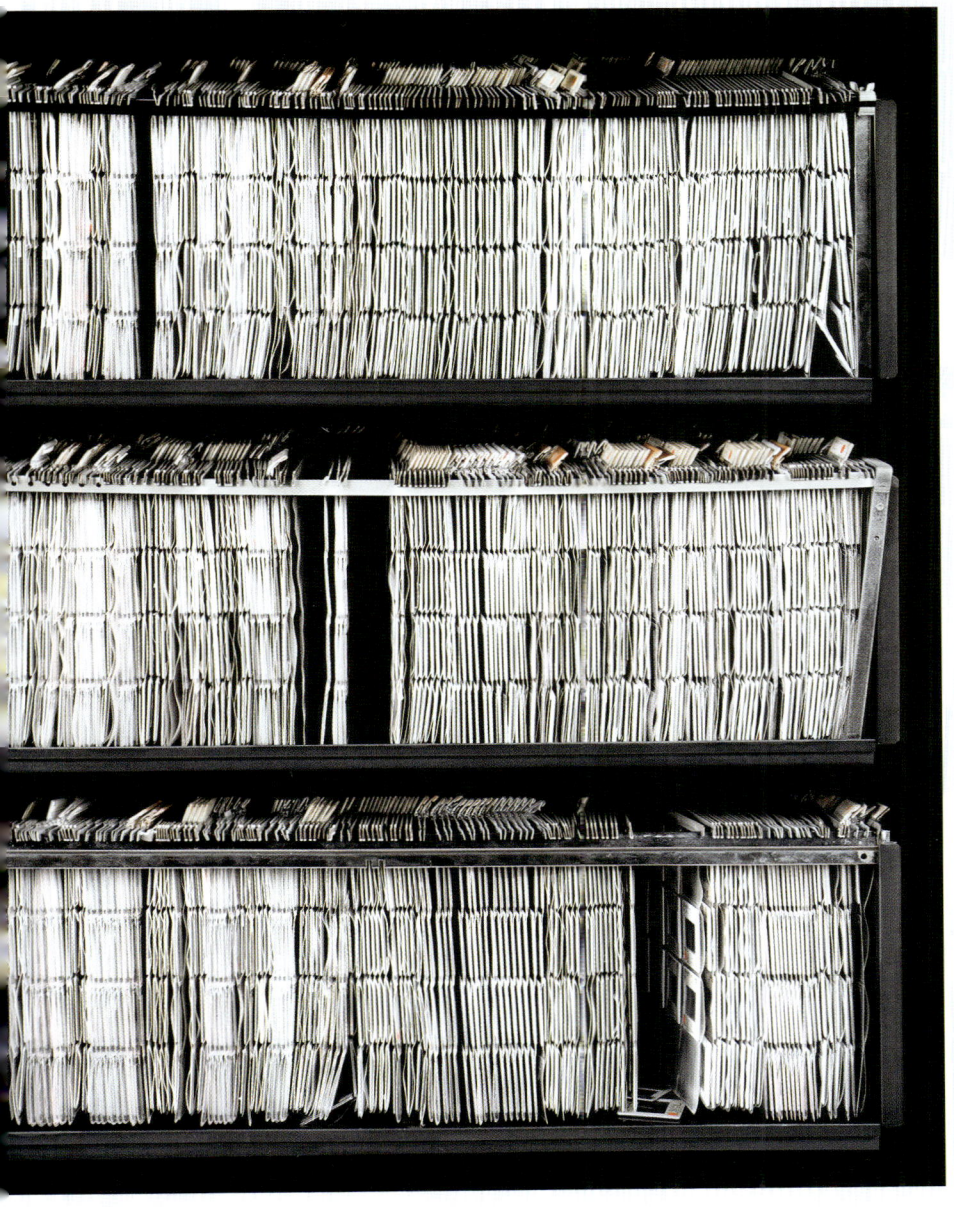

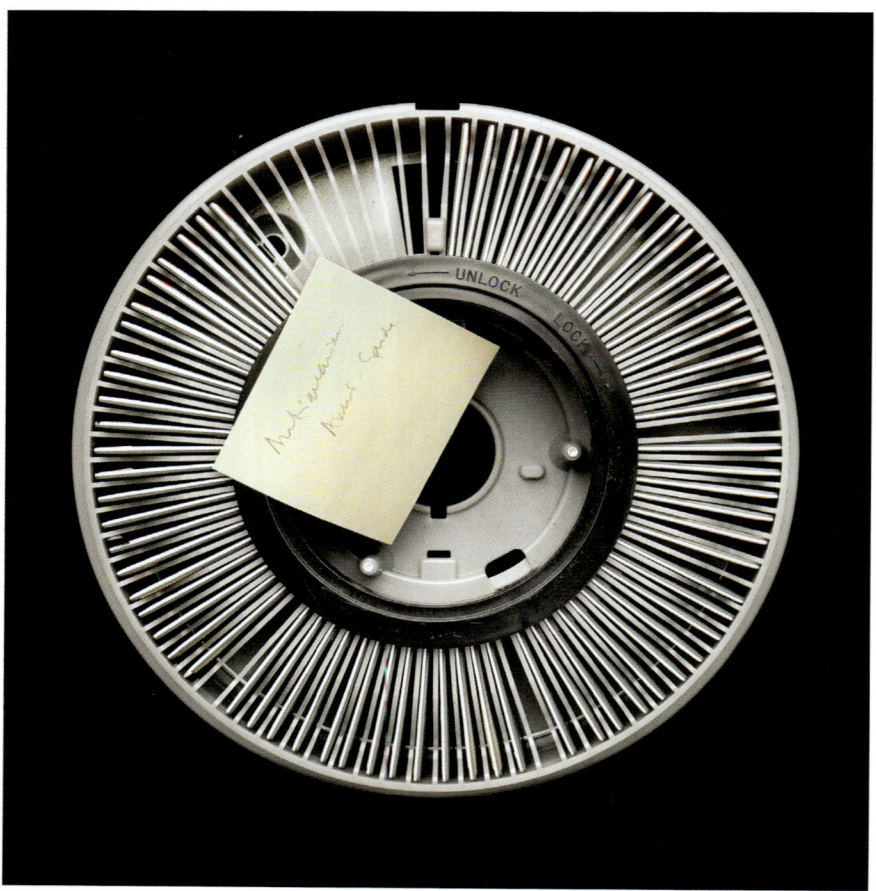

Figure 7.6 Susan Dobson: *Antiquarian Avant-Garde*. Archival pigment print, 2018, 35 in x 35 in (89 cm x 89 cm). Courtesy of the artist.

In Canada, photographer Susan Dobson has been working with similar material in her photographic series *Slide Library*. Dobson's photographs of projection apparatus as well as slides enable views of an imaging system as well as its results. In her 2017 *Slide Trays* installation at the Santa Cruz library in Tenerife, Spain, she created a 12 by 50-foot mural of side-on slides, organised by geographical subject matter, again using scaling up as a means to draw attention to material considered obsolete, as well as to its emphases and lacunae. Scale is key to the work's meaning; as Alison Nordström has put it of Dobson's work, 'as innumerable small fragments of knowledge, almost overwhelming in quantity and uniformity', it is in their number that slides matter (Nordström 2018). Dobson plays with scale in her final prints, where proportions are inverted; the architectural scale of slide drawers and slide carousels tower over the viewer in acts of estrangement (Figure 7.5 and Figure 7.6).

In the final example, Canadian multimedia artist Annie MacDonell describes her work as questioning 'the constitution, function, and circulation of images in the twenty-first century'. In an artistic commission for the National Media Museum-funded project *Either/And*, later reformulated as a photographic spread for *Photography Reframed* (Burbridge and Pollen 2018; Knelman and MacDonell 2018), the artist described how she found the slides 'next to the trash' at a higher education institution that asked not to be identified when the work was published. They were 'unlabeled, undated, and unsourced' (MacDonell 2012). Each slide image had been produced on a copy stand, variously from art monograph, fashion magazine or technical manual sources, and MacDonell highlighted the multiple transformations the images had undertaken in their journey from, say, paintings on walls to reproductions in print, to copying as slides, to viewing as a digital artwork. Showing edges and folds, reflections and loss of focus, the seeming errors in the slide reproductions – unselfconsciously betraying their status as copies – also reveal their multiply-reproduced genealogies (Figure 7.7 and Figure 7.8). As MacDonell puts it, 'the spine's interruption of the image reminds us of where they came from in the first place, and how our ways of

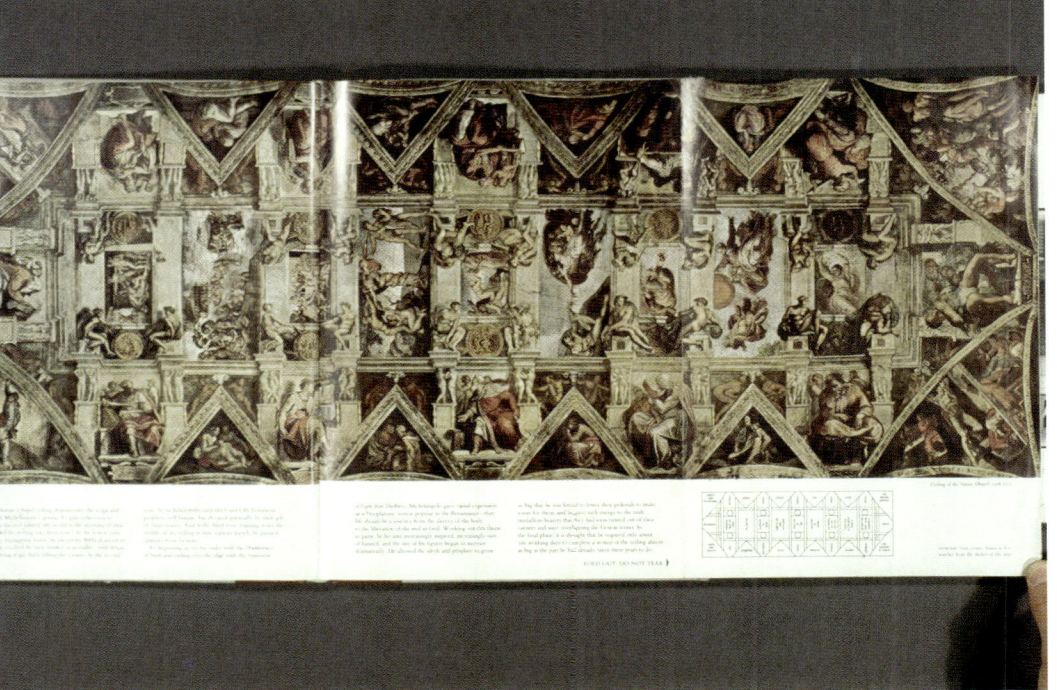

Figure 7.7 Annie MacDonell: digital photographs of deaccessioned slides from the series *Split Screen*, 2012. Courtesy of the artist.

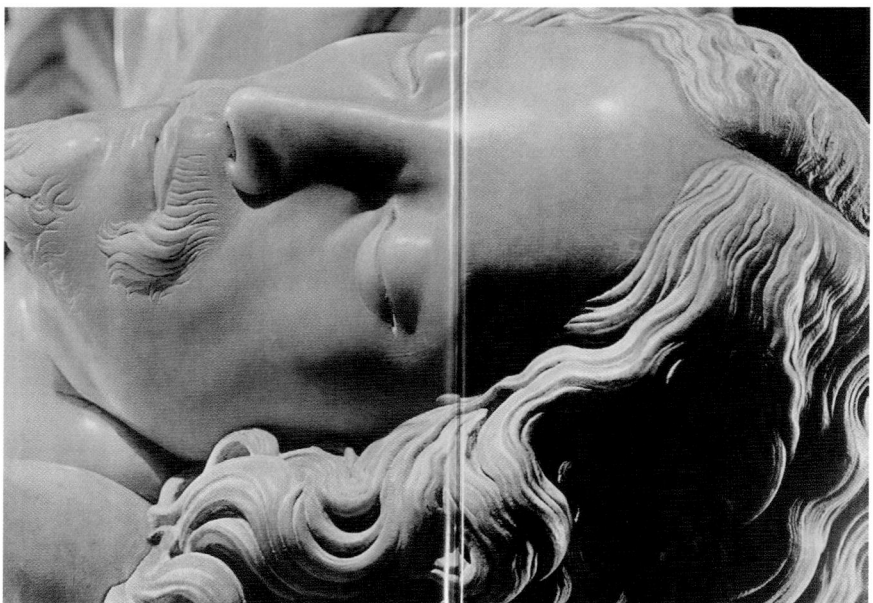

Figure 7.8 Annie MacDonell: digital photographs of deaccessioned slides from the series *Split Screen*, 2012. Courtesy of the artist.

encountering them continue to shift along with the technology that delivers them to us' (2012).

Slides as a Medium of Scale

While the recent artists' projects outlined above show a marked tendency to explore slides as a newly available source, they are not the first to work with slides as source material. An earlier moment took place in the 1960s and 1970s when conceptual artists increasingly turned to the projected image and its associated apparatus as a relatively innocent technological form capable of communicating information and imagery and, in the process, drawing attention to its own medium and materiality. As can be seen in the works gathered for the 2005 exhibition *Slide Show: The Projected Image in Contemporary Art*, scale mattered to the conceptual artists working with slides in this period, as did abundance (Alexander 2005). Slides were selected for their adaptability, cheapness and lack of material object in their immersive, impermanent displays. They combined forms (elements of photography, cinema, theatre, information technology) and their links to documentation/record/science/objectivity were also attractive; they were humble in dimension but could be scaled up to be cinematic. Now that slides are near-obsolete, as an artistic medium they provide a different commentary on their form; their material qualities and especially fallibilities remain part of their charm, but whereas they were once the means of 'preserving and projecting history' in the art classroom, now they record their own historical status (Alexander 2005).

The artists who work with slides today are in some ways in dialogue with earlier practitioners. Although their work expands artistic engagement with concepts of 'the archive' as a subject and a form in contemporary practice of more recent decades (Foster 2004), each work using art historical slides performs a metapictorial aesthetic. New work continues to provide ways of thinking about photography as mediation and remediation, but it also provides reflection on contemporary anxieties about scale. If scale is inherent to all photographic thinking, it also, by extension, becomes the subject matter for metapictorial photography about photography and art about art history. Scale in photography is not just about the too-large or the excessive; it is about the push-pull contrasts of the individual image, potentially full of detail and powerful in meaning, in juxtaposition with its enormous quantities. As such, art from slide collections moves from micro to macro view in a microscoping-telescoping oscillation, from piles, stacks, grids and multiple filing cabinets to single views of tiny details writ large. The large and small become the warp and weft of meaning; the individual element in the mass becomes a pictorial device to understand the meaning of the whole.

Metapictures and the Mise en Abyme

In my use of the term metapictorial, I draw on W. J. T. Mitchell's conceptualisations of metapictures. In *Picture Theory*, Mitchell delineated several categories of the form: 1) one that is self-referential, in which the picture represents itself as a kind of mise en abyme (a picture within a picture); 2) pictures that speak of pictures as a class, and are thus pictures about pictures; 3) pictures that are inherently about the nature of visual representation. In the end, however, his three-part schema – already showing some bleed between types – is overwritten by his broad assertion: 'Any picture that is used to reflect on the nature of pictures is a metapicture' (Mitchell 1994: 56.) Despite the metapictorial capacity of 'any picture or visible mark no matter how simple', Mitchell acknowledges their potential complexity of meaning: 'They don't just illustrate theories of picturing and vision: they show us what vision is, and picture theory' (1994: 57). In conclusion, Mitchell reflects:

> The metapicture is not a subgenre within the fine arts but a fundamental potentiality inherent in pictorial representation as such; it is the place

where pictures reveal and 'know' themselves, and where they reflect on the intersections of visuality, language, and similitude, where they engage in speculation and theorizing on their own nature and history. (1994: 82)

The idea of an image within an image, or a story within a story, was first encapsulated as a formal narrative device by novelist André Gide in 1893. He stated: 'In a work of art I rather like to find transposed, on the scale of the characters, the very subject of that work. Nothing throws a clearer light upon it or more surely establishes the proportions of the whole' (Gide 1984: 30–1). Proportion is the telling term here; the scaling up and down shows the innermost centre and its outside parameters. In the extended passage, Gide draws parallels with mirrors in painting and plays-within-plays but states that the most useful parallel is the shield within a shield in heraldry, 'that involves putting a second representation of the original shield "en abyme" within it' (1984: 30–1).

The concept of the 'mise en abyme', identified as an idea by Gide but coined as a term by Claude Magny in 1950, has been used extensively in literary criticism and has itself been the subject of intense scrutiny, not least by Lucien Dällenbach. In *The Mirror in the Text* Dällenbach explores the terms' origins, uses and misunderstandings. In heraldic terms, abyme/abyss has particular meaning, as Dällenbach explores. 'Semantically', he explains, 'the word "abyme" (abyss) evokes ideas of depth, of infinity, of vertigo and of falling, in that order' (1989: 189). Art critic Craig Owens explored the concept of mise en abyme in relation to photography in an influential article for *October*; here he used the concept to read photographs by Brassai, Lady Clementina Hawarden and Walker Evans that used mirrors, doubling and duplication centrally, and thus pictured photography's own condition as a mirror form and as a site of potentially endless reduplication (Owens 1978).

Regression and Expansion

In dialogue with these conceptualisations, then, I suggest that an application of the mise en abyme as a metapictorial device might illuminate some aspects of photographic excess as seen in the artistic methods of hundreds of thousands of slides tumbled across gallery floors, piled up by dustbins, and scaled up into monumental photographic portrayals. These are inherently pictures about pictures. Photographic historian Steffen Siegel has noted that Goldbach's *Sturm* display encapsulates both 'the big picture' of its overall effect and another perspective. The installation is made up of 'lots of little pictures'; these are also 'countless pictures of other pictures' (2014: 81). In *Sturm*, 'the viewer is confronted with the sheer and, in fact, astounding volume of such a collection'.

Despite this volume, Siegel notes that digital image repositories have 'amassed to proportions far greater than any of the largest collections imaginable in slide format' (2014: 83). We are looking at an enormity of slides but the edges that we can see signal a larger scale of images whose outer limits are so large as to stretch out of view.

Susan Dobson describes her own artistic strategy in *Slide Library* as an attempt 'to draw attention to my role in the cycle of material reproduction' (Dobson 2019). The work also invites this interpretation; as Nordström has put it, 'Dobson is a photographer photographing photographs of photographs' (Nordström 2018). In Sara Knelman's accompaniment to MacDonell's slide presentation, entitled 'On Images of Images of Images', the curator provides a set of frames that show if not infinite regress then a set of nesting practices that scale up and down:

> *On sculpture*
> *On photographs of sculpture*
> *(On photographs of people posed after sculpture*
> *On photographs of photographs of people posed after sculpture)*
> *On books of photographs of sculpture*
> *On slides of images in books of photographs of sculpture*
> *(On books of images of slides, including photographs of photographs*
>   *and photographs of sculpture)*
> *(On slideshows of images of sculpture and other arts, of family life and*
>   *travel and everything else)*
> *On digital scans of slides of images in books and magazines of photo-*
>   *graphs of sculpture*
> *On essays on digital scans of slides of images in books and magazines of*
>   *photographs of sculpture.*   (Knelman and MacDonell 2018)

The expansion and contraction of these points of view are meditations on the manifold versions of images that exist in a reproductive form of technology; the layers show excess in multiple.

MacDonell's examples also show another way in which excess has been discussed in relation to photography, in the context of the camera's capacity to record too much. Visual anthropologist Elizabeth Edwards has explored this aspect – what she describes as the 'random inclusivity of photographic inscription' as an important site of affect (2015: 237). The debate relates to the work of anthropologist Deborah Poole, who explored the way in which early anthropological photography was marked by a need to manage the medium's inherent informational 'excess' (Poole 2005). Photography's ability to record more than that which was required for the purposes of 'evidence' has been characterised by Poole as offering potential alternative readings; as a site of presence, 'it offers a space in which other histories might emerge' (Edwards 2015: 237). Edwards, like Hariman and Lucaites, shifts the language of scale from 'excess' to 'abundance' to open up possibilities that are not couched in problem and risk but grounded in 'plentifulness, plenitude and potential' (Edwards 2015: 237). As can be seen with MacDonell's slide choices, the places where the slide production has potentially 'gone wrong' – the too-wide framing, the reflected light, the edges of the page, the intruding folds – are the places that show peopled histories of labour and material practices of production.

Thus, 'where there is presence and affect, there remains abundance, excess and the possibility of recoding' (247), according to Edwards. Although she is speaking of alternative readings of historic photographs taken as part of anthropological endeavour, as artists rework art historical materials these excesses and abundances are the productive points of departure. For nineteenth-century anthropologists seeking scientific records, photography's excess was controlled through regulated framing and plain backdrops. Although the production of art historical information was not quite in pursuit of scientific objectivity, there were still exacting instructions provided by librarians about correct procedures for presenting image records that show fixed categories of right and wrong. The slides were meant to convey controlled and detailed information. If one was reading the hand of the librarian or the affordances of the medium (its crackling, discolouration or the materiality of its mounting) then one was missing its proper meaning. In the artists' practices I have foregrounded, missing the proper meaning is the pursuit. Slides' excess, in more ways than one, is what is wanted.

A Personal Mirror

The thoughts in this chapter have been prompted by a longstanding interest in mass photography and photography *en masse*, developed through a range of case studies (Pollen 2015, 2016, 2018, 2020). They are also specifically prompted by my own relationship to an institutional slide library and its deaccession, although this polite term implies a formality of disposal that did not exist in practice. Here, dialectics of the miniscule and the unmanageably large, the wanted and the unwanted, and of institutions and individuals played out in scaled relations. The Slide Library at the University of Brighton, comprising some 600,000 slides at its peak in 2009, was one of the very largest institutional collections. Numbers mattered. In one typical day in 1977, for example, to give a snapshot of usage, 411 Brighton slides were loaned to staff. In an audit conducted in 2011, when the slide library closed, only 255 slides had been loaned in the whole previous year; these were the quantities on which jobs and collections depended. In discussions about the slide library's closure, scale was often at the forefront of debates, which necessarily carried other values.

In a 2013 interview with former Brighton slide librarians Monica Brewis and Belinda Greenhalgh they noted the qualities of the slides as tiny, beautiful and brightly coloured; this was contrasted to the immersive scale of their theatrical projection, vast and luminous in a darkened space. An abundance of images in contemporary culture was negatively likened to white noise; contemporary looking was characterised as a distracted 'flitting' between multiples. This was contrasted with the rewarding hardships of looking deeply at one image for an hour, a day, a week; looking as a painter would look; looking so hard that it hurt (Goody 2013). These manoeuvres, from the tiny precious singular object to the howling mass, from the slow to the speedy, evoke values from depth to distraction and from care to carelessness; they reveal the affordances embodied in the slide.

In considering how to dispose of the Brighton slide library, it was initially argued that the slides could not be repurposed; their licensing related only to academic instruction in one specific institutional context. To be disposed of safely, as objects composed of glass, all 600,000 would have to be ground to powder. This violent image of destruction evoked an ashes-to-ashes, dust-to-dust demise as glass would be returned to sand. This prompted a series of passionate local efforts to 'rescue' the slides from this fate. As with other collections, including a rare few which have been preserved *in toto*, claims were made that they represented a history of the discipline and of the institution; they record changing histories of labour, material and technology; many of their images were unique productions (Davis 2012; Goody 2013). These points were forcefully made to no avail; the Brighton collection was disposed of in 2011. It was too big a problem; it took up too much room in a building under pressure to create further study space; individually the items were tiny transparent slivers; together they were a bulky burden that must be broken up. Under the guidance of slide librarians, art historians invested in the collection furtively filled crates when library managers were not looking. I took the entirety of the photography collection: tens of thousands of photographs of photographs of photographs, through which I learned my trade as a student and through which I taught my subject, in turn, as a tutor in the same lecture halls. What remained was taken as a whole, by artist Mary Goody, in a hundred banana boxes, with the intention of creative repurposing.

The slides of the Brighton photography collection, now sticky in their decomposing plastic sleeves, take up two filing cabinets in my office and

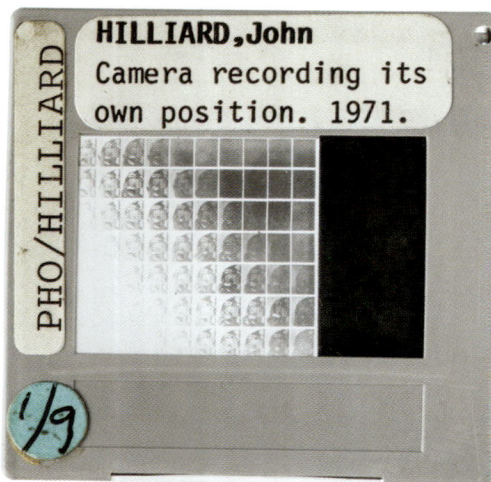

Figure 7.9 John Hilliard, 'Camera recording its own Position' [sic], 35 mm slide, 1971, as labelled in the former University of Brighton slide library. Photograph by Richard Boll, 2019.

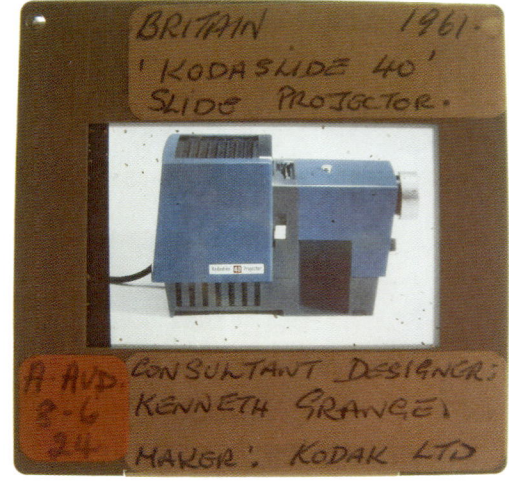

Figure 7.10 'Kodaslide 40' slide projector, 35 mm slide, 1961, as labelled in the former University of Brighton slide library. Photograph by Annebella Pollen, 2011.

are a potent metaphor for histories of photography. These slides were always to some extent metapictorial, as photographic means for telling photographic stories, but their status has become intensified as they stand outside immediate utility and take on a symbolic form. As Geoffrey Batchen has observed of snapshots, 'the advent of digital technologies means that this kind of photography has now taken on an extra memorial role, not of the subjects it depicts, but of its own operation as a system of representation' (2008: 130). In their form and quantity they embody fear and desire about loss and rescue, about the unwieldiness of analogue technologies and the unfathomable scale of what replaces it; they show dramatic shifts in medium and message and the scale and the speed at which these changes take place. As Henning has argued, 'specific techniques developed to make images available, searchable, viewable, such as the slideshow . . . can also be understood as ways of attempting to control or programme what might otherwise be experienced as an unmanageable and inassimilable onslaught or flood of images' (2018: 138). As their metapictorial qualities are enhanced, the slides provide multiple mises en abyme.

We might look, for example, to those conceptual artists of the 1960s and 1970s who embraced visual representation as their subject. John Hilliard's 'Camera Recording its own Condition' (7 Apertures, 10 Speeds, 2 Mirrors) appears several times as a slide in the Brighton collection, in various states of age, repair and format, and with labelling systems varying according to age, including some carrying incorrect information (Figure 7.9). As Hilliard's piece was constructed as a sequence where a camera considered itself, seventy times over, in seventy different settings, it already comprised scales and mirrors in both its subject and form; it is already fading out of view. For another example, we might consider an earlier slide, from when the slides belonged to what was then Brighton School of Art. This example (Figure 7.10) shows historic audiovisual technologies; a 1961 Kodak slide projector is recorded with slide film to illustrate changing times for a changing audience. Perhaps most poignant of all, however, is the slide labelled 'Wm. Henry Fox Talbot, Study of Leaves. 1839' (Figure 7.11). Under its full title of '*Two Hawthorn Leaves and a Fig Leaf*, photogenic drawing negative, 1939', it is now part of a freely downloadable online digital resource provided by the J. Paul Getty Museum; it is high quality, easily accessible and fully contextualised, everything that the slide is not (Getty Art Collection 2019).

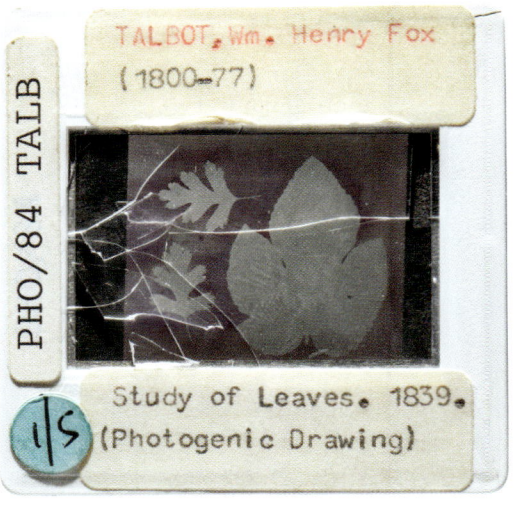

Figure 7.11 William Henry Fox Talbot, 'Study of Leaves', 35 mm slide, 1839, as labelled in the former University of Brighton slide library. Photograph by Richard Boll, 2019.

As photographic historian Larry Shaaf observes in the narrative provided by Getty, issues of scale were involved in the production of the photograph from the outset:

> One of Talbot's largest difficulties throughout 1839 remained the production and distribution of enough examples so that people could more readily understand what he had invented. The exceptionally poor weather that year limited the number of pictures that could be produced, and those that were accomplished passed through many hands and were repeatedly exposed to daylight. In spite of all his efforts in that first public year of photography, surviving examples made those first twelve months are relatively scarce. (Schaaf 2002: 24)

The example in the Brighton collection is a 'pinkie'. Its sepia tint has faded to the characteristic puce that marks failing slides, whose functional life only averages 5–8 years. The glass that surrounds it is smashed. Its information is too vague and its framing too cropped; it is simultaneously too little and too much to handle. From scarcity to excess, the image and its form speak of larger antagonisms and dialectics. 'Photographs are but one link in a potentially endless chain of reduplication', Owens has noted; 'themselves duplicates (of both their objects and, in a sense, their negatives), they are also subject to further duplication' (1978: 85). They ever were copies of copies of copies, and yet each transposition is never quite the same; its material matters.

Conclusion: 600,000 Problems and their Potential

Slides are fungible, fragile, and friable. They fade, break and get stuck in the fallible machinery. They come with requirements of etiquette and effort: they mustn't be shown for too long; they must be created, stored and loaned in structured systems: they require specialist equipment and particular personalities to produce and maintain them (Goody 2013). They take up space and they get in the way; they are hard work and their rewards are hard earned. They embody enormous quantities of investment; their tiny mounts will not contain the level of detail they are required to carry. The photographic abyss and its associations of depth, infinity, vertigo and falling play out in various ways in slide collections and their artistic reinterpretations. It is materialised in their vast scale, where they communicate their own unwieldiness, the scale of the problem of how to dispose of them, and the scale of the new media that replaces them. It is seen in photography's endless reproducibility and endless copies as an inherently mirrored multiple media form. It is also seen in the individual images' excesses as tiny fragments of abundant potential always implicated in interrelations of scale, of order and disorder. As such, as metapictorial pictures about pictures, the micro view of the individual slides and the macro view of artworks made with them speak of parts and wholes, of failure and promise, of the desires and the anxieties about photographic multiples and masses.

References

Alexander, Darsie (2005), *Slide Show: Projected Images in Contemporary Art*. London: Tate Modern.

Barron, James (2017), 'Donated Slides from the Met get a Second Life, and Showing', *New York Times*, 16 April 2017. Available at: <https://www.nytimes.com-2017-04-16-nyregion-slides-metropolitan-museum-of-art-materials-for-the-arts.html> (last accessed 12 August 2019).

Bouchard, Karen A. (2015), '"Now, Slides, Sail Thou Forth to Seek and Find": Facilitating a Slide and Photograph Diaspora', *VRA Bulletin*, 41(2). Available at: <https://online.vraweb.org-index.php-vrab-article-view-90> (last accessed 12 August 2019).

Burbridge, Ben, and Annebella Pollen (eds) (2018), *Photography Reframed: New Visions in Contemporary Photographic Culture*. London: Bloomsbury Academic.

Caraffa, Constanza (2011), 'From "Photo Libraries" to "Photo Archives": On the Epistemological Potential of Art-Historical Photo Collections', in Constanza Caraffa (ed.), *Photo Archives and the Photographic Memory of Art History*. Deutscher Kunstverlag.

Dällenbach, Lucien (1989), *The Mirror in the Text*. Oxford: Polity Press, 1989.

Davis, John (2015), *Adopt a Slide*. Available at: <https://pickaslide.wordpress.com-page-13> (last accessed 12 August 2019).

Dobson, Susan (2019), *Slide Library*. Available at: <https://susandobson.com-portfolio-portfolio-slide-library> (last accessed 12 August 2019).

Edwards, Elizabeth (2015), 'Anthropology and Photography: A Long History of Knowledge and Affect', *Photographies*, 8(3): 235–52.

Fisher, Andrew (2012), 'Photographic Scale'. *Philosophy of Photography*, 3(2): 310–29.

Fontcuberta, Joan (2015), *The Post-photographic Condition*. Montréal: Le Mois de la Photo à Montréal.

Foster, Hal (2004), 'The Archival Impulse', *October*, 110: 3–22.

Getty Art Collection (2019), 'William Henry Fox Talbot, Two Hawthorn Leaves and a Fig Leaf'. Available at: <http://www.getty.edu-art-collection-objects-33818-william-henry-fox-talbot-two-hawthorn-leaves-and-a-fig-leaf-british-1839> (last accessed 12 August 2019).

Gide, André (1984), *Journals 1889–1949*. London, Penguin.

Godfrey, Jenny (2014a), 'Dodo, Lame Duck or Phoenix? How Should we Consider the Slide Library?' *Art Libraries Journal*, 29(3): 28–33.

Godfrey, Jenny (2014b), 'Dodo, Lame Duck or Phoenix, part 2? Can or Should we Preserve a Slide Library for Research?' *Art Libraries Journal*, 29(3): 12–20.

Goldbach, Philipp (2019), Available at: <http://www.pgoldbach.de-works.html> (last accessed 12 August 2019).

Goody, Mary (2013), Interview with Monica Brewis, retired slide librarian, University of Brighton, and Belinda Greenhalgh, former Slide Library assistant, University of Brighton.

Hariman, Robert, and John Louis Lucaites (2016), 'Photography: The Abundant Art', *Photography and Culture*, 9(1): 39–58.

Henning, Michelle (2018), 'Image Flow: Photography on Tap', *Photographies*, 11(2–3): 133–48.

Kessels, Erik (2012), *Album Beauty: The Glory Days of the Photo Album*. Paris: RVB Books.

Knelman, Sara, and Annie MacDonell (2018), 'On Images of Images of Images', in Ben Burbridge and Annebella Pollen (eds), *Photography Reframed: New Visions in Contemporary Photographic Culture*. London: Bloomsbury Academic, n.p.

MacDonell, Annie (2012), 'Split Screen', *EitherAnd*. Available at: <http://either-and.org-eitherand-split-screen> (last accessed 12 August 2019).

McKeown, Roy, and Mary Edmunds Otter (1989), *National Survey of Slide Collections*, British Library Research Paper 67, The British Library Board.

Mitchell, W. J. T. (1994), *Picture Theory: Essays on Verbal and Visual Representation*. Chicago and London: University of Chicago Press.

Nordström, Alison (2018), 'The Things We Keep'. Available at: <https://susandobsonsite.files.wordpress.com-2018-10-essay-by-alison-nordstrom.pdf> (last accessed 12 August 2019).

Owens, Craig (1978), 'Photography "en abyme"', *October*, 5: 73–88.

Parsons, Sarah (2005), 'What Lies Beyond the Slide Library? Facing the Digital Future of Art History', RACAR: Revue d'Art Canadienne-Canadian Art Review, 30(1–2): 114–25.

Pollen, Annebella (2015), *Mass Photography: Collective Histories of Everyday Life*. London: Bloomsbury Academic.

Pollen, Annebella (2016), 'The Rising Tide of Photographs: Not Drowning but Waving?' *Captures: Figures, Théories et Pratiques de l'Imaginaire*, 1(1). Available at: <http://revuecaptures.org-node-249> (last accessed 12 August 2019).

Pollen, Annebella (2018), 'When is a Cliché not a Cliché: Reconsidering Mass Produced Sunsets', in Ben Burbridge and Annebella Pollen (eds), *Photography Reframed: New Visions in Contemporary Photographic Culture*. London: Bloomsbury Academic, pp. 74–84.

Pollen, Annebella (2020), 'Objects of Denigration and Desire: Taking the Amateur Photographer Seriously', in Gil Pasternak (ed.), *The Handbook of Photography Studies*. London: Bloomsbury Academic, pp. 292–309.

Poole, Deborah (2005), 'An Excess of Description: Ethnography, Race, and Visual Technologies', *Annual Review of Anthropology*, 34: 159–79.

Schaaf, Larry (2002), '*William Henry Fox Talbot*', In Focus: *Photographs from the J. Paul Getty Museum*. Los Angeles: Getty Publications.

Schoen, Molly (2017), 'Visual Resources: From Analogue to Digital and Beyond', in Paul Glassman and Julie Dyki (eds), *The Handbook of Art and Design Librarianship*, pp. 53–62.

Shore, Robert (2014), *Post-Photography: The Artist with a Camera*. New York: Laurence King Publishing.

Siegel, Steffen (2014), 'Recollections of the Sound of Pictures', in *Philipp Goldbach: Read Only Memory*. Wiesbaden, pp. 80–3.

Stojković, Jelena, Ulla Fischer-Westhauser and Uwe Schögl (2015), 'Editorial: Special Issue: Image after Image: Reconsidering the Fabric of Slide Shows', *PhotoResearcher*, 24: 1–9.

Vilanova, Oriol (2019). Available at: <http://www.oriol-vilanova.com> (last accessed 12 August 2019).

Visual Resources Association Slide and Transitional Media Task Force (2014), 'Tell Us Where Your Slides Are' Summary of Survey Results. Available at: <http://vraweb.org-wp-content-uploads-2016-01-VRA-STMTF-Slide-Survey-Results-Summary-2014.pdf> (last accessed 12 August 2019).

8 The Failed Photographs of Photography: On the Analogue and Slow Photography Movement

Michal Šimůnek

THE CURRENT EXCESS of photography is linked to the networked digital image, recognised as a critical determinant of the changes sweeping contemporary photography. In this respect, most accounts on the multiplicity and ubiquity of photography have addressed widespread practices of camera-phone photography and the networked digital image itself.[1] It is in this context that when considering the contemporary mass image, we must also address the 'mass-amateurization of photography' (Berge 2011: 177; Rubinstein and Sluis 2008: 11) – that is, the shift to a valorisation of amateur photography stimulated by online photo-sharing platforms and easy-to-handle photography tools – that has enabled so many not only to make photographs but also to make these photographs public. This chapter focuses on contemporary amateur photography, though instead of concentrating on dominant 'digital' practices it will centre on Lomography, which is often claimed to be a subversive 'analogue' variation directed against the masses of trivialised images flooding mainstream digital photographic culture.

Taking as a case study contemporary communities of analogue and slow photography enthusiasts, and in particular so-called Lomographers, this chapter examines mainstream photography through the perspective of practices and discourses which aim to slow down the pace of networked visual culture and 'leave the digital grind behind' (Lomography 2010). Questions raised have their origins in my experiences from my early research into the Lomography community. As I was becoming familiar with the online Lomography hub, I reached a moment at which I needed to decide how to cope with the 14,153,656 photographs shared by

Lomographers on their photo-sharing site.² In order to eliminate the epistemological limits of compressing multiple images in one 'statistical' image (see, for example, Hochman and Manovich 2013), and instead hoping to understand at least some of the photographs as unique images with their own histories and meanings, I engaged in auto-netnographic (Kozinets 2015; Villegas 2018) participant observation in the life of the Lomography community.³

The chapter proceeds in two moves. The first step presents and discusses core theories and concepts that have been employed for the interpretation of counter-practices in conceptual art and experimental photography, while the subsequent sections describe, interpret and conceptualise Lomography's discourses and practices in order to demonstrate that the frequent Lomography tactic against the digital image is based on producing photographs of photography, that is 'metaphotographs'. Nevertheless, as it is further argued, the subversive potential of this tactic fails to be realised; entangled in the branding strategies of the Lomographic Society International (LSI) and dwelling on the intersection between analogue and digital photography practices, the 'metapictoriality' (Mitchell 1994) of Lomography does not succeed in its quest to offer a consistent subversion of mainstream networked image culture.

Counter-practices of Photography

To engage critically and reflexively with the transformations of photography is commonly the domain of scholars and artists, who question and problematise the routine ways we use photography for our everyday purposes, often proposing new categories that address emerging socio-cultural and technological constellations. Hence, counter-practices in experimental photography should be part of a discussion of photography in digital culture, even if going against the grain of discourses of quantity and scale and the mass image. In my work, I draw mainly on the writings of Marc Lenot (2017a, 2017b) and Ernst van Alphen (2018), both of whom recently contributed significantly to the debate on photography and its counter-practices.

Lenot (2017b, see also 2017a) offers a comprehensive account of experimental photography practices in his book *Jouer contre les appareils*, which is part encyclopaedia of artists experimenting with the medium since the 1950s, part typology of experimental practices themselves, and part theoretical consideration attempting to define and evaluate experimental photography's position with regard to mainstream photography practices. Although Lenot does not attempt to define mainstream photography practices, he identifies the mainstream with realistic conception and uses of photography as the record of the real: 'Photography is for most of us, primarily an image, a representation. To describe a photograph, we can talk perhaps about its colours, composition, style or veracity, but we always describe its subject, that what is shown and represented' (Lenot 2017b: 15).

Lenot describes experimental photography as a heterogeneous set of photographic practices which question and oppose claims that photography is about realistic depiction and indexical preservation of the real: 'Experimental photography does not pretend to be an accurate representation of reality, but rather an exploration of photography's nature and the photographic process itself' (Lenot 2017b: 204–5). In this sense experimental photography is critical towards mainstream photography: it is 'a deliberate act of critical rejection of the rules of the apparatus of photographic production, whereby the photographer calls into question one or more established parameters of the photographic process' (Lenot 2017a: 16). In so doing, experimental photography 'reveals the medium to itself . . . and destabilises the usual spectator's relationship to photography' (Lenot 2017b: 9). It forces us to ask, 'is this still photography' (Lenot 2017b: 10)?

In order to question conventions and parameters of dominant photographic practices and the representative power of photography, experimental photographers employ diverse techniques. Lenot's typology distinguishes several types of these techniques that he categorises according to which aspect of photography-as-realistic-depiction is being questioned. Experimental photographers intervene in the relationship of photography to light in the sense that they push photography to the verge of the visible,[4] and they problematise photography's temporality using extremely long expositions lasting for months or even years; through this slow photography approach, they question the instantaneousness of the snapshot.[5] Other experimentations focus on photography's materiality, mainly in the form of interventions into the developing and printing processes, using expired photo-materials, under-developed or over-developed negatives, double or multiple expositions, unfixed, and thus, when exposed to the light, slowly degrading and disappearing photographs.[6] In addition, photography can be countered through a diverse range of hacks, re- and de-constructions of cameras – including camera-less photography – which are usually considered as one of the most contra-mainstream photography techniques (see Batchen 2016). These techniques are often mixed on the surface of a single photograph, and deliberately supplemented with a variety of errors and initiated acts of chance in order to stress aesthetics of imperfection as opposition to conventionalised expectations of what a good photograph should look like.

Similarly to Lenot, van Alphen (2018) understands counter-photography practices as those that 'challenge our everyday experience of the perceptual' (van Alphen 2018: 10) and 'deviate from the practice of the snapshot' (29). Van Alphen calls these kinds of images 'failed images' as they 'fail to comply with the dominant notion of photography' (van Alphen 2018: 56). Tracing historical and contemporary works of artist–photographers, he considers deliberately staged, blurred, under- or over-exposed photographs and archival images-as-inventories as deviating from the dominant photographic approach (on questions of poor images and social media, see Stejskalova's chapter in this volume). To take one example, in a section on staged photography, van Alphen interprets photographs by Cindy Sherman, arguing that 'one of the problems of staged photography is . . . the fact that the photographic image is supposed to continue outside the frame. A staged photograph only exists within it' (van Alphen 2018: 57). According to van Alphen, photographs of Cindy Sherman are, in this sense, illustrative, as she 'does not only stage her image, but also draws attention to the act of staging itself' (62). Although these forms of imperfection are also common in popular photography (see Chéroux 2003), they are most often the result of unintended mistakes, errors and acts of chance that occur during the picture-taking or photography process.

Both Lenot and van Alphen draw on Vilém Flusser (2000) in their theorisation of experimental photography, underlining how experimental photographers play against the programme of the apparatus, and in so doing may free us from the totality of the apparatus itself (see Flusser 2000: 81).[7] Reading Lenot and Flusser's accounts, one is able to elaborate on the statement that experimental photographs make visible 'the inside of the black box and the processes that occur within it' (Lenot 2017a: 4). The prominent approach of experimental photographers could also be considered by applying W. J. T. Mitchell's concept of 'metapictures' (on questions of artistic metapictorial strategies, see Pollen's chapter in this volume). Metapictures, as defined by Mitchell, are pictures that 'might be capable of reflection on themselves, capable of providing a second-order discourse that tells us – or at least shows us – something about pictures' (Mitchell 1994: 38). They are also understood as 'pictures that refer to themselves or to other pictures, pictures that are used to show what a picture is' (35). In this self-reflection lies the capacity of an image to reveal and question the processes and conventions of its production, 'its institutional setting, its historical positionally, its address to beholders' (Mitchell 1994: 36). Metapictures disrupt and expose to light those oppressive powers usually hidden behind the automated conventions and apparatuses that determine our media uses and practices. One of the most promising ways to answer Flusser's call for play against the programme of the apparatus thus remains in the production of metapictures; these images that record their own conditions of existence.

Nevertheless, this tactic is not always successful, as 'the apparatuses themselves automatically assimilate . . . attempts at liberation and enrich their programs with them' (Flusser 2000: 75). Forces of resistance can be incorporated into the programme of the apparatuses, thereby becoming deprived of their subversive potential. Practices of Lomography, as demonstrated below, are an example of this dynamic between subversive contra-mainstream practices and the power of dominant apparatuses to incorporate these practices into their programmes.

Situating Lomography as Analogue and Slow Photography Movement

In a contemporary digital and online photo-culture in which most photographs are taken with smartphones, making analogue photographs has undoubtedly become a peripheral photographic practice. However, this does not seem to apply to Lomography, as it has evolved from the 1990s artistic endeavour of select Vienna-based artists into a commercially successful and prosperous brand involving a vast global community of enthusiasts.

What follows is a conceptually developed report of my auto-netnographic (Kozinetz 2015; Villegas 2018) encounters with Lomographers, part of my investigative journey based on doing, living and researching Lomography. To my surprise, becoming a double-agent Lomographer-researcher (Šimůnek 2018a) and trying to understand the narratives and Lomography practices of other Lomographers, I discovered that the Lomography community is almost exclusively composed of 'metaphotographers'. Lomographers do not make and share their photographs in an attempt to represent the real, but instead, continuously produce and share a vast amount of Lomographs of Lomography, still-growing mounds of metapictures shared online. Hence, besides reporting, I want to understand these practices in relation to Flusser's conception of play against the programme of apparatus and Mitchell's notion of metapictures as a useful reference point.

The Lomography movement began with the foundation of the Lomographic Society International (LSI) in the early 1990s in Vienna. Nowadays, there are approximately 350 Lomography Embassies (Lomography Gallery Stores) around the world, and members of the LSI have, to date, uploaded almost 15 million photos on Lomography photo-sharing site.[8] The Lomography brand has survived the digital revolution: it has been able to stimulate the analogue photography market with the incessant introduction of new photography equipment and materials, maintaining a large community of enthusiasts through elaborate brand communication strategies.

However, the commercial and community success of Lomography is also supported by the broader situation in the photography industry – visual culture transformed by the networked digital image. In this regard, both Lenot (2017a, 2017b) and van Alphen (2018) argue that the boom of analogue experimental photography in the last thirty years can be explained as a consequence of the arrival of digital photography. Lenot compares the contemporary relationship between analogue and digital photography to the relationship between photography and painting in the nineteenth century, demonstrating that 'the development of digital photography in the late twentieth century freed analogue photography from its role of representing the real, allowing it to refocus on the photographic material, and thus on its essence' (Lenot 2017a: 11).

Van Alphen, drawing on Krauss's (1999) and Baker's (2005) idea of the 'expanded field', and what could be considered as photography, writes that the field of photography that first began to expand in the 1960s within postmodern art practices has undergone a further expansion since the 1990s, brought about by technological transformations of the digital revolution. However, at the same time, the expansion of photography also started to move in the opposite direction, expanding photography's 'inner field'; a revival of those photographic practices that were performed since the inception of the medium but were later marginalised by the dominant photographic approach (van Alphen 2018: 33). In a similar vein, for example, Margaret Iversen argues that 'it is only now, with the rise of digitalisation and the near-obsolescence of traditional technology, that we are becoming fully aware of the distinctive character of analogue photography' (Iversen 2012: 797). And in the words of Jussi Parikka (2012: 3), 'retro cultures seem to be as natural a part of the digital-culture landscape as high-definition screen technology and superfast broadband'.

An essential aspect of the analogue revival is found in the rhetoric of slowness. In the case of Lomography, analogue cameras and materials are celebrated as means that 'slow your photography way down, giving you time to think, compose, and shoot with patience' (Neanderthalis 2012). These references to slowness and slow photography should be recognised as a part of a broader trend of slow lifestyles and slow media practices celebrating manual, crafted and contemplative approaches to media production and consumption, all promising to fill one's life with authentic experiences (Koepnick 2014). It is especially against the presumed fast pace of the digital that the analogue is claimed to be 'slow'.

It is thus widely acknowledged that the arrival of the digital has conditioned the analogue revival, which in turn is driven by nostalgia about what is being lost in the digital revolution, and by laments over the malaises of the digital visual culture (acceleration of changes, increased automation, multiplicity and triviality of decontextualised photographs – Frosh 2001, 2002, 2003; Rubinstein and Sluis 2008; Rubenstein, Golding and Fisher 2013). In this sense, Lomography is, at least rhetorically, placed in opposition to the digital. The LSI, recalling this analogue/digital opposition, recently launched a microsite with ten digital prophecies declaring, in an expressive style, that 'The Digital Present is Over' and 'The Future is Analogue' (Lomography 2010). Similar statements about the 'Analogue Revolution' are further dispersed across most of the Lomography platforms and publications, where digital photography is labelled as inauthentic, glossy, perfect, superficial and trivial, while analogue photography is celebrated as authentically imperfect, meaningful and deeply contextualised in the given experience.

This Lomographic call for the analogue revolution is not at all meant radically – or even seriously. It is instead part of a broader, oppositional, 'against-any-rules' rhetoric of the Lomography brand lifestyle, which is expressed in condensed form by the 'Lomography prophecies' (Lomography 2018) and more broadly by 'The 10 Golden Rules of Lomography' (Lomography 2018). These rules are far from being practical advice on how to make Lomographs: instead, they reproduce abstract lifestyle values associated with Lomography, such as spontaneity, freedom, authenticity, entertainment, rebellion against any conventions – all values symbolised by the tenth golden rule: 'Don't worry about any rules' (Lomography 2010). However, it is critical to note that the analogue revolution could only be realised via digital means, which becomes apparent from LSI's 'Analogue vs Digital Survey' (Lomography 2012a) that confirmed a deep engagement of Lomographers with digital media. In this sense, the tenth Lomography prophecy is telling: '[L]iving analogue is sexy, contagious, tantalising . . . Yet, a little helping of digital technology is not a crime. Live offline but share online' (Lomography 2010). Lomography's success could not be possible without Lomography photo-sharing sites and, for example, the Lomography SmartPhone Scanner (Lomography 2019a) that enables Lomographers to transform their analogue images as fast as possible into an online shareable digital image. The Lomography's analogue revolution is significantly supported by digital technologies, and as such, it loses its potential to oppose the malaises of the digital visual culture.

However, as Kim Knowles (2016) argues, the recent association of analogue technology with slowness should be understood in relation to the materiality of analogue media and in opposition to material infinitude and speediness of digital media. In this sense, contemporary analogue media practices have a counter-cultural potential as they 'outwardly reject the forward drive of capitalist progress and its obsession with the relentlessly new' (Knowles 2016: 147). Artists working with analogue media have to 'enter into a temporal contract with its physical materials that is at odds with modern society's benchmark of speed, efficiency, and instantaneity' (147). The materiality of analogue photography is also essential in Lomography practices, at least until the moment when the analogue is transformed into the digital, as it is critical for metapictorial Lomography practices, which seem to have a counter-digital-photography potential.

Lomography's Metapictoriality

Academic literature on the Lomography movement is limited (Albers and Nowak 1999) but, in considering the practices of Lomography enthusiasts, one can find a telling description in Italo Calvino's (1984) short story 'The Adventure of a Photographer'. Antonino Paraggi, the protagonist of this story, is in search of true photography once he realises 'that photographing photographs was the only course that he had left – or, rather, the true course he had obscurely been seeking all this time' (Calvino 1984: 235). Paraggi recognises that the total photograph is a photograph of photography and that therefore 'antiphotographic polemic could be fought only from within the black box, setting one kind of photography against another' (Calvino 1984: 226). In this sense, Calvino's character is not just a fictional generalisation of an experimental photographer, but also of a Lomographer, who aims to oppose mainstream digital photography practices and whose prominent – and only – tactic of resistance against the digital is based on making photographs of photography. Still, Lomographic metapractices are not so much a result of critical reflection on photography and a deliberate decision to break with conventions and powers of the contemporary dominant photographic approach but rather should be understood as a consequence of the complex self-referential branding system of the LSI.

When considering Lomography's metapictoriality, it is essential to bear in mind that Lomography could not be understood only by looking at Lomographs themselves. Lomography is, as is the case of any other photographic practice (and after all, Lomographs are photographs), a network woven of diverse nodes: photographs, their users and uses, cameras, apparatuses, photographic materials and other material objects, rules and conventions, communications and interactions between community members, and marketing and branding appeals. My primary focus is thus to consider what is outside of the frame of images themselves. Since an inventory of all nodes from which a Lomography network is composed could be almost endless, I am focusing on those nodes that are important in considering Lomography's metapictorial practices.

LomoWalls: All Lomographs Are Equal in their Triviality

The branding and marketing strategies of the LSI are frequently praised by scholars from the fields of consumer culture studies (Schiavone 2013: 51–70) and marketing management (Hsu 2011). The LSI is considered an exemplar of building a brand identity through intensive engagement of brand consumers and users (Muñiz and Schau 2011); an essential part of the Lomography network is made up of Lomography exhibitions and an overall strategy of showing exhibited Lomographs almost exclusively in the form of so-called 'LomoWalls'. The aesthetics of LomoWalls also determines the graphic design of Lomography books (Lomography 2012b, 2012c) and other promotional materials. Similarly, LomoWalls are an inevitable part of each Lomography store. From the promotional perspective, the most visible and spectacular examples are the Lomo-Walls created as a part of festivals and trade fairs: for instance, at the first Lomographic World Congress in Madrid, in 1997, the LomoWall was composed of 35,000 Lomographs. At the Photokina trade fair in 2008, there was a LomoWall made of 100,000 Lomographs, and in Manchester in 2012, an open-air LomoWall consisted of 14,000 images.

LomoWalls are series, or more precisely, they are mosaics made of photographs. There are always several images made from a single frame of a negative, pictures are usually sorted by colour, hue and saturation, and are placed side by side into the mosaic layout. Individual images communicate with each other, but differently to conventional photo-stories and photo-sequences, in which 'the signifier of connotation is no longer to be found at the level of any one of the fragments of the sequence but at that . . . of the concatenation' (Barthes 1977: 24). In the case of LomoWalls, the connotation procedures are not based on concatenation, but on swarming. The meaning of individual images is reduced to colour and hue; the individual image has no meaning; what it depicts and represents is not important; it is irrelevant. LomoWalls communicate in their entirety, as a single image, not as a series of individual images.

The LSI explains this display strategy as an act of democratisation, solidarity and egalitarianism of all Lomographers and all Lomographs. Of course, it is always possible to look at individual images, but this is meaningless, as they are deliberately deprived of their connection with their referent. They become tiles in a mosaic; similar to pixels that make up the digital image. Furthermore, since it makes no sense to look at individual pixels in an image, it makes no sense to look at individual Lomographs in a LomoWall as all of them are de- and recontextualised in order to deliver a single message: this is a LomoWall composed of Lomographs. Lomographs are thus only able to whisper shyly: 'Hey, I am Lomography too'.

The LomoWall aesthetic is reproduced by the layout of the Lomography PhotoSharing site and the LomoHomes of Lomographers, where users can sort images into albums, and label them with captions and tags. Interestingly, Lomographers rarely anchor the meaning of their images with captions, limiting their textual description mostly to tagging. It is also noteworthy that all tags almost exclusively describe the technical qualities of Lomographs: type of a camera, film, lenses. Descriptions of depicted objects or of where the image was taken are seldom found. If there are captions, they almost always describe the process through which the images were created, or they deliver commentaries on errors and imperfections of the given image. In this sense, images shared on Lomography photo-sharing site are ripped from their referent, similar to images in LomoWalls; their meaning is anchored by tags and rarely used captions, but in both cases the message is again tautological, that is, Lomographs are Lomographs. Rubinstein and Sluis (2008) argue that metadata provides 'a new paradigm to "interface reality" providing a means for the image to escape its original context. Stripped of their interfaces, photo-sharing sites function as vast databases of indexed photographs which can be remixed and remapped online as mashups' (2008: 20). It is not surprising that this process of decontextualisation also applies to Lomography photo-sharing site. The LSI, with its LomoWalls, anticipated this decontextualisation long before photo-sharing site as its metadata structure became a dominant way of showing, archiving, searching and looking at images.

LomoWalls may have anticipated the contemporary intensification of photography's multiplicity, but they also play significantly on photography's scalability. As argued by Olivier Lugon, photography is 'an image without any specific scale' (2015: 388), but the actual size of a photograph has significant consequences affecting its cultural and social status. Lugon argues that large, even gigantic, enlargements are historically associated with photography-as-art, while miniaturisation of photography is associated mostly with the documentary function of photography-as-record, as in snapshot photography and family albums. In this respect, LomoWalls could be understood as a specific union of these two associations as they are large, art-like images composed of thousands of small photographs. LomoWalls thus bring together both elitist and populist responses; they are both private (single images) and public (mosaic); they have the status of both the industrial mass image and the artistic singular large print valued for its rarity and exclusivity. However, most importantly, they are an apotheosis of multiplication, industrial logic of quantity, mass production and mass consumption. LomoWalls, just like 1930s photomurals, are 'pictures of the crowd' (Lugon 2015: 394), which never survive their original display and, in this sense, symbolise the contemporary throwaway nature of the networked digital image, emphasising accelerated obsolescence, permanent renewal, multiplicity, ubiquity and triviality of a single photograph.

Aesthetic of Imperfection

Photography has always been prone to chance. Imperfections of the image – mainly in the form of material accidents of the photographic process – have always been an intrinsic feature of photography. However, it does not seem to be the case in contemporary popular photography dominated by digital images, camera-phone apparatuses and easy-to-use editing software. As mentioned by many commentators (Chesher 2012; Cruz and Meyer 2012), the easiness of creating impressive images is the result of the increased technological control by camera operators over picture-taking and editing processes. From this techno-industrial perspective, chance seems to be superseded by control, and accidental imperfections seem to disappear under a glut of flawless digital images. In this respect, imperfections serve Lomography in enabling it to distinguish itself from the perfect digital image – and this is a significant part of the rhetoric of Lomography's analogue revolution.

The LSI manufactures and sells only plastic toy cameras which guarantee the quality of imperfection to every image: vibrant colours, deep saturation, vignettes framing the shot, light leaks, over- or under expositions, mechanical damages of film, multiple exposures. A diverse array of interventions into the particular phases of image production further intensifies these camera-based imperfections: actions deliberately damage negatives, positive prints, or influence the process of digitisation of Lomographs for their sharing. In this regard, Lomographers use a similar set of 'intervening' and 'damaging' strategies as experimental photographers. Lomographers only very rarely hack cameras: it is not necessary since the LSI sells plastic toy cameras, pre-damaged photographic materials (for example, Revolog and Redscale films – Lomography 2019b, 2019c), as well as a wide range of conversion lenses and other tools intended to disrupt the parameters of the dominant photographic approach.

Because all Lomographs are equal, Lomographers usually scan all frames on the negative and share all of the exposed (or even unexposed) images without making any selections. Among the most popular are first frames on the film which were partly exposed when the film was loaded into the camera. Lomographers enjoy using expired film; negatives are often developed in alternative homemade developers; other times they are heated or frozen, washed in a dishwasher, boiled in diverse solutions, drawn or scratched on. There is no attempt to remove dust prior to digitisation in scanners, and sometimes old, low-resolution or deliberately damaged scanners are used.

As I have mentioned earlier, imperfect images are common in family snapshot photography, but in such cases they are not deprived of their relation to the referent. As Gillian Rose argues, 'a photo that is a blur of flesh and shadow is kept by a mother because it was the first time her daughter wanted to use the camera, not because it actually shows anything much at all . . .' (Rose 2014: 71). On the contrary, Lomographers keep the image precisely because it is imperfect: all imperfections are considered to be authentic as they are the result of unexpected or deliberately initiated acts of chance. As such, they are celebrated and appreciated.

Imperfections play a crucial role in experimental photography because of their metapictorial quality in questioning the photography itself. However, in the case of Lomography, the metapictoriality of imperfections is tautological, as the meaning of most of the Lomographs is limited to the single message: this imperfect photograph is Lomography. In this sense, the imperfections of Lomographs – and all Lomographs are imperfect with regard to breaking the rules of the conventional notion of what constitutes a good photograph – do not imply an oppositional or even revolutionary stance against the digital, but rather an affirmation of the contemporary flood of banal images. As such, every single Lomograph shares its fate with the poor, low-resolution digital image that is

> [N]o longer about the real thing – the originary original. Instead, it is about its own real conditions of existence: about swarm circulation, digital dispersion, fractured and flexible temporalities. It is about defiance and appropriation just as it is about conformism and exploitation. (Steyerl 2009)

Recently I created an album composed of photographs that were almost entirely black or grey, showing only white spots of dust and light streaks due to the automatic exposure failure of my LOMO LC-A camera (Šimůnek 2018b). The commentary of one Lomographer illustrates the fact that Lomographers never play against apparatus, but instead play with it or even let apparatuses play with images and, in addition, with Lomographers: 'Only autonomous machines are the true artists!' (Šimůnek 2018c). Depicted objects, if they are at all recognisable, are overlaid with imperfections in Lomography, which leaves the Lomographs with only one meaning; that is, that they are Lomographs. A triviality, taken to its absurd extreme.

Conclusion: Failed Images that Fail in their Failing

Technical images have always been prone to growth and spreading: as such, they also awaken disturbing feelings of image overload and urgent calls for the ecology of images. As Susan Sontag famously remarked, 'if there can be a better way for the real world to include the one of images, it will require an ecology not of real things but of images as well' (Sontag 2005: 141). But her call for an ecology of images, even as it is obvious at the present moment, remains unheard and unanswered.

This chapter has argued that metapictorial questioning of photography, as experimental photographers practise it, might be a way to cope with the contemporary triviality of the mass image, a way to play against the networked digital image apparatus. However, instead of following artists experimenting and working with the medium, the potential of metapictoriality to question and oppose contemporary image overload was investigated through the example of the Lomography movement that calls for an analogue revolution against the digital.

Focusing on selected metapictorial practices of Lomography, specifically the LomoWall exhibition strategy and the metapictoriality of Lomography's imperfections, this chapter has argued that the potential of resistance in metapictorial tactic has failed to be realised. The Lomography community dwells in a brilliantly crafted and self-referential environment curated by LSI, including its politics of consumption and brand community practices. To be a Lomographer means to find oneself in a space where everything and everybody inevitably follows the course, culminating in taking masses of Lomographs of Lomography, where every particular Lomography can represent only the tautological fact that it is itself a Lomography. The Lomography prophecies (Lomography 2010) blame digital media for being ever present and automated, but Lomography itself turns analogue photography into an ever-present and automated practice, resulting in the production of a growing mass of tautological and trivial metapictures.

Van Alphen considers failed images as images that are deviant, which fail to meet generally accepted and socially determined expectations of what is a photograph and what are the 'good' ways and means of their production, editing, dissemination and use. Lomography has been rhetorically designed as a sort of failed image, but Lomography practices have never been intended to become oppositional and contra-mainstream. It is in this sense that Lomography is just another contemporary practice reproducing the dominant photographic approach, and as such suffering the malaises of digital visual culture. More than 15 million Lomographs shared on the Lomography photo-sharing site are thus failed images that fail in their failing – insofar as it was meant to be a subversive gesture.

However, despite this failure – or perhaps for this very reason – Lomography, being both analogue and digital, could help us understand the nebulous and ever-changing identity of the contemporary photograph, and maybe also comprehend the multiplicity and triviality of photography itself.

Notes

1. Please see, for example, Ritchin 2009; Golding and Fisher 2013; Cruz and Meyer 2012; Lister 2013; Larsen and Sandbye 2014; Cruz and Lehmuskallio 2016; Kuc and Zylinska 2016; Manovich 2017; Rubinstein et al. 2013.
2. Available at: <https://www.lomography.com/photos> (last accessed 4 January 2018).
3. Netnography, being a compound word comprised of 'ethnography', 'network' and 'Internet', could be defined as ethnography adapted to the study of online social networks and communities. Auto-netnography is a form of nethnographic research that highlights the role of reflexive self-observation of the researcher's experiences with his/her engagement in the life of an online community. My research was focused mainly on the community gathered around the Lomography official online hub (lomography.com) that has more than 1 million users. Large communities of Lomographers are also on Flickr, Instagram and Facebook. See, for example, Flickr group Lomo. Available at: <https://www.flickr.com/groups/lomo> (last accessed 4 January 2018).
4. It is, for example, the case of American artist Lisa Oppenheim, who superposes negatives and positives of a single photograph in order to nullify and destroy the image itself. Available at: <https://lisaopp.net/hl-2009> (last accessed 28 October 2019).
5. As illustrative examples of such slow photography practices Japanese photographer Hiroshi Sugimoto and German photographer Michael Wesely are usually mentioned. Sugimoto photographed interiors of movie theatres during the entire screening time of a movie, thus producing photographs of projection screens mysteriously glowing in the middle of the darkened interior of cinemas. Wesely photographed railway stations with exposure times lasting from the moment of departure of a train until its scheduled arrival at its destination, or streets and squares in Berlin and other cities with exposure times lasting months or even years (Koepnick 2014).
6. As an example of slowly disappearing photographs we could mention Heather Ackroyd and Dan Harvey's Chlorophyll Prints. See, for example, Benandi and Antonini 2015: 184–9 or Ackroyd and Harvey's webpage: Available at <https://www.ackroydandharvey.com/category/works> (last accessed 28 October 2019).

7. In this regard, particularly Lenot (2017a, 2017b) uses Flusser's philosophy when interpreting works of conceptual and experimental photographers. For the similar use of Flusser's theory see, e.g., Fuller 2007; Berti 2010; Sandbye 2018.
8. Available at: <https://www.lomography.com/photos> (last accessed 28 October 2018).

References

Albers, Philipp, and Michal Nowak (1999), 'Lomography: Snapshot Photography in the Age of Digital Simulation', *History of Photography*, 23(1): 101–4.

Baker, George (2005), 'Photography's Expanded Field', *October*, 114: 120–40.

Barthes, Roland [1961] (1977), 'The Photographic Message', in Roland Barthes, *Image Music Text*, London: Fontana Press, pp. 15–31.

Batchen, Geoffrey (2016), *Emanations: The Art of the Cameraless Photograph*. Munich: DelMonico Books.

Bendandi, Luca, and Marco Antonini (2015), *Experimental Photography. A Handbook of Techniques*. London: Thames & Hudson.

Berge, Lynn (2011), 'Snapshot, or: Visual Culture's Clichés', *Photographies*, 4(2): 175–90.

Berti, August (2010), 'Kurtis' "Vandalised" Photographs: On the Problem of Technical Images in Post-Documentary Photography', *Flusser Studies*, 10: 1–19. Available at: <https://www.flusserstudies.net/sites/www.flusserstudies.net/files/media/attachments/berti-kurtis.pdf> (last accessed 28 October 2019).

Calvino, Italo (1984), 'The Adventure of a Photographer', in *Difficult Loves*, William Weaver (trans.), 1st ed. San Diego: Harcourt Brace Jovanovich, pp. 220–35.

Chéroux, Clément (2003), *Fautographie: Petite histoire de l'erreur photographique*. Crisnée, BE: Éditions Yellow Now.

Chesher, Chris (2012), 'Between Image and Information: The iPhone Camera in the History of Photography', in Larissa Hjorth, Jean Burgess and Ingrid Richardson (eds), *Studying Mobile Media: Cultural Technologies, Mobile Communication, and the iPhone*. New York: London: Routledge, pp. 98–117.

Cruz, Edgar Gómez, and Asko Lehmuskallio (eds) (2016), *Digital Photography and Everyday Life: Empirical Studies on Material Visual Culture*. Abingdon, NY: Routledge.

Cruz, Edgar Gómez, and Eric T. Meyer (2012), 'Creation and Control in the Photographic Process: iPhones and the Emerging Fifth Moment of Photography', *Photographies*, 5(2): 203–21.

Flusser, Vilém [1983] (2000), *Towards a Philosophy of Photography*. London: Reaktion Books.

Frosh, Paul (2001), 'Inside the Image Factory: Stock Photography and Cultural Production', *Media, Culture & Society*, 23(5): 625–46.

Frosh, Paul (2002), 'Rhetorics of the Overlooked: On the Communicative Modes of Stock Advertising Images', *Journal of Consumer Culture*, 2: 171–96.

Frosh, Paul (2003), *The Image Factory: Consumer Culture, Photography and the Visual Content Industry*. Oxford, New York: Berg.

Fuller, Mathew (2007), 'The Camera that Ate Itself', *Flusser Studies*, 4: 1–31. Available at: <https://www.flusserstudies.net/sites/www.flusserstudies.net/files/media/attachments/fuller_the_camera.pdf> (last accessed 28 October 2019).

Hochman, Nadav, and Lev Manovich (2013), 'Zooming into an Instagram City: Reading the Local through Social Media', *First Monday*, 18:7. Available at: <https://firstmonday.org/ojs/index.php/fm/article/view/4711/3698> (last accessed 28 October 2019).

Hsu, Ruby (2011), 'Lomography Strategy'. Available at: <https://www.rubyhsu.live/work/lomography-strategy> (last accessed 9 July 2020).

Iversen, Margaret (2012), 'Analogue: On Zoe Leonard and Tacita Dean', *Critical Inquiry*, 38: 797–819.

Knowles, Kim (2016), 'Slow, Methodical, and Mulled Over: Analog Film Practice in the Age of the Digital', *Cinema Journal*, 55(2): 146–51.

Koepnick, Lutz (2014), *On Slowness: Towards an Aesthetic of the Contemporary*. New York: Columbia University Press.

Kozinets, Robert V. (2015), *Netnography: Redefined*. Los Angeles, London: Sage.

Krauss, Rosalind (1999), *'A Voyage on the North Sea': Art in the Age of the Post-Medium Condition*. New York: Thames & Hudson.

Kuc, Kamila, and Joanna Zylinska (2016), *Photomeditaions: A Reader*. London: Open Humanities Press. Available at: <http://photomediationsopenbook.net> (last accessed 28 October 2019).

Larsen, Jonas, and Mette Sandbye (eds) (2014), *Digital Snaps: The New Face of Photography*. London, New York: I. B. Tauris.

Lenot, Marc (2017a), 'Flusser and Photographers, Photographers and Flusser', *Flusser Studies*, 24: 1–18. Available at: <http://www.flusserstudies.net/sites/www.flusserstudies.net/files/media/attachments/marc-lenot-flusser-photographers-photographers-flusser.pdf> (last accessed 28 October 2019).

Lenot, Marc (2017b), *Jouer contre les appareils: De la photographie expérimentale*. Paris: Libella.

Lister, Martin (ed.) (2013), *The Photographic Image in Digital Culture*. London, New York: Routledge.

Lomography (2010), 'The 10 Prophecies'. Available at: <https://microsites.lomography.com/prophecies> (last accessed 28 October 2019).

Lomography (2012a), 'How Do You Balance Analogue & Digital in Your Life?' Available at: <https://microsites.lomography.com/analogue-vs-digital/> (last accessed 28 October 2019).

Lomography (2012b), *Lomo Life: The Story. Vol. 1*. London: Thames & Hudson, 2012.

Lomography (2012c), *Lomo Life: The Cameras. Vol. 2*. London: Thames & Hudson, 2012.

Lomography (2018), 'The 10 Golden Rules'. Available at: <https://www.lomography.com/about/the-ten-golden-rules> (last accessed 28 October 2019).

Lomography (2019a), 'Lomography Smartphone Scanner'. Available at: <https://shop.lomography.com/en/smartphone-scanner> (last accessed 28 October 2019).

Lomography (2019b), 'Redscale XR 120 ISO 50-200 3 rolls'. Available at: <https://shop.lomography.com/en/lomography-redscale-xr-50200-120-3-pack> (last accessed 28 October 2019).

Lomography (2019c), 'Revolog & Bento Bundle'. Available at: <https://shop.lomography.com/en/revolog-bento-bundle> (last accessed 28 October 2019).

Lugon, Olivier (2015), 'Photography and Scale: Projection, Exhibition, Collection', *Art History*, 38(2): 386–403.

Manovich, Lev (2017), *Instagram and Contemporary Image*. Available at: <http://manovich.net/index.php/projects/instagram-and-contemporary-image> (last accessed 28 October 2019).

Mitchell, W. J. T. (1994), *Picture Theory: Essays on Verbal and Visual Representation*. Chicago and London: The University of Chicago Press.

Muñiz Albert M., and Hope J. Schau (2011), 'How to Inspire Value-laden Collaborative Consumer-generated Content', *Business Horizons*, 54: 209–17.

Neanderthalis (2012), 'Holga 120 WPC: Slowing it Way Down', *Lomography Magazine*. Available at: <https://www.lomography.com/magazine/159178-holga-120wpc-slowing-it-way-down> (last accessed 28 October 2019).

Parikka, Jussi (2012), *What is Media Archaeology?* Cambridge and Malden, MA: Polity Press.

Ritchin, Fred (2009), *After Photography*. New York: W. W. Norton & Company.

Rose, Gillian (2014), 'How Digital Technologies Do Family Snaps, Only Better', in Jonas Larsen and Mette Sandbye (eds), *Digital Snaps: The New Face of Photography*. London and New York: I. B. Tauris, pp. 67–86.

Rubinstein, Daniel, Johnny Golding and Andrew Fisher (2013), *On the Verge of Photography: Imaging Beyond Representation*. Birmingham: ARTicle Press.

Rubinstein, Daniel, and Katrina Sluis (2008), 'A Life More Photographic', *Photographies*, 1(1): 9–28.

Sandbye, Mette (2018), 'New Mixtures: Migration, War and Cultural Differences in Contemporary Art-documentary Photography', *Photographies*, 11(2–3): 267–87.

Schiavone, Francesco (2013), *Communities of Practice and Vintage Innovation: A Strategic Reaction to Technological Change*. New York: Springer.

Šimůnek, Michal (2018a), 'LomoHome double-agent', *Lomography Lomo-Homes*. Available at: <https://www.lomography.com/homes/double_agent> (last accessed 28 October 2019).

Šimůnek, Michal (2018b), 'Automatic Exposure Failure & Scanner Composition'. Available at: <https://www.lomography.com/homes/double_agent/albums/2174564-automatic-exposure-failure-scanner-composition> (last accessed 28 October 2019).

Šimůnek, Michal (2018c), 'R001-IMG03'. Available at: <https://www.lomography.com/homes/double_agent/albums/2174564-automatic-exposure-failure-scanner-composition/22787025> (last accessed 28 October 2019).

Sontag, Susan [1977] (2005), *On Photography*. New York: RosettaBooks.

Steyerl, Hito (2009), 'In Defence of the Poor Image', *e-flux*, 10. Available at: <https://www.e-flux.com/journal/10/61362/in-defense-of-the-poor-image/> (last accessed 28 October 2019).

van Alphen, Ernst (2018), *Failed Images: Photography and Its Counter-Practices*. Amsterdam: Valiz.

Villegas, Dino (2018), 'From the Self to the Screen: A Journey Guide for Auto-netnography in Online Communities', *Journal of Marketing Management*, 34(1–2): 243–62.

9 Strangely Unique: Pictorial Aesthetics in the Age of Image Abundance

Josef Ledvina

Introduction

ONE DAY IN 1922 László Moholy-Nagy picked up the phone and called an enamel sign factory in the small German town of Tannroda:

> I had the factory's colour chart before me, and I sketched my painting on graph paper. At the other end of the telephone, the factory supervisor had the same kind of paper, divided into squares. He took down the dictated shapes in the correct position. (It was like playing chess by correspondence.) One of these pictures was delivered in three different sizes so that I could study the subtle difference in the colour relations caused by the enlargement and reduction. (Mcholy-Nagy 1947: 79–80)

That is how Moholy-Nagy himself described the origin of *Telephone Pictures* some twenty years later. Yet subsequently this version of the events was challenged by photographer and Moholy-Nagy's first wife Lucia Moholy. According to her, the famous telephone story was a prank: 'I distinctly remember the timbre of his voice on this occasion – "I might even have done it over the telephone"' (Moholy 1972: 79).

Whatever the true course of events, the three *Telephone Pictures* are still with us (Figure 9.1). Or should we instead speak of just one image 'ordered in different sizes'? These three treasured artefacts share some aspects characteristic of the environment of the contemporary image, while at the same time conspicuously deviating from others. At first, the story (or prank) about the graph paper procedure bears a striking similarity to the digital 'identity' of contemporary images: having the same

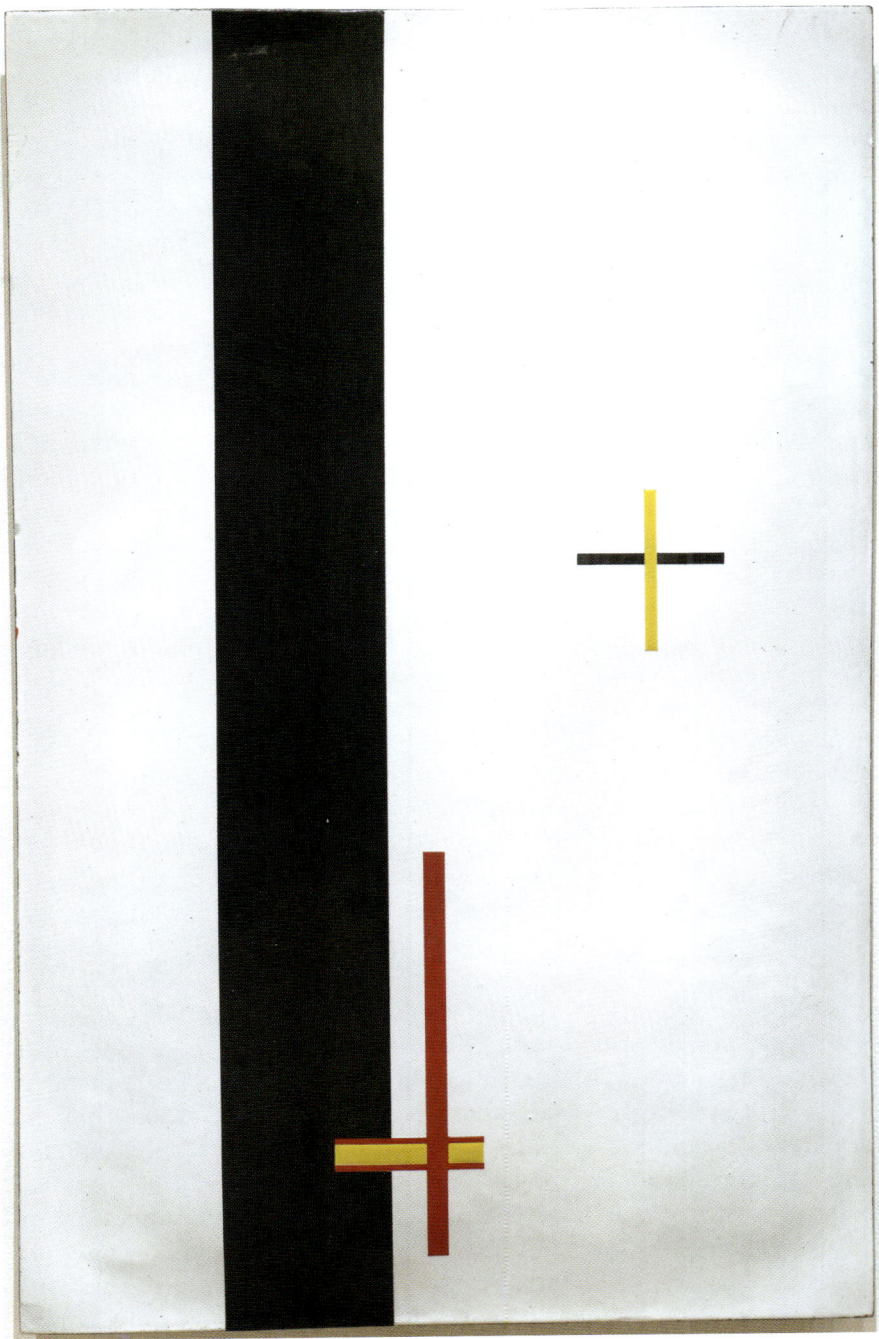

Figure 9.1 László Moholy-Nagy: *EM I Telefonbild*, 1923. Porcelain enamel on steel, 95.2 cm x 60.3 cm. New York, Museum of Modern Art (MoMA). © 2019. Digital image, The Museum of Modern Art, New York/Scala, Florence.

image, not just in three, but a myriad of different, algorithmically recounted and mechanically inscribed formats is something we live out every day. We share an image between devices; we display the image on a smartphone, then on a computer screen – once in a small window and another instance on a full screen – and then another time we project the same image onto a wall. There are also some stylistic similarities:[1] except for their size, in their mechanic industrial execution Moholy-Nagy's *Telephone Pictures* look almost exactly the same. And what is, after all, more 'identical' in such precise execution than different instances of the same image mechanically 'produced' from one dataset? Algorithmically screened images are as precise as they can be.

Here comes the difference, though; even if we treat *Telephone Pictures* as three instances of one and the same image, coded through the graph paper's units and the factory colour chart's set of colour values, they are, in stark contrast to the weightless circulation of digital images, 'heavy'. Set in tin and porcelain enamel, they insist on their lasting, material presence. The materiality of *Telephone Pictures* invites close scrutiny: in practice, they defy Moholy-Nagy's own formalist theory of 'absolute painting', that is, painting that carries its subject 'within itself, in its colour' and so consists of purely optical sensuous configurations (Moholy-Nagy 1969: 14). There is much more to see in *Telephone Pictures* than merely shapes and colours, beginning with the conspicuous fact that they are made from tin plates covered with a layer of porcelain enamel; a highly unusual material for art production at that time. This was, of course, a matter of special interest for Moholy-Nagy. It was he, after all, who further dramatised the relationship of this already industrial material to the field of factory mass production through the careful juxtaposition of three pictures in a 1924 presentation in the Sturm Gallery in Berlin. The precision, bordering on a pure notionality of geometrically defined lines and surfaces, is a stylistic feature of machine-made things (in contrast to more individuated artisan production);[2] it is also a feature that Moholy-Nagy – as a connoisseur of industrial and technological modernity – was very much attracted to. Another question is how he felt about the fact that closer scrutiny reveals imprecisions and inevitable deviations from the (apparently) sought after notionality of pure geometry. For example, along the edges, the porcelain layer recedes and thins, revealing the metal support of the configuration; in contrast, the narrower enamel bars are almost bulging from the notionally defined picture plane. In these and other similar ways, there are marked differences between the three *Telephone Pictures*; the subtle enamel relief of the thin bars is, for example, more pronounced in the case of the smaller versions.

In contrast, there is something strongly counter-intuitive to the conversation about different and unique artefacts when it comes to viewing the same image file on different devices; even more so if this happens on the same device. It is here that the popular discourse of 'dematerialisation', 'ephemerality' and 'fluidity' finds its breeding ground.[3] In the vast majority of non-art contexts, we treat images as transparent. We do not consider them as singular materialisations of the same image, as we, especially today, do in the case of old-fashioned enamel-on-tin 'hardware'. But, does it make sense to treat two different instances of opening the same image file as two distinct artefacts?

My answer to this question is an emphatic yes.[4] In what follows, I demonstrate a selection of specific ways for overcoming, countering or getting behind the ephemerality and interchangeability that governs the contemporary image environment. In other words, I explore ways to attend to what is continuously appearing and disappearing on our screens with the same sort of care and attention we usually reserve for the old and treasured. Many things have changed, but some truths still hold: despite their ephemerality, images are still artefacts, or, as I will argue, pieces of design, which means particular pieces of technology made from particular 'matter' in a particular way for a (more or less) particular purpose. That is, they are tools, and as such they can go 'strange'. Sometimes, when they are broken, they go strange by themselves, and other times, when they are works of art, for example, they are made strange on purpose. Images can thus be rescued from the flood of pictorial data and seen as strangely unique. What this all means will be developed in detail, after one more demonstrative jump located right in the middle of an aesthetically striking encounter with a set of non-depictive images that are identical yet different. In this case, they will be contemporary, digital and quite mundane.

Broken Pictures

Does it make any sense to treat two cases of the opening of the identical image file as two distinct artefacts? There unquestionably are occasions when it does. A digital image, when it is being viewed, is necessarily 'screened', and thus the screening device can make a difference – a difference that does not always go unnoticed. There is a considerable field of professional expertise, as well as popular connoisseurship, that makes subtle distinctions in this regard. The screen device market runs partially on comparing respective qualities of displays (for more information on 'flat panel display' technologies see Lee, Liu and Wu 2009), where pixel density is scrutinised as well as the advantages and disadvantages of newly introduced display technologies. One of the earlier examples is in-plane-switching (IPS) screen technology, implemented into marketed devices since the 1990s to compensate for strong viewing

angle dependence, previously one of the main limitations of Liquid Crystal Displays (LCDs). A more recent example is the introduction of Organic Light-Emitting Diodes (OLED) as an alternative to traditional LCDs, where the key advantage is the OLED screen's thinness and flexibility. For connoisseurs of the immaculate image, there is a price to pay for this: the view in bright light can be more difficult because of lower maximum brightness, and, more importantly, OLEDs are prone to image degradation over a relatively short period of time. This results in colour shifts as one colour fades faster than another, image persistence, and in extreme cases, image burn-in. Such effects are usually subtle, visible only to a trained eye, but can be disruptive and disturbing.

There is an image of striking beauty circulating on the web, depicting six identical LG OLED TV sets, with an identical red slide on their respective screens Even though the code of the embedded monochrome images is, no doubt, identical – as is the model of the TVs – it is difficult to see them as just the repetition of the same. This is because all of them are, to some degree, 'spoiled' with visible image burn-in traces or, as the popular metaphor goes, with 'ghosts'. On one of the TVs, even the ghost of the CNN channel logo can be recognised (Figure 9.2). As much as my interest in this unusual image constellation is an aesthetic one, the origin of my concerns stems from a practical interest: it is with regard to the result of the test which demonstrated that the life-span of the new LG OLED TV line is significantly shorter than the 30,000 hours promised by the manufacturer (O'Keeffe 2019). In general, the story of LG OLED TV sets leads to the fascinating realisation that, at least on the molecular level, no two screenings of what we usually see and handle as perfectly identical images are entirely the same pictures. Over time and through use, these screens are undergoing subtle changes, and so are, as a consequence, the images screened on them. Of course, it can be argued that these minute changes are almost imperceptible and thus aesthetically void. But where is the line separating what counts aesthetically and what doesn't? Perceptibility is a highly context-dependent quality; an expert or connoisseur can see more than an amateur. Are magnifying glasses to be prohibited? And if so, why not dioptric glasses too? The point is that that the very fact of degradation can create a horizon determining how we watch images on displays. We can always search for ghosts, burns and retention; there will always be some to be found.

I suggest that the aesthetic interest I find in unique image constellations comes, at least partially, from the relation between two aspects. First, there is the relish of the luminescent monochrome image plane.[5]

Figure 9.2 (previous page) Real Life OLED Burn-In Test on 6 TVs, week 94. Courtesy RTINGS.com

Second, what makes the set of red monochromes particularly aesthetically interesting, at a deeper level so to speak, is the fact that this image of the purest form is at the same time 'tainted'. In a way, the image splits into two folds: on the one hand, there is in the image a notionally uniform red colour; on the other hand, picture qua picture, it is an artefact or piece of technology. This experience of mine is a case of a particular attitude to images that has been discussed recently in philosophical aesthetics, usually under the rubric 'inflected seeing-in' (for varying conceptions of image inflexion see Podro 1998: 26; McIver Lopes 2005: 40, 128–9; Hopkins 2010: 151–80; Nanay 2010: 181–207; Nanay 2016). Malcolm Budd had already argued in 1995 that 'the interrelationship between the marks on the surface and what is depicted in them' is 'the crucial characteristic of pictorial art' (Budd 1995: 58). More recently, Bence Nanay proposed 'design-scene property' as the term for this peculiar 'characteristic', a 'relational property that cannot be fully characterized without reference to both the picture's design and to the depicted object' (Nanay 2010: 194). For Nanay, the aesthetic experience of images differs from how we experience them in non-aesthetic contexts, in that we consciously attend not just to what is 'in the image,' but at the same time to the 'picture surface'. I am particularly fond of Nanay's choice of terms as it helps to avoid some potential misconceptions. Philosophical aesthetics often say very little about the material 'fold' of inflected imagery, instead focusing on image surfaces and planes; this can easily lead to a Greenbergian idea that what shall be attended to – and what artists should put on display – are the purely optical qualities of shapes and colours or the optically active field.[6] But materialist interpretations of surface can lead to a different kind of popular misconception, namely, that what we explore in the 'second fold' is only 'matter' in some physicalist sense or, in Heideggerian terms as merely present-at-hand (*Vorhandensein*). What we often explore when we get behind image transparency is an artefact qua artefact, or a piece of design, which means a particular piece of technology made from a particular matter in a particular way for a (more or less) particular purpose, that is, as ready-to-hand (*Zuhandensein*) (Heidegger 1996).

I propose here to think about images, on a general level, as tools designed for delivering pictorial content or, in other terms, tools for seeing-in.[7] Inflected digital images are just one example of what Alva Nöe calls 'strange tools'. In his book of the same name, Nöe compares images to doorknobs: 'When you walk up to a door, you don't stop to inspect the doorknob. Doorknobs don't puzzle us' (Nöe 2016: 100). Yet this does not mean that those doorknobs are, in the true sense of the word, natural: 'Doorknobs exist in a context of a whole form of life, a whole biology – the existence of doors, and buildings, and passages, the

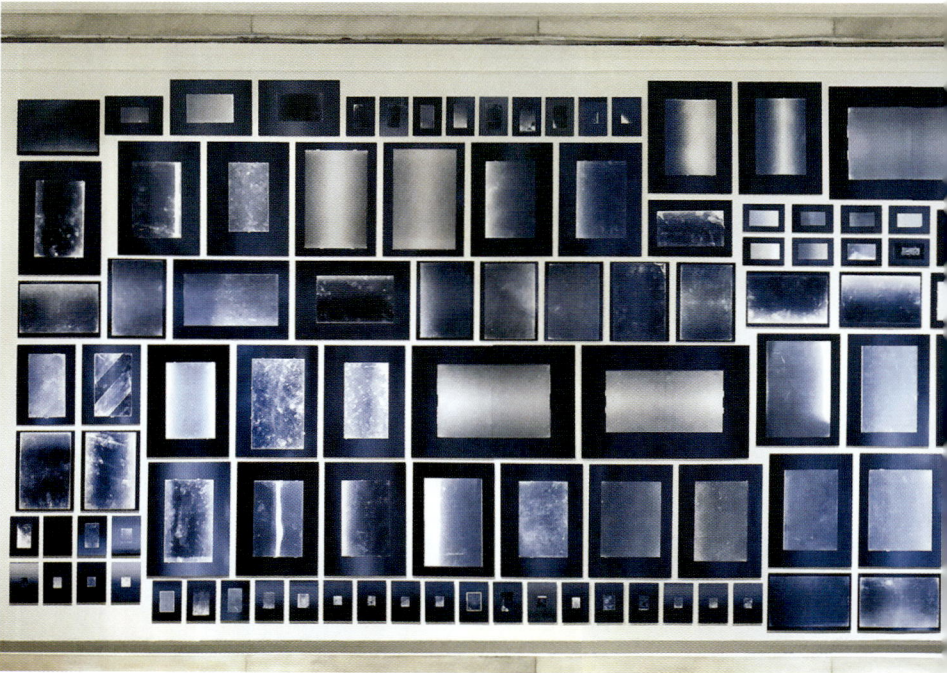

human body, the hand and so on' (Nöe 2016: 100). The reason they seem natural to us is that we take all of these complex and interrelated presuppositions for granted. The same can be said about images. 'The pictures in the daily newspaper or family album' – and here we can add to Nöe's examples our smartphones, computer screens and TV sets – 'strike us as self-evident and natural' (100). This is what constitutes their transparency: 'It seems to us as if they are transparencies through which we see the world' (100). But all of this works just because they are part of a very familiar 'communication game', a game in which we are 'at home' (100). As with the doorknobs, images are natural to us in the way good design is natural. Art starts, according to Nöe, 'when we lose the possibility of taking the background of our technologies for granted, when we can no longer take for granted what is, in fact, the precondition for our very natural-seeming intelligibility of such things as doorknobs and pictures' (Nöe 2016: 100).

Image burn-in and retention can also be seen as a case of the breakdown or malfunction of electronic image-tools that makes their inconspicuous presence visible or, speaking of images, makes transparencies opaque. While we are usually experiencing these breakdowns as disturbances, frictions, annoyances or hiccups, they can be mined for aesthetic and artistic purposes. Heideggerian underpinnings of Alva

THE AGE OF IMAGE ABUNDANCE   167

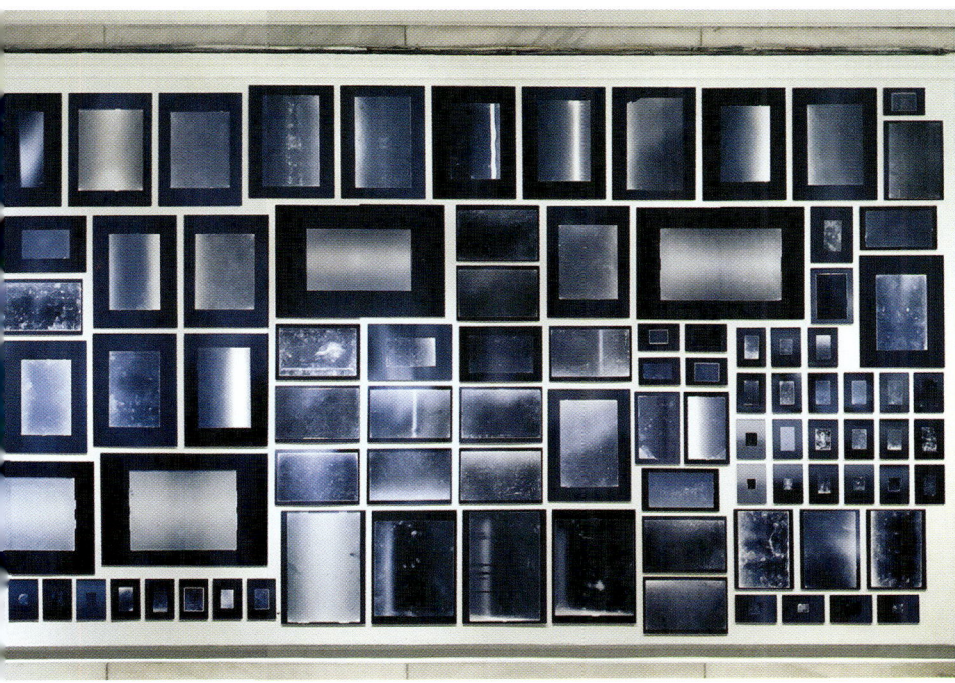

Figure 9.3 Penelope Umbrico: *Sun/Screen/Scan*, 2018. 185 archival pigment prints, variable: 17 in x 24 in; 17 in x 12 in; 12 in x 8.4 in; 6 in x 4.25 in. Courtesy of the artist and Bruce Silverstein Gallery, New York.

Nöe's aesthetics are obvious, and it was. in fact, Heidegger who explicitly reflected how 'broken tools' could complicate the transparent presence-at-hand of *Zuhandene* and make their own 'worldliness' apparent: 'When we discover its unusability, the thing becomes conspicuous' (Heidegger 1996: 68). This does not mean that what was previously ready-at-hand is now objectively something that 'just lies there'. Instead, the horizon of purpose is still determining our experiencing of a damaged tool: 'Pure objective presence makes itself known in the known thing only to withdraw again in the handiness of what is taken care of, that is, what is being put back into repair' (Heidegger 1996: 68). The tool does not change its objectively present properties, but it is lacking with regard to what it was originally designed for.

Opaque Images

There are many artistically and aesthetically productive ways that things can go wrong with digital images.[8] Some of the resulting 'strange pictures' are even more mundane than the degradation of organic compounds on which the OLED technology is based. As I write this chapter, I open a random image from the web: light falling through the window of the café I am working in reflects off the surface of my laptop screen. As a consequence, the image gets 'spoiled' with a unique and highly personalised pattern of specks, smudges and stains (reflecting, for example, my bad habit of eating and drinking over the computer).

Penelope Umbrico's artistic projects often and precisely draw our attention to this unique, individualised diversity of what is usually considered the interchangeable and transparent support of the mediums that deliver to us identical images, regardless of time and space. A prime example is her work *Sun/Screen/Scan*, exhibited for the first time in 2018 in the New York City Library (Figure 9.3). It consists of a cluster of over one hundred printed scans of screens extracted from disused computer monitors, laptops, tablets and smartphones. All of the devices that we, in Umbrico's words, 'touch, that we are intimate with, and that replace natural sunlight in our lives' (Umbrico n.d.). While not captured in the moment of screening an image, the screens are nevertheless transparent. Placed on the uniform module of scanning glass, they reveal undifferentiated greyish 'nothing' as if ready for an image to be put on display. However, it is the screens themselves that are being put on display; each of the pictured screens is, of course, unique. They differ significantly through their formats, and here the systematic differentiation of different categories of screen devices comes to fore, especially with regard to smartphones, being significantly smaller. More importantly, though, each of the screens has a unique pattern of indices from the routines of their past uses, seen through scratches, smudges, and sometimes clearly visible fingerprints. This incredible richness in the opacity of transparencies was achieved through a peculiar scanning procedure deployed by the artist. While making the scans, Umbrico placed the scanner in sunlight with the lid removed, thereby producing an effect analogous to what we sometimes experience with functioning screens, at those annoying moments when the artificial luminescence is overcome by the Sun.

Poor Resolution

The reflections, dirt, scratches and burns of the computer or smartphone screens may still feel somewhat external to the 'image itself'.[9] In the end 'the same image' can be opened on a different, 'unspoiled' device. But what is closer to the image 'as such'? Or, more precisely, what constitutes the identity of a digital image in its different inscriptions? The seemingly straightforward answer is at hand: 'the code'. If the data are identical, so is the image, regardless of contingencies such as scratches, burns or reflections of ambient light. This means that digital images are, in contrast to their analogous predecessors, in Nelson Goodman's terms 'notational'. One of the reasons why Goodman gives so much space to a detailed discussion of notational 'symbol schemes' in his *Languages of Art* is to explain why there are some artforms where forgery is logically impossible (Goodman 1976: 177–221). For Goodman, there can be fake Rembrandts, but no fake *Finnegans Wake*, and no fake Fifth Symphonies, though there can be fake first editions of *Finnegans Wake* and fake performances of the Fifth. Goodman explains that while painting is 'autographic', literature, as well as classical music based on musical notation, is 'allographic', which means that authorship consists in designing the notation, and 'performance of the piece' is provided by some other agency. A novel is set in definite notation; namely, the characters of a given script. Goodman states that

> [T]he fact that a literary work is in a definite notation, consisting of certain signs or characters that are to be combined in concatenation provides the means for distinguishing the properties constitutive of the work from all contingent properties, that is for fixing the required features and the limits for permissible variation in each. (Goodman 1976: 116)

In classical music, we have a composition set in a musical score and a variety of performances which all, if correct, are of the same piece and the same piece. They are, in Goodman's useful terminology, 'inscriptions' of the same 'character'. But this is obviously also the case for digital images: the 'author' provides the bits of bites – or concatenation of nulls and ones – and this 'definite notation' provides the means of distinguishing the constitutive properties of an image.[10] All the different screenings of the same image, however they may vary in multiple aspects, are merely different inscriptions (screenings) of the same character (image): they are performances of an identical piece.

Things are, to be sure, technically much more complicated than implied above. The move between the pattern of magnetised and non-magnetised electric particles on a hard drive and an image appearing on a computer screen is far from straightforward. The code changes all the time, often without us noticing; one version is in the storage capacity of the phone, another post on Facebook, yet another stored in Google Photos. Image standards, compression formats and device-specific screening algorithmic procedures make the identity of code a complex and, for our daily lives with images, a mostly irrelevant issue (for an introduction to compression formats see the 'Codecs' entry in Fuller 2008: 48–55). For most users, this is all a black-box. However, what is of interest for us here is what role the notation of digital images plays on an experiential or phenomenal level. The visible counterpart of the image data and its hidden process of the inscription are, of course, 'pixels'.

When opening an image file, the image is mechanically 'performed' through a matrix of a vast number of lit LEDs or OLEDs. Nevertheless, at present, we don't usually see these native pixels as something out of which the image is made; the image on the screen typically pictorialises as a homogenous whole. There are some exceptions, one of which was explored above; the OLED screens with their image burn-in draw our attention to this otherwise invisible or transparent screen design, as do many projects by Umbrico and the vast field of popular aesthetic preoccupation otherwise known as glitch art. But sometimes we see another and different meaning of the ambiguous term 'pixels'; when a stored image does not contain enough data to match the native resolution of the screen, it usually becomes pixelated.[11] These clearly visible pixels inscribed on the screen are, of course, materially composed of many native pixels lit in the same colour, and can thus be, for example, spoiled by burn-in degradation of the hardware pixelation. What is of importance for us is that when the pixels suddenly emerge, we are encountering another variety of image inflexion. In non-art contexts, pixelated images usually count as, to some degree, dysfunctional: they are poor images or images of low quality. These dysfunctional or lacking image-tools can perform well as strange tools of art.

Needless to say, this was not always the case. In the not-so-distant past, all digital images – even the best ones – were conspicuously pixelated, especially in comparison to finely grained analogue print. Returning to Goodman's analysis of digitality, the key difference between analogue and digital symbol schemes is based on the fact that the first symbol scheme is 'syntactically dense', meaning that it 'provides for infinitely many characters so ordered that between each two there is a third' (Goodman 1976: 136). This property of analogue imagery can be illustrated in one of Goodman's examples, Katsushika Hokusai's *Mount Fuji in Clear Weather*. In the case of *Mount Fuji*, every variation and modulation in the rising, falling, undulating, thickening and thinning line potentially depicts something of the volcanic mountain's silhouette, where even the slightest projection can represent a piece of rock or vegetation. In between any two points, there is some other semantically significant 'character' inscribed. Of course, if we magnify *Mount Fuji*, we arrive at some threshold of depiction; when we start to see discrete, spatially separated pieces of ink-dyed paper fibres. No one is likely to claim that these depict something of the mountain, but the density constitutes, in Whitney Davis's succinct terms, a 'horizon' of our perceiving and exploring of the picture (see the discussion of Goodman's Hokusai example in Davis 2006: 73–7). In contrast, digital images are notational and thus disjointed: there is an arbitrary and strictly set boundary of discrimination. When coloured square blocks of pixelation appear we do not see them as depictive, and no one, we can assume, would see a visibly pixelated digital silhouette of Mount Fuji and think that the mountain was formed from some seemingly odd cubic stone blocks; the pixels are of the inscription (of its design) and not of its character.

Today we do not very often see digital images as 'digital'; disjoint pixels as the constituent part of digital imagery notation have largely disappeared from our horizons. This way of describing the difference between digital and analogue images worked not just on a logical level but also on a phenomenological level in 1968, at the time of Goodman's *Languages of Art* first publication, and to a great degree until at least the 1990s. With the exponential rise of cheap computing power and data storage capacities coupled with the development of still higher and higher resolution screening devices, the situation has changed dramatically. In many contexts, we simply handle digital images analogically: we search in them for more and more detail, in between what we have already noticed. We even zoom in, assuming that there is always more to see. We open the same image on different devices with varying resolutions, unrestrained by the fear that the image will fail and the distracting noise of pixelation will come into view. All of this runs smoothly and without notice until it doesn't, and this is when things get strange.

The idea of an image that is stored somewhere, or rather nowhere or everywhere 'in clouds' and can be put at any time to any use, fails most often, or at least leads to unsatisfactory results, because of 'poor resolution'. The fluidity and flexibility of always-ready-at-handedness are the distinguishing characteristics of digital imagery, and indeed, what makes digitally notated images – compared to analogue ones – an immensely efficient tool from the point of view of storing and distribution. This is also where we can witness the breakdown of the digital image. Let us turn to a telling example, *Four Photographs of Rays of Sunlight in Grand Central*, Penelope Umbrico's beautiful project installed in 2016 in Grand Central Terminal in New York and at Bruce Silverstein Gallery. *Four Photographs* was based on her signature technique of appropriating a vast number of images from the web, in this case, hundreds of iconic pictures capturing fleeting moments when sunlight fell through the windows of the Manhattan station hall (see Umbrico, n.d.) (Figure 9.4). Presented also as a single-channel digital projection, all of the projected images are digital versions of what had previously been four analogue pictures, meaning that the viewers, in some respects, witness countless iterations of the original four. Yet the images are not seen only as repetition of the same; the digital versions vary widely due to cropping, flipping, filtering and colour calibration (some versions are in black and white scale, others capture tonal qualities of analogue prints in colours).

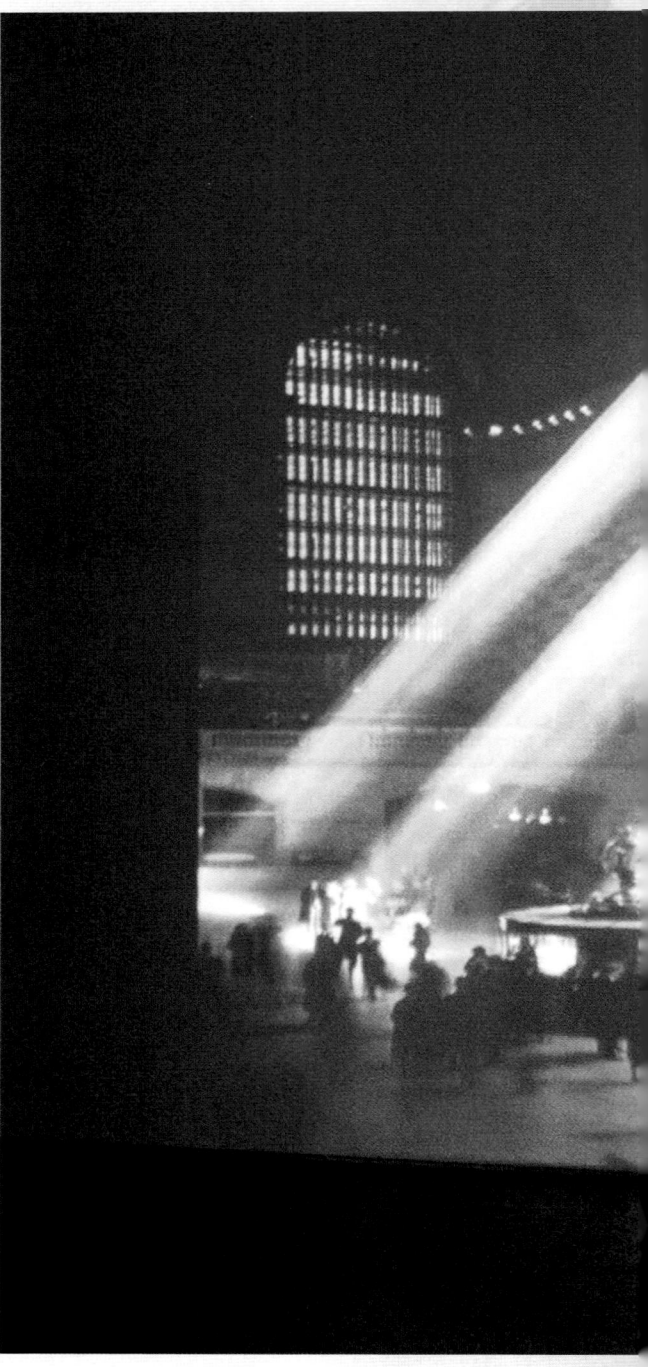

Figure 9.4 Penelope Umbrico: *Four photographs of Rays of Sunlight in Grand Central, Grand Central Terminal, 1903–1913, 1920, 1926, 1928, 1929, 1934, 1937, 1940, 1930–1940, 1935–1941, 1947, or 2010, by John Collier, Philip Gendreau Herbert, Edward Hulton, Kurt Hulton, Edward Lunch, Maxi, Hal Morey, Henry Silberman, Warren and Wetmore Trowbridge, Underwood & Underwood, Unknown, or Anonymous (Courtesy: Associated Press, the author, Bettmann/Corbis, Hal Morey/Getty Images, Getty Images, Hulton Collection, Hulton-Getty, Hutton Collection, New York City Municipal Archives, New York Transit Museum, New York City Parks and Landmarks, Royal Geographical Society, SuperStock/Corbis, Underwood & Underwood, Warren and Wetmore, or Image in Public Domain)*, 2013–2016, single-channel digital video, colour, 6:29 min. Courtesy of the artist and Bruce Silverstein Gallery, New York.

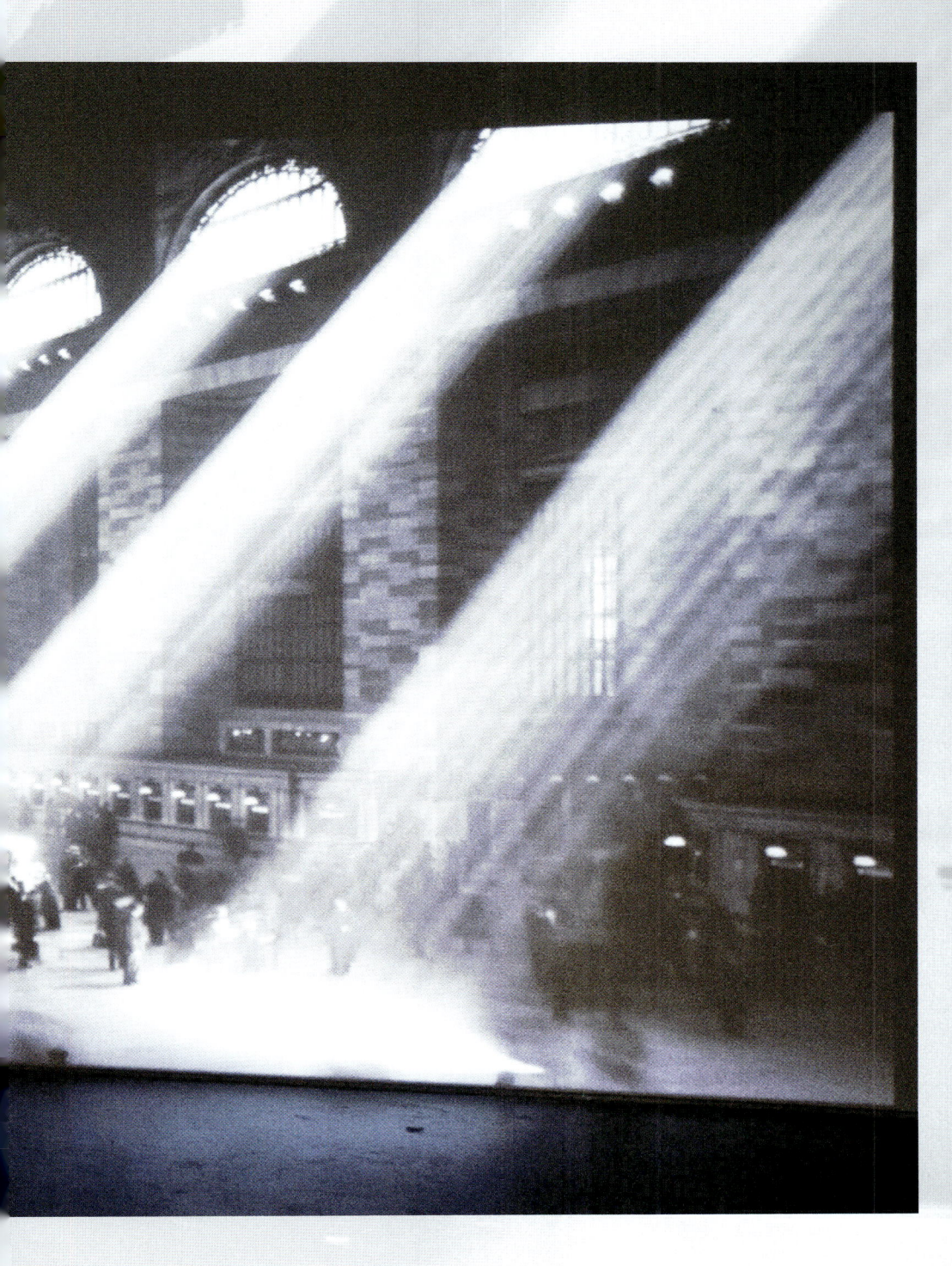

Most importantly for our purposes, all of them are, to some degree, 'bad'. Conspicuous pixelation gets between the image user and the depicted scene and also between what was already, before digitalisation, to some degree opaque: the aged and treasured analogue prints on paper. Here, a clash between the analogue richness of the finely grained pictures and the disjoint, gap-ridden digital 'reproductions' is being performed. But this is something that can be avoided; first, there are better versions available, somewhere in the non-space of the internet, and second, these images are not bad in and of themselves. They are just small, and when inscribed on an adequately small screen, such as in the small window of a computer's GUI or as thumbnails, they serve their purpose perfectly well. The breakdown occurs when we try to use them for something for which they are not good enough, or for which they were not designed. This breakdown is device- and use-dependent, and it happens right here, in front of us in an exhibition space, during projection.

In her *Defense of the Poor Image*, Hito Steyerl names thumbnails among the examples of 'poor images' (Steyerl 2009). But thumbnails are, in fact, rich enough as thumbnails. At the same time, from another point of view, Steyerl is right: they are bad in general because they are single-purpose tools, pragmatically rigid and thus lacking what we are tacitly counting on; the flexibility of use. When this flexibility fails, we can begin to learn how many notationally different images – with different stories and histories of editing, compressing and supplementing, serving different and sometimes highly specialised purposes – there are. However, until the moment of revelation, we treat these different 'characters' simply as identical, homogenous, dense, analogue wholes.

Resolution Overkill

Even in the age of high resolution, things with pixels can get strange in the opposite direction – in the arguably rare moments when we face analogue density, where some arbitrarily set threshold of discrimination is to be expected. The best example of this kind of strangeness is provided by Seth Price's recent work. In 2018, Price presented a series of large-format photographs in MoMA: printed on fabric and stretched on commercial lightboxes, they emanated a cloud of cold glow, similar to the projected-light-based images on computer screens. Titled *Danny, Mila, Hannah, Ariana, Bob, Brad*, the photographs depict sections of legs and arms of six different sitters, friends of the artist, identified informally by their first names (Figure 9.5). To say that these images are rich in detail is a gross understatement: the artist first took thousands of images with the aid of a special robotic camera, normally reserved for scientific research or forensic study. These images were then 'stitched' together using satellite-image software, retouched by professional retouchers, and then run through 3D modelling software.

The resulting effect is captivating; the viewer is drawn closer and closer, carefully scrutinising the details, searching in vain for the limit. Seth Price explains his original motivation as a search for a method to create 'large format print at extremely high resolution'. Interestingly, he also speaks about familiarity: 'We are familiar with seeing huge prints on the side of buildings or buses, but there is almost no data there, it's very low-res. Or you see super high-res images, but they are quite small' (Mellin 2019). Those who have had the opportunity to see a billboard print from up close know that digital printing also has its arbitrary set limit, even if the technology of subtractive CMYK colour representation is different from the additive RGB used in screen devices.

Translation between RGB and CMYK is an exciting topic in and of itself; strange things happen, and ample space for hiccups and failures appears in the process.[12] But let us not get involved in that lengthy discussion here: intricacies of halftoning and dithering aside, when we get closer to a large print, we expect, at some point, to see a raster of cyan, magenta, yellow and black dots on a white surface. Seth Price's bodily portraits are thus strange not because of a lack of transparency but because of transparency overkill. We simply see too much. Yes, Price's images are strange also for other reasons: we are not quite sure what they depict, the bodily surfaces are cropped details lacking context; they are simply too big; and it is strange to see a bit of hand three metres high. But here, too, the size and unusually high resolution for the format work together. There are, of course, many large images of bodily surfaces on billboards, but they are supposed to be seen from a distance, and when we get closer to them the raster quickly tells us to back away. Under the specific decorum governing the way we look at pictures in art museums, the situation is somewhat different – close-up viewing and backing-off is part of the game. The usual reason for this is to explore the design-scene properties, to see how the image is designed from marks on the surface, whether these are brush strokes, the grain of analogue photography, a bulging enamel layer, or the raster of a digital print. But *Danny, Mila, Hannah, Ariana, Bob, Brad* defies this attitude. Instead of exploring the border between the becoming of an image and its dissolution into a non-depictive configuration of marks – and the relation between both – we delve deeper and deeper into the hidden microcosms of skin anatomy. It is indeed a strange idea to have one image that depicts a hand, and at the same time, when viewed close enough, also shows something of the

Figure 9.5 (next page) Seth Price: *Danny, Mila, Hannah, Ariana, Bob, Brad*, installation view, MoMA PS1, New York, 2018. Courtesy of the artist and Petzel, New York, Photograph by Ron Amstutz.

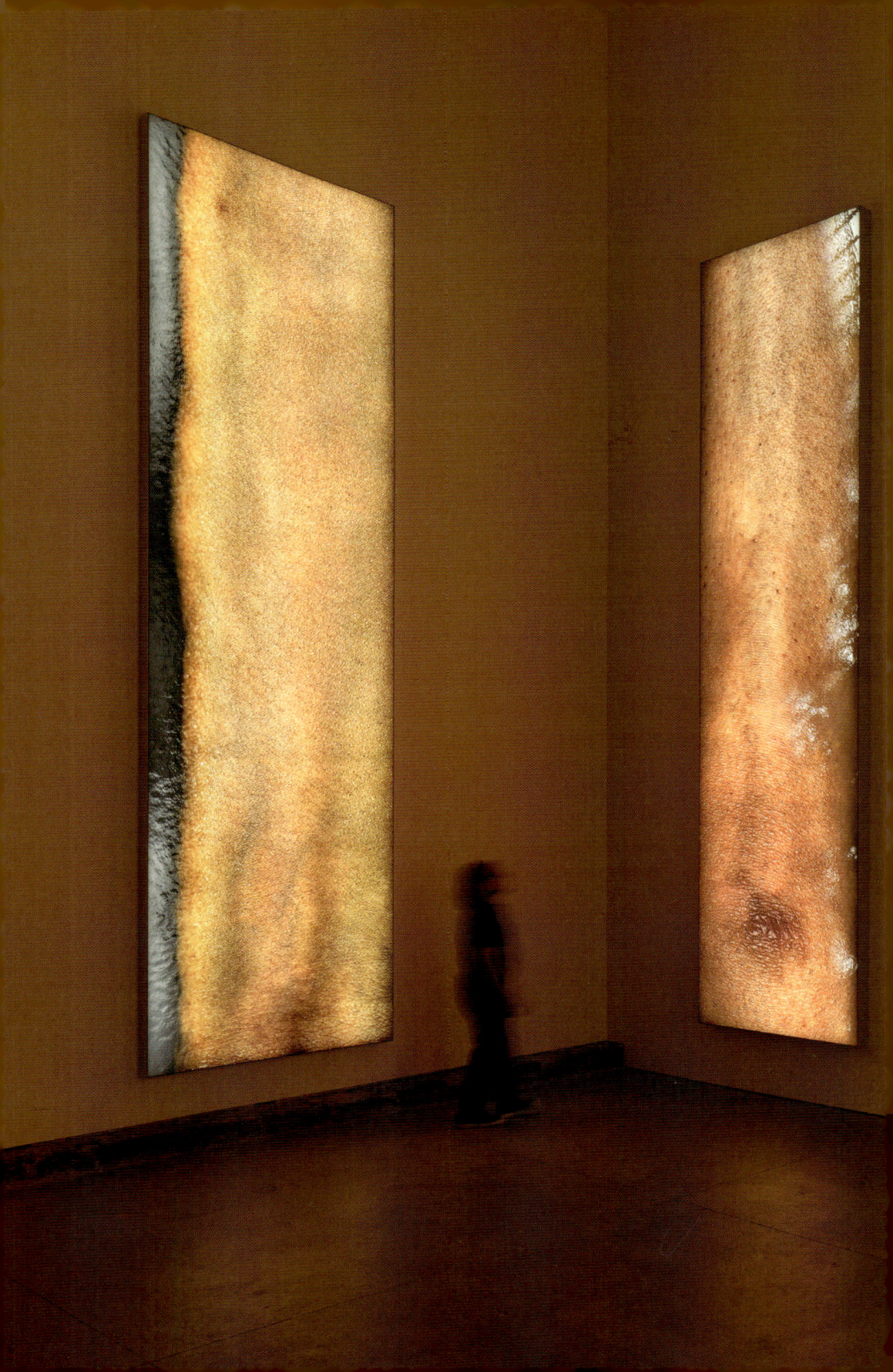

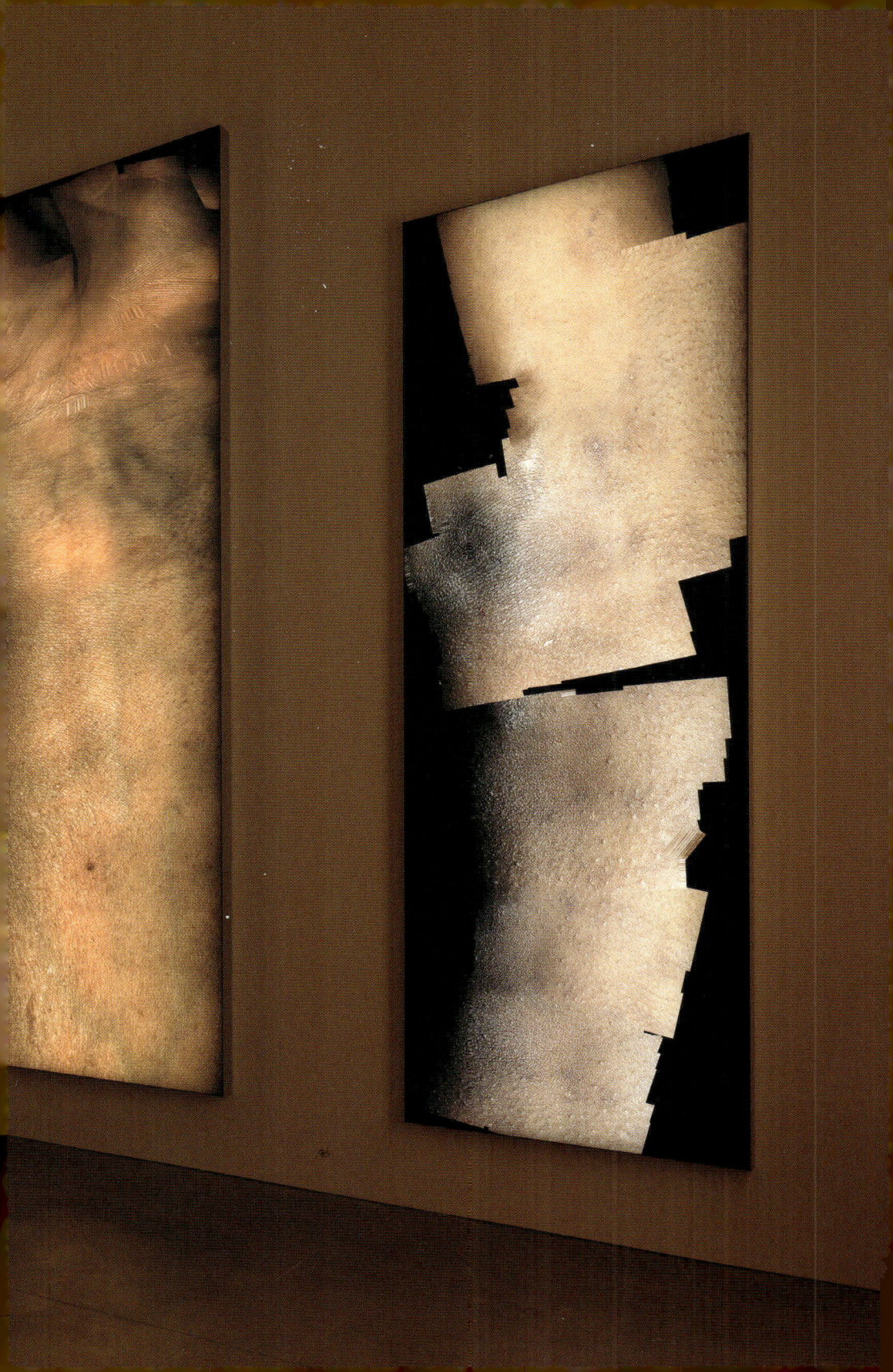

physiognomy of the hand at the almost cellular level. Usually, for each of these two things, we reserve images of different registers.

About the strangeness of Price's image-tools there is likely to be no disagreement, but are they in some sense 'broken'? It depends upon the interpretation. As I have tried to demonstrate, they fail to depict what their titles suggest they are: it is hard, if not impossible, to see Danny, Mila, Hannah, Ariana, Bob or Brad in them. From a more general perspective, imagine if this kind of image took the place of the ready-at-hand images we so often choose from the web when we want to see what someone or something or someplace looks like, or to show something to someone else, to use a picture in a lecture or yet another as wallpaper for your computer. With most standard devices you would not be able to open them, and in some, it would take an exhaustively long time; you would physically experience something more commonly experienced in the recent past – time. And though it still takes time for the machine to take the stored data and process them into an image on the screen, this time is usually counted in measures beyond the reach of human experience. The sought-after flexibility of the tool, that is, the idea of one image for every occasion, would be lost. We would not necessarily say that this tool is broken, but rather that it has become useless, inconvenient and, in most contexts, extremely wasteful.

Conclusions

Digitalisation brought, without doubt, a fundamental change in how we handle and experience images. They are produced and reproduced, displayed and discarded, inscribed and reinscribed at scales that were unimaginable some twenty years ago. This also means that we care much less about them, simply because it is easier to have them or to get them; they have lost the value they used to enjoy. This also means that we are much less prone to look at them as attentively as we do, for example, at Moholy-Nagy's *Telephone Pictures*.

Nevertheless, here I have proposed a way to rescue such images from the never-ceasing flux of visual information, applying to them the same amount of careful study that we usually reserve for the old and the treasured. Does this imply that I am disregarding what is new about images, what makes them different, and in effect, arguing that the change is not as fundamental as it would seem? The answer is both yes and no. Yes, images are still images and they are still tools for seeing in, but no, if it should imply that the aesthetic experience of contemporary imagery is or should be the same as in the age of relative image scarcity. The very idea that every single image inscription is unique and that we should treat it as such is strange indeed. But this is precisely why its realisation in practice is aesthetically so rewarding: it helps us reflect upon contemporary conditions when particular images are seemingly nowhere and everywhere.

Notes

1. It is important here to distinguish between stylistic analysis and formalism in the vein of Whitney Davis: 'Unlike formalism, however, stylistic analysis investigates the *causes* of an apparent configuration' (Davis 2011: 46).
2. Here, I borrow a useful concept of notionality from Summers, closely related to the abstraction from size. For Summers, '*notional* refers to generalized *dimensional* relations, usually ratios' (Summers 2003: 685). This generalisation is based on abstraction from facture, that is, from the aspects of how the artefact has been made.
3. Compare Geoffrey Batchen's characterisation of the present condition: 'The old, familiar distinctions between reality and its representation, original and reproduction, nature and culture – the very infrastructure of our modern worldview – seem to have collapsed in on each other. More specifically, the substance of an image, the matter of its identity, no longer has to do with paper or particles of silver or pictorial appearance or place of origin; it instead comprises a pliable sequence of digital codes and electrical impulses' (Batchen 2001: 155). Though Batchen, at the same time, argues that these conditions were already present with the 'invention' of photography.
4. I am, of course, not the only one who thinks that it makes sense to study singular articulations of identical digital images. For an inspiring and, in some respects, related discussion of what the author calls 'apparitions of images' see Batchen 2018.
5. This predilection can be partially based on my intimate art-historical acquaintance with modernist monochrome painting tradition in general and dematerialising luminescent opticality of monochromes made in the 1960s by Yves Klein in his signature 'International Ives Klein's blue' in particular.
6. According to Clement Greenberg, this pure opticality is the only legitimate 'subject' for modernist painting, which means that, at least in theory, the true aesthetic experience must be un-inflected. Compare (Greenberg 1995: 89): 'With Manet and the Impressionists, the question ceased to be defined as one of color versus drawing, and became instead a question of purely optical experience as against optical experience modified or revised by tactile associations. It was in the name of the purely and literally optical, not in that of color, that the Impressionists set themselves to undermining shading and modelling and everything else that seemed to connote the sculptural.'
7. This is, of course, simplification; we use images for a great variety of purposes, and some of their properties are determined by these widely

differing uses. Nevertheless, what makes imagehood of an image is that it is pictorially contentful. This is the property on which all uses of images in widely differing communication games to some degree depend, at least in the cases where they are used as images (and not for example as characters of script or ironing boards). So, any general theory of pictures needs to explain first the phenomenon of pictorial contentfulness. For one such inspiring attempt at a general theory of images see McIver Lopes 2004. This line of argument for the explanatory priority of phenomenon of pictorial contentfulness is somewhat similar to Robert Brandom's criticism of the pragmatist conception of language that rests on the level of pointing at the 'plurality of language games'. And it is for Brandom also a starting point for a monumental attempt at a pragmatic explanation of the phenomenon of representational contentfulness of language (Brandom 1994: 89–91).

8. What follows is not meant to be, in any respect, an exhaustive typology. The whole field of vernacular 'glitch art' would be, for example, relevant here. For a basic orientation, see 'Glitch' by Olga Goriunova and Alexei Shulgin (Fuller 2008: 110–19).

9. The question of what constitutes the identity of an image is a complex one and has been formulated in a variety of ways. Following a discussion of Goodman's ideas about digital representations will not provide any answers in this regard. Inspirational ideas as to the question of identity can be, for example, found in Hans Belting, who distinguishes image and medium, latter defined as a 'carrier of representation' (Belting 2011: 9–13). But this 'carrier' is for Belting not just the material support of representation; it is constituted in the relation between the matter and the body of the beholder, where the body is 'guided by cultural patterns and pictorial technologies' (2011: 9–13). All this makes Belting's conception of pictures similar to Nöe's idea that images are kinds of tools. The question of what makes images identical could thus be productively rephrased as: what makes two pictorial tools identical? It may very well be that in answering this question, the distinction between analogue and digital would become relatively less revolutionary than it appears.

10. Here, I avoid a discussion of who is the author in the case of technical images. Of course, it can be a machine or apparatus, but it deserves to be mentioned that characters have their 'authors' as well as their inscriptions. In some artforms, inscription authorship is aesthetically significant: Beethoven's Fifth Symphony performed by the Vienna Philharmonic under Herbert von Karajan is something other than the same performed by the Los Angeles Philharmonic under Gustavo Dudamel. But who are the authors in the case of image inscriptions of digital images? Usually, we don't care, but when we do, we usually see the machine as their 'author'. Although it is the machine that is malfunctioning, on another level, it can fail due to bad

design that has already its name or, in the current state of affairs, many names (or a name of some collective agency – for example LG development department).
11. Usually, there is the possibility for advanced algorithmic supplementation of the missing data besides just repeating (on your screen) pixels of the same value.
12. To get an idea of how diverse digital print techniques are, see Martin Jürgens *The Eye* (n.d.). Anachronistic paper print is also a popular strategy among contemporary artists for 'freezing' the inherent instability of electronic image circulation. A prime example is the 'Printed Web' project by Paul Soulellis (n.d.).

References

Batchen, Geoffrey (2001), *Each Wild Idea: Writing, Photography, History*. Cambridge, MA: MIT Press.
Batchen, Geoffrey (2018), *Apparitions: Photography and Dissemination*. Prague and Sydney: Power Publications and the Academy of Performing Arts in Prague (AMU Press).
Belting, Hans (2011), *An Anthropology of Images: Picture, Medium, Body*. Princeton: Princeton University Press.
Brandom, Robert B. (1994), *Making It Explicit: Reasoning, Representing, and Discursive Commitment*. Cambridge, MA: Harvard University Press.
Budd, Malcom (1995), *Values of Art: Pictures, Poetry and Music*. London: Allen Lane.
Davis, Whitney (2006), 'How to Make Analogies in a Digital Age', *October*, 117: 71–98.
Davis, Whitney (2011), *A General Theory of Visual Culture*. Princeton and Oxford: Princeton University Press.
Fuller, Matthew (ed.) (2008), *Software Studies: A Lexicon*. Cambridge, MA: MIT Press.
Goodman, Nelson (1976), *Languages of Art: An Approach to a Theory of Symbols*. Indianapolis: Bobbs-Merrill Company.
Greenberg, Clement (1995), 'Modernist Painting', in Clement Greenberg, *The Collected Essays and Criticism, Volume 4: Modernism with a Vengeance, 1957–1969*. Chicago: University of Chicago Press.
Heidegger, Martin (1996), *Being and Time*, Joan Stambaugh (trans.). Albany: SUNY Press.
Hopkins, Robert (2010), 'Inflected Pictorial Experience: Its Treatment and Significance', in Catherine Abell and Katerina Bantinaki (eds), *Philosophical Perspectives on Depiction*. Oxford: Oxford University Press, pp. 151–80.
Jürgens, Martin (n.d), *The Eye*, <http://the-eye.nl> (last accessed 11 November 2019).

Lee, Jiun-Haw, David N. Liu and Shin-Tson Wu (2009), *Introduction to Flat Panel Displays*. Hoboken, NJ: Wiley.
McIver Lopes, Dominic (2004), *Understanding Pictures*. Oxford: Oxford University Press.
McIver Lopes, Dominic (2005), *Sight and Sensibility*. Oxford: Oxford University Press.
Mellin, Haley (2019), 'Seth Price's Self as Tube', *Garage*, 18 July 2019. Available at: <https://garage.vice.com-en-us-article-ywy8kg-seth-prices-self-as-tube> (last accessed 11 November 2019).
Moholy, Lucia (1972), *Marginal Notes*. London and Krefeld: Scherpe Verlag.
Moholy-Nagy, László (1947), *The New Vision*. New York: Wittenborn.
Moholy-Nagy, László [1925] (1969), *Painting, Photography, Film*. London: Lund Humphries.
Nanay, Bence (2010), 'Inflected and Uninflected Experience of Pictures', in Catherine Abell and Katerina Bantinaki (eds), *Philosophical Perspectives on Depiction*. Oxford: Oxford University Press, pp. 181–207.
Nanay, Bence (2016), *Aesthetic as Philosophy of Perception*. Oxford: Oxford University Press.
Nöe, Alva (2016), *Strange Tools: Art and Human Nature*. New York: Hill and Wang.
O'Keeffe, Daniel (2019), 'Real Life OLED Burn-In Test on 6 TVs', *Rtings.com*. Available at: <https://www.rtings.com-tv-learn-real-life-oled-burn-in-test> (last accessed 11 November 2019).
Podro, Michael (1998), *Depiction*. Cambridge, MA: Harvard University Press.
Soulellis, Paul (n.d.), *Printed Web*. Available at: <https://printedweb.org> (last accessed 11 November 2019).
Steyerl, Hito (2009), 'In Defense of the Poor Image', *e-flux*, 10. Available at: <https://www.e-flux.com-journal-10-61362-in-defense-of-the-poor-image> (last accessed 11 November 2019).
Summers, David (2003), *Real Spaces: World Art History and the Rise of Western Modernism*. London: Phaidon.
Umbrico, Penelope (n.d.), 'Four Photographs of Rays of Sunlight in Grand Central . . .', Penelopeumbrico.net. Available at: <http://www.penelopeumbrico.net-index.php-project-grand-central-> (last accessed 11 November 2019).
Umbrico, Penelope (n.d.), 'Sun-Screen-Scan . . .', Penelopeumbrico.net. Available at: <http://www.penelopeumbrico.net-index.php-project-sunscreenscan> (last accessed 11 November 2019).
Wollheim, Richard (1980), 'Seeing-As, Seeing-In and Pictorial Representation', in *Art and Its Objects*, 2nd edn. Cambridge: Cambridge University Press, pp. 205–26.

III Models, Scans and AI

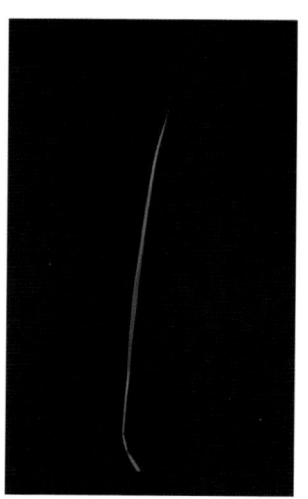

10 On Seeing Where There's Nothing to See: Practices of Light beyond Photography

Jussi Parikka

WiFi Vision

IN A RECENT PAPER, Person-in-WiFi: Fine-grained Person Perception using WiFi, a team of researchers suggested that WiFi antennas and signals are, in principle, sensors capable of detecting body postures and movement. This form of seeing beyond the visual spectrum is introduced as an alternative to camera-based, radar, and lidar (Light Detection and Ranging) technologies that have already been used in the context of 'people perception' (Wang et al. 2019). In a city – nowadays, almost any city – that is cut through by an extensive range of wireless signals between signal stations, this means that, in effect, the city is continuously forming images. These images, however, take a detour via WiFi, where transmission turns into photography and signal processing into spatial modelling, in a reminder that everything that exists as a signal can also exist as an image.

This is not the first paper to claim the usefulness of WiFi as a form of perception: the authors list earlier work in which 1D signal space has been reconstructed into '2D fine-grained spatial information of human bodies', itself questioning the theoretical focus on the visual spectrum through the mapping of opening doors, keystrokes, dancing and even static objects. Out of this broader ontology of 'wirelessness' (Mackenzie 2010) emerges the possibility of mapping, visualising and modelling space, humans, animals, objects – anything that reflects back, so to speak, the signals from WiFi traffic and antennae. This quirky detail also reveals how vision, or even a metaphorical extension of 'seeing' in this technological context, is not a distinct sensorial capacity to be understood in relation to other human-based sensoria (hearing, touching) but is something modelled according to sampling rates: 'lidars have sampling rate in the range of 5–20 Hz, which is much lower than other sensors such as cameras (20–60 Hz) or WiFi adapters (100 Hz)' (Wang 2019: 2). The image, then, is a sampling of a spatio-temporal situation: a constantly produced entity that cuts across the dynamics of a city as part of an operational processing of what is being seen, at what time, in which relations, and to what ends.

How does this relate to our concern, photography off the scale? Most visual theory and photographic studies have only now started to deal with the not so new media discoveries of the early nineteenth century such as the infrared (by Frederick William Herschel) and ultraviolet (by Johann Wilhelm Ritter) as visual realities that form – alongside the more traditional focus on photography, cinema, television and computer images – an alternative genealogy to the technical media of the past 100 to 150 years. Of course, the two lineages are not separated, even if photographic theory and history have had a tendency to focus more on seeing through things we call 'cameras' instead of, for example, sensors (Gabrys 2016). Such a view of images sees them as one subset in the larger field of 'measurement', whether as photogrammetry or as pattern recognition, that then forms a fundamental background for the contemporary contexts of AI, where images somehow persist as part of computational culture. However, it is the assemblage of 'seeing' by other means – seeing as measurement and seeing off the visible spectrum – that has thrown photography off the scale, alongside many other traditional forms of evaluating the techniques, discourses and habits of seeing in the cultural context of 200 years of machine vision (Virilio 1994). These assemblages can be coined post-lenticular landscapes, following the works of the artistic design team ScanLAB, and others.

Alternative contexts of seeing, with a specific focus on technologies of pulse and light, have emerged as one particular type of time-critical (Ernst 2016) and post-human (Zylinska 2017) visual measurement and observation. Of the multiple technologies of pulse and light, lidar stands out as one of the most discussed examples in the contexts of architecture and urbanism and one which has become a widely used technique across a range of fields in scientific measuring, including architectural modelling. It is increasingly used in artistically driven projects that mobilise lidar imagery as a way to survey and map landscapes and urban areas, engaging with emerging mobile units, such as autonomous vehicles, as key elements of these landscapes. The light-scanning technology developed earlier in the context of atmospheric modelling (Synge 1930) becomes a recurring reference point for some of the insights that articulate both genealogies of seeing through signals and pulses of light and sound, and contemporary technologies that map the city as one intensive, complex landscape of dynamics and navigation.[1] This same genealogy links research into light waves and far-away planetary objects by Christian Doppler in the 1840s, the realisation that the physical world is (often a light-emitting) broadcasting station in the 1920s and 1930s (Canales 2014: 23), the discovery of radar as the ultimate synesthetic transformation of sounds to images in the 1930s, and the recent discussions about lidar imaging and autonomous cars as a light echo pulse of the city. In many ways, it is also clear that this form of imaging is not about visuality per se, but about navigation: these are not images to be seen, but terrains to manoeuvre (see Mende 2017). In this context of images that echo across the city, to speak of the 'pulse of the city' is not a metaphoric description but a technical one: lidar as light radar is a technology of millions of directed (ultraviolet or near-infrared) light pulses per second, where the returning signal is then recorded and modelled accordingly. An image of the city, an image of clouds, an image of complex formations; each is measured in front of our eyes.

Consider the city as an already complex formation, a pattern of dynamics upon which technologies attempt to build their networks of images. Cities are full of signals and light; they are full of cameras and techniques of observation, of surfaces that refract and reflect light; from shop windows to closed-circuit televisions, the city is continuously being seen and registered and measured. However, an increasing amount of the technological 'seeing' that takes place in the large-scale visual landscapes of the city works to question traditional photographic modes of understanding visual power while introducing different genealogies of what the city is, as an assemblage of materials and seeing, as movement and large-scale dynamics. The city is a perfect test case – a laboratory even – for technologies and images off the scale. This is not merely because cities are large in scale, but because they exhibit such a vast multiscalar complexity that speaks to many of the changes that are taking place at the level of human perception and visuality and in the culture of the city itself. The city becomes a site of post-human forms of sensing – if this refers to the various autonomous systems that now process the majority of the things we still call 'images'. If the theoretically outlined media archaeology of the camera has been, until now, focused on the detachment of the seeing eye from the human body and from the act of seeing (Silverman 1993), we can now articulate how this camera-eye got stuck on the (autonomous) car, where it sees in ways that are not just seeing but modelling, mapping, measuring, predicting, and a range of other cultural techniques that pave the way for a wider set of infrastructural implications. In other words, the forms of seeing now introduced – whether through WiFi signals, lidar, radar or camera as measurements – are part of the operative ontologies (Siegert 2017) that do not focus on the act of seeing at the site of the device or the body of the perceiver, but in the connected networks where multiple feeds are a part of the dynamic formation of an image in real time.

What Is It Like to See Like a Computer?

At the centre of this chapter are themes that have been discussed earlier by Paul Virilio, Harun Farocki and other theorist–artists, each contending with machines that form images, and images that are part of computational systems. Machine vision, computer-assisted technologies of scanning, and the nonhuman; all have already entered the photographic focus, questioning divisions between media-specific analyses such as cinema and photography (see, for example, Anderson 2017). In recent years, artistic projects have attempted to understand the changing visual landscapes of things unseen, from computer vision to AI, and the neural network processing of image data. For Trevor Paglen (2016), images turn to look at you in a complex assemblage of visuality where it is becoming more and more difficult to pinpoint where the actual seeing happens along chains of multiple operations that are connected to this network of events.

Another example of this difficulty is Ben Grosser's computational algorithm piece *Computers Watching Movies* (2013; Figure 10.1), the staging of a situation in which humans are given a glimpse of what (and how) a computer might see as it watches a film. Grosser's work is primarily focused on the software that 'uses computer vision algorithms and artificial intelligence routines to give the system some degree of agency, allowing it to decide what it watches and what it does not'.[2] Films such as *2001: A Space Odyssey*, *American Beauty*, *Inception*, *Taxi Driver*, *The Matrix*, and *Annie Hall* are each mapped as simple moving vector spaces, while the soundtrack makes way for the possibility of the viewer recalling what the films look like for humans. Sound calls forth a nostalgia for the visuals that have already left the human's visual spectrum. The visual space is mapped in a different measure and becomes something other than visual in the sense of seen and observed. It becomes part of the regime of pattern recognition with multiple technical, aesthetic and political implications (see Apprich et al. 2018).

While systems of machine vision are no longer limited to military-operated large-scale analytical and targeting machines, they are still relatively new in the context of contemporary visual arts. Although architecture and speculative design are dealing with this at an ever-increasing pace, there remains much to discuss in relation to the transformation I pointed out earlier in this chapter: when and where visuality turns into navigation; navigation functions as part of large-scale infrastructures; and images are both seen and processed as data (cf. Bridle 2019). Our sense of machine vision is often metaphorical when it tries to cater to the human assumption about what the machine sees. In many contexts, the cultural, artistic and humanities responses to non-human vision are simply versions of philosopher Thomas Nagel's (1974) famous question 'what is it like to be a bat?' In the case of autonomous and technological vision systems, the question should be: what it is like to see like a machine? A more refined version of this move would be to educate ourselves in machine ways of seeing, as a recent project and a workshop put it, adapting the original words of John Berger in inventive ways (Cox 2016). This means: not just speculating about what the machine sees when it sees something – as if it would or could see something in the same register of things we consider to be perception – but what this seeing means in the broader sense of processing patterns, organising culture, or designing large-scale distributed nonhuman agent systems. As Geoff Cox (2016) puts it:

> In this we should not try to oppose machine and human seeing but take them to be more thoroughly entangled – a more 'posthuman' or 'new materialist' position that challenges the onto-epistemological character of seeing – and produces new kinds of knowledge-power that both challenges as well as extends the anthropomorphism of vision and its attachment to dominant forms of rationality.

The sort of imaging/imagining practices that actively avoid the assumed primacy of human eyes and interpretation seem to be themselves one particular aspect of what we relate to as the automation of images, but also, as I want to elaborate, the urban environment of images. This refers to the images of the environment in the context of the ongoing mass-scale disaster of climate change, global warming and toxic planetary inhabitability, but also to the images as fundamentally involved in those environments in ways that hark back to discussions about remote sensing, large-scale visualisation practices and ultimately, images as data and incorporated as elements in large-data sets (Anderson 2017).

The impact of such imaging becomes evident when considering the range of automated image and machine vision systems that function in large-scale, embedded and dynamic systems – from cityscapes to meteorological systems, from military scanning of landscapes to development of experimental ways of environmental visualisation. Each of these, in many ways, detaches images from the usual register of what visuality means as optical perception or quality. For example, different forms of sensors would be one source that only leads to data visualisation that

Figure 10.1 (next page) Still frame from *Computers Watching Movies* (*The Matrix*), 2013. <https://bengrosser.com> , used with permission.

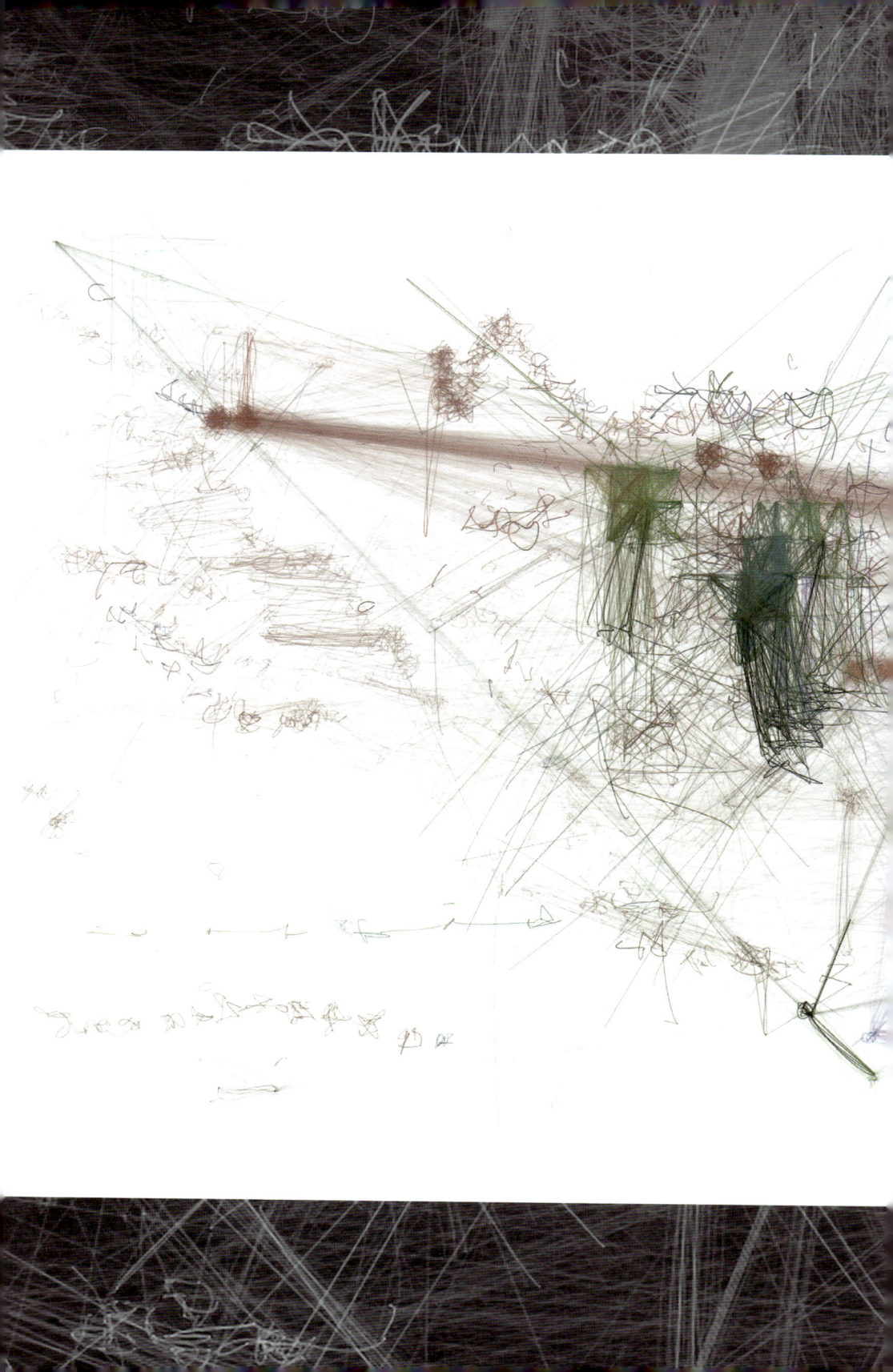

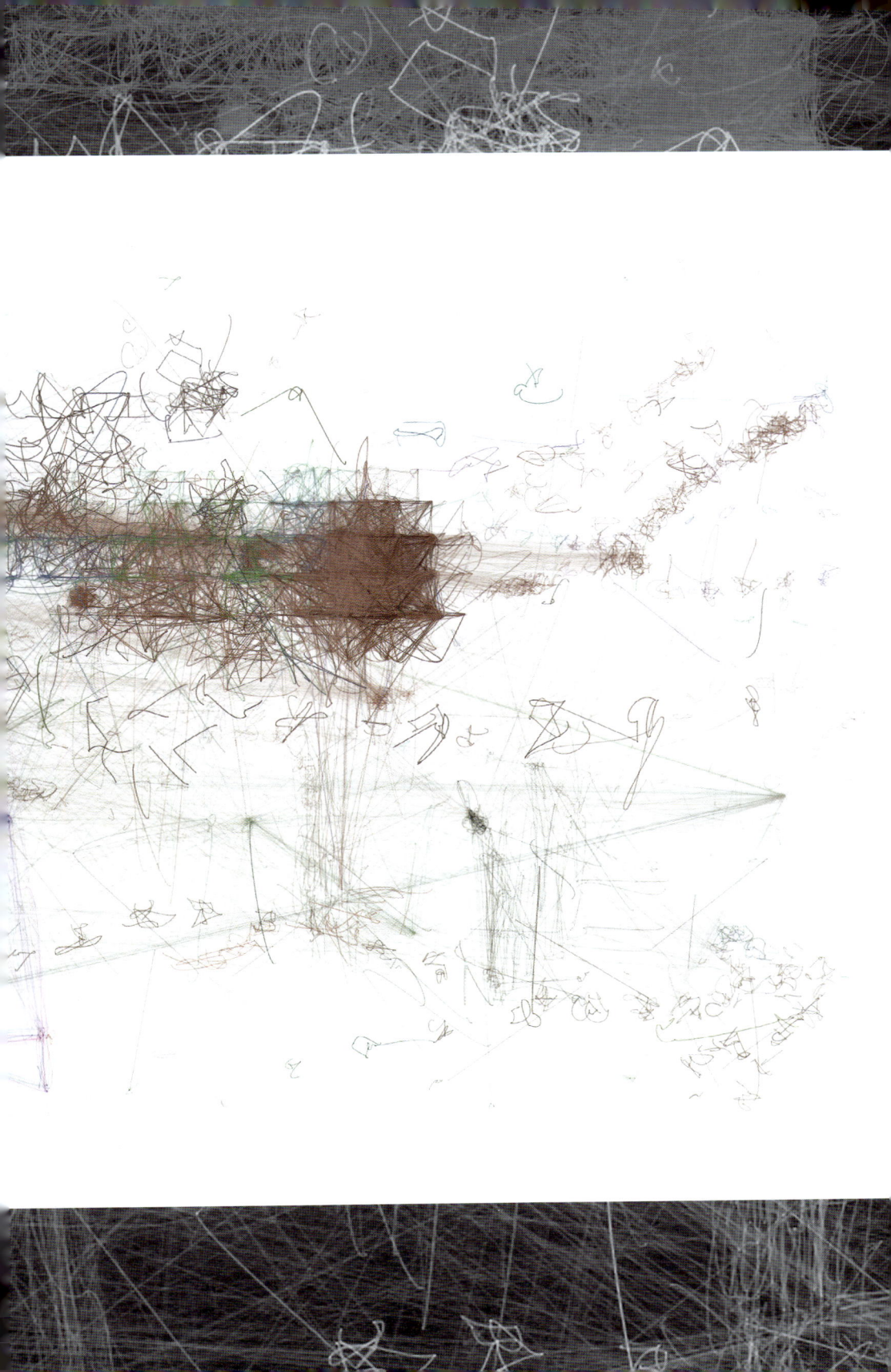

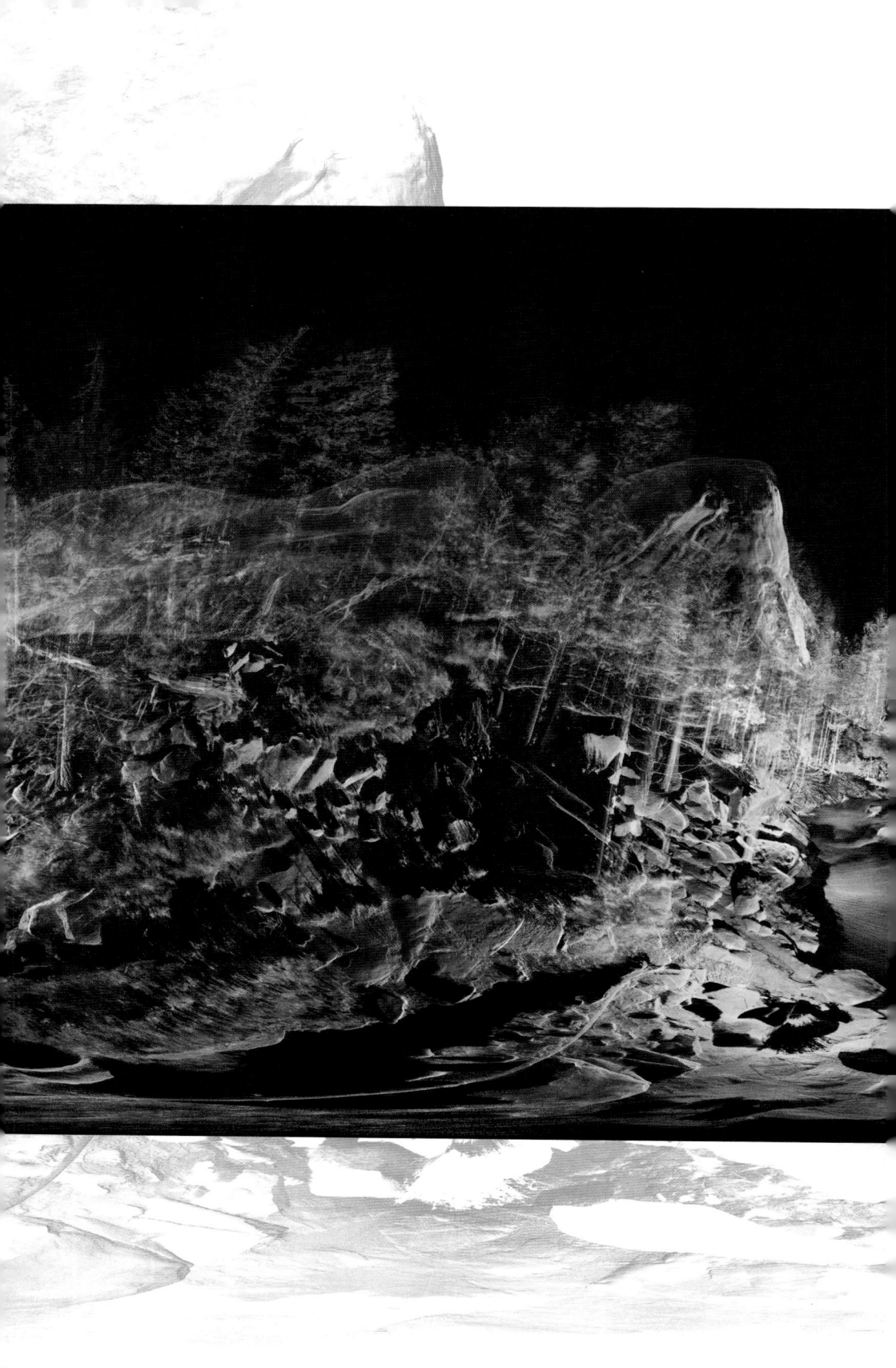

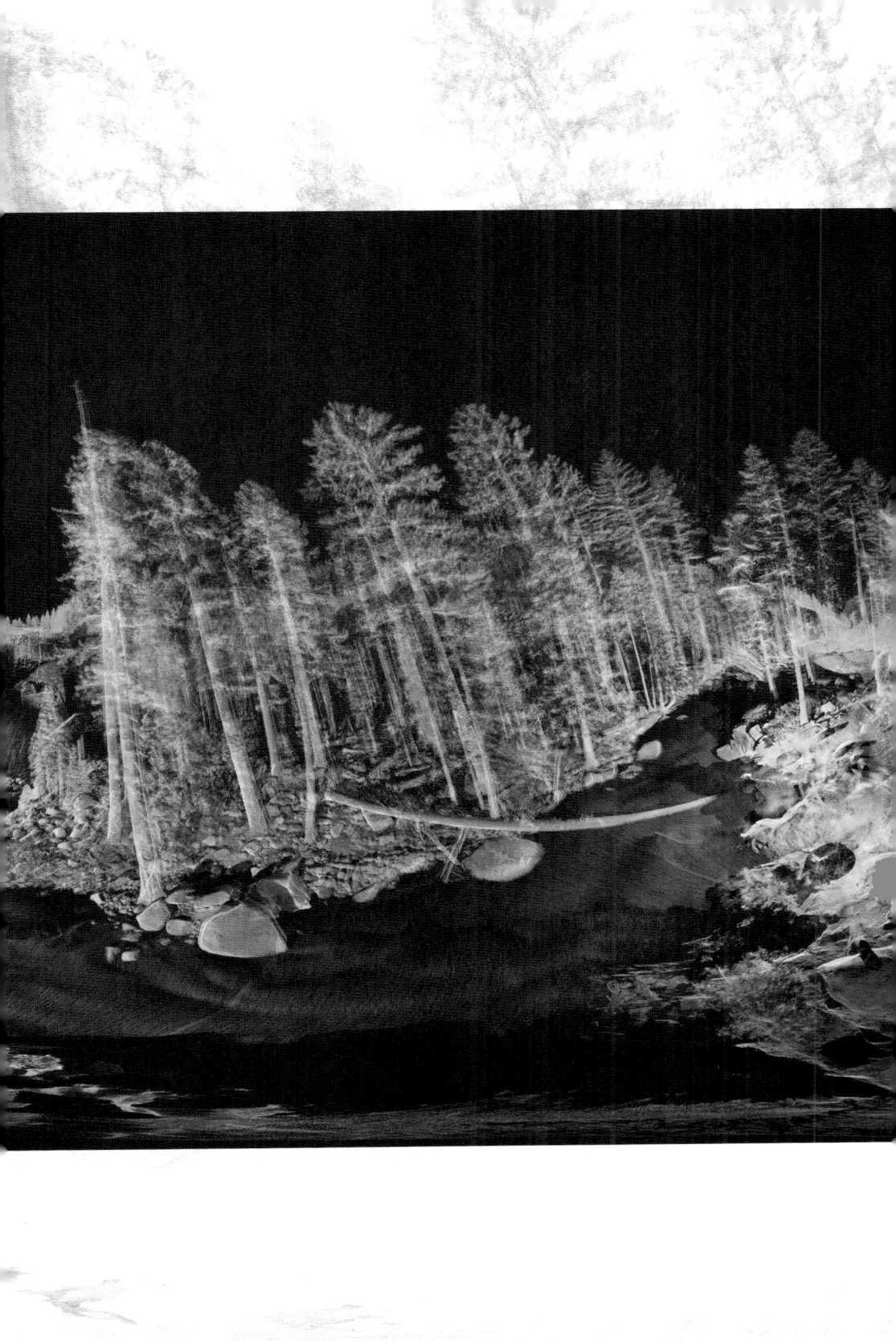

provides something even remotely resembling 'an image'. Of course, the latter point should not itself be mistaken for something new or revolutionary: for a long time visuality was governed in relation to geometrics and calculation, including the perspectival calculations for painters (as famously outlined by Alberti) as well as the metrics of measurement through images for architects (also introduced by Alberti). In our context, this relates directly to the genealogy of photogrammetry (Carpo 2017: 115). Hence, while there could be a longer narrative about the genealogy of visuality as measurement (see Tomáš Dvořák's chapter in this volume) and as environmental analysis of the (architectural) image, I want to turn to some recent examples that deal with alternative genealogies of machine vision and post-lenticular landscapes.

The Urban Pulse

While the term post-lenticular landscape could be seen as describing a wider shift in visual technologies and photography, it is also the title of a work, *Post-lenticular Landscapes* (2016–17; Figure 10.2), by ScanLAB Projects, who in the summer of 2016 travelled to Yosemite National Park to produce a 3D model – a hologram – of Yosemite Valley with laser scanning technology. From lenticular photography to laser-based pulses, from scanning to modelling, the work was contextualised as part of the history of landscape photography, extending from Eadweard Muybridge's famous Yosemite series of the 1870s through the various professional and amateur images produced since. Besides the legacy of the site itself, the work is situated in relation to the legacy of photogrammetric modelling of geological landscapes where Edouard Deville's large-scale experiments 'with dry plate cameras within the Rocky Mountains beginning in 1887' (Mattison 2008: 949) is but one of many significant reference points for the surveys and models that are contextually necessary to see where post-lenticular landscapes fit in: to measure and to survey.

For ScanLAB, and somewhat in the spirit of landscape surveys, the cameraless 3D scanning of the national park becomes a test case for the still rather new form of imaging that fits into the lineage of photography. But like the example of the WiFi imaging of people we began with, laser scanning also represents a different set of concerns that move the focus from apparatus of seeing to the forms of sensors, processing and infrastructure in which 'seeing' (even without lenticular mediation) is produced. Large-scale landscapes, as well as urban dynamics, become

Figure 10.2 (previous pages) *Equirectangular Landscapes 05: Nevada Falls (After Muybridge)*, based on 3D scan data captured in Yosemite National Park in 2016. Source: ScanLAB Projects, used with permission.

the objects of this form of modelling that emerges from history of landscapes and architecture and becomes integrated into contemporary contexts of AI as we will see later. As ScanLAB articulate the use of laser scanning, this shifts the focus from camera to scanning, but it also returns to 'Muybridge's original endeavour to capture the scenes in three dimensions as stereograms'[3] (Figure 10.3).

Over a period of two weeks, ScanLAB traversed the valley with a team of eight to scan the landscapes, and converging on the 4 x 4 car that they'd turned into a digital base camp to process images, the stereogrammatic view was updated in multiple ways with a particular awareness of the infrastructure required of imaging: 'The logistics of taking such high tech equipment into a comparatively inaccessible environment formed a major part of the re-enactment, mirroring the epic nature of the early pioneer photographers' (ScanLAB n.d.). This underlines that these technologies of imaging are

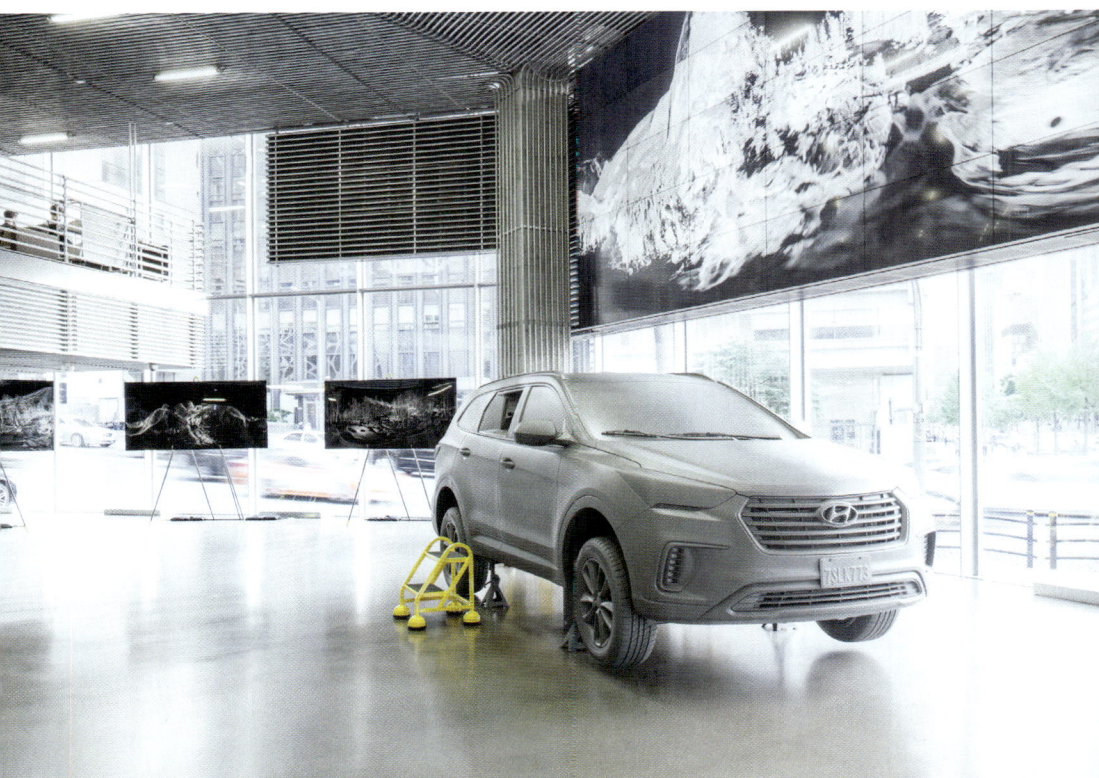

Figure 10.3 *Post-lenticular Landscapes*. Installation view at Hyundai ARTLAB, Seoul 2018, originally commissioned by LACMA. On view are *Urban Diorama* (holographic vehicle), 2016, *Post-lenticular Landscapes* (4k animation), 2017, *Equirectangular Landscapes 01–06* (prints on aluminium), 2018. Source: ScanLAB Projects, used with permission.

fundamentally about logistics and infrastructure – a point that becomes clear in the context of lidar applications of contemporary urbanism and autonomous cars. However, it also points out that traditional genres of imaging and photography, aesthetics and cultural history are entangled through the many and speculative uses of new technologies. In such experiments of ScanLAB, photographic and rhetorical tropes such as landscapes and Romanticism, as Geoff Manaugh writes (2015), shift gear and site:

> If the conceptual premise of the Romantic Movement can somewhat hastily be described as the experience and documentation of extreme landscapes – as an art of remote mountain peaks, abyssal river valleys and vast tracts of uninhabited land – then ScanLAB is suggesting that a new kind of Romanticism is emerging through the sensing packages of autonomous machines.

We can also read ScanLAB's *Post-lenticular Landscapes* in direct relation to their project the *Dream Life of Driverless Cars*,[4] where lidar takes a central role as the standard technology of imaging, processing and transmitting movement in movement. The intensity of imaging practices that relate to autonomous cars is due to their (by necessity) capacity to be able to process *in-situ* a wealth of incoming data in relation to their environment while simultaneously transmitting this data in real time with the wider network in which they are connected. In this sense autonomous cars are both an issue of data transmission and also reserve a place for images as part of this data circulation and movement navigation.

> As the scanner moves through the city, slowing for speed bumps and stopping in traffic, the city map created warps and extends depending on the speed at which we move. Stuck in traffic a Routemaster bus becomes an elongated, narrow corridor, broken only by the shadow of a passing cyclist. Turning the corner into Parliament Square duplicates Big Ben as we observe the tower for a second time.[5]

The *Dream Life of Driverless Cars* offers a ghostly apparition of the scanned city, shifting through street scenes without humans or other organic life, passing by semi-transparent buildings with their collective architectural layers. The scanner moves through the city, a second-order record of movement as it observes, tracks and facilitates the vehicle among the multiple other moving and unmoving parts of the city. Lidar, beaming its pulsing, millions of light bursts per second across urban surfaces, acts like the laser version of flash photography and the probe light, each of which had a revelatory impact on the history of photography: artificial light that enables seeing by a pulse quicker than the human eye. The invention of flash in the mid-nineteenth century introduced an artificial form of light that escapes even the blink of an eye, producing a register of light essential to photography. While it allows seeing, the flash itself remains beyond the register of the eye's reaction (Canales 2011). However, the autonomous car's lidar system is not the flash of photojournalism, but one of laser-based scanning operating on a different frequency spectrum. These laser images are at the centre of ScanLAB's work and include both the modern version of Edward Muybridge's Yosemite images and the new photoscapes of cities as large-scale systems, where seeing is not limited to the humanly visible.

Geoff Manaugh (2015) proposes that ScanLAB's *Dream Life of Driverless Cars* is a form of the transformation of cityscapes *and* visuality, images *and* data, movement *and* seeing movement, echoing some of the concerns that Virilio tracked even earlier as a central part of the transformation of visual culture since the beginning of modern technical images (Figure 10.4). Manaugh outlines the case of autonomous cars as a way to understand the visual change of environments as follows: the use of 3D scanning lidar sensors in autonomous cars relates to a particular navigational way of mapping the city not merely as one image but as an ecology of machine-flickering that captures 'extremely detailed, millimeter-scale measurements of the surrounding environment, far more accurate than anything achievable by the human eye' (Manaugh 2015). Such large-scale images are premised on a particular ecology of time when millions of light bursts per second echoed back their pulsations at great speeds. In many ways, this is the contemporary version of the Doppler effect, named after Christian Doppler's mid-nineteenth-century investigations, insofar as it includes some early ideas about the echo-pulse principle of measuring objects and their movement by way of light. Doppler's influential research, which can be quoted in relation to multiple engineering and research innovations that characterise media of the twentieth century, was focused on planetary movements and measuring light. According to Doppler, colour being dependent on the frequency of light led to the observation that objects in movement emit a different frequency in relation to each other. This implied that a transmitted pulse signal returning from a measured source can communicate the location of said object based on its frequency, leading to all sorts of implications in navigation, observation, location and, of course, frequency. So, while the 1842 paper *Über das farbige Licht der Doppelsterne und einiger anderer Gestirne des Himmels* (Doppler 1992) was indeed about the extra-planetary scale of the measurement of light and movement, it also began to speak to measurements at other scales too: the world is measurable as a function of signals and their echoes, of pulses and their reverberations.

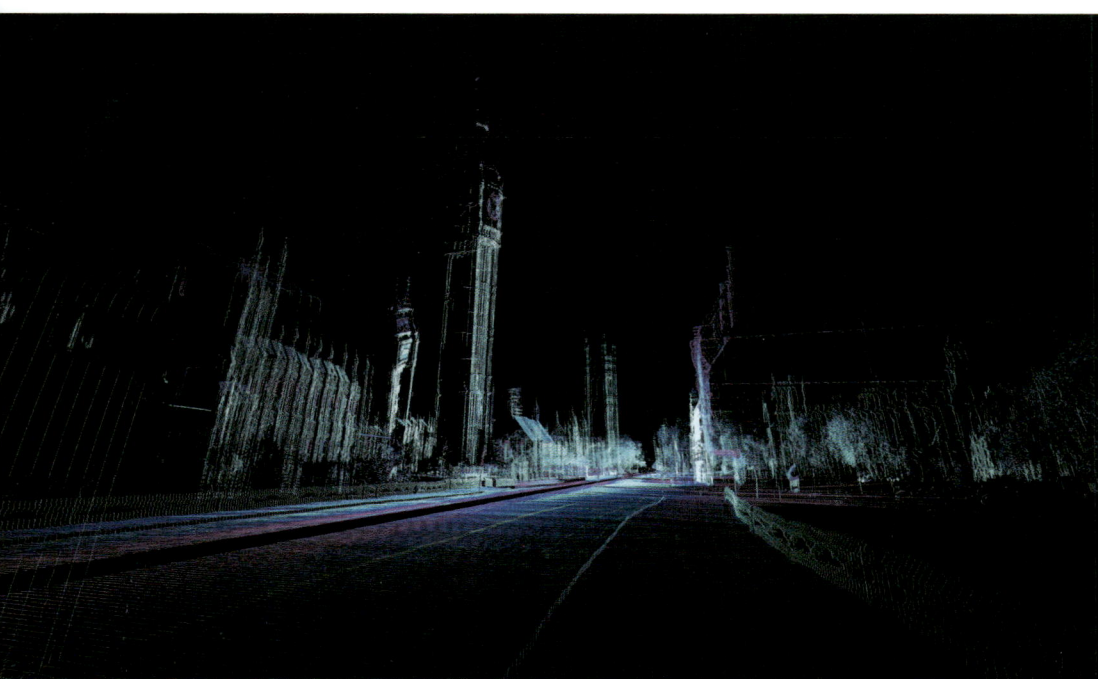

Figure 10.4 *Dream Life of Driverless Cars*, originally produced for the *New York Times*, 2015. Source: ScanLAB Projects, used with permission.

Twentieth-century variations of this include the array of military technologies that occupy this sphere of observation—seeing without eyes, synaesthesia where sound turns into image (radar), and echo pulse signal into visual perception. Indeed, as Ryan Bishop and John Phillips (2010: 101) write, 'radar technology allows soundwaves to see', which echoes as a trait through modernist aesthetics and the military-technological infrastructure that reorganised forms of seeing and perception, and visibility and invisibility, across the twentieth century. In many ways, the navigational images of autonomous cars and the pulsing landscapes recorded through the laser scanning of lidar are part of this story.

However, the nature of the scanned lidar image that emerges is not of the usual scale because of the millions of tiny images, or light bursts, that form the technical ontology of this sort of imaging practice: it also relates to the complexity of the technological laser scan records both as a movement across the city and as a sensitive way of dealing with light as a living entity that records the complexity of the multiple surfaces of the city, itself as an image, a trajectory of light. Besides the apparent technological accuracy, these are also systems of imaging that are particularly vulnerable to over-seeing, where all sorts of things like 'complex architectural forms, reflective surfaces, unpredictable weather and temporary construction sites' (Manaugh 2015) can throw sensors off, and lead them to perceive the cityscape in surprising, accidental ways. But this reflective reality, the over-seeing of light, also hints at what Manaugh aptly describes as 'a parallel landscape seen only by machine-sensing technology in which objects and signs invisible to human beings nevertheless have real effects in the operation of the city' (Manaugh 2015).

Such accidents of over-seeing can cascade and be multiplied, and they can be taken as guidelines for investigations into contemporary visual, photographic, scanning technologies. In other words, as glitches, they become ways to understand the functions of this form of imagining. Indeed, ScanLAB's *Dream Life of Driverless Cars* (Figure 10.5) was not meant as a technical demonstration of the accuracy of lidar, but rather, as an experimental framework for a scanning device that also records its own conditions of existence:

> Their goal, Shaw said, is to explore 'the peripheral vision of driverless vehicles,' or what he calls 'the sideline stuff,' the overlooked edges of the city that autonomous cars and their unblinking scanners will 'perpetually, accidentally see.' By deliberately disabling certain aspects of their scanner's sensors, ScanLAB discovered that they could tweak the equipment into revealing its overlooked artistic potential. While a self-driving car would normally use corrective algorithms to account for things like long periods stuck in traffic, Trossell and Shaw instead let those flaws accumulate. Moments of inadvertent information density become part of the resulting aesthetic. (Manaugh 2015)

A range of methodological implications emerge: on the one hand, contemporary uses of lidar as it (and other alternative forms of imagining whether WiFi, radar, or other) rearticulates its relation to lenticular histories of photography, and, on the other hand, the alternative genealogies of imaging that are but one way to explore lidar as the echo and the pulse of the city, all the way from Doppler's research into spectra of light to the forms of flash and photography that define the technological configurations of images in the age of photography. These scans, to echo a theme articulated by Benjamin Bratton (2017), are part of the discourse of the smart city and its multiple skins.

Large-scale Computable Scans

From the perspective articulated above, we can assert the following claim: while these contemporary images are part of the history of scientific photography, they also take a particular place in contemporary computational cityscapes as scans, as infrastructure, and as interfacial skins

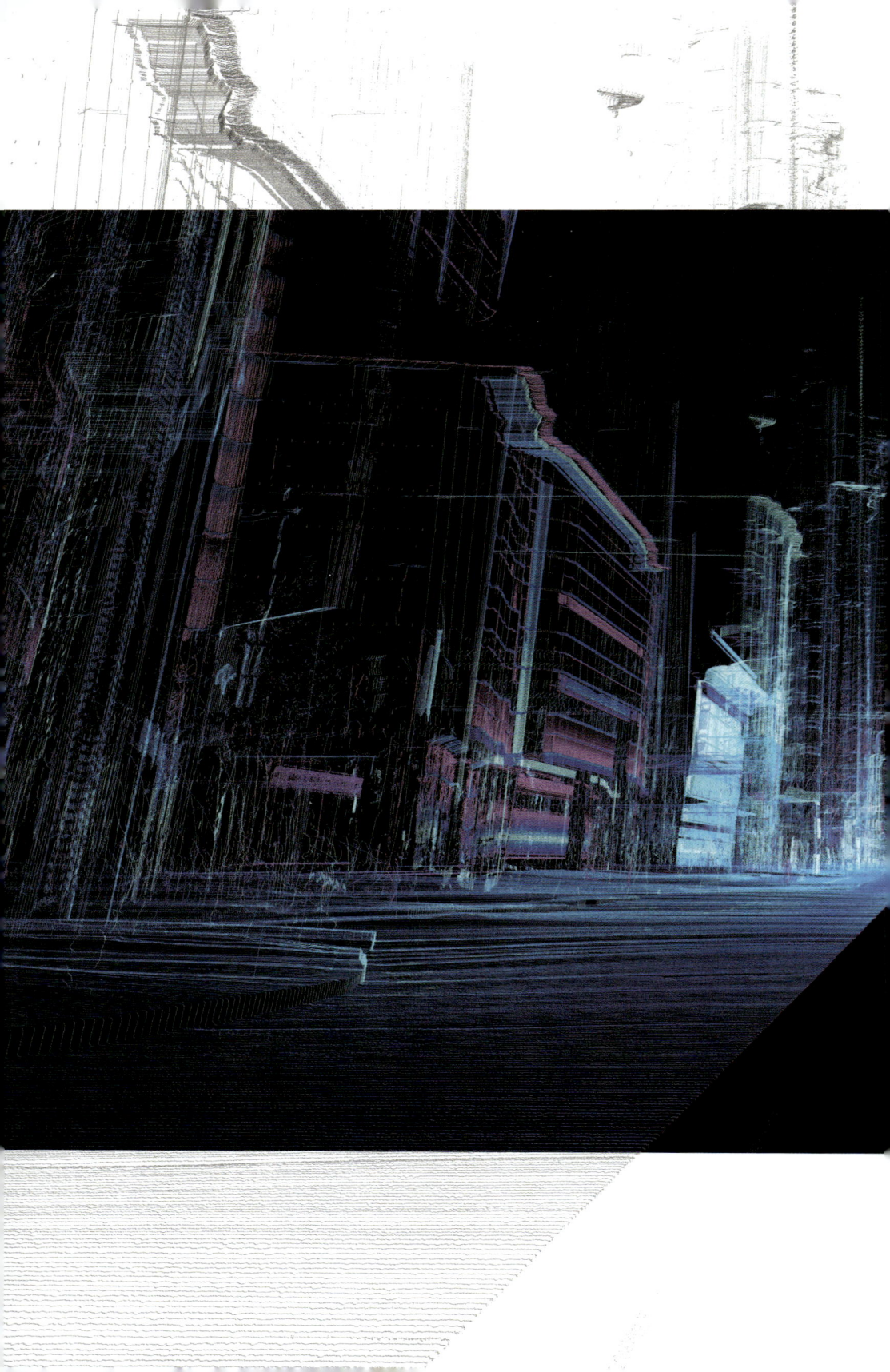

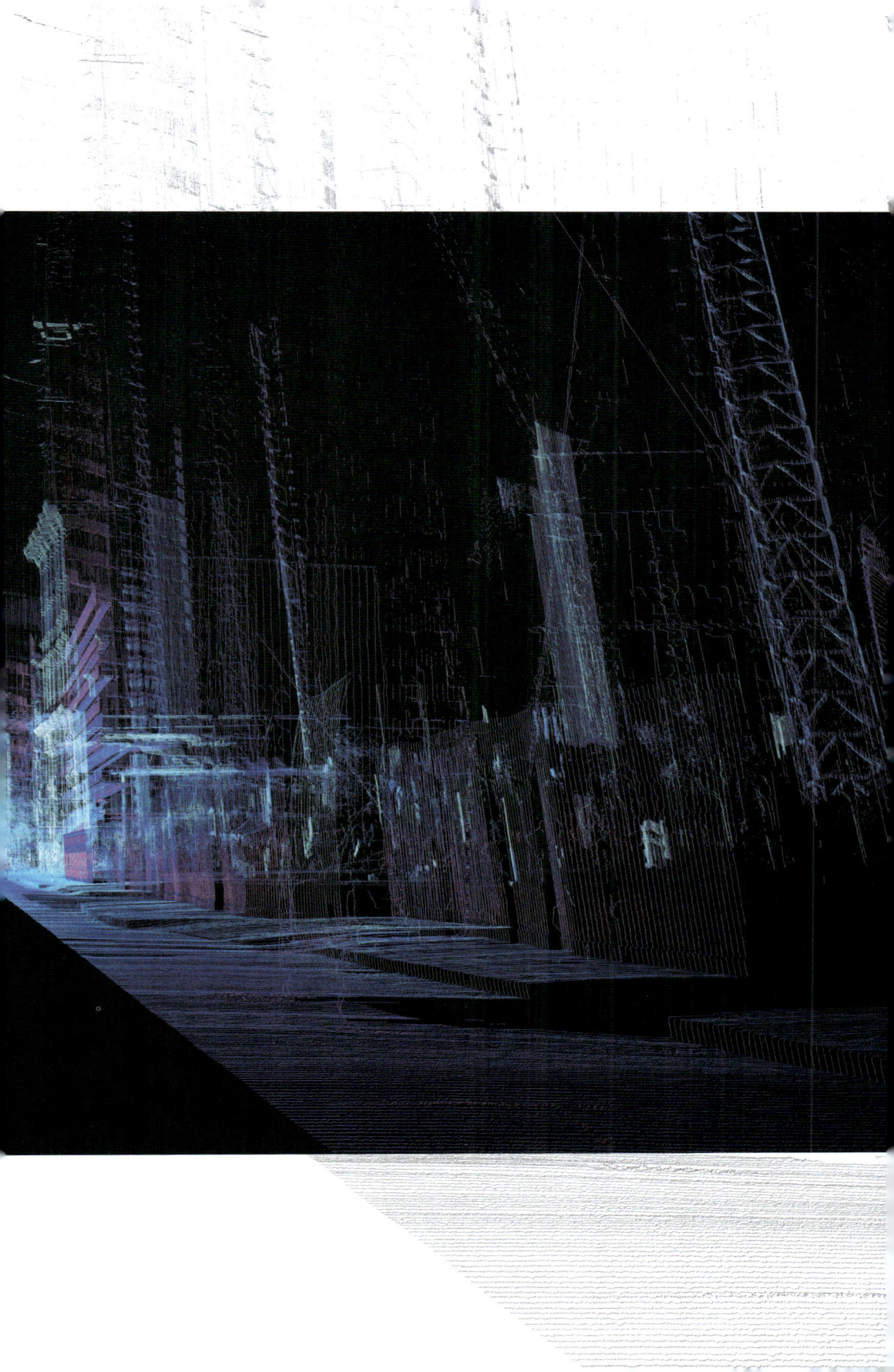

(Bratton 2017). Consequently, they are folded into multiple operations as components in large-scale systems. In this sense, these images continue the legacy of photogrammetry and plotting as computational solutions to problems of measurement and analytics[6] – although, in the contemporary situation, the extent and scale of computation are of a completely different order and the processing of images becomes automated as part of these operative chains. This is amplified with the automation of events from image sensors as part of the distributed network of computing (of which the mobile car unit is only one part) that tries to keep up with the already existing complexity of the moving landscape. As Geoff Manaugh writes (2015), '[h]umans are not the only things now sensing and experiencing the modern landscape – that something else is here, with an altogether different, and fundamentally inhuman, perspective on the built environment.' This is precisely where we shift our question from 'what does the computer see' to 'what does the sensor and the scan *do* in the context of sensing and movement'.

As Florian Sprenger (2019) demonstrates, lidar and related sensorial systems sit as part of the history of environmentally sensitive robotics, which, we should remind ourselves, are now also part of large-scale systems. Adaptive systems that are continually producing information about their environment have gradually become the solution to problems of manoeuvring and movement in robotics. From the experimental robotic systems of the 1950s to the more recent robotics turn in the 1980s, these forms of autonomous systems became conceptually and technologically dependent on sensing: instead of trying to upload a map of the environment into the autonomous system, the goal is now to create multiple layers of perception and sensing that situate the system in its location. As Sprenger (2019) also argues, autonomous systems and their forms of scan-based sensing, including lidar, can be seen as special cases of robotics that were premised on being context aware and reliant on adaptation to environmental conditions. For us, this also helps to address the argument about contemporary forms of sensing and sensors as mobile systems. Indeed, as mentioned earlier, the case for understanding these imaging systems as inherently about navigation becomes clear.[7]

Following this navigational focus, we can also claim that these images are instrumental if we follow Allan Sekula's use of the term: these sorts of images operate in automated systems and as part of large-scale infrastructural technologies, where such images include those used in aerial imaging, military systems, automated navigation or robotic object

Figure 10.5 (previous page) *Dream Life of Driverless Cars*, originally produced for the *New York Times*, 2015. Source: ScanLAB Projects, used with permission.

recognition guided movement (an example being the factory assembly reliance on automatism and action) (Keenan 2014). In our case, the laser-scanned images and landscape are directly related to the instrumental role these systems play in coordinating (in) a city, its multiple levels of agents and events, and in other contexts, other forms of navigation in complex ecologies. Consider Benjamin Bratton's (2017) summary about the tight coupling of sensors, images and the infrastructure of autonomous cars:

> . . . driverless cars are emblematic of big heavy machines sensing/learning in the streets. Their proprioceptive sensors include wheel speed sensors, altimeters, gyroscopes, tachymeters, touch sensors, while their exteroceptive sensors include multiple visual light cameras, lidar range finding, short- and long-range RADAR, ultrasonic sensors on the wheels, global positioning satellite systems/geolocation aerials, etc. Several systems overlap between sensing and interpretation, such as road sign and feature detection and interpretation algorithms, model maps of upcoming roads, and inter-car interaction behavior algorithms.

It becomes difficult to detach the imaging systems from their role in the overlapping systems in which they are operational. Even if for the sake of genealogical arguments (like those briefly rehearsed in this chapter) some of their histories are related to an expanded, transformed notion of photography, they become emphasised as connective images. In other words, the urban images produced are more akin to the skins and interfaces (Bratton 2017) that regularly guide and process, predict and instruct. The computational – in its multiple manifestations and as multiple platforms across the city and its devices – becomes a key reference point for images that are the operational elements of an infrastructure.

Hence, in the midst of the car and its sensorial technologies, we have to look beyond the image – or even the sensor – as a stand-alone unit, and instead understand that the image is, at best, an interface (Bratton 2015: 220–6; Andersen and Pold 2018) that allows a kind of access to other scales of infrastructural action that mobilise multiple kinds of knowledge of large-scale, dynamic systems including maps, information systems, AI, sensors, data-transfer, and so on. Environmental perception and localisation in relation to external data and maps become a form of synchronisation that adds to the work of actual sensing that can be seen as one crystallisation of what images have become in the complex and distributed large-scale autonomous systems of the twenty-first century.

This infrastructure can be understood as an operational bundle of technologies that is also part of a political economy of innovation that aims to reformat the city according to its ideals of the 'city as computer'. As Shannon Mattern (2017) argues, this trope assumes – and rhetorically

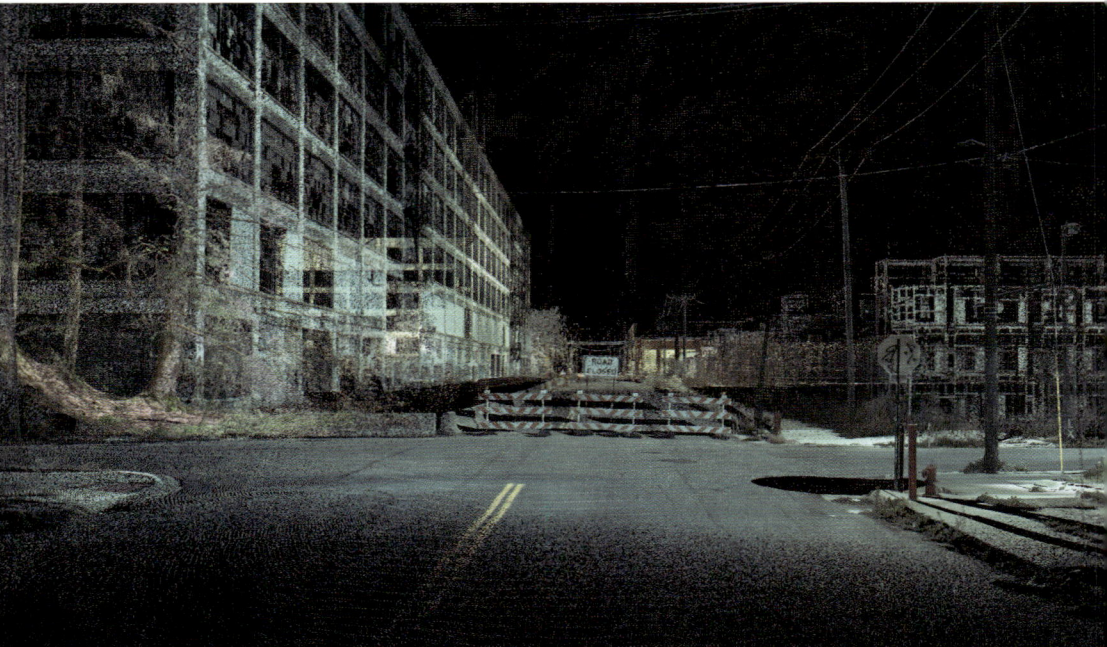

Figure 10.6 Still for *Where the City Can't See*, directed by Liam Young, written by Tim Maughan, 2016.

produces – a frictionless programmability of the city as its modus operandi and aim, producing a particular corporate vision of what various interlinking parts of movement and sensing can add up to. As Mattern (2017) summarises, one can also track this infrastructure through its corporate financial attachments that mobilise their own views of operative ontology through the employment of different forms of data feeds, maps, location systems, and other variations on the theme of 'seeing' and 'imagining': digital data platforms connected to technologies of self-driving cars, to multiple scales of navigational infrastructure, to urban technologies (for example, Sidewalk Labs), and to various forms of maps, robotics, engineering and expertise that form the links between technological discourse and corporate hype (Figure 10.6).

We move from what the computer sees, and what the sensor and scan do, to focus on those complex ecologies in which 'seeing' is embedded in technological, corporate and aesthetic systems and discourses. The question as to what sort of perception or agency an autonomous system exercises is replaced with questions that underline the distributed complexity of such systems in which images function, and moves to survey speculative design in its attempts to offer glimpses of the broader landscapes and cityscapes in which those systems function.

The echo light pulse systems of laser scanning become one emblematic aesthetic face for the transition to complex systems which operate within the genealogies of photography and also in the context of the contemporary corporate mapping of what the city is transforming into. While ScanLAB's work turns towards technological and aesthetic questions, a similar short film operates in the imaginary political near future of laser scanning and corporate surveillance. Liam Young's audiovisual work, *Where the City Can't See* (2016), written by Tim Maughan, relates to the same bundle of issues that unfold when considering these images as interfaces. Young's speculative design version of these visible/invisible interfaces is introduced as 'the first fiction film shot entirely through laser scanning technology' and is 'set in the Chinese owned and controlled Detroit Economic Zone (DEZ), in a not-too-distant future where Google maps, urban management systems and CCTV surveillance are not only mapping our cities, but ruling them'.[8] Speculative fiction about automated governance of cityscapes becomes a way to continue the discourse about scanning, but with a particular focus on urban politics. Or, in other words, scanning becomes a form of control, emphasising how this survey of a landscape and this scan of a city is part of the reordering and rethinking of what images do, positioned somewhere between the traditional visual image and their role as digital measures of relations, movement, events and management of large-scale dynamic entities. Young's film also engages with what could be coined as post-lenticular subcultures:

> Exploring the subcultures that could emerge from these new technologies, the film follows a collection of young factory workers across a single night, as they drift through the smart city in a driverless taxi, searching for a place they know exists, but that the map doesn't show. They are part of an underground community that work on the production lines by day, by night adorn themselves in machine vision camouflage and the tribal masks of anti-facial recognition, enacting their escapist fantasies in the hidden spaces of the city. They hack the city and journey through a network of stealth buildings, ruinous landscapes, ghost architectures, anomalies, glitches and sprites, searching for the wilds beyond the machines.[9]

In some ways similar to ScanLAB's investigation of laser scanning as a technology that records its own glitches, the speculative fiction of Young's film works with corresponding themes. In the glitching of a cityscape, the WiFi sees alongside other sampling rates that form the perceived quality of the city. The city is itself a connected entity of sensing and sensors, but what stands out is the transversal interconnection of agencies. The images are not merely there as representational, but as agential entities that enable and hinder perception as they hide and they seek as operational entities of machine vision. Paradoxically, to understand the transformation of visuality and the photographic, one needs to look away from the representational quality of images and towards their infrastructural coupling with large-scale systems of sensing and computation. The city itself is a large-scale analytical and synthetic, even synthesising, unit (cf. Bratton 2015) that presents a particular case for ecologies of images that are embedded in multiple sites, functions, vehicles and passages to do a multitude of things. In other words, a discussion of nonhuman photography is complemented with an infrastructural angle that links images to the conditions of their existence outside of their own frame of visibility. Logistics would be one word for this, thus also implying connections to issues of labour, technology, and political economy of contemporary financially driven circulation of data and goods. Any discussion of the digital that obsesses with the isolated ontology of representation based on the technical qualities of the image is somewhat misguided – at least when it comes to the attempt to understand what images have transformed into. It is only when situated and considered in terms of their infrastructure that one starts to understand the functions of invisible images and photography off the scale.

Environmental Media of Pulse and Light

The echo pulse of light bounces across city surfaces, registered by machines that in the very act of registration also register their own conditions of existence; their own algorithmic hiccups and glitches, affordances and limitations, all part of their machine ways of seeing that are algorithmic as well as infrastructural (Cox 2016). Looking at machine vision as an ensemble of applications such as embedded sensors in automobiles, drones, security and, for example, supply chain management industries becomes a way to begin to see the wider distributed link of the image: the image is itself a measurement of environmental relations and, as such, a non-representational part of data capture that acts within the large-scale systems. Hence, to see the environment through a visual modelling of WiFi marks a larger shift in what is considered the visible spectrum and in what can be considered as part of the broader environment of visibility that does not cater to the usual understanding of images.

This topic of what is visible extends to a range of post-lenticular forms of imaging that in some cases refer back to histories of photography – whether photogrammetry or examples such as Muybridge's Yosemite photographic surveys – but also shift gear in how these images function as scans, as data, and as components in a larger infrastructural set that defines the computational city (both as corporate rhetoric and as technological programming of what connects where in the platform of sensing, movement, navigation, mapping and control). From the scanned city that pulses with millions of light beats that model the real-time movement of and within the landscape, we come to a realisation about the function of autonomous vehicles as not only cars but also as (data) platforms. In our case, we consider the (lidar) image itself as merely one entry point into a large-scale system, nested within a set of relations that are there to mobilise the image as part of an array of functional uses: identification or object-detection; prediction; big data analysis; among others. To be accurate, one should say that the particular terminology of 'image' here becomes somewhat inaccurate insofar as we are dealing with different channels of registering the world.

The examples of work that speculate what the computer sees should extend to situations in which seeing is seen as part of an infrastructural system of operations, including navigation. In terms of autonomous vehicles, for example, this relates to data pooling from the camera, light detection, lidar, radar, ultrasonic sensor and vehicle motion data feeds; furthermore, this data pool of combined sources – that may or may not be images – is not only for on-site processing but for a variety of other scales of uses, such as simulation and modelling (Meyer 2018). As a network platform, this system becomes part of the flows but also the design and engineering problems of storage and transmission, including how to transmit in real time such a massive amount of data that consists of multiple moving entities in an environment that itself is dynamic on multiple scales, including the reflective surfaces of the city registered by laser scanning. But here is the proposition that emerges: it is necessary to discuss the image – including the broader category of the photographic – as part of a bundle of other forms of measure and infrastructure where forms of imaging are actioned; the image becomes entangled, even conflated, with its own sensors which, in turn, act as the necessary prism through which the image and the photographic too can be seen anew.

In other words, I argue that earlier photographic discourse about the instrumental image must be updated to include the infrastructural image: although these are not necessarily images that represent or depict infrastructure, their mode of existence as environmental media (Hansen 2015; Gabrys 2016; Hörl 2018; Sprenger 2019) is premised on what they action in particular situations. It is in this vein that I am interested in the aesthetic of the infrastructural that does not merely depict or represent but *operates* in that broad category of image-data-environment.

This chapter has offered some potential ways to respond to this question, especially in the context of lidar and its briefly outlined genealogical contexts (though this can be extended into various levels of further investigation). This imagining infrastructural image deals with photography off the scale as it deals with large-scale systems, remote sensing, automated systems and the complex situations of dynamic data wherein the image functions. From the artistic works of ScanLAB to Liam Young and others, there is a common line that runs through these various practices that track images that track, that observe images that observe, and that try to gather a sense of how images make sense outside the scope of standardised human vision. It is this lineage that speaks to post-human photography (Zylinska 2017) and its multiple variations across the non-visible spectrum of pulse and light.

Notes

1. This was also one theme that emerged in the context of the event Art after Culture: Navigation Beyond Vision, 5–6 April 2019. The event was partly a response to Harun Farocki's work on navigation and computer images, especially in his *Parallelen* series.
2. See the project website for more fulsome descriptions at: <https://bengrosser.com/projects/computers-watching-movies>
3. Quotes from ScanLAB Projects can be found on their website at: <https://ScanLABprojects.co.uk/work/post-lenticular-landscapes>
4. A short film produced for the *New York Times*, an online version of the project and the video can be viewed at: <https://ScanLABprojects.co.uk/work/dreamlife-of-driverless-cars>
5. Directly quoted from the project page at: <https://ScanLABprojects.co.uk/work/dreamlife-of-driverless-cars>
6. As Otto von Gruber (1932: 276) put it in the 1930s, '[t]he problem of automatic plotting instruments concerns the representation on a map of an object shown on photograms, without the need for carrying out computations point by point or for graphical constructions.'
7. On the navigational image, see Mende 2017.
8. Quoted from the Abandon Normal Devices festival website (2016), at: <https://www.andfestival.org.uk/city-cant-see> . *Where the City Can't See* was commissioned by Abandon Normal Devices, St Helens Heart of Glass and University of Salford Art Collection.
9. A trailer of the film is available at <https://vimeo.com/188626212>

References

Andersen, Christian Ulrik, and Søren Bro Pold (2018), *The Metainterface: The Art of Platforms, Cities, and Clouds*. Cambridge, MA: The MIT Press.

Anderson, Steve F. (2017), *Technologies of Vision: The War Between Data and Images*. Cambridge, MA: The MIT Press.

Apprich, Clemens, Wendy Hui Kyong Chun, Florian Cramer and Hito Steyerl (2018), *Pattern Discrimination*. Luneburg: Meson Press.

Bishop, Ryan, and John Phillips (2010), *Modernist Avant-Garde Aesthetics and Contemporary Military Technology: Technicities of Perception*. Edinburgh: Edinburgh University Press.
Bratton, Benjamin H. (2015), *The Stack: On Software and Sovereignty*. Cambridge, MA: The MIT Press.
Bratton, Benjamin H. (2017), 'The City Wears Us: Notes on the Scope of Distributed Sensing and Sensation', *Glass Bead*, Site 1, 2017. Available at: <http://www.glass-bead.org-article-city-wears-us-notes-scope-distributed-sensing-sensation-?lang=enview> (last accessed 11 July 2020).
Bridle, James (2019), A Talk at the Navigation Beyond Vision conference, Berlin, HKW, 5 April 2019.
Canales, Jimena (2011), 'Flash Force: A Visual History of Might, Right, and Light', in Elena Agudio and Ivana Franke (eds), *Seeing with Eyes Closed*. Berlin: Association of Neuroesthetics, 34–41
Canales, Jimena (2014), 'Einstein's Discourse Networks', *Zeitschrift für Medien- und Kulturforschung*, 5(1): 11–39.
Carpo, Mario (2017), *The Second Digital Turn: Design Beyond Intelligence*. Cambridge, MA: The MIT Press.
Cox, Geoffrey (2016), 'Ways of Machine Seeing', Unthinking Photography, November 2016. Available at: <https://unthinking.photography-articles-ways-of-machine-seeing> (last accessed 11 July 2020).
Doppler, Christian [1842] (1992), 'Über das farbige Licht der Doppelsterne und einiger anderer Gestirne des Himmels', facsimile reproduced with a translation in Alec Eden, *The Search for Christian Doppler*. Vienna: Springer Verlag.
Ernst, Wolfgang (2016), *Chronopoetics: The Temporal Being and Operativity of Technological Media*, Anthony Enns (trans.). London: Rowman & Littlefield.
Gabrys, Jennifer (2016), *Program Earth: Environmental Sensing Technology and the Making of a Computational Planet*. Minneapolis: University of Minnesota Press.
Hansen, Mark (2015), *Feed Forward: On the Future of Twenty-First Century Media*. Chicago: The University of Chicago Press.
Hörl, Erich (2018), 'The Environmentalitarian Situation: Reflections on the Becoming-Environmental of Thinking, Power, and Capital', *Cultural Politics*, 14(2): 153–73.
Keenan, Thomas, (2014) 'Counter-forensics and Photography', *Grey Room*, 55: 58–77.
Mackenzie, Adrian (2010), *Wirelessness: Radical Empiricism in Network Cultures*. Cambridge, MA: The MIT Press.
Manaugh, Geoff (2015), 'The Dream Life of Driverless Cars', *New York Times*, 11 November 2015. Available at: <https://www.nytimes.com-2015-11-15-magazine-the-dream-life-of-driverless-cars.html> (last accessed 11 July 2020).

Mattern, Shannon (2017), 'A City Is Not a Computer', *Places*, February 2017. Available at: <https://placesjournal.org-article-a-city-is-not-a-computer> (last accessed 11 July 2020).

Mattison, David (2008), 'Mountain Photography', in John Hannavy (ed.), *Encyclopedia of Nineteenth Century Photography*, Vol. 1. London and New York: Routledge, pp. 947–50.

Mende, Doreen (2017), 'The Navigation Principle: Slow Image', e-flux lectures, November 2017. Available at: <https://www.e-flux.com-video-176025-e-flux-lectures-doreen-mende-the-navigation-principle-slow-image> (last accessed 11 July 2020).

Meyer, David (2018), 'How Cloud Computing Contributes to Autonomous Driving – A Thought Experiment'. Blog post, July 11, 2018. Available at: <https://mse238blog.stanford.edu-2018-07-davidmyr-how-cloud-computing-contributes-to-autonomous-driving-a-thought-experiment> (last accessed 11 July 2020).

Nagel, Thomas (1974), 'What Is It Like to Be a Bat?', *The Philosophical Review*, 83(4): 435–50.

Paglen, Trevor (2016), 'Invisible Images (Your Pictures Are Looking at You)', *The New Inquiry*, 8 December 2016. Available at: <https://thenewinquiry.com-invisible-images-your-pictures-are-looking-at-you> (last accessed 11 July 2020).

ScanLAB (n.d.), 'Post-lenticular Landscapes'. Available at: <https://scanlabprojects.co.uk-work-post-lenticular-landscapes> (last accessed 11 July 2020)

Siegert, Bernhard (2017), 'Öffnen, Schließen, Zerstreuen, Verdichten. Die operative Ontologien der Kulturtechnik', *Zeitschrift für Medien- und Kulturforschung* 8(2): 95–113.

Silverman, Kaja (1993), 'What is a Camera, or: History in the Field of Vision', *Discourse*, 15(3): 3–56.

Sprenger, Florian (2019), *Epistemologien des Umgebens. Zur Geschichte, Ökologie und Biopolitik künstlicher environments*. Transcript: Bielefeld.

Synge, Edward Hutchinson (1930), 'XCI: A Method of Investigating The Higher Atmosphere' *The London, Edinburgh, and Dublin Philosophical Magazine and Journal of Science*, Series 7, 9(60): 1014–20.

Wang, Fei, Sanping Zhou, Stanislav Panev, Jinsong Han and Dong Huang (2019), 'Person-in-WiFi: Fine-grained Person Perception using WiFi', arXiv:1904.00276 [cs.CV]. Available at: <https://arxiv.org-abs-1904.00276> (last accessed 11 July 2020).

Virilio, Paul (1994), *The Vision Machine*, Julie Rose (trans.). Bloomington: Indiana University Press.

Von Gruber, Otto (1932), *Photogrammetry: Collected Lectures and Essays*. London: Chapman & Hall Limited.

Zylinska, Joanna (2017), *Nonhuman Photography*. Cambridge, MA: The MIT Press.

11 Planetary Diagrams: Towards an Autographic Theory of Climate Emergency

Lukáš Likavčan and Paul Heinicker

Introduction: The Earth Revealing Itself

ON A PEDESTAL in Musée d'Orsay in Paris stands a sculpture by Louis-Ernest Barrias called *Nature Unveiling Herself Before Science* (1899). It depicts a heavily gendered imagination of nature, personified by a young woman who reveals her breasts to the male gaze of Western science. Seduced by their instruments, she is imagined to be ready to reveal her secrets to those who approach her. Since the end of the nineteenth century, this trope of nature unveiling itself has mutated many times. Its most recent instantiation is the climate crisis; a situation when the planet turns into a massive diagram of anthropogenic destruction, revealing itself in hurricanes, heatwaves, droughts, sea level rises, loss of wildlife or the acidification of the oceans. Defying patriarchal reveries of the nineteenth century, the Earth responds to our celebrated technologies of modernity and progress in a rather destructive manner.

An original and contemporary variation on this trope is Susan Schuppli's *Nature Represents Itself* (2018), a piece that investigates aesthetic and jurisdictional aspects of BP's Deepwater Horizon oil spill of 2020 in the Gulf of Mexico. This video, commissioned by the SculptureCenter in New York, confronts us with a massive, literal oil painting: streams of petroleum diagram the ecological disaster on the surface of the water (Schuppli 2019a), while underwater cameras live-streaming the oil bubbling up from corrupted pipes provide us with a glimpse of the Anthropocene in action. In this chapter, we wonder whether we can read climate crisis in a similar vein, as a diagram of destruction that can be captured by the very apparatus that contributes to the emergence of climate emergency as a stand-alone 'epistemic object': the human-made apparatus of sensing and modelling the Earth, a 'knowledge infrastructure' called 'a vast machine' by Paul Edwards (2010).

Our use of the notion of diagram requires additional explanation. In political philosophy, 'diagram' happens to have a prescriptive connotation, as an organising, disciplining tool (see Bratton 2006; Pasquinelli 2009). In data visualisation scholarship, diagrams are usually defined as schematic visualisations of relations or processes. However, our notion of a diagram is broader, and it differs from its usual connotations in order to grasp a labour of 'diagramming' as a procedure when some object or process reveals itself. Here, 'diagram', 'diagramming' or 'diagrammatisation' ceases to maintain its standard representational character and, instead, tends towards an instrumental dimension of its meaning, but not in the sense of a political tool. In our use, 'diagram' retains its prescriptive character only to a certain degree, that is, to such an extent that 'diagram' is a trace of the process itself: it retains some interpretative authority, and it is taken as a product of the phenomenon at its face value. To understand, then, how we can interpret climate change as a diagrammatic process, we need to update our theory of visualisation to give us a different perspective on what can count as a visualisation of human-altered planetary dynamics.

Today, it has become customary for us to encounter representations of the planet – satellite photographs, videos and time-lapses, live streams from the International Space Station or orbital spacewalks, and so on. Interestingly, they resemble what Harun Farocki (2015: 659) described as phantom shots: '. . . film recordings taken from a position that a human cannot normally occupy . . . for example, shots from a camera that had been hung under a train,' or photographic images by cameras on military missiles and drones. To call an image 'a phantom shot' simply means that it is produced by – or with the great aid of – nonhuman machinic apparatuses, but still, it remain the result of direct observation of the Earth's surface. Nowadays, this is also the case of global map apps, such as Google, Baidu or Bing Maps.

Similarly, we have become accustomed to computational models and simulations of the planet, which emerged as the primary means of visualisation of climate emergency. While these models and simulations still retain their representational nature – at least to some extent – they also move to the register of operational images, that is, images that 'do not represent an object, but rather are part of an operation' (Farocki 2015: 660). They are operational to the degree to which they are synthetic: human labour is joined and sometimes overwhelmed by the labour of computational algorithms, which is also the case for satellite footage stitched together into a planetary patchwork of Google Earth (Kurgan 2013: 11, 20). These images remain many times invisible to us (Paglen 2016), and they serve as inputs for further algorithmic operations in the computational apparatus of the vast machine. Moreover, they are reconstructed from information on opacity, reflectivity and properties of light emitted by objects below the satellite, broken down to individual wavelengths in colour spectrum, and only then rendered as images that can be seen by us humans.

Yet, this chapter argues, there is a third register of planetary visualisation that is not operational in a standard sense and is by no means representational. We call this register 'autographic', following recent elaborations on the theory of visualisation crafted by Dietmar Offenhuber (2019a, 2019b). This alludes to cases when nature has revealed itself – such as the oil spillage that Schuppli's piece concerns – and serve as localised examples of this register of visualisation. Ultimately, we claim that the planet gains a peculiar autographic feature under the conditions of climate emergency – it becomes an image of the slow violence that cannot be adequately visualised in computational models. These models can yield visualisations of discontiguous processes, but they cannot offer an urgency at scale; an urgency that comes with the planet itself turning into a photographic surface of the integral catastrophe of the Anthropocene.

In this chapter we thus aim to analyse the emergence of autographic visualisations produced by the Earth itself, and processed by a vast machine of sensing and modelling the Earth. First, we introduce the general framework of autographic visualisation theory as sketched by Dietmar Offenhuber (2019a, 2019b), and we compare it to the notion of operational images crafted by Farocki (2015). While doing so, we argue that autographic visualisations are non-representational – which principally distinguishes them from photographs of the Earth – and sensitive towards the socio-material context of the emergence of data – which makes them different from operational images. In the second part of the chapter we explore the infrastructural context of the emergence of autographic visualisations on the global scale, answering the question of whom or what is the primary witness of planetary autographic visualisations. Ultimately, our claim is that autographic visualisations bring our attention back to the ways in which the opaque reality of the planet unveils itself in productive or destructive alignments between its human and nonhuman elements, for better or worse.

'The Language of Phenomena Themselves': Foundations of Autographic Visualisation Theory

Another work by Susan Schuppli can serve as an entry point to our discussion of autographic visualisation – the 2014 video *Can the Sun Lie?* that contemplates the nature of photography and its evidentiary role in court hearings and juridical processes. The question – 'Can the Sun lie?' – was originally posed by 'a US court in 1886 when reflecting upon the probative value of new forms of technical evidence, specifically photographs and film' (Schuppli 2014). The main problem of the dispute was whether a photograph can be a reliable witness, which was contingent on understanding the causality of photographic processes that would rule out any chance that the image might be illusionary or deceptive. As a result of the trial, photographs were judged as reliable evidence, since they are a direct imprint of nature – they are traces of interaction between light and chemical surface, an interaction that belongs under the jurisdiction of exact, natural sciences. Hence, in a way, photographs were considered to be instances of nature revealing itself.

An autographic theory of visualisation uses different examples to arrive at a similar conclusion – around us, there are naturally occurring diagrammatisations of physical, chemical and biological process, or so the argument goes. This conception is developed by contemporary visualisation scholar Dietmar Offenhuber (2019a, 2019b), and it provides a significant rearticulation of his earlier work on indexical visualisation (Offenhuber & Telhan 2015), which follows the Peircean triad of icon – index – symbol and offers a standard interpretation of data visualisation as representation that uses indexical signs instead of symbols (as would be the case in linguistic or para-linguistic representation).

To put it bluntly, 'autographic visualisation is a set of techniques for revealing material phenomena as visible traces and guiding their interpretation' (Offenhuber 2019a: 2). Just as in Schuppli's work on the Deepwater Horizon tragedy, autographic visualisation stands for those cases of diagrammatical processes concerning 'phenomena that reveal themselves' (Offenhuber 2019a: 2), 'present themselves' (Offenhuber 2019a: 7) and 'inscribe themselves' (Offenhuber 2019a: 2). Autographic visualisation is thus not a representation of something absent but a diagrammatic trace of the presence of the phenomenon (Offenhuber 2019a: 2): wind reveals itself in the movement of grass (Offenhuber 2019a: 6); air pollution reveals itself in the filter of a dust mask (Offenhuber 2019a: 5). However, what is crucial here is that autographic visualisations must be 'triggered': they do not happen by themselves, but the context of their emergence must be arranged or designed in a particular way; only then do the phenomena reveal their material information

PLANETARY DIAGRAMS   215

(Offenhuber 2019a: 2). For this reason, a theory of autographic visualisation also accounts for those design operations that might serve as triggering conditions of autographic processes. As an example, take the case of tree rings as material traces of the plant's ageing. In order to gather the information required to know the age of a tree, we need first to cut the plant itself, in this case, the trunk: a paradigmatic case of an autographic design operation. At other times, we have to force the phenomenon to appear in a specific environment, such as gas chambers that allow us to see the otherwise invisible movement of subatomic particles.

Some of the primary references Offenhuber uses in his exposition of autographic visualisation are the chronophotographs by Étienne-Jules Marey, who spoke about his famous footage of running horses, falling cats or flying birds as presenting 'the language of the phenomena themselves' (Marey 1885 cited in Offenhuber 2019a: 2). The crucial trait of these pictures is that they are dealing with processes unfolding over time, which allows the claim that in general, all autographic visualisations are diagrams intimately related to temporality (Offenhuber 2019b). Such is also the case of the seismometer, which translates motions of tectonic plates into a chart, creating a temporal diagram of earthquakes

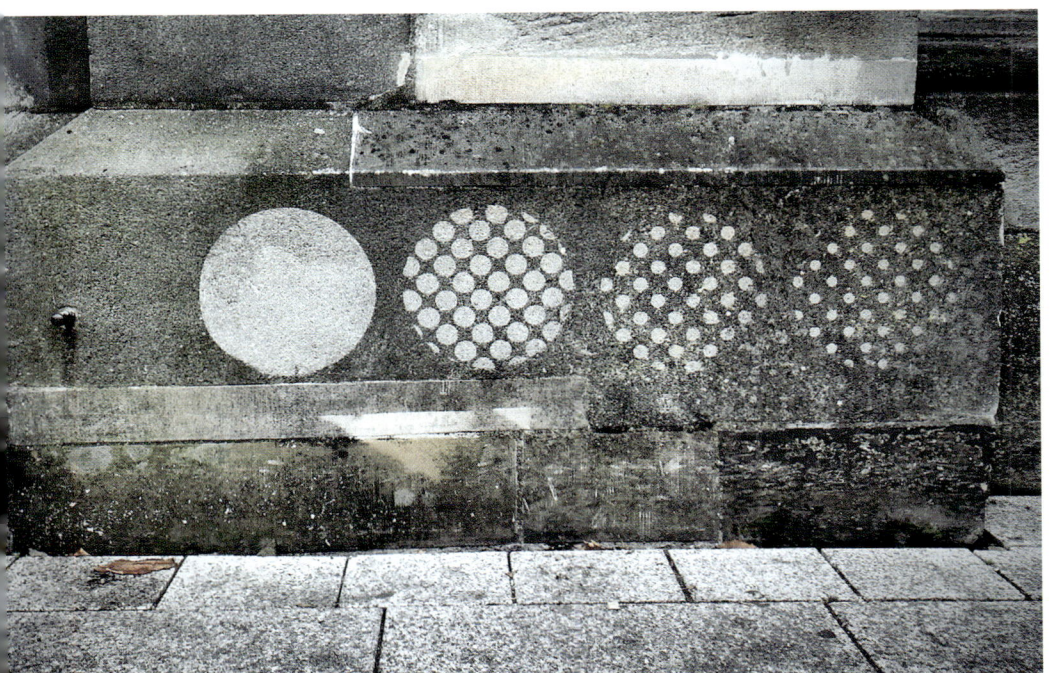

Figure 11.1 *Dust Marks*, Dietmar Offenhuber, 2018. Courtesy of the artist.

(Offenhuber 2019a: 2, 3). This even holds for an example constructed by Offenhuber himself – a work called *Dust Marks* (2018) that visualises air pollution by spraying a kind of 'reverse graffiti' on urban surfaces: removing pollution accumulated on them over time and letting it reaccumulate (Figure 11.1).

Close Relatives: Early Photography, Operational Images and Autographic Visualisations

With Offenhuber's interest in photographic approaches towards revealing material traces of real-world phenomena, we can conceptualise the historical tradition of autographic visualisations in line with other forms of evidence-seeking artistic practices. Photography, in particular, provides a rich culture of asking about the relation between the representation and the material cause of its creation. While data visualisation studies seldom examine indexicality of this mode of visual production (except for a few attempts such as Offenhuber's earlier notion of indexical visualisation), examinations of photography's indexicality are more established. For example, Jäger (2005: 349–61) crafted a classification of photography that structures photographic strategies of image production into four types, one of them being 'structural images'. He claims that this category no longer deals with the mere representational intention but creates its own world of images. Here, the character of photography as a transparent medium is suppressed and instead –unique for photographic processes – conditions of light and light-sensitive material are intentionally negotiated. Historical examples are the Rayograms by Man Ray (1963) and the photograms by László Moholy-Nagy (1946). Structural images reveal the camera as a generative system which allows the decoding of the underlying complexities and the creation of a type of imagery that focuses on patterned symptoms of a material reality.

This 'evidentiary tradition' of photographic images is central to the work of Harun Farocki (see Cirio 2019). He attempted to deconstruct complex systems of power by seeking traces of capitalist mode of production in increasing mechanisation and automation of vision, resulting in his conceptualisation of a new genre of visual production, labelled by him as 'operational images'. This term was originally coined in Farocki's installation work *Eye/Machine* (2000). He cites Roland Barthes's model of operative language as a source of inspiration (see Eschkötter and Pantenburg 2014: 207) and claims that operational images describe a type of imagery that does not represent a process, but rather is a part of a process.

Nowadays, one of the primary examples of operational images is imagery meant for mediation of computational operations – graphic user interfaces, QR codes, images produced by artificial neural networks, and so on. As an example, Jussi Parikka engages in this volume in an investigation of different modes of 'post-human forms of sensing', based on processing 'things we still call "images"' (see Chapter 10). Since Farocki's observations, it seems that the quantity of images produced by machines and/or meant to be read by machine audiences has far exceeded the number of images produced by and meant to be seen by humans (Bratton 2018). This, coupled with the proliferation of operational images, has brought us to the point of culmination, our visual culture rotating towards a nonhuman mode of its evolution, defying 'the assumed primacy of human eyes and interpretation' (Parikka in Chapter 10). What is more, these machine-produced images significantly differ from photographs or videos taken by humans. In terms of their use, they cease to be objects of aesthetic appreciation; instead, they become interfaces, or diagrammatic surfaces, that actively hide some algorithmic processes in order to make other processes visible or possible in the first place.

However, when using the notion of operational images as an analytical framework, we have to keep in mind its original purposes, since its primary intent was not to capture nonhuman algorithmic visual cultures. Since the 1980s Farocki was primarily interested in the disappearance of eye labour and its replacement by technical processes in a broader sense (not just computation). In this sense, operational images work by themselves. They are on the same level as objects and procedural executions, and due to their operativity, they lose their status of representations. Taken together with Farocki's background in political filmmaking, which ironically made him drop out of film school in the 1960s, we can see that his investment in the notion of operational images lies in their capacity to describe mechanisms between society, labour, and visibility in a Marxist tradition (Pantenburg 2001: 15). This helps to reveal that the agency of operational images in Farocki's conception is a human one.

Despite these comments, it is still true that the 'operativity' of operational images threatens their pictorial character. They are not needed as images anymore, but only as mathematical or technological operations. As Farocki puts it, these images are without social agenda, not meant for edification or reflection. This leads to a reading of operational images as clearly having non-representational character, which allows us to compare them to autographic visualisations, since – as mentioned earlier – one of the main differences of autographic visualisations (compared to earlier kinds of data visualisation) is that they are also non-representational. While traditional data visualisation encodes visual variables in order to represent patterns in the analysis of a phenomenon, autographic visualisation isolates some qualities of the phenomenon itself and uses them as traces of the occurrence of the given phenomenon or process (Offenhuber 2019a: 5).

Compared to data visualisation, autographic visualisation allows for a phenomenon to present itself, thus defying the logic of representation and incorporating the process-driven identity of operational images.

Further, just as in the case of operational images, autographic visualisation equally demands design interventions so that processes reveal themselves in front of a human eye. Both approaches gather strategies to cope with evidence in complex systems; however, the conceptual framework of operational images is more interested in decoding power relations produced by data, whereas the notion of autographic visualisation is sensitive towards the socio-material contextualisation of data generation itself (Offenhuber 2019a: 1, 5).

This leads to the main difference between operational images and autographic visualisations. While the non-representational aspect is shared by both concepts, they diverge in relation to predominant 'data-centric' perspectives on the production of different visualisations. The standard positivist or affirmative approach to visualisation techniques takes data as something given and decontextualised (Mareis 2015), and the myth of data as a rhetorical mode of naturalisation is maintained by the equalisation of data with reality. Essentially, there are two underlying assumptions which lead to this equation. Firstly, the idea that data is prior to human observation; a form of raw material which merely needs to be discovered and processed (Gitelman 2013). Secondly, what is also implied when we talk about data is objectivity. The strong confidence in numbers builds on a longer existing process that Western capitalism has been able to assert as a widespread phenomenon since at least the nineteenth century, with its computing practices, political authorities and use of statistics (Vollmer and Mennicken 007).

This dominant approach to data and their emergence is not explicitly questioned by the concept of operational images. On the contrary, it

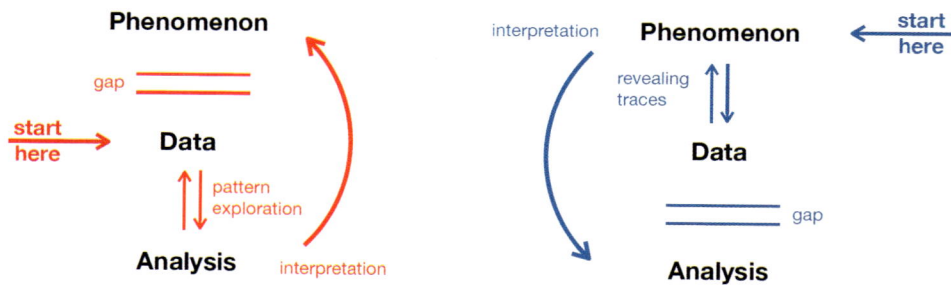

seems that its frequent use in contemporary writings on digital media unveils the political role of these images, but not the socio-material context of the production of data. In contrast to this dominant approach, the notion of autographic visualisation does not rely on data as raw material processed in visual representation but takes some aspect of the phenomenon itself, triggered by some design operation as its (always critically examined) source or input. As noted by Drucker (2011), 'data are capta, taken not given, constructed as an interpretation of the phenomenal world, not inherent in it'. This allows for a focus on the socio-material conditions of datasets, as well as a self-reflective and critical understanding of visual modelling. As Offenhuber (2019a: 9) also points out, autographic visualisations reveal actual processes of data generation; instead of putting data at the beginning of analysis to find patterns within them, they begin with a phenomenon itself and end with data as their final artefact (Figure 11.2).

Autographic visualisations also promote design agency. In order to visualise material traces, someone or something needs to ensure the emergence of autographic context through the combination of several design operations. Against naive readings of material traces as natural occurrences, autographic visualisations can clearly emphasise the former's artificiality. The concept of autographic visualisation thus also changes the role of design operations: they are meant to isolate the qualities of a phenomenon instead of purely encoding data into form. This comes with an assumption that in an autographic design we are leaving the comfort of the computational realm. Instead of creating endless iterations in a short amount of time within a generative computational system, autographic systems have to follow a different temporal and spatial scale. Relying, for instance, on biochemical and physical processes, the creation of autographic visualisations is slower and in need of

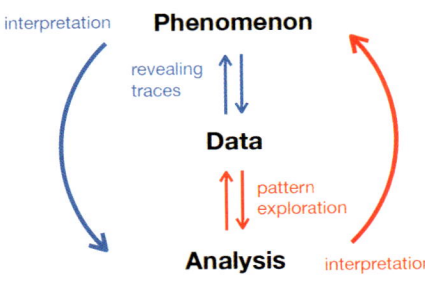

Figure 11.2 Models of traditional information visualisation, autographic visualisation and combined, Dietmar Offenhuber, 2018. Courtesy of the artist.

various resources. However, this limitation is, at the same time, the kernel of their critical potential. With the help of autographic visualisations and their dependence on external, observer-independent scales, we can conceptualise our interest in phenomena of a planetary or more-than-human scale, which we will discuss in the next section.

Scaling Up: Climate Emergency as an Autographic Process

Seeing how the theory of autographic visualisation stands in relation to the concepts of representation, operational images and data visualisation more broadly, we may ask broader questions about the applications of Offenhuber's approach outside of the scope of his initial proposal. In this respect, our main research question relates to the climate crisis, and its capacity to be a trigger of autographic processes: Can we have an autographic theory of climate emergency? What would it mean? How would an autographic visualisation of global heating look like?

First, we assume that if local biological and environmental processes have an autographic capacity (tree rings, the flow of wind, and so on), the same holds on a planetary scale – the planet itself might provoke procedures of visualising its changes over time in an autographic manner. Second, this scaling also influences the extent of urgency that an autographic process reports about – it does not tell the story of some local environmental damage but of a planetary emergency situation. From this point on, far-reaching environmental disasters, extreme weather patterns on a global scale and climate crisis in general become perceptible indicators for profound Earth-system changes. The autographic theory of climate crisis thus proposes a reading of the Earth as an ever-changing archive, in line with Weizman's (2017: 274) description of the planetary surface as a photographic inscription of human and nonhuman processes.

For example, climate emergency reveals past traces of human design activities on a large scale which are no longer visible under standard conditions. We think of last year's heatwave in the UK, which re-visualised former archaeological sites in the form of patterns on the fields (Royal Commission on the Ancient and Historical Monuments of Wales: 2018). Here inscriptions of domestication and geopolitics were conserved in geological memory and re-emerged due to the anthropogenically triggered change of temperature and precipitation. In a sort of epistemic serendipity, these archaeological traces also become indexes of the climate crisis itself, just as an oil spill in the Gulf of Mexico is not only a visible trace of a spatially limited event but an index of larger ecological collapse on the planetary scale, induced by the fossil fuel industry. Another example includes historical revelations in Poland in 2015, where new record lows of the Vistula river near Warsaw revealed Jewish tombstones, pointing to a dark period of industrial genocide (Associated Press 2015). In this case, instead of water being a cleansing substance, it preserves and curates access to traces of modernity. And just as in the case of the 2018 British Isles heatwave and droughts, these revelations do additional labour in diagramming the ongoing climate crisis, since the low water levels in the river are a direct result of this damaging process. We might assume that such accidental diagrams of climate emergency will be more frequent as global heating further escalates.

Returning to Susan Schuppli's practice, we find this same approach in her work on ice core samples. Her *Learning from Ice* (2019–21) research project 'investigates Arctic environments as a vast information network composed of material as well as cultural "sensors" that are registering and transmitting the signals of pollution and climate change' (Schuppli 2019b). Through the prism of autographic visualisation theory, Schuppli's description can be read as an apt allusion to those self-diagramming processes of the Earth that provide visible and decipherable traces of ongoing climate collapse – the ice core sample, for instance, becomes a material device for inscription of changing temperature over time, just as tree rings inscribe the process of ageing, or as sedimentation of soil and rocks into thick layers inscribes geological processes.

However, it is not just different environments but also biological species that might serve as autographic visualisations of climate emergency. Jennifer Gabrys, for example, writes about organisms as environmental proxies and indexes of ecosystem conditions: '. . . indicator species of lichens and mosses and other organisms that can be studied as expressions of environmental processes, whether for atmospheric pollutant levels, radioactivity, or different types of mineral depositions in soil' (Gabrys 2016: 124). This means that, for example, the decrease of marine calcifiers species in the oceans turns their diminishing population into the autographic diagram of global ocean acidification. The same idea is expressed by Offenhuber (2019) when he refers to synthetic biology as offering possibilities to design objects and organisms with autographic qualities. So whether by direct (bio-)design intervention or by naturally occurring capacities in some individuals or the whole population of some organisms, autographic visualisations diagram the change that massively influences their modes of existence. This should not be that surprising given how organisms are irrevocably tied to their

Figure 11.3 (next page) Cropmarks in Wales during the heatwave of summer 2018. RCAHMW/SWNS, 2018. Source: Royal Commission on the Ancient and Historical Monuments of Wales, South West News Service.

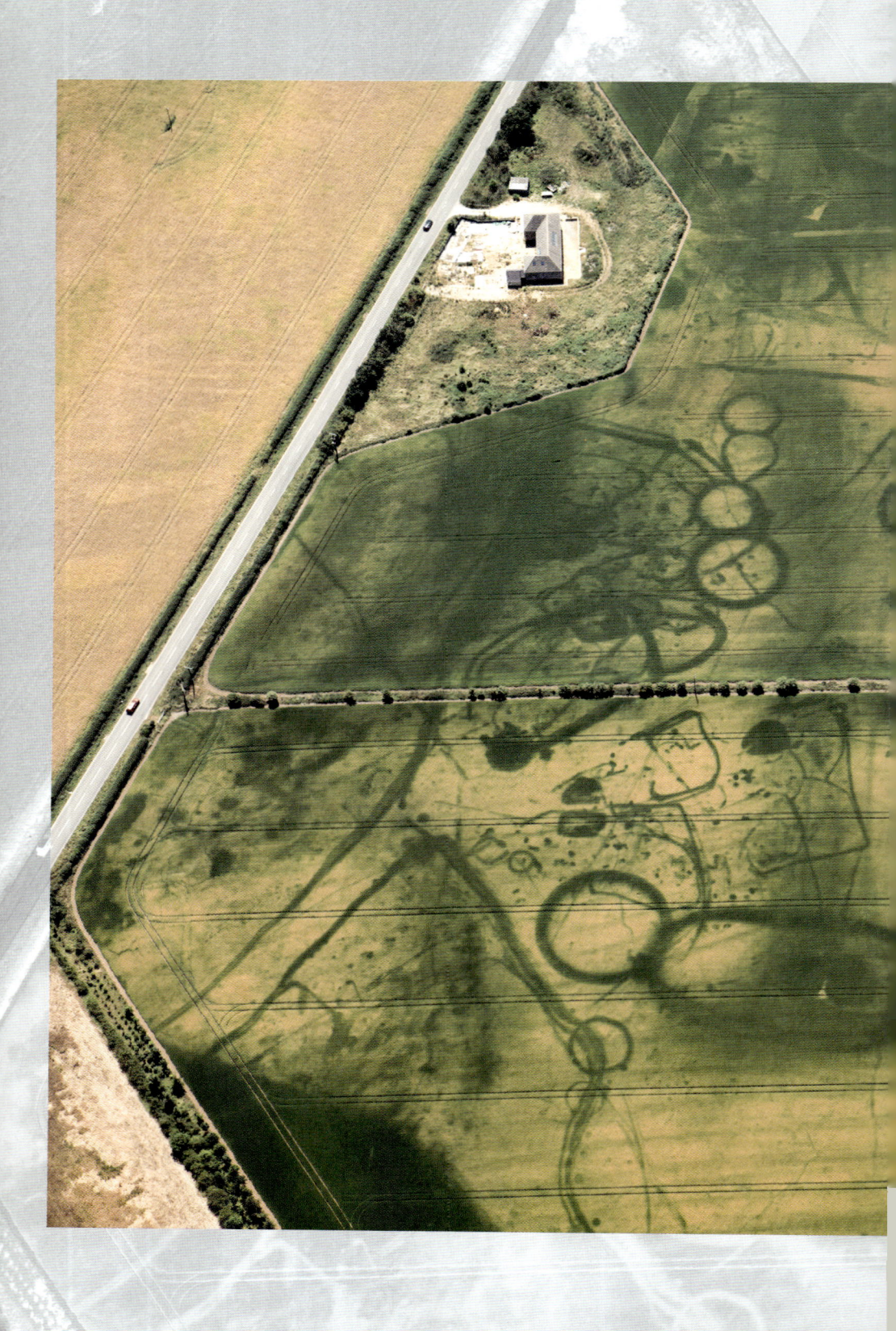

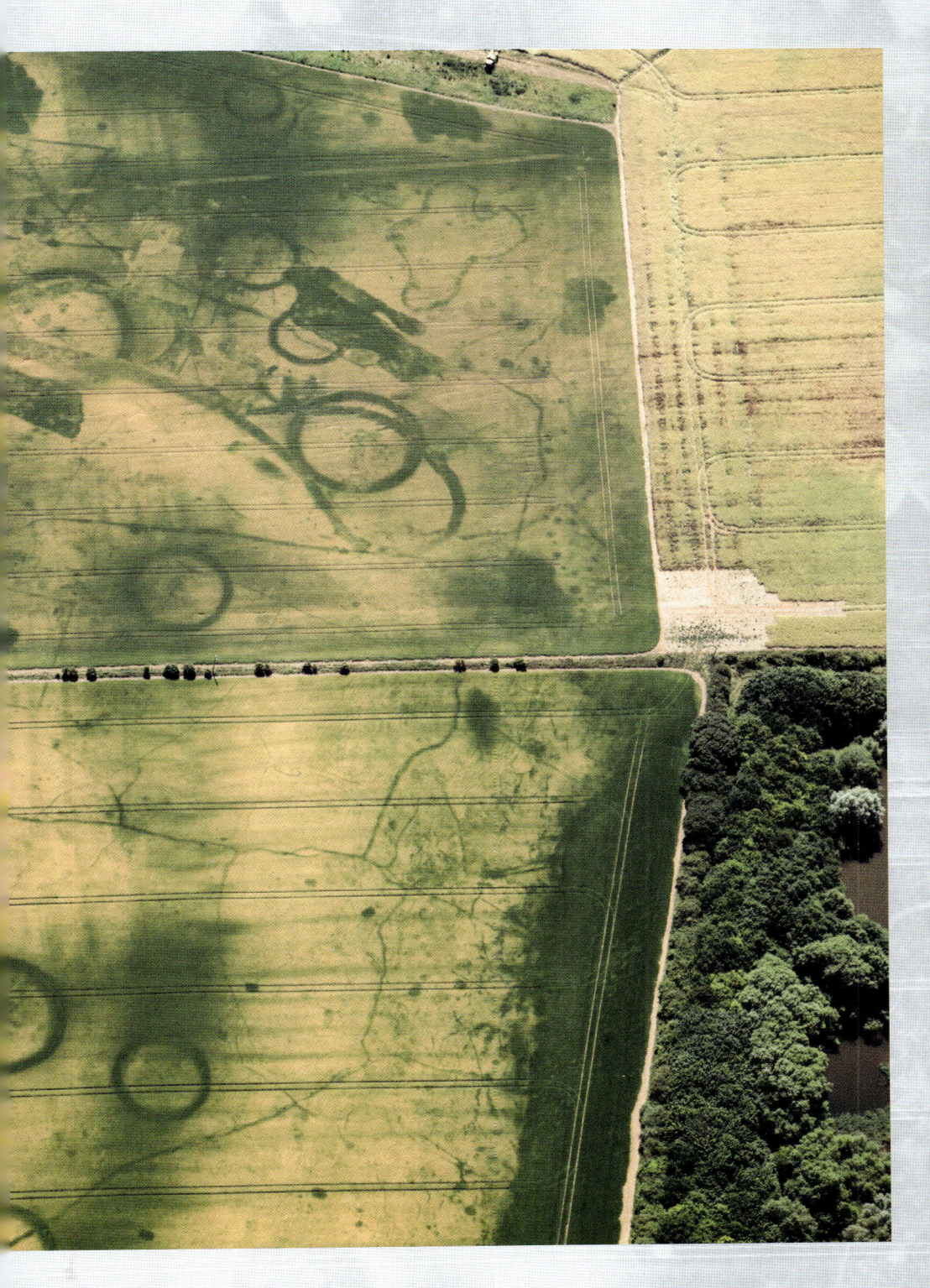

environment, in a sort of metabolic flux where each life-form stands for the temporary compression of its external conditions, following, for example, von Uexküll's theory of *Umwelt* (2010).

Given these examples, we declare the human-made climate emergency as a medium of indication and planetary framing of the archival processes of the Earth that unfolds through different environments and biological species (Figure 11.3). Human-accelerated ecological processes thus become a method of autographic design. In opposition to material traces that can be simply observed with some training, human-induced climate change is a large-scale autographic design operation that was not even planned to be one. Without explicit human intention, effects of climate change reveal the archival processes of human cultural activities by the Earth: a geo-epistemic serendipity which implies nonhuman processes of distancing and distinguishing that are too sensitive for human perception of the world. Hence, the climate crisis enables a specific mode of more-than-human visualisation to emerge, an opportunity to reveal the dimensions of the memory space of the Earth itself.

A Vast Machine: Planetary Diagrams and their Nonhuman Witnesses

We propose to further speculate on the possibility of autographic visualisations of the climate emergency as images neither produced by us, nor meant for us: it is not visual culture about the Earth but visual culture by the Earth. Here, apparatuses of sensing and modelling the Earth can spark or catalyse the framing process of an accidental autopoietic visualisation on a planetary scale, revealing the Earth as a nonhuman archive emerging from conspiratorial activity between biological, geological *and* technological agents. To explain this point, Offenhuber also states in relation to autographic visualisations that while being confronted with them, 'an observer becomes a participant, has to *tune into* the phenomenon' (Offenhuber 2019b). The last question to ask in relation to an autographic theory of climate crisis then is: who or what is the observer of planetary self-diagrammatisation processes? Who or what does the labour of *tuning into* the planet itself? Answering this question will also help us to better see how autographic visualisations are mediated, evacuating this visualisation theory from certain perils of naive epistemological realism.

Given the scope of the armature necessary to witness such an autographic process, the answer must be a planetary infrastructure, in this case, an infrastructure that captures the Earth as a geophysical unit, which nowadays happens through satellite imagery or computational models and climate simulations. Especially these models and simulations stand for one of the many instances of a general contemporary shift towards nonhuman visual cultures. These visual cultures can capture phenomena beyond the range of our human sensibility – be it a '*longue durée*' of climate patterns and geological movements or slow violence of environmental catastrophes (Nixon 2011: 2). Nonhuman visual cultures facilitate evidence for current Anthropocene discourse, which is intertwined with the temporality of deep, geological time (Parikka 2015: 37–45). What is more, they are examples of widespread automation of image-making that reaches far beyond the scope of the automation of the infrastructure of sensing and modelling the Earth.

The provisional history of the infrastructure of planetary sensing and modelling might have several points of departure. Some authors, such as Kurgan (2013: 9), choose to depart from the first pictures of the Earth, especially the paradigmatic examples of *Earthrise* (1968) and *Blue Marble* (1972). Gabrys (2016: 1), however, focuses on pre-visual planetary sensations, such as the auditory landscape of beeps and noises produced by the first human-made satellite, *Sputnik 1*. Since the end of the 1950s, the planet has been gradually enveloped by a great number of artificial objects, surveying the surface of the planet, and giving us an overview of environmental conditions around the world. And as mentioned before, it is not just satellites that comprise this planetary infrastructure of sensing and modelling: we can also see massive deployment of climate and biological stations, 'airborne instruments, ..., ocean vessels, and buoys, as well as terrestrial monitoring stations such as carbon flux towers that can be found dotted around the globe' (Gabrys 2016: 116). All of these coalesce into what Edwards (2010: 17) calls a 'knowledge infrastructure' of the 'vast machine'. This infrastructure represents a planetary socio-technical system that comprises 'robust networks of people, artifacts, and institutions that generate, share, and maintain specific knowledge about the human and natural worlds' (2010: 17). This vast machine of meteorological calculations and planetary visualisation also propagates a special regime of infrastructural globalism, which means that the vast machine does not only produce planetary-scale images but is also in itself a planetary-scale machine (Edwards 2010: 25).

However, this infrastructure is not a giant monument but rather a discontiguous network (Bishop 2016: 303). As Gabrys notes, it is not holistic. Instead, it tends towards the proliferation of many fragmented perspectives stitched together by the labour of computational algorithms:

> If the satellite view has largely been narrated as a project of making a global observation system and of seeing the earth as a whole object, then the more distributed monitoring performed by environmental sensors

points to the ways in which the earth might be rendered not as one world, but as many. (Gabrys 2016: 14)

This leads to observations on how the vast machine – and mainly its computational infrastructure – is, according to Gabrys (2016: 1), undergoing a process of becoming environmental: digital technologies become the general infrastructural background not just of scientific inquiries regarding our planet, but also of our everyday activities. This holds increasingly not just for humans, but also for nonhuman actors. What is more, this process leads to computation being generative of new environments and technological ensembles: 'The becoming environmental of computation then signals that environments are not fixed backdrops for the implementation of sensor devices, but rather are involved in processes of becoming along with these technologies' (Gabrys 2016: 9).

With this realisation that computational models of the Earth are slowly becoming the Earth itself, we can see how the 'becoming environmental of computation' might be interpreted as the vast machine's literal, physical tuning into the planetary reality, witnessing its autographic processes. However, the vast machine is not just generative in terms of visual representation of the Earth and observing its labour of self-diagrammatisation but also in terms of actually reformatting Earth's ecologies. Here, we can follow once more Gabrys's suggestion that sensing infrastructures inform the environments: they give shape to new ecological relations and transform the environments they monitor and in which they are deployed (Gabrys 2016: 14). Descriptions and observations of the planet become propositional, meaning that they 'translate from an observation of any single variable to a control of any single variable, such as proposals for geo-engineering or ecosystem services where environmental processes are one more data point to be engineered' (Gabrys 2016: 134).

This leads to our last speculative remark. The general 'tragedy' of visualisation is that when we try to visualise things, we tend to modify or even destroy them at the same time. This might be caused, in part, by our urge to visualise things not by 'tuning into' their autographic processes and harvesting their self-diagramming capacities but by overlaying them with our culturally produced frameworks and regimes of representation. These idealised counterparts are then treated as proxies of the things we aim to represent, and we end up in a situation resembling what Baudrillard (1981: 9–12) called the 'precession of simulacra'. Representations and even operational images of the planet thus enact – many times over – a replacement of the authority of the thing with the authority of its image.

This 'tragedy' might be further conceptualised in Virilio's (2003; see also Bratton 2006: 21) vocabulary of integral accidents, where every technology is treated from the point of view of the new genre of the accident it generates: the blackout comes with the electric grid, the plane crash comes with the aeroplane. If nowadays images are technical tools rather than simple representations – as is the case with operational images – even images and visualisation techniques might be judged as bringing a new kind of catastrophe into the world: the disappearance of the external object the image used to relate to. Even planetary imagery then carries its integral accident: our visualisations of the Earth are eating the Earth at the same time they capture it, as it is the technological infrastructure of the vast machine, largely dependent on the fossil fuel industry, that drives the climate crisis modelled by the very same infrastructures (Hu 2015: 79–80). To see the ageing of the tree diagrammed in the tree rings, we cut the tree. To see the planetary dynamics, we set the planet on fire.

Conclusion: Three Registers of Planetary Imagery

To sum up, our argument interprets different biological and environmental processes, as well as artistic practices that build upon observation of these processes, as cases of autographic visualisations, when some phenomenon reveals itself through traces of its own activity. Scaling to the level of the unfolding climate emergency, we interpret this tragedy as an autographic process, triggered by the human fossil fuel economy, witnessed by nonhuman apparatus that sense and model the Earth, themselves by-products of economic and political globalisation. With respect to this sensing infrastructure, we are now able to read three categories of planetary imagery in the following manner:

1. 'Representations of the planet', such as satellite photographs, which are instances of aesthetic products of the Earth-sensing infrastructure;
2. 'Operational images of the planet', such as climate models and simulations, which are instances of algorithmic processes of the Earth-sensing infrastructure; and,
3. 'Autographic visualisations of the planet', such as oil spills and ice cores, like those examined in Schuppli's practice, extreme weather patterns or heatwaves that reveal archaeological sites and turn them into diagrams of climate collapse, all of which are instances of the catastrophe triggered by the failure of global infrastructure to escape the curse of fossil-fuel extractivism.

It is the identification of and speculation on the last of these categories that we treat as the primary contribution of our chapter. Demonstrating how autographic visualisations differ from mere representations, as well as from otherwise extremely useful registers of operational images, we have examined, in-depth, the infrastructure that contributes to witnessing their emergence, as well as their persistence on the photographic surface of the Earth that is within the spontaneous, nonhuman archive of climate emergency. These 'planetary diagrams' demonstrate what 'photography off the scale' might mean in the context of climate emergency, both literally and metaphorically: our notion of the 'photographic image' needs to be scaled up to fit the genre of planetary autographic processes, and it also needs to be accommodated to identify these autographic processes as 'photographic' in a broader sense.

References

Associated Press (2015), 'Poland drought: Jewish tombstones and fighter plane uncovered as rivers run dry', *The Guardian*, 26 August 2015.

Baudrillard, Jean (1981), *Simulacres et simulation*. Paris: Éditions Galilée.

Bishop, Ryan (2016), 'The Protean Munus and Nomos of the Political Subject in Polyscalar Autonomous Remote Sensing Systems', in Ryan Bishop, Kristoffer Gansing, Jussi Parikka and Elvia Wilk (eds), *Across & Beyond – A Transmediale Reader on Post-digital Practices, Concepts, and Institutions*. Berlin: Sternberg Press and transmediale e.V., pp. 290–305.

Bratton, Benjamin H. (2006), 'Logistics of Habitable Circulation', in Paul Virilio (ed.), *Speed and Politics*. Los Angeles: Semiotext(e), pp. 7–25.

Bratton, Benjamin H. (2018), 'For You-For You Not: On Representation and AI', in Beatrix Ruf (ed.), *Size Matters! (De)Growth of the 21st Century Art Museum*. London: Koenig Books.

Drucker, Johanna (2011), 'Humanities Approaches to Graphical Display', *Digital Humanities Quarterly*, 5(1).

Cirio, Paolo (2019), *Evidentiary Realism*. Berlin: NOME.

Edwards, Paul (2010), *A Vast Machine*. Cambridge, MA: MIT Press.

Eschkötter, Daniel, and Volker Pantenburg (2014), 'Was Farocki lehrt', in *Zeitschrift für Medienwissenschaften*, 6(11): 207–11.

Farocki, Harun (2015), 'Phantom Images', in Walead Beshty (ed.), *Picture Industry*. Annandale-On-Hudson, NY: Luma-CCS Bard.

Gabrys, Jennifer (2016), *Program Earth*. Minneapolis: University of Minnesota Press.

Gitelman, Lisa (ed.) (2013), *'Raw Data' Is an Oxymoron*. Cambridge, MA: The MIT Press.

Hu, Tung-Hui (2015), *A Prehistory of the Cloud*. Cambridge, MA: MIT Press.

Jäger, Gottfried (2005), 'Bildsystem Fotografie', in *Bildwissenschaften*. Frankfurt: Suhrkamp, pp. 349–61.

Kurgan, Laura (2013), *Close Up at a Distance: Mapping, Technology, and Politics*. New York: Zone Books.

Man Ray (1963), *Self Portrait*. Boston: Little, Brown and Company.

Mareis, Claudia (2015), 'The End of Representation', in Sabine Himmelsbach and Claudia Mareis (eds), *Poetics and Politics of Data*. Basel: HeK Basel.

Moholy-Nagy, László (1946), *Vision in Motion*. Chicago: Paul Theobald.

Nixon, Rob (2011), *Slow Violence and the Environmentalism of the Poor*. Cambridge, MA: Harvard University Press.

Offenhuber, Dietmar, and Orkan Telhan (2015), 'Indexical visualisation', in Ulrik Ekman, Jay David Bolter, Lily Diaz, Morten Søndergaard, and Maria Engberg (eds), *Ubiquitous Computing, Complexity and Culture*. New York: Routledge, pp. 288–303.

Offenhuber, Dietmar (2018), *Dust Zone*. Available at: <http://dust.zone> (last accessed 8 July 2020).

Offenhuber, Dietmar (2019a), 'Data by Proxy – Material Traces as Autographic Visualisations', *arxiv.org*. Available at: <https://arxiv.org-pdf-1907.05454v1.pdf> (last accessed 8 July 2020).

Offenhuber, Dietmar (2019b), 'Autographic Visualisation – Traces, Symptoms, Evidence', Google Cambridge-Boston, 19 February 2019. Available at: <https://www.youtube.com-watch?v=aT-tKIFNVl0> (last accessed 8 July 2020).

Paglen, Trevor (2016), 'Invisible Images (Your Pictures Are Looking at You)', *The New Inquiry*, 8 December 2016.

Pantenburg, Volker (2001), 'Sichtbarkeiten: Farocki zwischen Bild und Text', Vorwerk, in Susanne Gaensheimer and Nicolaus Schafhausen (eds), *Harun Farocki: Nachdruck-Imprint. Texte-Writings*. Berlin: Frankfurter Kunstverein, pp. 8, 15.

Parikka, Jussi (2015), *A Geology of Media*, Minneapolis: University of Minnesota Press.

Pasquinelli, Matteo (2009), 'Google's PageRank Algorithm: A Diagram of the Cognitive Capitalism and the Rentier of the Common Intellect', in Konrad Becker and Felix Stalder (eds), *Deep Search*. London: Transaction Publishers.

Royal Commission on the Ancient and Historical Monuments of Wales (2018), 'Cropmarks 2018'. Available at: <https://rcahmw.gov.uk-cropmarks-2018> (last accessed 8 July 2020).

Schuppli, Susan (2014), 'Can the Sun lie?'. Available at: <http://susanschuppli.com-videos-can-the-sun-lie-2> (last accessed 8 July 2020).

Schuppli, Susan (2019a), 'Nature Represents Itself'. Available at: <http://susanschuppli.com-exhibition-naturerepresentsitself> (last accessed 8 July 2020).

Schuppli, Susan (2019b), 'Learning from Ice'. Available at: <http://susanschuppli.com-exhibition-learning-from-ice> (last accessed 8 July 2020).

Virilio, Paul (2003), *Unknown Quantity*. London: Thames & Hudson-Fondation Cartier pour l'art contemporain.

Virilio, Paul (2006), *Speed and Politics*. Los Angeles: Semiotext(e).

Vollmer, Hendrik, and Andrea Mennicken (2007), *Zahlenwerk. Kalkulation, Organisation und Gesellschaft*. Berlin: Springer.

von Uexküll, Jakob (2010), *A Foray Into the Worlds of Animals and Humans: With A Theory of Meaning*. Minneapolis: University of Minnesota Press.

Weizman, Eyal (2017), *Forensic Architecture: Violence at the Threshold of Detectability*. New York: Zone Books.

12 Undigital Photography: Image-Making beyond Computation and AI

Joanna Zylinska

Photography Off the (Human) Scale

IN JULY 2018 the electronics manufacturer Huawei held a photographic competition which was judged by photographer Alex Lambrechts and a Huawei P20 Pro AI (artificial intelligence) smartphone. Building on its previous claims that the Huawei P20 was equipped with 'Master AI' which automatically set the most optimum camera mode for every situation as well as learning to adapt to user behaviour (Huawei 2018), the Chinese 'AI-powered' flagship was not just making photos but also evaluating them, 'using its artificial intelligence to rate thousands of images alongside a professional Leica photographer'.[2] Art festivals and competitions now regularly include AI-generated images, with an algorithm partly taking on the role of the artist. This recent outpouring of computer-made creative decisions and artefacts has been accompanied by the unfolding of public interest in artificial intelligence, from fascination with AI's creative capabilities to anxiety related to the impending automation of the labour force or even the possible annihilation of the human species.

Responding to the developments outlined above, this chapter discusses the current rescaling of photographic practice and output by examining the relationship between artificial intelligence and mechanical image-making. With this, I propose to go beyond the question of scale understood principally in terms of volume, whereby the human's cognitive and perceptive capacities are seen as fundamentally challenged or even stumped by the sheer quantity of photographic acts and images. Instead, I want to engage with the question of the nonhuman scale as something that offers a different ontological understanding of photographic practice, at a time when the function of the image maker *and* image recipient has been expanded to, or even taken over by, machines.

Traversing the oft-posed question: 'Can computers be creative?', the chapter analyses the nexus between machine vision and human labour in current AI research with a view to offering a critique of the political underpinnings of AI and the way it feeds into image-making today. By way of theoretical grounding, in the first part of the chapter I bring into conversation artist Trevor Paglen's understanding of photography in terms of 'seeing machines' with my own earlier work on nonhuman photography, in order to probe the algorithmic aspect of perception and vision across apparatuses, species and time scales. The discussion of my own image-based piece which engages with AI, presented in the second part of the chapter, leads to a broader interrogation of spaces and institutions where critical thinking and learning about technology, image-making and creativity takes place today: the public university, the liberal arts college, the art school.

Trevor Paglen's Seeing Machines

In his visual practice Paglen has always investigated how we see the world, focusing on the way in which the logic of total transparency promoted by the socio-political apparatus translates into global surveillance while also creating zones of opacity that hide the actual operations of power. And thus in *The Other Night Sky* (2010–11) he drew on data obtained from amateur satellite observers to track and photograph classified American satellites and space debris, in *Limit Telephotography* (2012) he used powerful telescopes to capture images of classified military bases, while in *Deep Web Dive* (2016) he photographed NSA-tapped underwater internet cables at the bottom of the Atlantic. In all of those works the human–nonhuman assemblage was still driven by the human artist, who had mobilised the hybrid apparatus to reveal the limitations of human vision. Through this, Paglen raised questions about the inhumane aspects of some of the viewing practices installed by the current political regimes yet hidden from general view. The problem of seeing has been very much of interest to the artist in his more recent work, which engages with AI technology. He frames his current approach as follows: 'Over the last ten years or so, powerful algorithms and artificial intelligence networks have enabled computers to "see" autonomously. What does it mean that "seeing" no longer requires a human "seer" in the loop?' (in Strecker non-dated). In an interview associated with his 2017 exhibition 'A Study of Invisible Images' at Metro Pictures in New York, Paglen highlights the fact that the majority of images produced today are not only generated automatically, without human intentionality or oversight, but are also intended for a nonhuman recipient: this or that section of the planetary computational system that Benjamin Bratton has deemed 'the stack' (Bratton 2016). The artist has in mind here photographs produced via face recognition technology which are increasingly used in policing, surveillance and access; computer vision directing the self-driving cars; or cameras on drones used to allow algorithm-driven 'killer robots' to determine worthy targets.

Paglen's project *It Began as a Military Experiment* (2017) included in the Metro exhibition features rows of colour portrait photographs, showing seemingly regular subjects of different genders, ethnicities and ages – with the display looking like an updated version of August Sander's *People of the 20th Century*. Only a very close look allows the viewer to detect grid-like white symbols, which have been superimposed on the subjects' faces. From the accompanying materials we learn that the photos had been drawn from the so-called FERET database containing thousands of photos of people – many of them workers at a military base in Maryland – which had been collected on behest of DARPA (the Defense Advanced Research Projects Agency) to help develop facial recognition technology. To advance the technology, the military needed to train algorithms in correct pattern recognition by feeding the network thousands of similar faces and teaching it to recognise variations between them. Paglen spent months going through the FERET database to select individual images, which he subsequently retouched and colour-corrected, and then ran them through an algorithm to identify key points in the faces. '[T]hese photos represent some of the original faces of facial recognition – the "Adams and Eves" that nearly all subsequent facial recognition research has been built upon' (in Strecker non-dated). In this sense, they not only hint at Sander's totalising humanism but also reference Edward Steichen's *The Family of Man* photographic exhibition held at MoMA in 1955, whose ambition was to reveal a supposed universality of human experience while also promoting a soft version of US imperialism. And yet a strange shift occurs in this presumed Adamism – a term Roland Barthes used ironically in *Mythologies* to refer not just to the presupposed originary unity of 'all men' in Steichen's exhibition that the FERET database perpetuates, but also to a 'lyricism' which immobilises humans in their place by making their social condition look eternal (Barthes 1973: 102). What is new about the FERET images is that they are not aimed at human eyes: as a training set for a facial recognition algorithm, their goal is to establish this commonality-in-difference for machine vision. Indeed, these images are not meant to be seen at all by humans but are rather going inside the black box that AI has become. The fact that most of AI research has been funded by the military, with

DARPA, the original funders of internet development, also sponsoring 'more AI research than private corporations and any other branch of the government' (Barrat 2013: 180) from the 1960s through to the 1990s, means that AI is literally a military project, even if developed by external companies and research universities. It is precisely the impossibility of knowing what is *in* the database – not only due to the lack of access but also the sheer physical impossibility on the part of humans to sift through all the data – that drives Paglen's work.

This black-boxing of AI technology hides, for example, the data bias of human engineers who construct the supposedly universal datasets. As Alexander Strecker, editor of *LensCulture*, wrote in his review of Paglen's exhibition:

> imagine the first time a self-driving car has to choose between two children who have run out into the road, one white and one black. If the computer 'sees' the black child as a small animal, due to the bias of the training sets it has been given, its choice will be clear. (Strecker undated)

Yet it is not only the question of data bias – which some AI researchers argue can be overcome by feeding the system a wider set of data, training people in labelling the data better, making them undergo bias awareness training or simply paying them more – that emerges as a concern here. A deeper problem lies in the very idea of organising the world according to supposedly representative datasets and having decisions made on the basis of these, in advance and supposedly objectively. Such technologies are of course already in use: we can mention here not only face recognition at border control and other security access points, but also Facebook photo-tagging algorithms, identification of bank cheque deposits or rapid decisions about credit. One might even go so far as to argue that what we humans perceive as ethical decisions are first and foremost corporal reactions, executed by an 'algorithm' of DNA, hormones and other chemicals that push the body to act in a certain way, rather than outcomes of a process of ethical deliberation concerning the concept of the good and the value of human life.

I am therefore reluctant to analyse AI developments by pitching the human against the machine in order to wonder whether 'they' are going to get 'us' or not. But I do want to throw some light on the very debate about AI by shifting from a polarised and dualist narrative to one that interrogates entangled human–nonhuman agency while also raising political questions. Technologically aware art can open up a space for interrogating who funds, trains and owns our algorithms. This interrogation is important because, as shown by Safiya Noble in *Algorithms of Oppression: How Search Engines Reinforce Racism*

[D]ata and computing have become so profoundly their own 'truth' that even in the face of evidence, the public still struggles to hold tech companies accountable for the products and errors of their ways. These errors increasingly lead to racial and gender profiling, misrepresentation, and even economic redlining. (Noble 2018)

Critical projects such as those by Paglen encourage us to ask: Whose vision is AI promoting? Who is doing the looking, in what way and to what purpose?

Paglen's project *Sight Machine* (2017) was aimed at exploring precisely these questions. A collaboration with Kronos Quartet and light installation company Obscura Digital, it involved staging a concert in a San Francisco warehouse (replayed at London's Barbican Centre in 2019), accompanied by the projections of various bits of data driven by AI algorithms. As well as displaying, in frequent motion, one of the face recognition training datasets discussed above, the artist had installed a number of cameras in the warehouse, with feeds going into the video mixer and the hardware. The cameras then made visible on the screen behind the band renderings of outlines of the human members of the band in the form of multicoloured squiggles, circles and squares. The artist and his team occasionally turned the camera on the audience to allow them to see themselves being seen by the computers, with their faces identified as faces and also rendered as rectangles. The idea behind the project was to examine the architecture of different computer vision systems by trying to learn what it was that they were seeing. Yet we should ask to what extent this is still actually 'seeing'. And are we still talking about intelligence? Or are they just behaviours that *look like* seeing and intelligence to us, their human interpreters? Echoing a quip that is popular with AI researchers, 'Can the submarine swim?', these questions are important because the systems put in motion that enable computer vision and other forms of AI determine who and what is allowed in and what isn't.

Much translation work had been involved in Paglen's *Sight Machine*, yet ultimately the performance revealed the basic untranslatability of data between different recipients, resulting from the opacity of code (from brute force algorithms of the 1960s systems to contemporary AI systems such as TensorFlow, Torch and Caffe). It is precisely in that very gesture of attempting to undertake the work of translation that the incompatibility between different cognitive frameworks and different forms in which intelligence is embodied was revealed. The project thus succeeded and failed at the same time: it failed at transparency, at revealing (to us) what and how computers supposedly see, but it succeeded at unveiling this translation gap – which is also an epistemological and ontological gap.

And even though the project failed the classic Marxian promise that revealing the conditions of injustice would lead to increased political activity and eventual liberation, that promise itself has been debunked by the public responses to platform capitalism. It would be naive to think that people are unaware that, for example, Amazon is spying on them, that Google tracks their every move or that Facebook mines their personal data for commercial gain, yet the percentage of those who permanently sign off social media or remove their personal data from the cloud is – and indeed *can* be – very slim. Yet what Paglen unveils is precisely the fact that vision itself is changing and that we cannot ever truly see the conditions of our material existence. He also shows us that a new network of visibility, much of which remains permanently obscured from human vision, has now emerged which has the potential to redefine radically what counts as visible and what doesn't – or *what counts, full stop*.

We could therefore conclude that Paglen's work reveals the impossibility of 'seeing it all' on the part of the human, while also demonstrating how the link between seeing and knowing has been ultimately severed in the algorithmic culture that organises our social and political lives. And yet, as with his previous projects, there is something romantically futile about this artistic gesture, premised as it is on unveiling the dark machinations of 'the stack'. To say this is not to dismiss his artistic undertakings but rather to suggest that the success of Paglen's work lies in its parergonal nature: to really 'get' what he is showing we need to engage not just with the images he produces but also with the narrative about machine vision, the human intervention into the limits of the image and the discourse about art-making. The term 'parergon', referring to a supplementary remark, additional material or ornament whose function is merely to embellish the main work (i.e. the 'ergon'), has been immortalised in art theory by Jacques Derrida. In his reading of Kant's *Critique of Judgement* included in *The Truth in Painting*, Derrida takes issue with the idea of a self-contained nature of the work of art, conveyed by the belief in its supposed intrinsic value and beauty, by literally bringing the work's framing into the picture.

> A parergon comes against, beside, and in addition to the ergon, the work done [*fait*], the fact [*le fait*], the work, but it does not fall to one side, it touches and cooperates within the operation, from a certain outside. Neither simply outside nor simply inside. (Derrida 1987: 54)

The supposedly secondary function of the framing, be it literal or conceptual, is argued to be actually foundational to the artwork's existence and recognition as an artwork, as its very existence delineates and preserves the artwork's identity. For Derrida, a work of art is therefore never self-contained; it always depends on its parerga – frames, ornaments, commentaries – if it is to be recognised in its supposed uniqueness and singularity. And thus to say that Paglen's work is parergonal is not to criticise it for its supposed lack but rather to acknowledge its (perhaps knowing) reliance on the grid, the network and the cloud. In other words, Paglen's projects about seeing machines mobilise human intelligence and machinic technology to say and show us something, while also revealing our own cognitive and political limits and blind spots. His practice does not amount to producing political art per se, but it does engage our sense *and* sensibility to reprogram the human cognitive-sensory apparatus – and maybe to open it up to a different hack.

Paglen actually uses the notion of 'seeing machines' to describe the contemporary condition of photography. In a series of blog posts written for Fotomuseum Winterthur in 2014, he proposed an expanded understanding of the photographic medium, encompassing 'the myriad ways that not only humans use technology to "see" the world, but the ways machines see the world for other machines' (Paglen 2014). His definition includes various image-capture apparatuses, from mobile phones through to satellite cameras, but also incorporates data, storage systems, interpretation algorithms and, last but not least, the technologies of perception that emerge as part of the networked photographic practices – and that establish and legitimate particular regimes of visibility. Most importantly, the concept of photography-as-seeing-machines highlights the fact that to focus 'too closely on individual images is entirely to miss the point' (Paglen 2014). With this argument Paglen offers a blow to the art-historical understanding of photography in terms of singular historical records and framed artefacts. It is not even that digital technology has resulted in the supposed over-production of images today, with singular photographs giving way to image and data flows but rather that photographs cannot be treated as discrete entities because they are part of the wider technological network of production and perception: they are both objects to be looked at and vision-shaping technologies, for humans *and* machines. Their identity as discrete images is thus performatively established by the very acts of looking at them. But we must bear in mind that the 'looker' is not always human.

After Nonhuman Photography

There is an affinity between Paglen's conceptualisation of photography in terms of 'seeing machines' and my own notion of 'nonhuman photography', developed in the book of the same title (Zylinska 2017). The book's argument was premised on my conviction about the inadequacy of the traditional photography theory for analysing the image landscape today, because, as Paglen points out, 'Susan Sontag's seminal work has little to say about the infrared imaging system on a Reaper drone' while 'applying Roland Barthes' ideas to the billions of images in London's city-wide surveillance archives would be utterly absurd' (Paglen 2014). For me, the concept of 'nonhuman photography' refers to photographs that are not *of*, *by* or *for* the human (see Zylinska 2017: 5), encompassing images as diverse as depopulated vistas, satellite pictures and QR codes. Even though the opening premise of *Nonhuman Photography* was that today, in the age of CCTV, drone media, medical body scans and satellite imaging, photography has become increasingly decoupled from human agency and human vision, I also suggested that even those images that have been taken by the human entail a nonhuman element. This element, executed by means of technical and cultural algorithms, is revealed by the fact that most people's wedding photographs, holiday snapshots and Instagram feeds look very similar.

The recognition of this cultural iterability allowed me to suggest that humans have always been technological, i.e. that we have run on algorithms – from DNA to behavioural instructions developed in various cultures to legitimate and promote certain ways of doing things over others. If we accept this premise, we will then have to conclude that all manifestations of art, and specifically all images, starting from cave paintings, have depended on bodily prostheses, cognitive extensions and expanded modes of intelligence. My concept of 'nonhuman photography' thus arguably goes further (or deeper) than Paglen's idea of 'seeing machines' because it not only studies humans as seen by machines or machines that see things outside the human spectrum, but also because it understands humans as seeing machines. Last but not least, it also reaches towards the geological past, with the universe positioned as a giant camera making photo-imagistic impressions on a variety of surfaces, from rocks through to skin.

Yet, rather than enter into terminological competition with Paglen, whose work I greatly admire, I am more interested in bringing his theory of machinic sight into a conversation with my own work that probes the algorithmic aspect of perception and vision across apparatuses, species and time scales. The rationale for this conversation is an attempt on my part to imagine better ways of seeing the world at a time when it is being re-shaped by the discourses and practices of AI. It is also to envisage better ways of acting in the world. While I acknowledge that both seeing and acting will be undertaken by human and nonhuman agents, the reflective process on what constitutes this goodness and what forms it may take, and also on the competing claims as to its validity – depending on one's political and ontological constitution – will be uniquely human. To enact this encounter, I want to offer a new conceptual figuration:

'undigital photography'. The term is not fully mine: I have borrowed it from the academic discipline of computational photography, a field which deals with images captured and processed by means of digital computation rather than as a result of optical processes. 'Undigital photography' is the alternative moniker given to this new field in which 'the snap is only the start' (Kelion 2013) and where changes to focus, lighting, framing or depth of field can take place *after* an image has been taken. It goes without saying that computation has been part of mechanical image-making for a long time now: we can think here of Photoshop or internal processing of jpg or even raw files by various digital cameras. What changes with computational photography is the *inherent* instability of the outcome of the imaging process, with its openness to manipulation constituting the very ontology of the undigital image – and not just a possibility aimed at professionals or advanced amateurs, as it was with more traditional digital images produced by early mobile phone or DSLR cameras. Yet in the term 'undigital photography' I also see a conceptual and poetic promise for rethinking our current frameworks and modes of understanding image-making as developed in both media theory and visual culture. The term thus offers new possibilities for thinking photographically in the age of AI. This terminological reinscription is made partly in jest: my real goal is to cut through the smoke and mirrors that envelop the discourses of computation and AI. But I also want to raise broader questions about the conditions of image-making, creativity and labour today.

Undigital photography recognises the (human) history of photography: its artistic legacy, affective attachments and technological residues. But it repositions this history as premised on events undertaken by human agents along the lines of technical assemblages – assemblages which *also* include humans. This repositioning is undertaken with a view to offering a more complex understanding of the relations of causality, influence and change, but also of human responsibility and the possibilities of its enactment as part of such assemblages. It is an attempt to respond to Flusser's probing question as to what humans can do in a universe driven by geophysical forces which are not of our making (see Flusser 2011: 16–19) – and to explore what form human creativity can take, be it on an artistic, engineering or political level. This attempt also entails questioning to what extent such creativity can ever be *solely* human. The renewed interest in, and research into, artificial intelligence makes such an enquiry ever more urgent. My contribution to this enquiry has taken the form of an (un)photographic project that has engaged with 'artificial artificial intelligence'. The latter term is what Amazon has been informally calling its Mechanical Turk (MTurk) platform, an online 'marketplace' connecting labour suppliers with providers worldwide.

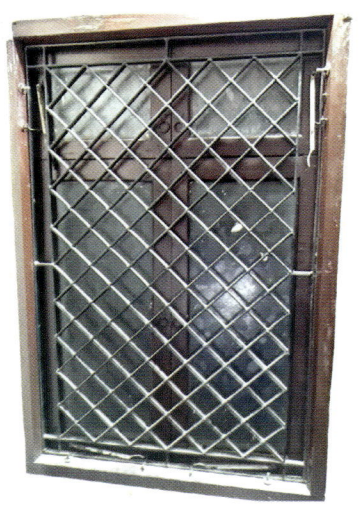
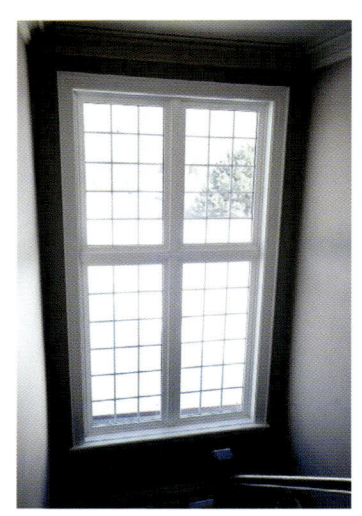
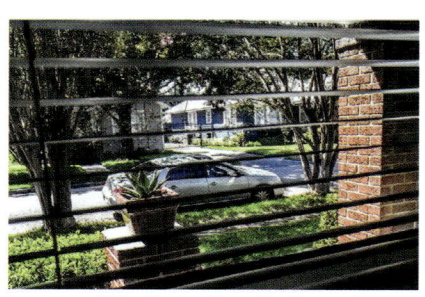
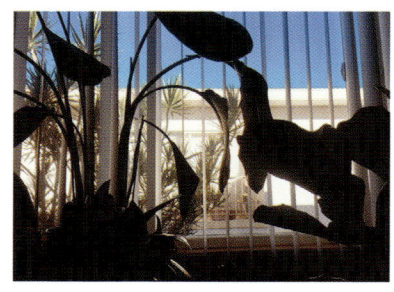
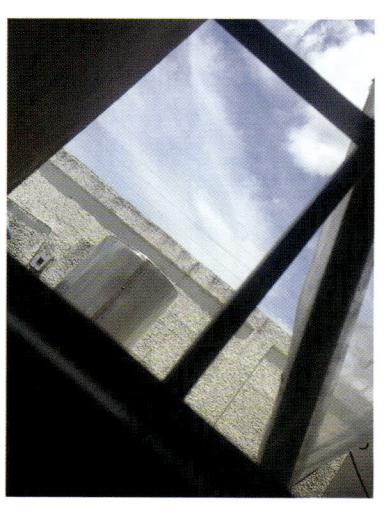
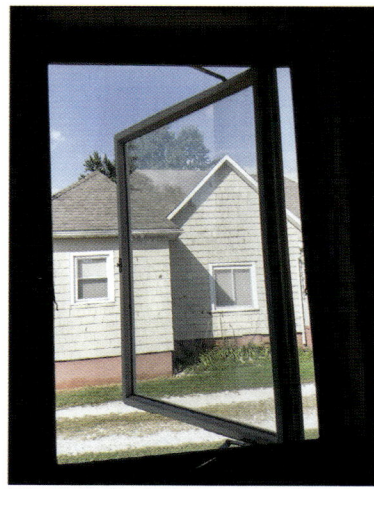

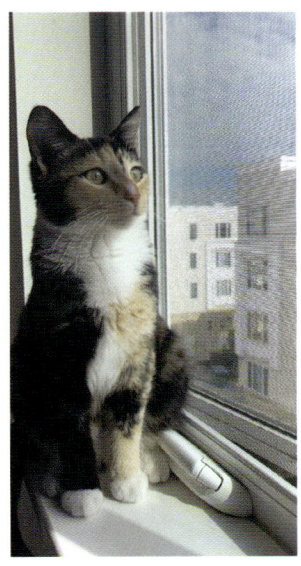
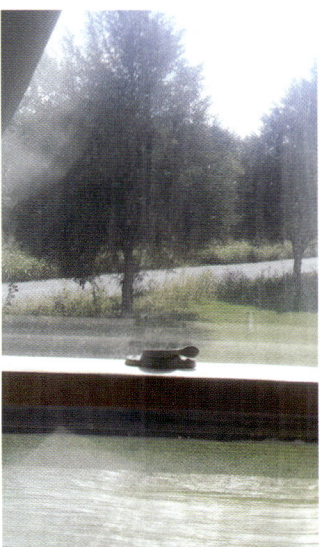

Figures 12.1 to 12.5 Joanna Zylinska: excerpts from *View from the Window*, 2018. The complete project is available at: <https://vimeo.com/344979151> or it can be viewed by scanning the QR code at the end of this chapter> (Figure 12.7).

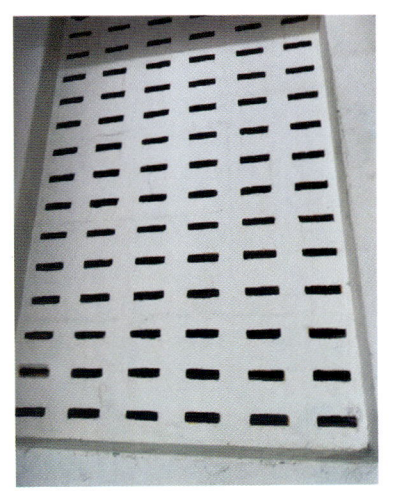
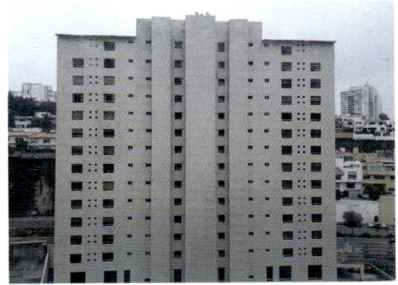

The 'labour' here consists of HITs, 'human intelligence tasks' usually involving simple mechanical actions performed on digital data, such as tagging photographs or filling in surveys, priced very cheaply (from 0.01 to 0.25 cents per task on average). The project basically puts humans in the role of machines, as it would be too impractical and costly to program a computer to perform such tasks.

Imaging (as) Off-the-Scale Labour

For my project I commissioned 100 MTurkers to take one photo of a view from a window of the room they were in at the time (see Figures 12.1 to 12.5). The instructions clearly stipulated that if there was no window in the room, they should go to the next available room with a window and take a photo from there. They were also asked not to upload stock photos, existing images from the web or their old photos. I explained that this HIT was for a research/art project which studied human and machinic creativity. The participants were asked to make their photo look beautiful, according to their own idea of what this meant. Post-processing was allowed but not required. The HIT was priced at double the US living wage (per hour), which probably explains why all the tasks had been snapped up and fulfilled almost immediately – although, given that the task was to take 1–2 minutes on average (precisely because I wanted a somewhat automatic production of the scene, to be executed by time-poor humans in assembly with their heavily automated phone cameras), I could hardly be said to be alleviating world poverty.[3] Indeed, the very act of using MTurk for this project was not unproblematic, as I will show further on, and can actually be seen to be perpetuating unfair labour conditions worldwide by validating Amazon's platform. The exploration of these issues and conditions also forms the fabric of my project.

I do not know where the MTurkers that responded to my call came from, although it is possible to make some guesses from the images themselves, using clues from signage, architecture and vegetation. According to a 2018 study, 'Most of the [MTurk] workers are from the USA (75%), with India (16%) being second, followed by Canada (1.1%), Great Britain (0.7%), Philippines (0.35%), and Germany (0.27%)' (Difallah et al. 2018: 3). The composition of a group of available workers at any one time also depends on what time it is in different time zones. The geographical concentration of the platform's workers is unsurprising given that, even though many of the advertised tasks are very simple, they require a command of the English language to understand and perform them, which puts native and near-native speakers at an advantage. Yet MTurkers operate anonymously and are only identified through their assigned number, creating an illusion of a fluid mobile labour force that forms part of the digital cloud.

The idea behind my project was to re-materialise the cloudy vapour behind this narrative by creating a group portrait of MTurkers' locations. Neither conventional portraiture nor landscape photography, the collective image-base of *View from the Window* offers instead a non-comprehensive demographic snapshot of the global workforce, looking out. The concept and the title entail a return to the mythical 'first photo' in the history of photography: Joseph Nicéphore Niépce's *View from the Window at Le Gras* (1826 or 1827) (Figure 12.6). Due to the limited sensitivity of photographic materials – namely, the pewter plate covered with bitumen – at the time, Niépce's image of a view from a window of his country house in Bourgogne took eight hours to expose. It resulted in 'a scene which the human eye could never see', with sunlight and shadow being visible on two sides of the buildings at left and right (see Anthes in

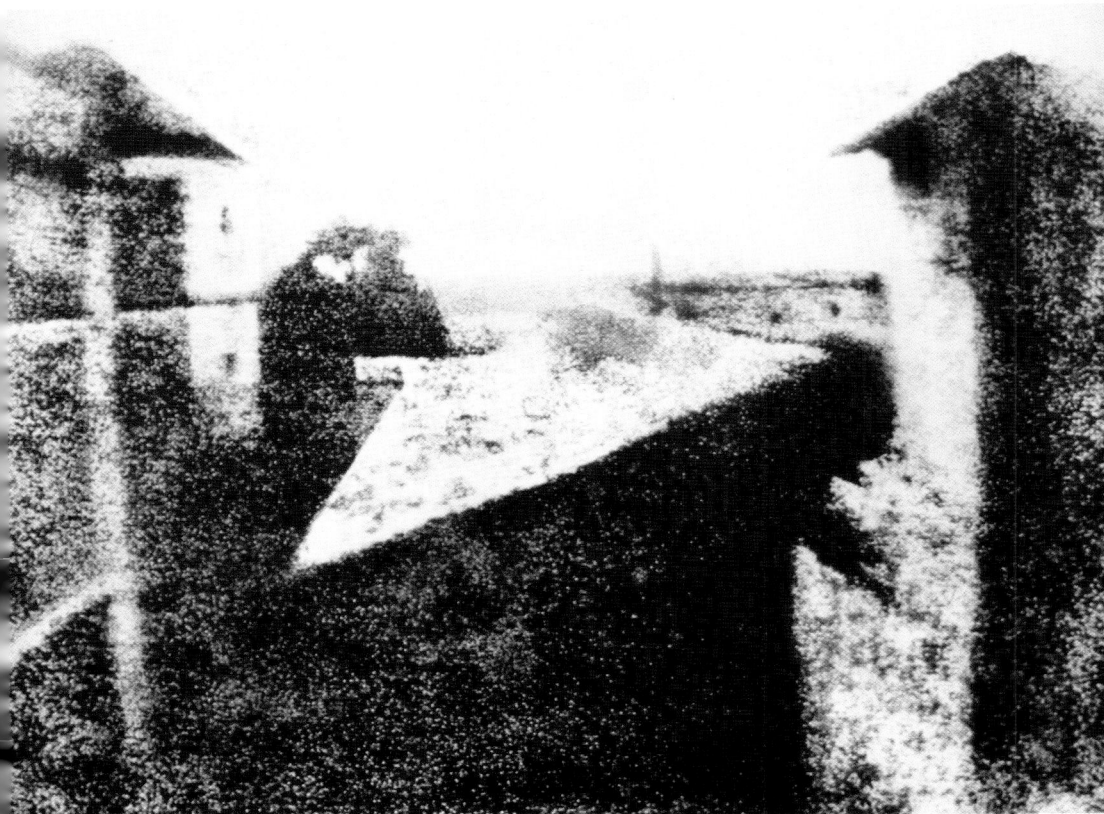

Figure 12.6 Enhanced version of Joseph Nicéphore Niépce's *View from the Window* at Le Gras, 1826 or 1827. Public domain.

Modrak 2011: 112). I argued elsewhere that the first image in the history of photography therefore presented a distinctly nonhuman vision (Zylinska 2017: 21–2), while also enacting a nonhuman agency at the heart of its production. It is also for this reason that I chose Niépce's image as a conceptual frame for my MTurk project. The 'artificial artificial intelligence' of Amazon's invisible and distributed labour force can therefore be described as 'undigital' in the sense that, even though it uses digital technology to perform at least partially digital tasks, simulating the work of machines in its quiet efficiency, it also ruptures the seamless narrative and visualisation of the machine world. It does this by bringing the material traces of human bodies and their locations into the picture, literally. The view from the window also shows us that *there is a window* in the first place (or not). This window is not just a rectangular visualisation of the software interface patented by Microsoft and used by other operating systems as part of their user-friendly GUI, but also a metal or wooden frame holding a glass pane (and, occasionally, curtains, shutters or a mosquito net) that brings in the outside world. It simultaneously keeps this outside world at bay, precisely as 'the outside', the place where the person looking out *is not*.

In her book provocatively titled book, *Artificial Unintelligence*, which deals with a misguided belief that computation can solve all complex social issues (see Broussard 2018: 11), Meredith Broussard argues that 'How you define AI depends on what you want to believe about the future' (89). Yet, unlike Brossard's effort to humanise technology and bring the human back to the centre of the technological assembly, *View from the Window* (Figures 12.1 to 12.5) aims to do something different. Indeed, for me such a well-meaning effort at humanisation can only ever be misguided because it is premised on severing the human's constitutive relationship with technology. What the project does offer, though, is a different vantage point for perceiving this relationship at this particular moment in time – and, more importantly, a recognition *that there is a vantage point*, and that the 'view from nowhere' (see Haraway 1998) promoted by most AI designers ends up putting a very specific (white, male, ahistorical) human in the picture. *View from the Window* thus also suggests that, as well as breaking through the glass ceiling, (un)digital workers may be ready at any time to start smashing their virtual windows. How is that for the 'AI breakout' many AI researchers are supposedly scared of?

Computer scientists Djellel Difallah, Elena Filatova and Panos Ipeirotis have conducted a 28-month survey which revealed that 'the number of available workers on Mechanical Turk is at least 100K, with approximately 2K workers being active at any given moment' (Difallah et al. 2018: 2). They have also demonstrated that 'the MTurk workers' half-life is 12–18 months, indicating that the population refreshes significantly over time' (2). Branded a 'virtual sweatshop', MTurk basically offers labour as performed by not yet quite artificial intelligence. The platform's name is borrowed from the late eighteenth-century chess-playing automaton constructed by Wolfgang von Kempelen and displayed at European courts and other venues of prominence. In the game of magic often associated with new technologies and the promises made in their name, tinted by the orientalist fantasies of the day, von Kempelen's automaton featured a turban-sporting sculpture ('The Turk') positioned above all sorts of contraptions that hinted at the complex mechanisms inside. Yet what the inside really hid was a human chess master, whose intelligence was needed to power the illusion of a chess-playing machine.

Given that the tasks required by Amazon's low-price anonymous labourers are infinite, it is understandable why artists may flock to the platform. Driven by opportunism, curiosity or even a desire to unveil the hidden conditions of global labour in the digital age, they have asked MTurks to 'draw a sheep facing to the left' that later made up a massive digital tapestry, paint small sections of a $100 bill without realising it was to become part of a larger picture, literally and metaphorically (both projects by Aaron Koblin), photographing themselves holding a sign which revealed why they did this work (Andy Baio), realise webcam performances (Eva and Franco Mattes) and even write poetry (Nick Thurston). There is a long history of artists exploring the multiple dimensions of creativity while challenging their own singular role in the process by 'crowdsourcing' their works – from André Breton's *Exquisite Corpse*, which involved collectively assembling words and images, through to mail art, smart mobs and Harrell Fletcher and Miranda July's *LearningToLoveYouMore.com*, where participants were asked to perform simple tasks (e.g. 'Take a picture of strangers holding hands') and upload the results to a website (see Grover 2006; Holmes 2011). What is new about using MTurk is that crowdsourced art is really an outcome of extremely cheap labour undertaken by those who rely on Amazon's platform for income, rather than of playful participation in a shared activity. Yet artists sometimes flatter themselves or alleviate their conscience by saying that they are providing a diversion to workers exposed to the chain of otherwise mindless HITs by allowing them to do something 'creative'.

An Uber for Art?

Koblin's work has garnered particular criticism. LABoral, a Spanish Centre for Art and Industrial Creation, has argued that 'Exploitation of creative labour, albeit in a humorous way, is built into this system of participatory art making', while at the same time acknowledging that

The Sheep Market 'questions the commodification of networked "human intelligence" and cultural production' (LABoral non-dated). M. C. Elish has pointed out that in projects of this kind '[t]he implications and the stakes of Mechanical Turk as an economic system are left untouched' (Elish 2010). These implications have been addressed by many scholars of labour in the networked global economy, but they have also become a focus of artists working explicitly with crowdsourced material. Nick Thurston's book *Of the Subcontract* contains poems written by MTurkers as part of their HIT and is prefaced by a foreword which Marxist critic McKenzie Wark had commissioned, via Freelancer.com, from a ghost-writer in Pakistan for $75. The poems veer between naive and self-knowing, crafty and well-crafted, but, in being framed by the MTurk pricing and the time dedicated to the fulfilment of the task, they all serve as a basic lesson in classic materialism: there is no 'pure' aesthetic experience outside the wider social conditions of labour, even if the artist or the recipient want to use the work to create an illusion of its existence. While many of the poems deal with supposedly universal topics such as pain, love and beauty, several are knowingly self-reflexive about the task – and the life – at hand:

> 0.04 [written in response to the offered payment of 0.02 cents]
> Would you do work for this measly amount?
> Would you take it seriously, would it even count.
> ('Am I Blind, or Maybe Dumb?', in Thurston 2013: 24)

> 00.17 [payment of 0.17 cents]
> To write a poem for you
> That would surely not do
> For you to take it and make it your own.
> ('A Poem You Did Not Write', in Thurston 2013: 38)

Thurston's book thus foregrounds the MTurkers' conditions of labour, which turn them into an '"elastic staffing pool" to whom the employer has no obligation beyond the agreed payment' (Thurston in Voyce 2014: 105). Clone-like in their anonymity, MTurkers are 'differentiated only by their listed efficiency relative to the efficiency of the latest Master Workers, just as all computers are the computer, differentiated only by their inbuilt processing capacity relative to the capacity of the latest market-leading computers' (Thurston in Voyce 2014: 108). The artificial artificial intelligence of the MTurk labour force is thus both a representation of a labour ideal in the times of global capital flows and a premonition of things to come, for the majority of workers, in the majority of jobs and careers. Yet the worry that AI-driven robots will take over, that they are going to replace us, is often dismissed by technocapitalists with the breezy reassurance that new jobs will be created, poverty diminished, and that, as a result of widespread automation, 'we' will simply have more free time. The rebranding of unemployment and precarity as freedom sounds particularly ominous in the positive reports about the supposed desirability of the gig economy, with its 'flexibility' and 'freedom'. In the aptly titled article, 'The Internet Is Enabling a New Kind of Poorly Paid Hell', published in *The Atlantic* in January 2018, Alana Semuels explains:

> A research paper published in December that analyzed 3.8 million tasks on Mechanical Turk, performed by 2,676 workers, found that those workers earned a median hourly wage of about $2 an hour. Only 4 percent of workers earned more than $7.25 an hour. Kotaro Hara, the lead author of the study and a professor at Singapore Management University, told me that workers earn so little because it's hard to secure enough tasks to be working every minute they're in front of the computer. He says workers spend a lot of time looking for tasks, waiting for the interface to load, and trying to complete poorly explained tasks before deciding to return them ... How is it legal to compensate workers so poorly? The federal minimum wage in America, after all, is $7.25 an hour. But ... crowdsourced workers do not have to receive the minimum wage because they are considered independent contractors, not employees. (Semuels 2018)

This problem of underemployment and underpayment affects not only workers on labour-sourcing platforms such as MTurk, CrowdFlower, Clickworker, Toluna or Fiverr, but also other actors in the 'disruptive' gig economy, bankrolled by Silicon Valley capital, such as Uber and Deliveroo drivers, zero-hours contract shop assistants and, last but not least, casualised academic staff.

Darren Wershler's afterword to Thurston's *Of The Subcontract* makes an important suggestion with regard to the force of such projects. More than as a critique of a particular form of creativity (in this case, poetry, with all its forms and conventions) or even of the economics of MTurk, he suggests that Thurston's project can be read as an institutional critique of the conditions of the production of art, with fame and glory attached to the singular auteur, but with the labour and infrastructure provided by 'legion'. (This applies to fine art made by the likes of Damien Hirst, to which of course there are historical antecedents predating the era of industrial capitalism – if not that of the celebration of the individual/ist human subject – as much as it does to fashion or entertainment media.) Wershler recognises Thurston's gesture as 'fully ironised' (Wershler 2013: 138), revealing as it does that

> [T]he once-lauded cultural value of the work of poets is now so close to nothing as to be indistinguishable from it, and that the work of precarious labourers in a networked digital milieu, which is remunerated far below minimum wage, without benefits or the collective bargaining power of unionisation, is nevertheless dignified.

Wershler proposes to read *Of the Subcontract* not as a solution but rather as a symptom of an age in which all sorts of activities are reconfigured as Human Intelligence Tasks. This reconfiguration goes hand in hand with the full automation of typically human creative tasks such as reporting, journalism and data analysis, with a growing list of jobs and careers threatened by being lost to AI. 'Poets and professors can point to this change', says Wershler, 'but, so far, have not been able to move beyond it. As we are being to realise, our tasks, too, can be outsourced' (Wershler 2013: 139). This state of events, deemed 'the uberfication of the university' by Gary Hall in his book of the same name (2016), hints at a near future in which we all become 'entrepreneurs of the self', with every aspect of our lives – from inhabiting a room or sleeping on someone's sofa, making friends and dating through to walking – monetised both as a 'shareable' good and a data point. Yet any wealth generated as part of this so-called sharing economy is 'concentrated in the hands of relatively few', who 'also centrally control the platform, software, algorithm, data, and associated ecosystem, deciding on pricing and wage levels, work allocation, standards, conditions, and preferred user and laborer profiles' (Hall 2016).

Significantly, Hall offers more than just a critique of the precarious labour conditions in the digital economy – or of the extension of these conditions to professions and careers that were previously seen as safe from the disruptive logic of its algorithms: Wershler's 'poets and professors'. He also issues a call to arms aimed at those *in* the academic world, highlighting that 'the university provides one of the few spaces in postindustrial society where the forces of contemporary neoliberalism's anti-public sector regime are still being overtly opposed, to a certain extent at least'. The most important question we are posed here is not therefore whether robots and algorithms *can* replace us as artists, poets and professors. Although, to answer that underlying question, 'they' surely can – by being able to produce singular artefacts that will 'take us in', evoke the sensation of beauty, become popular or even sell well, and by producing online books, classes and whole courses made up of the existing and rehashed content that 'will do', for a while at least. The question rather is how to create conditions in which creativity with its accompanying institutions, especially those not driven by the logic of innovation, profit and capital – institutions such as public universities and art schools, state-owned galleries, museums and cultural centres – still count *for us embodied humans with material and other needs*.

Scaling Back: A Conclusion (and an Opening)

The belief in the wisdom of the crowd associated with the optimism of the early internet era, and driven by the spirit of communitarianism and collaboration, has lost its shine in the age of global digital surveillance, fake news, Twitter bubbles and possible election manipulation via social media. The crowd has now been revealed to be not so much wise as mouldable and subject to all sorts of exploitation. We have also learnt not only that 'they' are really watching us but also that we are all doing it to one another: we are all MTurks in Jeff Bezos's or Mark Zuckerberg's digital factories. Crowdsourcing therefore becomes a form of crowd-mobbing. And thus, even if I argue that we have always been artificially intelligent, the specific historical and cultural labour practices of humans at a given point in time do matter. *View from the Window* can therefore be seen as an indictment of inhumane labour practices, of the supposed ease with which an erasure of the human is being enacted. In its photographic legacy and epistemological ambition to see otherwise, it casts light on the lingering shadows of the globalised digital labour market. Presented as diptychs in an automated photobook, the photographs in the project foreground the mediation processes shaping the production of knowledge, while also revealing the human signal points involved in the process. We see in them different labour distribution from what looks like the suburbs in the US, possibly in India, maybe somewhere in Latin America. Through the uneasy parallelism of the image pairs, the work asks whose interests are bring represented – and who can afford to be creative, where, when and for how long.

The defence of art practices and institutions for the human offered in this chapter has little to do with any residual humanism, a desire to preserve 'our human uniqueness', 'our sense of beauty' or any other humanist niceties of this kind. Instead, it has to do with asking poets and professors to keep fighting against the uberfication of the university and the art school, of knowledge production and art production. In other words, it is a form of 'scaling back'. With *View form the Window*, and the wider project of undigital photography, I thus want to show that, even though we are all entangled in algorithms, it matters how we use them, what visions and vistas they will be made to produce, who will get to see them, who (or what) will take the picture, of what, in what circumstances, to what purpose and for what price. Building on the legacy of the term in computer science, undigital photography thus becomes for me a way of reframing the picture after it's been taken, of looking askew and anew, of refocusing and re-zooming in on what matters, and of rethinking what matters to begin with. It is also a way of seeing photography and image-making as a practice that is inherently unfinished. Moving beyond the uniqueness of the single image on a gallery wall or the predictability of the Instagram flow, undigital photography becomes an ethico-political opening towards the unknown, coupled with a demand for this knowledge not to be computed too quickly.

Notes

This chapter has been adapted from Joanna Zylinska, *AI Art: Machine Visions and Warped Dreams* (London: Open Humanities Press, 2020).

1. Competition announcement available at: <https://consumer.huawei.com/uk/campaign/sparkarenaissance> (last accessed 4 March 2019).
2. I had to reject 20% of the original tasks I had received because, contrary to the instructions, some participants had just used stock photos or because the download link to the image did not work, so I reopened the HIT to get up to a hundred images.

References

Barrat, James (2013), *Our Final Invention: Artificial Intelligence and the End of the Human Era*. New York: Thomas Dunne Books-St Martin's Press.
Barthes, Roland (1973), *Mythologies*. London: Paladin Books.
Bratton, Benjamim H. (2016), *The Stack: On Software and Sovereignty*. Cambridge, MA: MIT Press.
Broussard, Meredith (2018), *Artificial Unintelligence: How Computers Misunderstand the World*. Cambridge, MA: MIT Press.
Derrida, Jacques (1987), *The Truth in Painting*. Chicago: University of Chicago Press.
Difallah, Djellel, Elena Filatova and Panos Ipeirotis (2018), 'Demographics and Dynamics of Mechanical Turk Workers', in *Proceedings of WSDM 2018: The Eleventh ACM International Conference on Web Search and Data Mining*. Marina Del Rey, CA, USA, February 5–9 (WSDM 2018), 9 pages. Available at: <https://dl.acm.org/doi/10.1145/3159652.3159661> (last accessed 11 July 2020).
Elish, M. C. (2010), 'Representing Labor: Ten Thousand Cents and Amazon's Mechanical Turk', *Furtherfield*, 29 January. Available at: <https://www.furtherfield.org-representing-labor-ten-thousand-cents-and-amazons-mechanical-turk> (last accessed 11 July 2020).
Flusser, Vilém (2011), *Into the Universe of Technical Images*. Minneapolis: University of Minnesota Press.

Grover, Andrea (2006), 'Phantom Captain: Art and Crowdsourcing', *Apexart*. Available at: <https://apexart.org-exhibitions-grover.htm> (last accessed 11 July 2020).
Hall, Gary (2016), *The Uberfication of the University*. Minneapolis: University of Minnesota Press. Kindle edition.
Haraway, Donna (1998), 'Situated Knowledges: The Science Question in Feminism and the Privilege of Partial Perspective', *Feminist Studies*, 14(3): 575–99.
Holmes, Kevin (2011), 'Creativity Bytes: A Brief Guide to Crowdsourced Art', *Vice*, 23 March. Available at: <https://www.vice.com-en-uk-article-xyvmwd-creativity-bytes-a-brief-guide-to-crowdsourced-art> (last accessed 16 January 2020).
Huawei (2018), 'Professional Phonetography at Anytime: A Look into HUAWEI P20's Master AI', 8 June. Available at: <https://huaweiarmenia.am-gb-blog-post-55> (last accessed 11 July 2020).
Kant, Immanuel (1952), *The Critique of Judgement*. Oxford: Clarendon Press.
Kelion, Leo (2013), 'Computational Photography: The Snap is Only the Start', *BBC News*, Technology, 11 July. Available at: <https://www.bbc.co.uk-news-technology-23235771> (last accessed 16 January 2020).
LABoral: Centro de Arte y Creación Industrial (Non-dated), 'The Sheep Market'. Available at: <http://www.laboralcentrodearte.org-en-recursos-obras-the-sheep-market-view> (last accessed 16 January 2020).
Modrak, Rebekah, with Bill Anthes (2011), *Reframing Photography: Theory and Practice*. London and New York: Routledge.
Noble, Safiya (2018), *Algorithms of Oppression: How Search Engines Reinforce Racism*. New York: New York University Press. Kindle edition.
Paglen, Trevor (2014), 'Seeing Machines': posting in the Fotomuseum Winterthur series 'Is Photography Over?', 13 March. Available at: <https://www.fotomuseum.ch-en-explore-still-searching-articles-26978-seeing-machines> (last accessed 16 January 2020).
Semuels, Alana (2018), 'The Internet Is Enabling a New Kind of Poorly Paid Hell', *The Atlantic*, 23 January. Available at: <https://www.theatlantic.com-business-archive-2018-01-amazon-mechanical-turk-551192> (last accessed 16 January 2020).
Strecker, Alexander (Non-dated), 'An Urgent Look at How Artificial Intelligence Will See the World', *LensCulture*. Available at: <https://www.lensculture.com-articles-trevor-paglen-an-urgent-look-at-how-artificial-intelligence-will-see-the-world> (last accessed 16 January 2020).
Thurston, Nick (2013), *Of the Subcontract, Or Principles of Poetic Right*, York: information as material.
Voyce, Stephen (2014), 'Of the Subcontract: An Interview with Nick Thurston', *The Iowa Review*, 43(3): 94–108.

Wershler, Darren (2013), 'Afterword', in Nick Thurston, *Of the Subcontract, Or Principles of Poetic Right*. York: information as material.

Zylinska, Joanna (2017), *Nonhuman Photography*. Cambridge, MA: MIT Press.

Coda: Photography in the Age of Massification

A Correspondence between Joan Fontcuberta and Geoffrey Batchen

'CORRESPONDENCE' is an online project created by the Foto Colectania Foundation, in collaboration with the Banco Sabadell Foundation, which aims to reflect upon the relevance that photography has had in contemporary visual culture, keeping in mind historical perspective and the original contexts in which photographs have been created and disseminated. The Spanish artist Joan Fontcuberta and the Australian theorist and historian Geoffrey Batchen exchanged a number of letters about the role of the photographer in contemporary culture between October 2016 and January 2017. This chapter presents an edited version of that exchange.

6 October 2016

Hi Geoff,

If Foto Colectania have asked me to 'correspond' with you about the role of the photographer today and the general question of the status of copyright and of the author, it's because they are aware that these are crucial issues for me. So crucial, in fact, that I've been harping on the subject for some time now, not least in my interventions as a guest at Foto Colectania and, more recently, and in a more focused manner with the publication of a book, *La furia de las imágenes: Notas sobre la postfotografía* [The Fury of the Images: Notes on Postphotography] – in which, by the way, I quote you profusely. There are very good reasons why you are one of the *maîtres-à-penser* of photography who have most guided my own thoughts and reflections.

In line with previous projects of mine based on a more or less semiotic approach to elucidating the degree zero of photographic writing (I'm thinking, for example, of *Blow Up Blow Up* and *Gastrópoda*), my *Trauma* series adopts the hypothesis that images have an organic metabolism: they are born, they grow, reproduce and die, to restart the cycle of life. In 1928 Paul Valéry wrote that images 'will be created and melt away at the slightest gesture'. In *Trauma* I put forward the idea of sick images, images that suffer: photographs with some kind of pathological condition or impairment that interferes with their documentary function and renders them unable to 'live' in an archive. The paradox is that this disease, though it can eliminate the identifiable information content of a picture, acts like the cancer which gives an orchid its dazzling beauty, endowing it with an extraordinary graphic uniqueness. In the photo book, the only clue to guide the reader is on the cover, which plays with the title of Freud's 1899/1900 *Die Traumdeutung* (*The Interpretation of Dreams*): with a slight conceptual manipulation, the German *Traum* (dream) has been replaced by *Trauma*. My working process, then, consists in prowling around photo libraries and archives in search of patients in a state of trauma. Like the great foundational work of psychoanalysis, the cover of my book includes a quote from the *Aeneid*, 'Flectere si nequeo superos, Acheronta movebo', in which Virgil invites us to turn to the gods of the underworld if the gods of heaven pay us no heed. So we are speaking of a heaven and a hell of images, and speaking, too, as Andrés Hispano has noted, of a limbo and a purgatory.

The archaeological operation carried out in *Trauma* has yielded a rich harvest of insights. The first is that on crossing the threshold of recognition or intelligibility, the image does not become hyper-realistic in the sense that it continues to provide data at increasingly precise scales; instead, it becomes abstract and ambiguous. The paradox is that in going so far beyond a discernible scale of representation, the visual information of the initial scene disappears, to make way for the information intrinsic to the actual substance of the photograph itself (grain, oxidation, scratches, mildew . . .). *Trauma* is an ode to the materiality that subsists in the chemical photograph, its residues and its excrescences – an ode intoned in melancholic recognition of the irremediable and overwhelming dematerialisation of the digital image. But it also – and hence the relevance of this project in prompting a debate about the authorship, its residues and its excrescences – makes clear the extent of these images' debt to earlier images. Recycling as an act of creation relies on the prior existence of a wealth of materials that can be recovered, selected and 'metabolised' – to continue my simile of the biology of the images. This

Figure 13.1 Joan Fontcuberta: *Trauma #2862*, 2016.

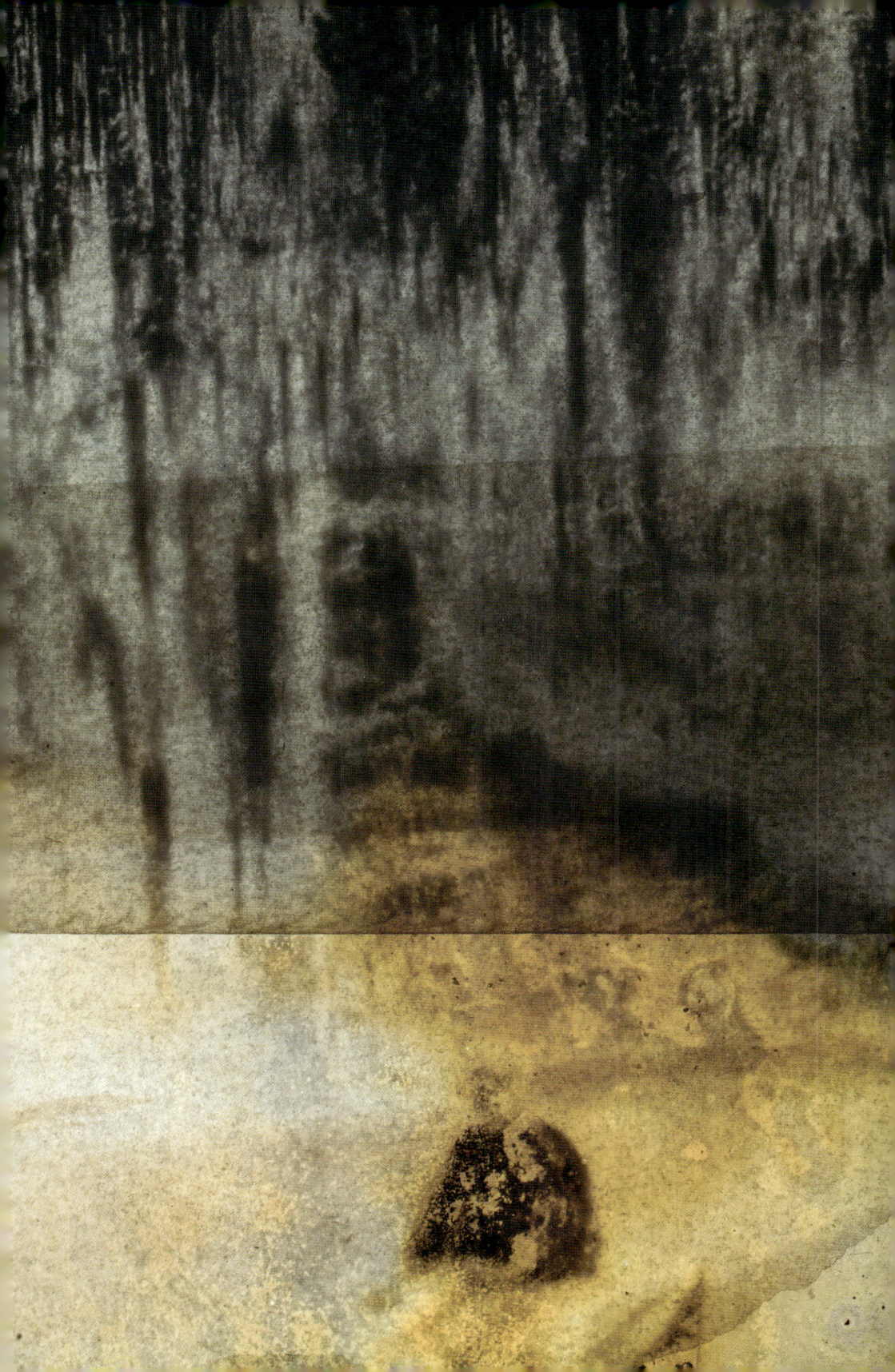

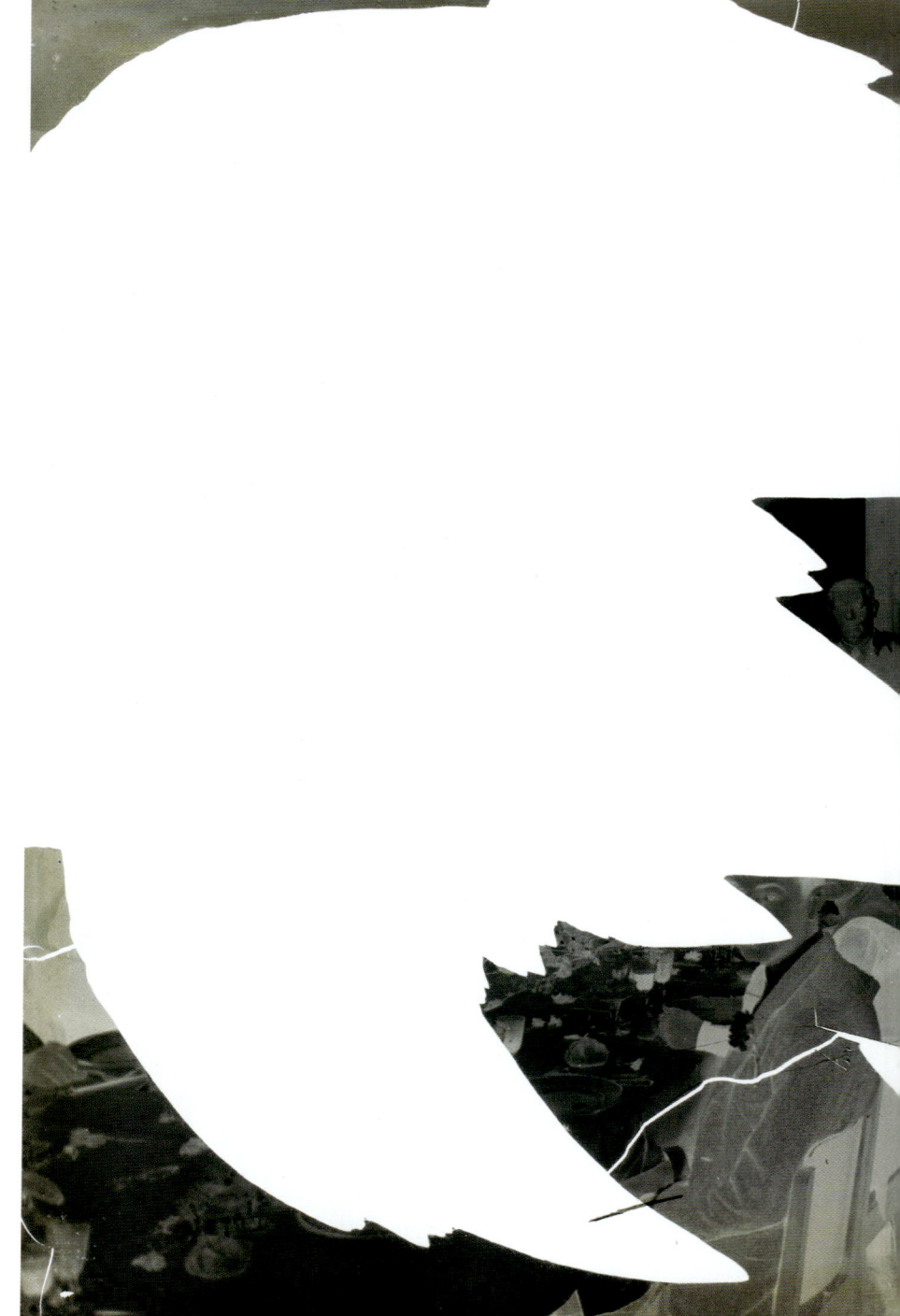

Figure 13.2 Joan Fontcuberta: *Trauma #2879*, 2016.

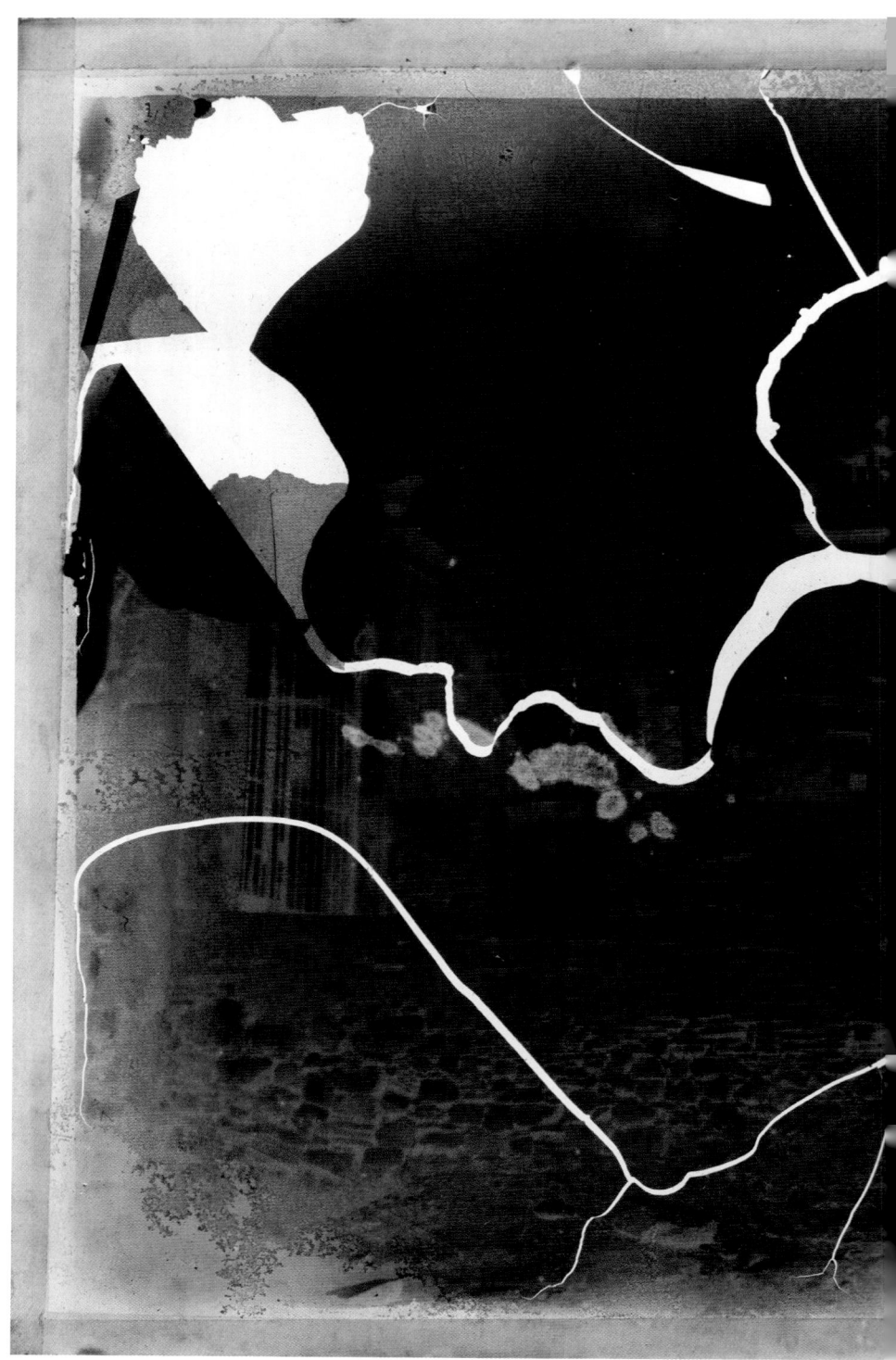

Figure 13.3 Joan Fontcuberta: *Trauma #2897*, 2016.

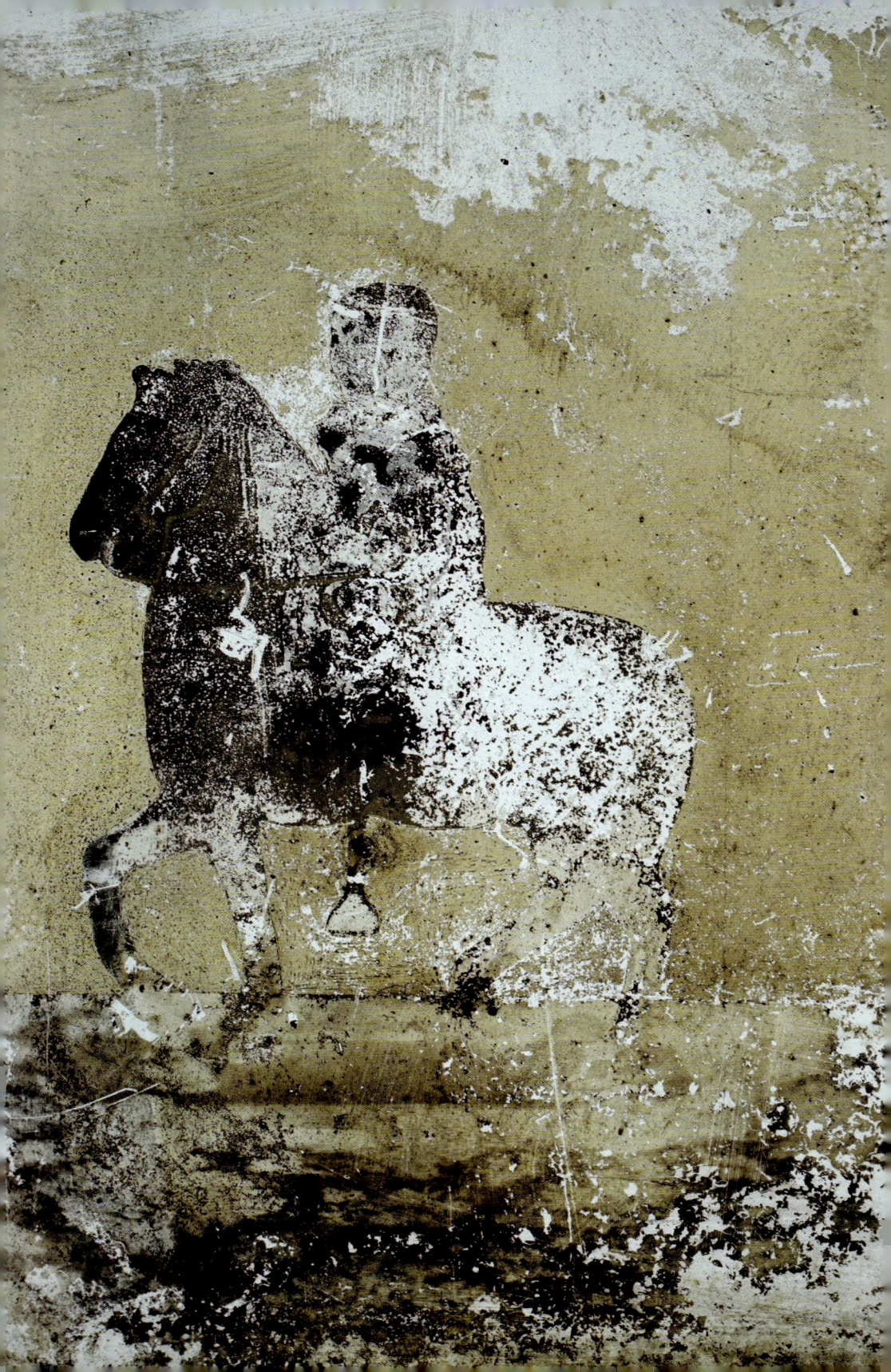

would entail acknowledging the notion of an iconic habitat: our life unfolds *in* images.

Ingrid Guardiola expressed this idea very well in her inaugural lecture at EINA art and design school. She cited a parable by the late David Foster Wallace: 'There are these two young fish swimming along and they happen to meet an older fish swimming the other way, who nods at them and says "Morning, boys. How's the water?" And the two young fish swim on for a bit, and then eventually one of them looks over at the other and goes "What the hell is water?"' Guardiola went on to unpack this for us: 'Foster Wallace was alluding here to the fact that the most obvious and important realities are the hardest to see and the most difficult to speak about. At a time like the present in which we are swimming in images, it is normal to ask ourselves: what are images? And this is not a case of naive "not knowing" but a question that goes to the heart of the matter. If, as Rancière says, "everything is image", we had better learn to swim among the images' (Guardiola 2016).

Indeed: we have to ask ourselves what images are – or rather, what they have become. In attempting to trace this seam, which runs through philosophy from Plato to the Visual Studies of Gottfried Boehm and W. J. T. Mitchell, I would suggest that when creation – as in *Trauma* – consists not in extracting an image from reality but in revealing how the image forms part of reality, and when the creative act consists in awakening 'dormant' images, the status of photographer (or author) is not attained simply by producing more photographs but by striving to make the photographs reveal what they are.

In conclusion, let me jump from Virgil to Homer. The exhibition in the Àngels Barcelona gallery that mine will follow is entitled *Penelope* and is a new work by Pep Agut, an artist who uses both painting and photography. According to the Homeric account, Odysseus sailed from Ithaca to fight in the Trojan War. For more than twenty years his wife Penelope awaited his return, resisting the proposals of the many suitors who courted her in the belief that her husband will not return. When the impatient suitors urge her to accept one of them, Penelope agrees to give her decision when she has completed the burial shroud she is weaving. This is evidently a ploy to gain time, because each night she unpicks what she has woven during the day. Agut takes the story of Penelope as a metaphor for representation and the meaning this may have. Penelope cannot

Figure 13.4 (previous page) Joan Fontcuberta: *Trauma #4123*, 2016.

offer her shroud to Odysseus 'because, continually interrupted, continually unwoven, it represents nothing . . . Penelope is the expectation of representation. She is the making and unmaking engaged in by every artist's mind and hands' (Agut 2016). Agut seems to be giving us a poetic message: it is only by making and unmaking the photograph that we become photographers.[1]

17 October 2016

Dear Joan,

Your letter was a welcome one, opening onto all sorts of issues that appear to concern us both. And this is the case even with the one you chose to put to one side at the outset, the question of copyright. For this too bears on the question of what an image is. Indeed, it might even be argued that this question is the incubator within which photography came into being.

In January 1839, for example, when photography was announced by both Louis Daguerre in France and Henry Talbot in England, there were already 72 print sellers working in London, servicing a growing middle-class market that was anxious to buy engraved reproductions of contemporary paintings. So lucrative was this market in reproductions that the copyright for a painting was sometimes worth twice the cost of the painting itself. In June 1846, for example, the *Art-Union* reported that, 'for the four pictures painted by Mr Edwin Landseer this year, he received nearly seven thousand pounds – ie. £2,400 for the paintings and £4,450 for the "Copyrights"' (Maas 1975: 20). Print publishers were even known to commission paintings so that engravings could then be made after them; in effect, the prospect of a copy came before the creation of an original, confusing that very distinction. A similar situation existed in France. In 1841 the painter Horace Vernet published a pamphlet in which he pointed out that 'the painter has two means of drawing pecuniary gain from his picture, namely: the sale of the picture itself, and the assignment of engraving rights' (quoted in Bann 2001: 36). As if to prove his point, in the following year he received 2,000 francs from Jean-Pierre-Marie Jazet for the right to engrave his *Napoleon Reviewing the Guard in the Place du Carrousel*, painted in 1838. Importantly, Vernet's text argues that a painter produces both a 'material object' and an 'intellectual object' – that is, both a painting and an image – and that these are separate commodities that can, if necessary, be sold to different parties.

Although English photographers were not granted legal copyright protection until 1861, commercial studios immediately recognised the pecuniary advantages of separating an image from a photograph and selling both. The first studios to be established in London frequently organised for their photographic images to be reproduced in the form of wood engravings or lithographs, and thereby to be distributed in vast quantities all around the globe. As the original daguerreotype was usually destroyed or discarded during the process of transmutation, these reproduced images are like ghosts, haunting the history of photography with their ephemeral, ink on paper presence (Batchen 2016). They are photographic images but not photographs (and therefore have been largely absented from that history). This raises the question of what kind of history must be forged to properly represent photography's complex identity (a history, I'd suggest, that has to be more like a cobweb than a chronicle). But it also raises the question of what happens to a photograph when it gives up its image, when it 'gives up the ghost', as we say in English. What is left when a photograph no longer indexically points outside of itself, when there is nothing left but the substrate, the residue, just a smear of light-sensitive chemicals? What happens when a photograph's only remaining referent is 'photography' itself?

Your own investigation of this condition, gathered under the title *Trauma*, chooses to riff off the legacy of Freud and present your found photographs as signs to photography's unconscious. The archive becomes a kind of hospital from which you have extracted its sickest patients, perhaps even the ones beyond help. Under this rubric, these ruined photographs, a ruination made all the more poignant by occasional glimpses of image, by momentary flashes of sanity, are turned into so many Rorschach tests, as if their study could reveal otherwise hidden thought disorders. You describe them as 'crossing the threshold of recognition or intelligibility', but perhaps some of them (as with the abstractions used in a Rorschach test) could be said to hover on the border between intelligibility and its other? I'm interested in this possibility, as it might help me move away from your biological/psychological metaphor, with its inferences of a photographic pathology perhaps beyond our control, to a discourse I'm a little more comfortable with: politics.

This leads me to reflect on the political identity of these eviscerated photographs of yours, a reflection made possible by your displacement of them from archive to art world. This shifting of context implies that a photograph reduced to a palimpsest of its former self enacts 'an erasure which allows what it obliterates to be read', (Derrida 1981: 6) or, as you put it, 'make[s] way for the information intrinsic to the actual substance of the photograph itself.' But how can one articulate a politics for this information, for this substance that comes both before and after the photograph?

I wonder, for example, how you would locate *Trauma*, as an 'ode to the materiality that subsists in the chemical photograph', in relation to the so-called New Materialism that currently preoccupies certain philosophers? The adherents of New Materialism claim to be offering a counter to what they regard as the orthodox view propagated by both deconstruction and psychoanalysis, the view that there is nothing outside of discourse (Cox et al. 2015). 'Everything is image,' you say, quoting Rancière. But in those instances where image and substance are presented as inseparable states of being, where an image is celebrated for being only itself and nothing more, are we in fact yearning for an *a priori* reality, for a world that exists before and outside of its interpretation by either a camera or a sovereign viewing subject (and therefore outside the mediations of politics or critical thought)?

I'm skeptical about these kinds of arguments myself, if only because I regard the materiality of the photograph as always already of political substance. For me, photography and modernity are synonyms, so closely enmeshed is one with the other. The conception of photography reproduced a representational schema derived from peculiarly modern notions of power, knowledge and subjectivity. The photographic apparatus emerged with the industrial revolution and has always been dependent on a certain combination of chemicals, plates, papers, and machined parts made possible by it. The circulation of photographs and photographic images has similarly depended on the exchange systems established by consumer capitalism. If anything, this symbiotic relationship has become even closer in the digital age, with most photographs being generated by devices designed in the United States and manufactured in China using rare earths extracted from the third world. The cell-phone camera is, in other words, the very embodiment of globalism, as are its photographic outputs, whether their manifestations be organic or electronic. In short, to excavate photography – to extract from it a something that is neither photograph nor non-photograph, and yet belongs to both categories – is to disembowel modernity itself, to turn what seems so certain and incontestable inside out and available for further inspection. It is, in other words, a political act.

In this context, let me offer a supplement to the once-were-images you have gathered in *Trauma*. I'm thinking of the 750,000 scoured and weathered snapshots found after the earthquake and tsunami that swept over eastern Japan in March 2011 (Takahashi 2014). Over 19,000 people were killed during this event and millions continue to struggle to recover from a natural disaster that was demonstrably exacerbated by our modern society's voracious appetite for housing and electricity. The disaster is by no means over. Three nuclear power plants went into meltdown after the tsunami breached their defenses, with as yet unknown consequences. Even now highly radioactive water continues to leak into the sea from these damaged plants. This catastrophe is conjured by the look of the photographs that survived, with the image on each piece of paper seemingly eaten away, as if by a fungus or disease. The spectral surfaces of these snapshots evoke the erasure of both the people depicted and, shortly thereafter, the means of their depiction (I am referring, of course, to Kodak's bankruptcy in January 2012).

As you say, a making that is also an unmaking seems like a potent means of engaging with photography at the moment. And indeed, perhaps at any moment. After all, the English poet Samuel Taylor Coleridge, who called himself 'an Eye-servant of the Goddess Nature' and was close to three of the inventors of photography, also conjured Homer (a Homer channelled through Herder and German idealist philosophy) when moved to speak of this same divinity as 'an ever industrious Penelope for

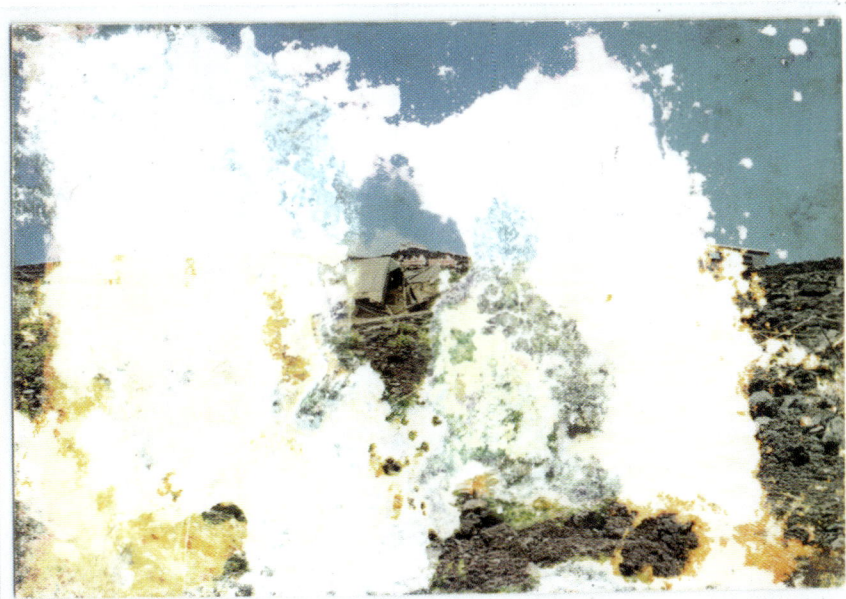

Figure 13.5 Unknown (Japan): Weathered colour snapshot, c. 2011.

ever unravelling what she had woven, for ever weaving what she had unravelled' (Batchen 1997: 60). But I wonder if, for our purposes, the critical capacity of this gesture is enhanced in significant ways when it is freighted with a specific history of the sort I have just described? Surely our challenge is to make (or make over) photographs such that they refer inwards to the political economy of photography but also outwards to a situation grounded in the complex agency of social life.

27 October 2016

Dear Geoff,

A few days ago the IVAM in Valencia inaugurated an exhibition curated by Jorge Luis Marzo, *Fake. It Is Not True, It Is Not A Lie*, which offers a comprehensive and well-documented overview of counter-information strategies in contemporary art and political activism. In one of the actions presented in the show, *The Ballad of Use Value* (2011–12), the artist Octavi Comeron engaged with a question which touches on our concerns here, by exhibiting a perfectly ordinary mass-produced car – a SEAT León – in a gallery and describing it as a work of art. One of the artist's associates then bought the car-cum-artwork from him and, as the sales invoice shows, paid VAT at the rate applied to works of art, 8%, instead of the standard rate for motor vehicles of 18%. In fact the whole thing was a ruse, a stratagem to provoke a response from the Spanish tax authorities, which duly sent Comeron a letter demanding that the sale be rectified and the outstanding tax paid. This gave Comeron the opportunity he was looking for – an exchange of correspondence with the Spanish Finance Ministry that lured the bureaucrats into debating what was or wasn't art. Of course the officials didn't want to know about Duchamp or theories of appropriation, refused to accept that a utilitarian object could be a work of art, and stuck to the bureaucratic and administrative formulas with which the law in force – essentially framed in the nineteenth century – classifies artworks: paintings, prints, sculptures, tapestries, enamels . . . and 'photographs taken by the artist, printed by him or under his supervision, signed and numbered and limited to thirty copies in total, whatever the formats and media' (Law 37/1992 of Value Added Tax). Unfortunately, the artist's untimely death in 2013 left the case unresolved, but the seed of subversion had been planted.

I mention this project because it illustrates the contradictions between a hegemonic value system established from power – a *doxa* – and an alternative counter-system of paradoxes – para-*doxas* – which is the prerogative of critical thinking. And as I see it, Geoff, our duty is to behave, intellectually, like hooligans: as hooligans defying not only the *doxa* of the arms and branches of the state, but also every kind of *doxa* that is imposed by any structure of cultural, social or political authority – art, science, history, academia or whatever.

So I really appreciate your comments in response, which open new windows from which to scan the landscape. And though it seems to me that we don't have the time or the space to deal with everything out there, we can engage with a number of significant points. You note, for example, that I ignored the issue of copyright, and it's true. The right to reproduce an image is part of a more general idea of authors' rights and copyright *in extenso*, and this being so I find it problematic to refer to the rights assigned to a faculty – that of authorship – which we question and have not managed to define. In other words, any discussion of authors' rights and copyright today must be subordinated to a previous discussion on the very notion of the author, which is precisely where we get bogged down in the sand.

For example, the law here recognises a duality in the artistic sphere between a *corpus misticum* (the creative essence of the work) and a *corpus mechanicum* (the material result of that essence of the work as a physical object). The existence of this *corpus misticum* is what enabled the nineteenth-century artists you mentioned to claim and receive remuneration when derivative works and reproductions exploited their original creative work – reproductions that, as you very well say, would go on to become ghost images, remaining in circulation long after the original matrix, plate or mould had been destroyed.

And here you make a very interesting ontological distinction between 'photographs' and 'photographic images', which would correspond to the distinction between an original photograph and derived photographs. But I want to return to your metaphor, which fired my imagination because it can also be taken as a distinction between body (flesh) and ghost: that is, between body-image and ghost-image. And given that Foto Colectania invited us to discuss the status of the photographer today, at this point I suggest that we set two things aside. The first thing we need to avoid has to do with the specificity of the different photographic processes, or with how certain images lead to others: we are well aware that making prints from a daguerreotype is quite a different thing from making positives from a negative, and the genealogy by way of which an image is derived from another previous image counts for more here than the technical dependence of the one on the other. The second thing has to do with the whole Benjaminian theory of the aura and the dialectic between original and reproduction. If these two premises are accepted as hypotheses for reflection – and I realise that this is a lot to ask – then assigning the condition of body (work, original) or of ghost (copy, reproduction) is entirely the decision of the author (the photographer), who has complete authority when it comes to categorising – for example, between intermediate materials or final results. The problem, once again, is the difficulty in legitimising the figure of the author when that figure is dissociated from the actual photographer. The photographer may be whoever presses the shutter release on the camera, but the author is the person who manages the meaning and the use value of the image.

I agree with your elegantly expressed perception that 'to excavate photography . . . is to disembowel modernity itself', and this being so is a political act. I am convinced that images are the very substance of politics, so that generating and managing images is a political activity. My perspective is not an attempt to deny or evade this political condition of photography; it's just that I feel more inclined to privilege a line of semiotic inquiry and poetic speculation – I have never tried to pass myself off as a theoretician.

In a recent article entitled 'Buried by Images', the philosopher Xavier Antich points out that an estimated 800 million images are uploaded to Snapchat every day, together with 350 million to Facebook and 80 million to Instagram (Antich 2016). If you were to devote one second to each of these images, it would take you more than 39 years to look at them all. And we're talking about just three platforms, not all of them. We shouldn't play down the brutality of these data: a level of photographic inflation far beyond all precedent, an asphyxiating visual pollution and a hypercapitalism of images. This rampant excess radically transforms our relationship with images, which are our primary means of engaging with the world, and therefore also changes our relationship with the world. Hence its inescapable political repercussions.

It is beyond doubt now that photography has become much more than a 'writing with light' practised by a few privileged scribes: it is a universal language, one that we all use naturally in most of the many areas of our lives. This is the phenomenon I propose to call the advent of *Homo photographicus*. At the same time it is also true that this excess of images is a symptom of a hypermodernity that manifests itself in cut-throat globalisation and cataleptic consumerism.

That said, the thing that troubles me now is: this being the situation, what is my responsibility as a photographer? Having arrived at a more or less plausible diagnosis, what do we do? For my part, and pending whatever suggestions you have, I can think of a dual response to the question of what we are to do. In the first instance, the strategy of containment that I pointed to in my previous missive: a refusal to contribute to this enormous proliferation by replacing accumulation with recycling. The second response would be to search for those images that – despite the fatigue and the superabundance – are still wanting: images that are in short supply, missing images, images that have been hidden, images of what is secret, images that do not yet exist . . . the void that these non-images evoke presents us with the great challenge.

8 November 2016

Dear Joan,

Thank you for your latest missive and its call for a little more intellectual hooliganism. Your opening story about the agitational work of Octavi Comeron reminded me of an action undertaken by Igor Vamos, an American MFA student I once taught. He also tangled with the agents of the state, only his story reverses the arc of the one you have told. In Igor's case, he parked his motorcycle outside his studio at the university and soon was issued with a parking fine. He then wrote to the campus police and claimed that his vehicle was in fact an artwork and therefore should be exempt from the fine. Much correspondence ensued. As if to prove his point, he exhibited the end results, presenting his motorcycle as a ready-made sculpture in the middle of a gallery, with the surrounding walls covered in the letters back and forth between himself and the long-suffering parking officers. This included the final letter from those officers that withdrew the fine.

Igor's success encourages me to take you at your word and become the hooligan you most fear, the one who ignores your prohibition on talk about process and aura and insists on speaking about nothing else. I am further prompted to do so when you (a man who claims not to be a theoretician, but who, in your very next sentence, refers to a recent article by a philosopher) ask me about the radical transformation of our relationship with images that occurs when we are faced with today's extraordinary photographic inflation. You pose two questions in the midst of that gesture: what is the nature of that transformation and what is our responsibility in the face of it?

I am not entirely persuaded that the quantity of photographs now being produced utterly transforms the nature of our relationship with images. After all, photography's numbers have always been overwhelming. One could argue that billions of digital images are no more debilitating to one's critical faculties than the millions of analogue photographs that used to be churned out each year during the second half of the twentieth century, or, for that matter, than the forty daguerreotypes per day produced by Richard Beard's London studio in 1841. In each case, an individual observer only encounters a tiny fraction of these photographs, usually just enough to recognise that both personal and commercial photography has always been driven by an economy of repetition and sameness. Seen a handful and you've seen them all, more or less. This allows the possibility of some critical purchase on particular genres of photograph. After all, Roland Barthes attempted to deduce the essence of photography from his examination of just one (unreproduced) personal photograph in *Camera Lucida*. A number of artists have produced interesting work that allows a similar reflection on our contemporary imagescape, including yourself, Joachim Schmid, Erik Kessels, and Penelope Umbrico. Such artists, all of them dedicated to an intelligent recycling of digital photographs, give me hope that critical thinking is still possible within and about this excessive image environment you describe.

I wonder also if the very theorist you want to put to one side, Walter Benjamin, still might have something useful to say about our current situation. Like you, I am no theoretician. So my interest is not in what Benjamin himself might have intended by his essay (if that could ever be deduced from what remains a strangely incoherent piece of writing) or even in trying to work out what the essay might mean in its own terms. No, my interest is in what can still be made of it for our own times. I want to rewrite this text in terms that make sense to me. I suggest that its bottom line is that the reproduction of images does something, to the images and to us. And as you imply, what overwhelms about the digital environment is not just the sheer number of images but the banal repetition of their form, their sameness, their abject surrender to the forces of reproduction. Such a repetition does indeed represent a 'hypercapitalism of images'. But again, this state of being merely reproduces to infinity what has always been that most basic condition of the photograph: its capacity to endlessly reproduce itself, to be one of many copies, to be a copy for which there is no original.

When Benjamin reflected on these issues in the 1930s, he chose to equate the reproductive capacities of photography with the processes of mass production, and thus with the most basic operations of capitalism itself.

For Benjamin, these processes are fraught with an inherent contradiction, an alienating inversion of social and commodity relations, such that reproduction is simultaneously capitalism's lifeblood and its poison.[2] Photography, he suggested, contained within it this same contradiction, being equally capable of sustaining capitalism and of destroying it. For him, reproducibility is a politically charged capacity that can be either exploited or suppressed but should definitely not be ignored.

It is easy to be distracted from this bigger political argument by debates about the meaning of 'aura'. Benjamin describes aura as 'a strange tissue of time and space: the unique apparition of a distance, however near it may be' (Benjamin 2008: 23).[3] I take this to be his attempt to account for the hallucinatory effects of commodity fetishism, such that unequal relations of power are experienced by individuals in very real, if often invisible, phenomenological and psychological terms. According to Karl Marx, commodity fetishism enables the subjugation of all social conditions and relationships to the needs of capital: 'a definite social relation between men . . . assumes, in their eyes, the fantastic form of a relation between things' (Marx 1990: 165). This form is 'fantastic' because the commodity comes to be invested with unearthly powers beyond its capacity to deliver. As Paul Wood explains the process: 'the commodity becomes a power in society. Rather than a use value *for* people it assumes a power *over* people, becoming a kind of god to be worshipped, sought after, and possessed. And in a reverse movement, as the commodity, the thing, becomes personified, so relations between people become objectified and thinglike' (Wood 1996: 263–4).

Accordingly, the endless reproduction of an artwork like the *Mona Lisa* brings this painting close to us, but at the considerable cost of the commodification of our relationship to it. In reproduction form the artwork is near, physically and temporally, but its cult value has been exponentially enhanced by this same reproduction and thus we are simultaneously distanced from it. We might flock with enthusiasm to see the original, to see (and photographically copy for ourselves) the source of this torrent of copies, but this copying has transformed the nature of our experience even before we get there. Its celebrity status, a consequence of its constant reiteration in reproduced form, denies us access to the painting in its own terms. We see a star, rather than an actor; a masterpiece to be worshipped rather than a piece of painting to be analysed. Alienated by processes inherent to capitalism, we are thus prevented from having anything like an authentic relationship to the products of our own culture.

This gets me back to the 'radical transformation' of our relationship to images that you worry about in your letter. Yes, photographs are being made and posted in ever greater numbers. Yes, most of those photographs are banal and unthinking, mere copies of what everyone else is doing. But still, I would suggest that people respond to photographs much as they always have, with heightened sentiment or dutiful boredom according to their connection to the subjects being depicted. Mostly, I suspect, people look at these photographs for confirmation of their own place in space and time, and to reiterate their stake within a comforting network of familial and emotional bonds. Photographs are posted as elements of a system of exchange, a system devoted to the mutual affirmation of shared values. The automatic reiteration of those values, their naturalisation by photography's continued association with what is real, is where the alienation effect comes into play. We feel like we are closer to those with whom we exchange photographs even as that friendship is made dependent on distance and estrangement, but also on a relatively invisible, seemingly innocent version of digital capitalism. To intervene within that system of exchange is once again to engage with this larger political economy.

But your anxiety seems to be directed at the fate of the professional photographer, rather than at the ennui of the on-line amateur. 'Has photography exhausted its potential? Have photographers burned out, got tired?' I'd put it another way: can photographs still offer some critical purchase on the world, including on the world of photography itself? I think your own work, as a photographer and as a writer, shows that it still can. And not just because you have often adopted the admirably sustainable practice of recycling existing images, although this is certainly an interesting strategy. As our colleague Joachim Schmid has declared: 'No new photos until the old ones are used up' (see Sachsse 2000; MacDonald and Weber 2007; Schmid 2008; Batchen 2013). This strategy is itself a form of hooliganism, if only because it contests the value judgements of the photography world's power brokers by making use of photographs that institutions like museums and dealers don't care about (this, incidentally, is Schmid's declared field of study). But a recycling of vernacular photographs also contests the usual investments of that world in the author function, another of your stated concerns. Schmid turns reproduction against itself by the deadpan manner with which he presents his plundered but otherwise nondescript images, refusing to provide them with meaning or embellishment. He simply implies that their re-presentation is itself meaningful. This orchestrates a shift in authorial responsibility from the maker to the viewer, from the singular act of production to the multiplicity of readings made available during the activity of looking. According to Roland Barthes, this kind of shift 'liberates what may be called an anti-theological activity, an activity that is truly revolutionary since to refuse to fix meaning is, in the end, to refuse God and his hypostases – reason, science, law' (Barthes 1977: 147).[4]

Magnum photographers tend to prefer a fixed meaning, and to favour the politics of revelation. They imagine that if they could but show us the truth of a situation, then we would do something about it. But, as your own work has shown, truth is a weak political weapon, for all sorts of reasons. For a start, it grants its recipients a passive role; photographs dedicated to the revelation of truth again distance their viewers from the situation at issue, they grant us a freedom from any complicity in that situation. As I've already implied, I prefer an approach, to photography but also to any other kind of critical activity, that makes complicity a central plank. As Barthes once proposed, 'ultimately, Photography is subversive not when it frightens, repels, or even stigmatizes, but when it is *pensive*, when it thinks' (Barthes 1981: 38). Our job, as intellectual hooligans, is to make the viewing of photographs more pensive, more thoughtful, than it might otherwise be.

18 November 2016

Dear Geoff,

Your response gives us a great deal of lucidity and encouragement to go on turning over and mulling over the issues that concern us. Equally welcome is the fact that you raise doubts about some of my statements, which I perhaps threw out, if not frivolously, then in an excess of high spirits. It's true that I base my observations not on scientific studies grounded in hard data and statistics but simply on impressions which are derived from intuition and as such entirely refutable. But trusting that the antennae that guide me are usually well oriented, I would like to consider two points on which I think we disagree: 1) I *do* believe that what has triggered the transformations that photography is undergoing is its massification (to a great extent, at least); and 2) I also believe that this massification substantially alters our relationship with the image.

Figure 13.6 (next page) Joachim Schmid (Germany): pages from Self (in the Other People's Photographs series), 2008, printed book, 17.6 cm x 37.0 cm (open). Courtesy of the artist.

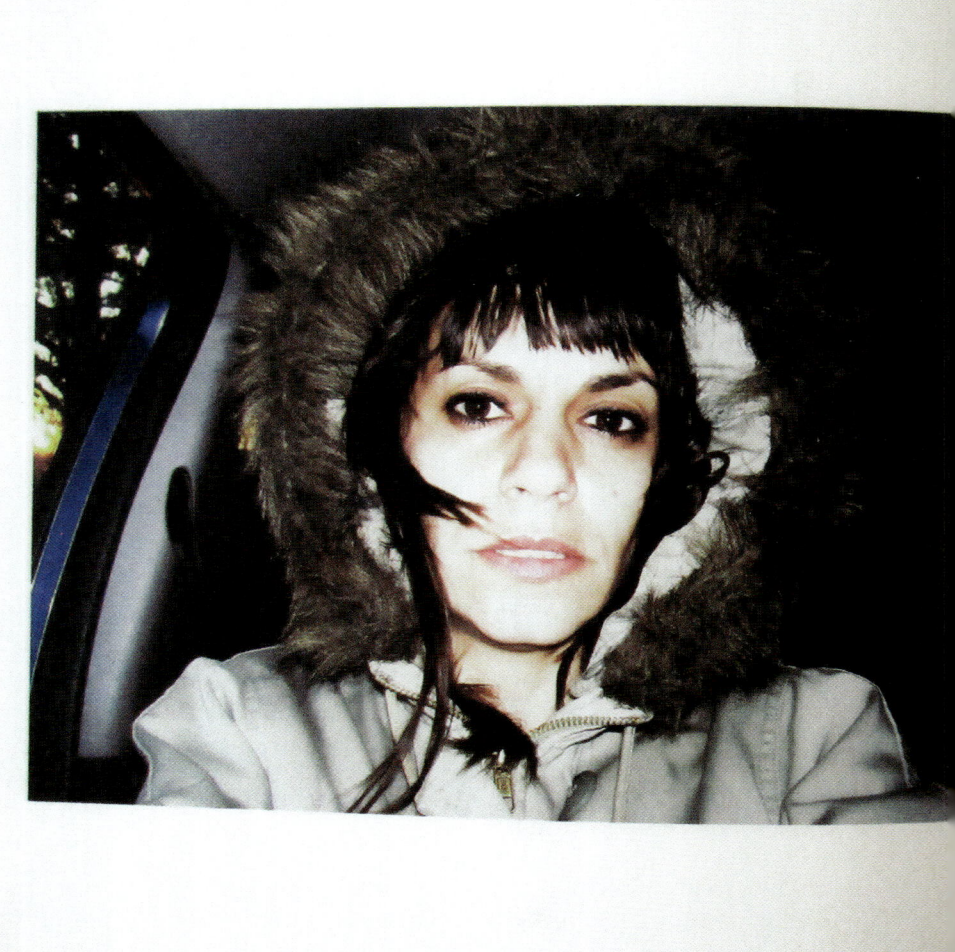

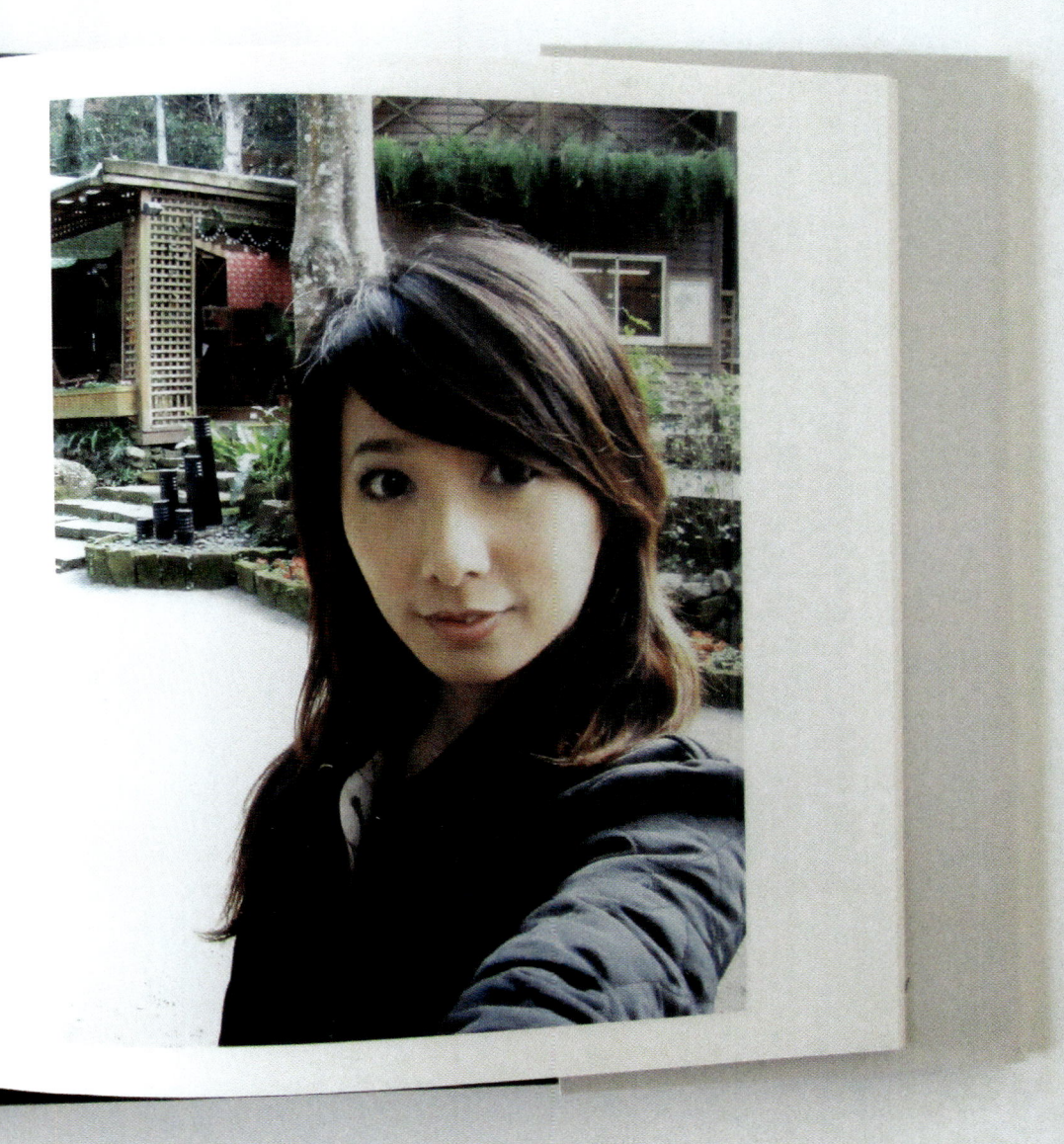

In the past there have been instances of photographs being produced in the huge quantities you mention, but it seems plain common sense to say that this was never on anything like the same scale as we are seeing now. In a text for the catalogue of the exhibition *From Now On: Post-photography in the Age of the Internet and the Mobile Phone* I related the circumstances of our understanding of images with the circumstances of physics.[5] The story goes that Mr Newton was taking a nap under an apple tree when a ripe fruit chanced to fall on his head and he cried out 'Eureka! Gravity!' The bit about the siesta would have been far more credible if Newton had been Spanish, but what holds good about the fable is the principle that bodies are attracted with a force proportional to their mass and inversely proportional to their separation. For centuries the Newtonian laws based on gravitational forces plausibly governed the observable phenomena of nature, but when we began to study subatomic particles and reach out into deep space – that is, when we radically shifted scale to the infinitely large or the infinitely small – those laws ceased to apply and we needed more sophisticated explanations. Along came quantum physics and the theory of relativity, not as a negation of Newtonian physics but as an adjustment in the application of its precepts. This simile invites us to think that a photograph that borders on infinity also requires its own particular quantum revolution to adapt it from phenomena that are measurable in kilometres to those measurable in light years. The disciplines that have allowed us to approach the analysis of the image from different perspectives (aesthetics, semiotics, epistemology, anthropology, sociology, and so on) therefore need to be revised in accordance with a new superlative scale. To put it another way: the rules have changed.

This revision affects fundamental aspects of the theory of the image. For example, it discredits the sacrosanct myth of aura – hence my reluctance to set foot in this particular quagmire. The aura emanates from the dialectic between original and reproduction, but the old binomial opposition there has lost much of its meaning in the post-photographic era. The proliferation of images is not so much a result of the serial copying or reproduction of a primordial matrix which acts as guarantor of the aura as of the multiplication of originals. The fact that there are so many photos today is not because they are being cloned but because a given scene generates an overabundance of 'original' versions. The aura then vanishes by exhaustion, from the sheer excess of originals, and this effect can also be expressed in terms of saturation.

Visual saturation is in my opinion one of the main consequences of the capitalism of images you referred to. Saturation de-sacralises and deprives the image of its magical dimension. It also pushes us towards insensibility and a new mode of censorship: concealment by smothering and fatigue. 'Art has become iconoclastic', Baudrillard tells us. 'Modern iconoclasm no longer consists in destroying images, but in manufacturing a profusion of images where there is nothing to see' (Baudrillard 2005: 118). Saturation actually causes blindness.⁶ Just as an excess of information amounts to an absence of information, so the superabundance and omnipresence of images is tantamount to their suppression. In fact, the idea is merely an exaggeration of notes that were already being formulated in the avant-gardes. For example, Magritte and Man Ray both produced pieces that anticipated the collapse of the image. In 1928 Magritte painted *L'image parfaite* (*The Perfect Image*) and in 1929 Man Ray dedicated to his friend Louis Aragon 'Ma dernière photographie' (My last photograph). In the first we see, from behind and to one side, a young woman looking at a picture frame containing a completely black canvas, while the second is nothing other than a veiled photograph. In both cases the blackness evokes the superimposed accumulation of all possible images – hence their perfection – and the assumption that a final image has been reached – hence it's being the last one possible. That darkness, in which nothing can be discerned any more, gives the measure of the exhaustion of any further capacity for representation. More than works of art, these are semiotic proclamations, gestures that bring to an end the long journey of the image and explain its saturation or satiation.

We are now suffering the consequences of Magritte's and Man Ray's clairvoyance and it is natural that we should worry about finding the right political and economic solutions with which to alleviate a crisis of which that saturation is no more than a symptom. For example, Serge Latouche proposes the notion of degrowth. He emerged as a leading apostle of the commitment to rethinking accumulation with the publication of his *Petit traité de la décroissance sereine* in 2007. Latouche likes to refer to himself as a 'growth objector' and proposes eight interdependent actions that will contribute to the 'virtuous circle of serene, convivial and sustainable degrowth: revalue, reconceptualise, restructure, redistribute, relocate, reduce, reuse and recycle' – eight Rs we must constantly bear in mind. But there is another R, and this is the one that invigorates and gives meaning to all of the previous eight: resist. Against excess and saturation, resistance.

The other question was whether we react in the same way or in a different way to images when they are scarce or abundant. We can think of photographs as symbolic substitutes for the real, but the strength of that substitution value has been weakened. Value, in terms of appreciation, is dependent on scarcity, on singularity. A century or two ago, images were luxury goods that adorned privileged spaces such as churches and palaces; these days almost all of us carry around a smartphone storing hundreds, even thousands of photos – photos that, precisely because they are obtained at no cost at all, are reiterative and banal, the balance of an excessive, compulsive and unrestrained production. Indeed, the photographic act itself often prevails over the content of the photograph. Inserted into processes that are more conversational than descriptive or documentary, the life of the image becomes ephemeral. Many photos are now being taken not to last but to interact and connect. The phenomenon of Snapchat is eloquent: an electronic messaging system in which the photos or videos you send are automatically deleted ten seconds after they are received. Having fulfilled its function, the image disappears. Our appreciation of and regard for a photograph will depend on that simple economic equation.

30 November 2016

Dear Joan,

Your latest letter, at once eloquent and provocative, gives me a much better understanding of, among other things, the motivations behind your own work as an artist. Our discussion could perhaps be reduced to a single question: does size matter? Or, to put it another way, does the overwhelming quantity of photographs being produced today mediate the quality of our relationship to the photograph in general? I tried to persuade you that any individual observer sees only a small fraction of the available photographic universe and that each individual's reaction to those photographs is much as it has always been. To use your own analogy, the rules may have changed (from Newtonian physics to quantum theory) but any apples that fall on our heads continue to hurt or not hurt according to the height of the fall and the hardness of our heads, regardless of those rules or our understanding of them. You stress the effect of visual saturation and the insensibility and even blindness it generates, but then quote the words of Jean Baudrillard to support your case; words spoken during a lecture presented in 1987, before the advent of the internet or digital cameras or social media.[7] Baudrillard, it seems, identifies these effects with postmodernity (or even with the media explosion of the 1960s, when he first started writing about the culture of simulacra) rather than with a 'post-photographic era'. Similarly, the scholars who worried about the desensitisation that might result from exposure to an excess of atrocity pictures – Roland Barthes (1979), Susan Sontag (1977) and John Berger (1980) – were writing in the 1960s and 1970s, in the age of illustrated magazines and television.

So I suggest we need to be cautious as we explore the issue of 'massification'. But let me be clear: I wouldn't want to pretend that nothing has changed in recent years. That would be as unwise as saying that everything has changed. What we are debating is the nature of those changes and the best way to respond to them. We have reached, you say, a darkness in which nothing can be discerned any more, a darkness already declared in the late 1920s by the Surrealists but now fully descended upon us as a consequence of the 'culture of excess' you describe. The excessive amount of photographs in the world is joined by their devaluation: people don't value what they don't have to pay for, or what they can produce in seemingly infinite numbers.

So where is the crisis here? For you, this crisis might be summed up thus: '[t]he photographic act itself often prevails over the content of the photograph . . . many photos are now being taken, not to last but to interact and connect . . . having fulfilled its function, the image disappears.' For a professional photographer, who makes images for a living and as a necessity, this is a crisis indeed. As a historian of photography, however, I can't help but be more dispassionate about it. The death of photography has been declared so many times that I regard such declarations as signs of life, as an inevitable marker of the rise of yet another photographic phoenix from the ashes of its predecessor. Indeed, your remarks made me recall an essay I wrote for another of my exhibition catalogues, this time for *Suspending Time* in 2010. I refer to a statistic claiming that Americans alone take about 550 snapshots per second, 'a statistic that, however it has been concocted, suggests that the taking of such photographs might best be regarded as a neurosis rather than a pleasure'. I go on to suggest that this neurosis could be taken 'as a declaration of faith in the midst of an increasingly secular world'. 'Photographers', I argue, 'take snapshots to allay their own fears about forgetting and being forgotten. It's the act that matters, not the photograph. This is why this act is endlessly repeated, even when we never intend to print the results' (Batchen 2010: 122–3, 126). Photography, it seems, continues to have meaning (and a profound meaning at that) even in the absence of photographs.

However, the fact is that we have never had more photographs than now. Not only is social media inundated with a surfeit of bad ones, but our museums, galleries and auction houses have never before presented us with so many good ones, have never, in fact, valued photographs more highly. This may well be a necessary corollary to the neoliberal economy in which we find ourselves; the rich get ever richer and the poor are left behind to fend for themselves. You propose that artists should respond to this excessive embrace by the art world (another example of photo-saturation) with a course of 'degrowth' and point us to Serge Latouche's eight actions (revalue, reconceptualise, restructure, redistribute, relocate, reduce, reuse and recycle), even while adding another: resistance. I've already indicated my strong support for all nine of these actions and have written approvingly about the work of a number of artists who have sought to enact them, yours included.

But, as a historian, I also note another response witnessed in the work of many contemporary artists working with photography, a response we might call retromodernism. As you have yourself, in your letter to me, a lot of artists are looking back to the utopian experiments of the mid-century avant-garde, to a period before the somewhat mournful, cynical and theory-laden moment we call postmodernism, and are seeking to re-explore and reinvigorate (two more 'Rs' for you) the critical capacities of modernism itself. This is a tendency that has been widely recognised, with exhibitions devoted to it, or to some aspect of it, having already taken place at the J. Paul Getty Museum in Los Angeles, the V&A in London, the Pompidou Centre in Paris, the International Center of Photography in New York, and the Govett-Brewster Art Gallery in New Plymouth, New Zealand – in this last case, one of my own exhibitions, *Emanations: The Art of the Cameraless Photograph*.[8] Making photographs without a camera, and thus returning to a mode of working associated with Man Ray and Moholy-Nagy in particular (the patron saints for many contemporary photo-artists), is one aspect of this response. But more generally, one might identify it with work that is self-conscious about the materiality of both the photograph and the act of producing it. These are photographs one is asked to look at, rather than through. Many artists, it seems, want to present us with photographs that are not just of something: they are something.

Whether consciously or not, photographers have often felt the need to take their medium back to first principles as a way of setting recent history aside and starting again. I might go even further and say that they have periodically sought to put the meaning of photography into crisis precisely in order to signal and respond to a greater crisis that is always already happening around them. In the case of the artists I am thinking about, the image has been erased from the photographic experience precisely so that the photograph can be brought back into our consciousness.

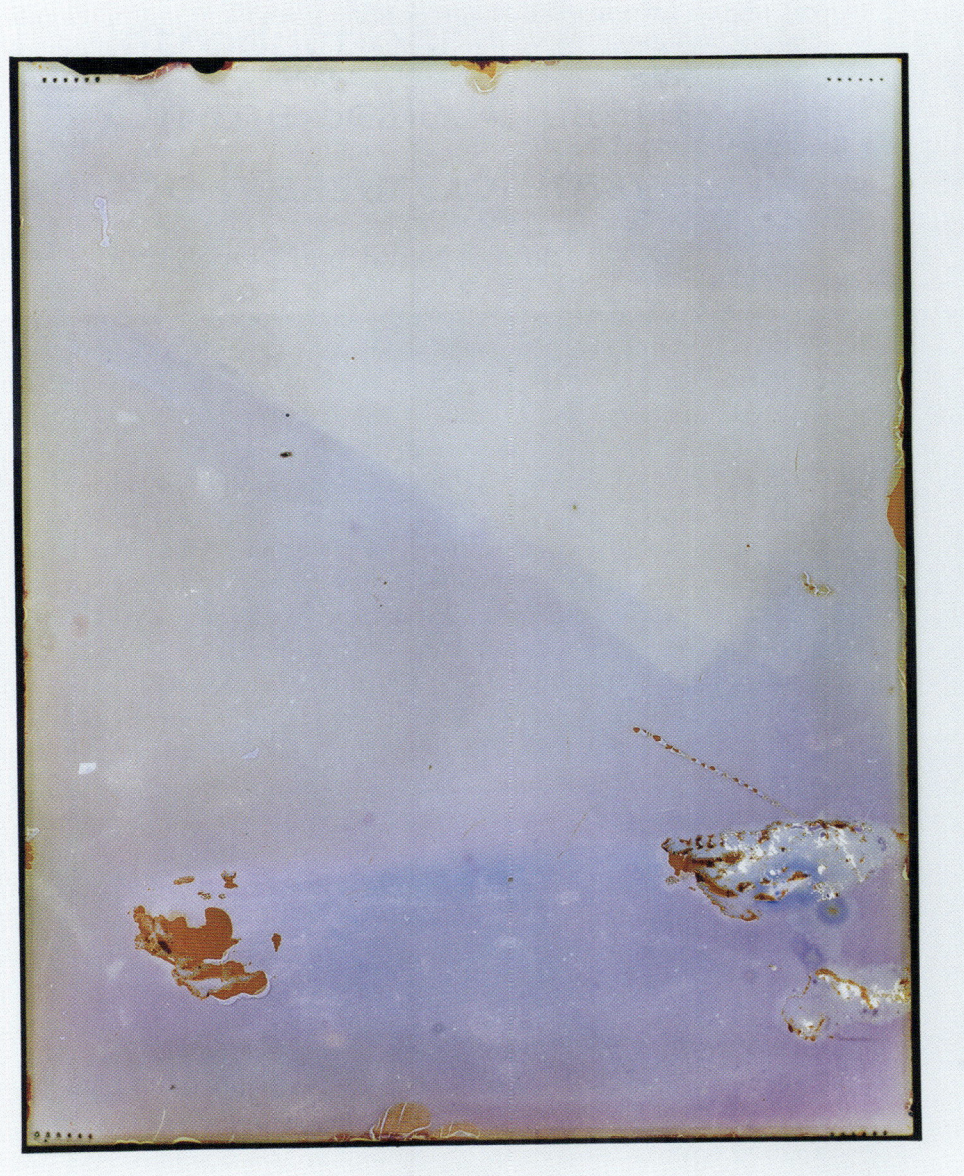

Figure 13.7 Justine Varga: *Desklamp* from the series *Film Object*, 2011-12, chromogenic photograph, 105.0 cm x 83.8 cm (image). Courtesy of the artist, Hugo Michell Gallery, Adelaide and Tolarno Galleries, Melbourne.

Australian artist Justine Varga, for example, creates photographic works from an intimate and often prolonged exchange between a large-format strip of film and the world that comes to be inscribed on it. *Desklamp*, produced during 2011–12, involved the year-long exposure of a colour negative placed on top of the artist's desk. Common sense and the laws of physics would suggest that this piece of film would be completely fogged by this extended duration. It should, in other words, be the embodiment of that complete darkness you have already described as a metaphor of our moment. But something strange has happened to Varga's film, as though it reached its representational limits, died, and then passed to the other side of those limits and came back to life, registering its hundreds of exposures to light and dark, and to whatever else may have touched it over this year, as luscious swathes of colour and accumulated incidental marks. As an act of photography, it promises the possibility, not of death, but of resurrection.

All this is made visible when the film is developed and printed from and enlarged. Immersing us in its chromatic atmosphere, the final work dispassionately documents the artist's presence in a particular place while also offering a sublime manifestation of her physical interaction with the activity of photographing. Varga's work has an autobiographical cast, but some of these 'retromodern' photographs ground their material form in a specific set of historical circumstances. It is this grounding that should displace the word 'abstraction' from our vocabulary and send us back to the dictionary for a better term. In my first exchange with you, I mentioned the 2011 earthquake and tsunami in Japan, with its devastating consequences, including nuclear contamination. Seeking to make visible this otherwise invisible threat to his country's inhabitants, the Japanese artist Shimpei Takeda collected contaminated soil samples from twelve locations throughout Japan, each of them of historical and symbolic significance ('with a strong memory of life and death', as the artist put it), and then placed the samples on sheets of photo-sensitive film, leaving them like that for a month (quoted in Baillargeon 2014). About half the resulting images remained almost black, but some were soon speckled with a blizzard of radioactive emissions, abstractions that nevertheless indelibly recorded the fragile state of the Japanese ecology. Here we see an automatic recording of a radiation that threatens the ecology and well-being of a specific place at a specific time. This specificity matters, to the form and meaning of the work, and perhaps also to our own survival as a species.

Although resembling abstract paintings, photographs of this kind enjoy, even exploit, photography's indexical grounding in a world of chemical and physical reactions to physical phenomena. They all are documents of their own coming into being, rather than just of a world outside the photograph. Despite appearances, they are, in other words, as realist as photographs can get. Exercising long durations rather than instantaneous exposures, these artists return photography to a handmade craft and away from an automatic subservience to global capitalism and its vast economies of mass production and exploitation. In short, this kind of work puts 'photography' into inverted commas and, by exacerbating it into visibility, asks us to ponder what something's photographicness might mean and why it might matter. Having abandoned the perspectival focus provided both by the camera and a centralised referent, such photographs also actively decentre the observer. They force us to cast our eyes back and forth over their opaque surfaces because these offer no singular resting point, and thus no visual confirmation of a stable position in space and time. They insist on their identity as photographs but keep us, and the world we inhabit, in flux and on the move.

You'll note, too, how a picture of this kind collapses any distinction between figure and ground (as well as between up and down), and how its edge is allowed to become an arbitrary cut within a field of potentially infinite elements, rather than a rational frame surrounding a discrete object. These are pictures, in short, that decisively break with all received conventions for camera-derived picture-making, and thus with the camera's comforting humanism too. In front of such photographs, we are freed from the passifying grip of this humanism and forced to seek another kind of viewing position, even another kind of subjectivity; indeed, another kind of position in the world at large.

I am suggesting, therefore, that there are varieties of resistance to the current situation, and even that 'degrowth' and 'retromodernism' are two sides of the same coin. Both seek to provide a counter to the photo-saturated environment of the present, to slow down our perception of that environment, and to encourage a more thoughtful consideration of its consequences. A politicised photographic poetry, in other words, is still possible and has never been more necessary.

Figure 13.8 (next page) Shimpei Takeda: *Trace #7*, Nihonmatsu Castle (Nihonmatsu, Fukushima), 2012, gelatin silver photograph, 40.0 cm x 50.5 cm. Courtesy of the artist, Tokyo.

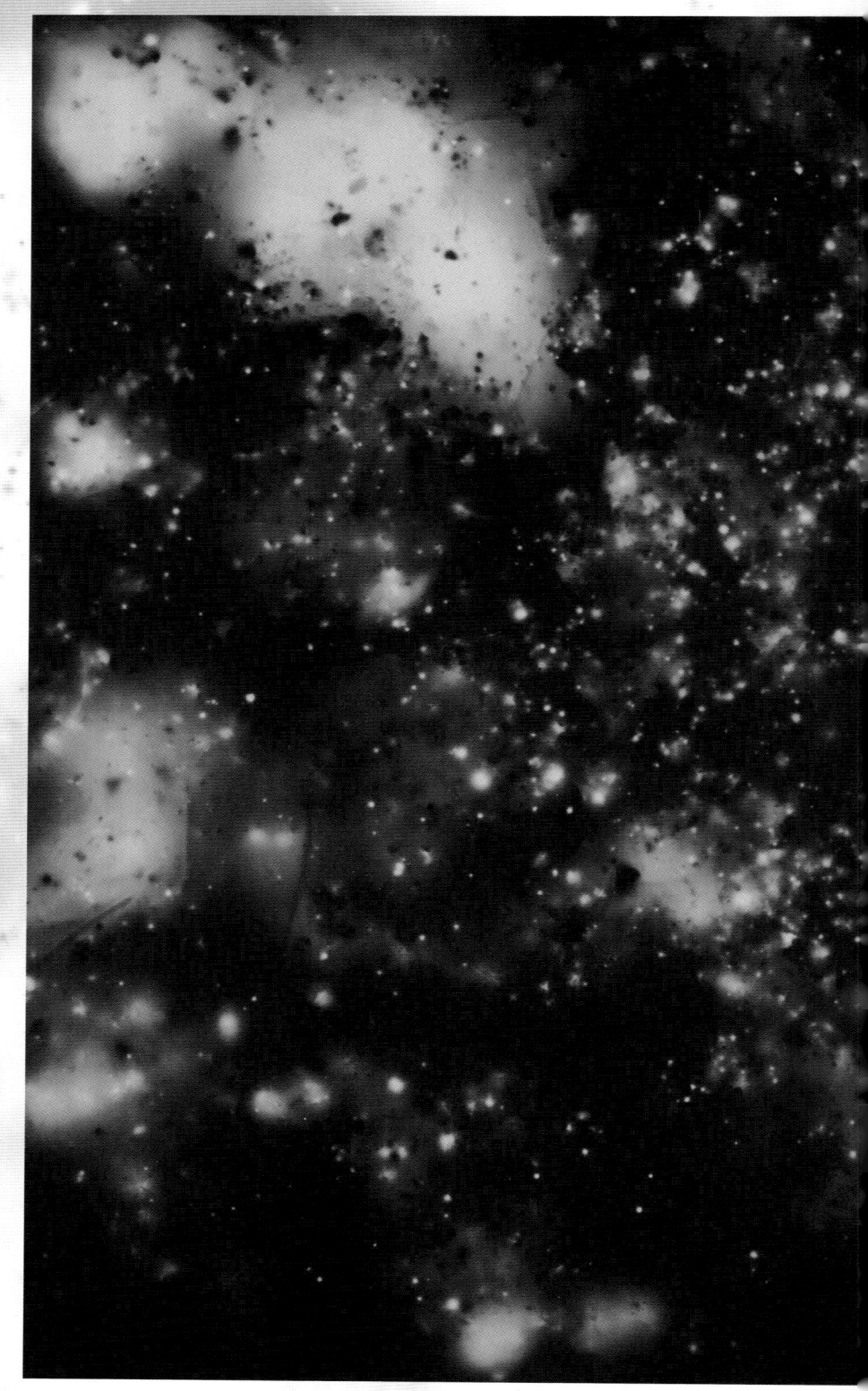

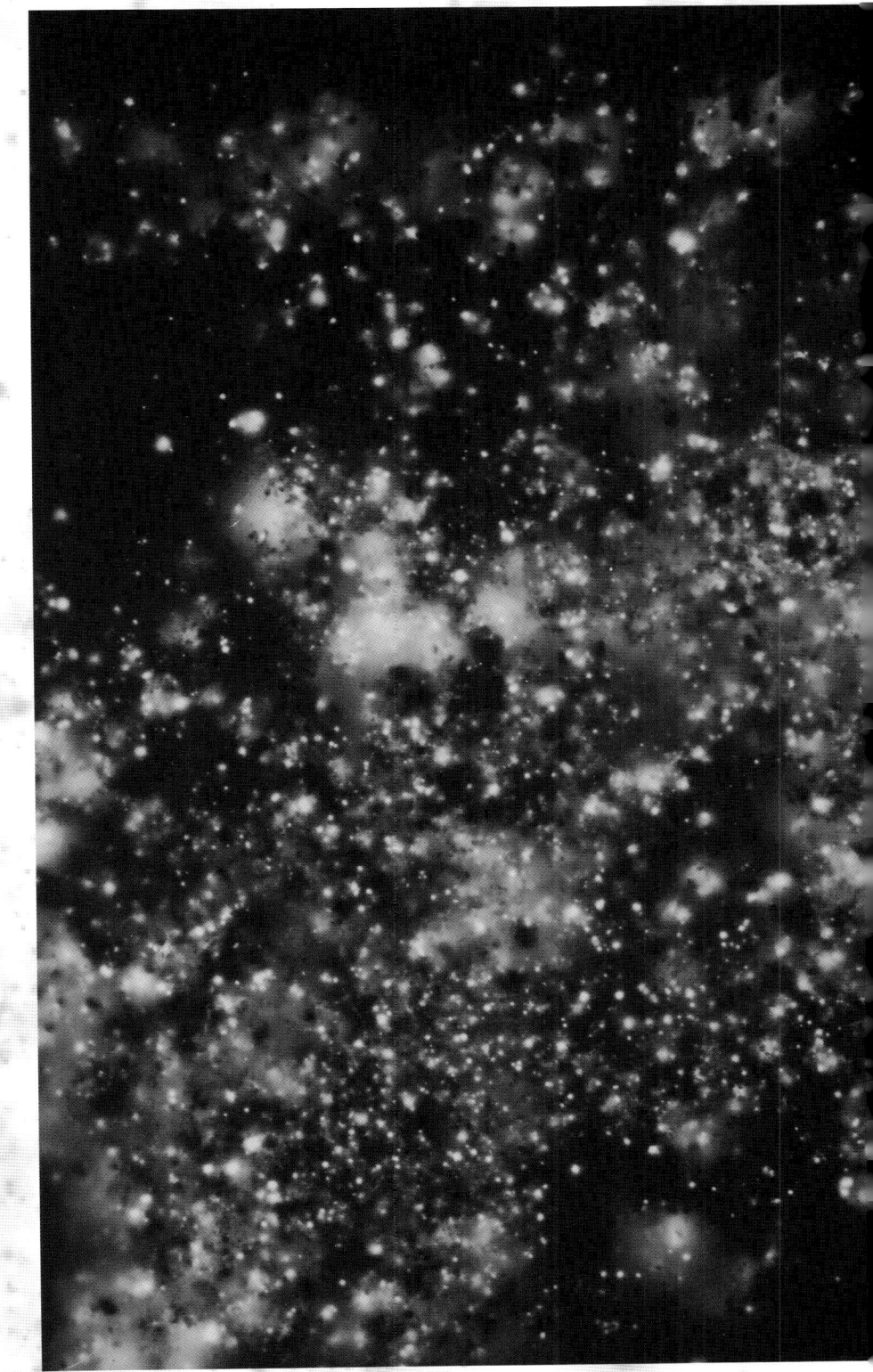

Notes

1. Joan Fontcuberta's letters were translated into English by Graham Thomson.
2. Benjamin establishes the contradictory logic of his argument in his first paragraph: 'Going back to the basic conditions of capitalist production, . . . what could be expected, it emerged, was not only an increasingly harsh exploitation of the proletariat but, ultimately, the creation of conditions which would make it possible for capitalism to abolish itself' (Benjamin 2008).
3. Anne McCauley concludes that 'Benjamin failed to see that the aura, as he defined it, was untouched by mechanical replication'. Pointing out that visitors still flocked to see original paintings, despite their reproduction in other media, she asserts that 'their aura certainly remains intact' (McCauley 1994: 300). I am trying to complicate this understanding of 'aura', shifting it from a quality embedded in a work of art to a social dynamic enacted in the relationship between a work and its audience.
4. Barthes's comment follows his earlier proposition: 'We know now that a text is not a line of words releasing a single "theological" meaning (the "message" of the Author-God) but a multi-dimensional space in which a variety of writings, none of them original, blend and clash. The text is a tissue of quotations drawn from the innumerable centers of culture' (Barthes 1977: 146).
5. An exhibition curated by Erik Kessels, Joachim Schmid, Martin Parr, Clément Chéroux and Joan Fontcuberta at Arts Santa Mònica, Barcelona, in 2013. The show had previously been presented at the Rencontres Inernationales de la Photographie in Arles in 2011. The catalogue was published jointly with R. M., Barcelona/Mexico City.
6. Saturation also anaesthetises us and neutralises the document's power to shock, especially in the case of the depiction of violence and horror. This is a subject you will be familiar with as co-editor of *Picturing Atrocity: Photography in Crisis*, Reaktion Books, London, 2012.
7. Your quotation was taken from Jean Baudrillard, 'Simulation and Transaesthetics: Towards the Vanishing Point of Art', the script of a lecture Baudrillard gave at the Whitney Museum of American Art in New York in 1987.
8. These exhibitions include Martin Barnes, *Shadow Catchers: Camera-less Photography* (London: Victoria and Albert Museum, 2010); Carol Squiers, *What is a Photograph?* (New York: Prestel/International Center of Photography, 2014); Virginia Heckert, *Light, Paper, Process: Reinventing Photography* (Los Angeles: Getty Museum, 2015); Clément Chéroux and Karolina Ziebinska-Lewandowska, *Qu'est-ce que la photographie?* (Paris: Centre Pompidou, 2015); Geoffrey Batchen, *Emanations: The Art of the*

Cameraless Photograph (New Plymouth, NZ: Govett-Brewster Art Gallery, 2016). Justine Varga's *Desklamp* (2011–12) was featured in this last exhibition, but also in *New Matter: Recent Forms of Photography*, curated by Isobel Parker Philip for the Art Gallery of New South Wales in Sydney in late 2016.

References

Agut, Pep (2016), artist's statement. Available at: <http://angelsbarcelona.com-files-160-NP-PEP%20AGUT-Penelope-CAST-LAST.pdf?mc-cid=274bd25caf&mc-eid=23aa6759a1>

Antich, Xavier (2016), 'Sepultats per les imatges'. Available at: <https://www.ara.cat-suplements-diumenge-Sepultats-imatges-0-1661233868.html>

Baillargeon, Claude (2014), *Shadows of the Invisible*. Rochester, MI: Oakland University Art Gallery.

Bann, Stephen (2001), *Parallel Lines: Printmakers, Painters, and Photographers in Nineteenth-Century France*. New Haven: Yale University Press.

Barthes, Roland (1977), 'The Death of the Author', in *Image-Music-Text*, Stephen Heath (trans.). London: Fontana.

Barthes, Roland (1979), 'Shock-Photos' in *The Eiffel Tower and Other Mythologies*, Richard Howard (trans.). New York: Hill and Wang, pp. 71–3.

Barthes, Roland (1981), *Camera Lucida: Reflections on Photography*. New York: Hill and Wang.

Batchen, Geoffrey (1997), *Burning with Desire: The Conception of Photography*. Cambridge, MA: The MIT Press.

Batchen, Geoffrey (2010), *Suspending Time: Life, Photography, Death*. Shizuoko: Izu Photo Museum.

Batchen, Geoffrey (2013), 'Observing by Watching: Joachim Schmid and the Art of Exchange', *Aperture*, 210: 46–9.

Batchen, Geoffrey (2016), 'Double Displacement: Photography and Dissemination', in Thierry Gervais (ed.), *The 'Public' Life of Photographs*. Toronto: Ryerson Image Center-The MIT Press, pp. 38–73.

Baudrillard, Jean (2005), *The Conspiracy of Art: Manifestos, Interviews, Essays*. Los Angeles: Semiotext(e).

Benjamin, Walter (2008), 'The Work of Art in the Age of its Technological Reproducibility' (1935–36), in Michael W. Jennings, Brigid Doherty and Thomas Y. Levin (eds), *The Work of Art in the Age of Its Technical Reproducibility, and Other Writings on Media*. Cambridge, MA: The Belknap Press, pp. 19–55.

Berger, John (1980), 'Photographs of Agony' (1972), in John Berger, *About Looking*. New York: Vintage, pp. 41–4.

Cox, Christoph, Jenny Jaskey and Suhail Malik (2015), 'Introduction', in Christoph Cox, Jenny Jaskey and Suhail Malik (eds), *Realism Materialism Art*. Sternberg Press, pp. 15–31.

Derrida, Jacques (1981), 'Implications: Interview with Henri Ronse' (1967), *Positions*. Chicago: University of Chicago Press.

Guardiola, Ingrid (2016), Inaugural lecture of the 2016–2017 course at EINA. Centre Universitari de Disseny i Art de Barcelona, given on 19 September. Available at: <https://blog.eina.cat-ca-audio-conferencia-inaugural-del-curs-20162017---ingrid-guardiola-57d923a1c01af1060ec4b0b3>

Latouche, Serge (2007), *Petit traité de la décroissance sereine*. Collection Les Petits Libres nr 70. Paris: Éditions Les Mille et Une Nuits.

Maas, Jeremy (1975), *Gambart: Prince of the Victorian Art World*. London: Barrie & Jenkins.

McCauley, Anne (1994), *Industrial Madness: Commercial Photography in Paris 1848–1871*. New Haven: Yale University Press.

MacDonald, Gordon and John S. Weber (eds) (2007), *Joachim Schmid: Photoworks 1982–2007*. Göttingen: Steidl.

Marx, Karl (1990), *Capital*, Volume 1, London: Penguin.

Sachsse, Rolf (2000), 'Joachim Schmid's Archiv', *History of Photography*, 24(3): 255–61.

Schmid, Joachim (2008), 'Reload Currywurst', in Joan Fontcuberta (ed.), *Soñarán los androides con cámaras fotográficas?* [Do Androids Dream of Cameras?], Madrid: Secretaría General Técnica, pp. 286–99.

Sontag, Susan (1977), *On Photography*. New York: Farrar, Straus and Giroux.

Takahashi, Munemasa (ed.) (2014), 津波、写真、それから *Tsunami, Photographs, and Then: Lost & Found Project; Family Photographs swept away by 3.11 East Japan Tsunami*. Kyoto: Akaaka Art Publishing.

Wood, Paul (1996), 'Commodity', in Robert Nelson and Richard Shiff (eds), *Critical Terms for Art History*. Chicago: University of Chicago Press, pp. 263–4.

Names index

Alberti, 194
Alphen, Ernst van, 17, 141, 143, 145, 152, 157
Andrejevic, Mark, 85–6, 89, 93–4
Antich, Xavier, 268, 287
Aragon, Louis, 277
Atget, Eugene, 9
Azoulay, Ariella, 64, 75, 92, 94

Ball, Harvey, 83–4
Barrias, Louis-Ernest, 211
Barthes, Roland, 7, 9, 19, 81–2, 92, 94, 148, 154, 216, 233, 238, 250, 270, 273, 279, 286–7
Batchen, Geoffrey, 10–11, 16, 19, 74–5, 134, 142, 154, 179, 181
Baudrillard, Jean, 25, 228, 277–8, 286–7
Beard, Richard, 270
Benjamin, Walter, 7, 9, 19, 27, 32, 39, 58–9, 268, 270–1, 286–7
Berger, John, 189, 279, 287
Berlant, Lauren, 16, 102–4, 109
Binkley, Sam, 83, 92, 94
Bishop, Ryan, 14, 20, 198, 209, 225, 228
Blumenberg, Hans, 49–50, 59
Boehm, Gottfried, 261
Bonnet, René, 51–2
Boudinet, Daniel, 7, 9
Bratton, Benjamin, 75, 199, 202–3, 206, 209, 212, 217, 226–7, 233, 250

Brewster, David, 6, 20, 280, 287

Calvino, Italo, 147, 154
Campbell, Sue, 81–2, 94
Caraffa, Constanza, 116–17, 137
Chakrabarty, Dipesh, 39
Coleridge, Samuel Taylor, 265
Comeron, Octavi, 266, 269
Cox, Geoff, 189, 206, 209, 264, 287
Crawford, Kate, 85, 96
Cubitt, Sean, 6–7, 12, 14–15, 20, 98, 100, 109

Dällenbach, Lucien, 130, 137
Darius, Jon, 57, 59
Davies, William, 85–6, 90, 94
Derrida, Jacques, 63, 75, 236, 250, 264, 288
Didi-Huberman, Georges, 57, 59, 82, 92, 94
Difallah, Djellel, 242, 244, 250
Dijck, Jan van, 86–7, 96
Dobson, Susan, 104, 109, 124, 126, 131, 137
Doppler, Christian, 187, 197, 199, 209

Edwards, Paul, 30, 39, 225, 228
Emerson, Ralph Waldo, 41, 59
Engels, Friedrich, 44
Ernst, Wolfgang, 17, 141, 157, 186, 209

Farocki, Harun, 188, 208, 212–13, 216–17, 228
Filatova, Elena, 244, 250
Fisher, Andrew, 4–5, 15–16, 20, 114, 146, 153, 156
Flusser, Vilém, 7, 9–10, 17, 20, 28, 39, 88, 94, 143–4, 239, 250
Fontcuberta, Joan, 11, 16, 19, 114, 137, 256, 258, 261–2, 286, 288
Freud, Sigmund, 31, 254, 263
Frosh, Paul, 77, 80, 87, 93–4, 146, 155

Gabrys, Jennifer, 29, 39, 186, 207, 209, 221, 225–6, 228
Getty, Jean Paul, 101, 135–7, 139, 172, 280, 286
Gide, André, 130, 137
Goldbach, Philipp, 117, 120, 122–3, 130, 138
Goodman, Nelson, 17, 168–71, 180–1
Gotthold Ephraim Lessing, 50–1, 60
Greenberg, Clement, 82, 95, 165, 179, 181
Grosser, Ben, 188–9, 208
Groys, Boris, 100–1, 104, 109
Guardiola, Ingrid, 261, 288

Haraway, Donna, 95, 103, 244, 251
Hariman, Robert, 114, 132, 138
Hegel, Georg Wilhelm Friedrich, 44–5, 60, 74
Heidegger, Martin, 45–6, 60, 74–5, 165–7, 181
Henning, Michelle, 11, 15–16, 114, 134, 138
Herder, Johann Gottfried, 266
Herschel, Frederick William, 186
Hilliard, John, 134–5
Hispano, Andrés, 254
Hochschild, Arlie, 82, 95
Hokusai, Katsushika, 170

Holmes, Oliver Wendell, 47–8, 58, 60, 245, 251
Homer, 261, 265

Illouz, Eva, 80–2, 85, 95
Ipeirotis, Panos, 250

Jäger, Gottfried, 216, 228
Jameson, Fredric, 42, 60

Kant, Immanuel, 236, 251
Kempelen, Wolfgang von, 245
Kessels, Erik, 1, 4, 16, 116, 138, 270, 286
Knowles, Kim, 146–7, 155
Koblin, Aaron, 245
Kundera, Milan, 82, 95
Kurdi, Alan, 64–5, 76

La Bruyère, Jean de, 53, 60
Latouche, Serge, 277, 280, 288
Leibniz, Gottfried Wilhelm, 51
Lenot, Marc, 17, 141–1, 145, 154–5
Lessing, Gotthold Ephraim, 50–1, 60
Lovejoy, Josh, 11, 20, 52, 60
Lozano-Hemmer, Rafael, 41–2
Lucaites, John Louis, 114, 132, 138
Lugon, Olivier, 149–50, 156
Luther, Martin, 31
Luxemburg, Rosa, 34, 39
Lysenko, Trofim, 44

Magny, Claude, 130
Magritte, René, 277
Majewska, Ewa, 100–2, 109–10
Malraux, André, 46–7, 60
Man Ray, 216, 229, 277
Manaugh, Geoff, 196–7, 199, 202, 209
Manovich, Lev, 12–13, 20, 141, 153, 155–6
Marey, Étienne-Jules, 215

Marx, Karl, 32, 39, 44, 104, 217, 236, 246, 271, 288
Massumi, Brian, 107
May, John, 12, 20
McLuhan, Marshall, 103
Michurin, Ivan Vladimirovič, 44
Mitchell, William John T., 16, 20, 90, 95, 113, 129, 138, 141, 143–4, 156, 261
Moholy-Nagy, László, 17, 158–60, 178, 182, 216, 229, 280
Mumford, Lewis, 41, 60
Muybridge, Edward, 194–5, 197, 206

Nagel, Thomas, 189, 210
Nakamura, Lisa, 105–6, 110
Nanay, Bence, 165, 182
Nancy, Jean-Luc, 15, 61–3, 66, 67–76
Neurath, Otto, 79, 84, 92–3, 95
Niépce, Joseph Nicéphore, 9, 243–4
Nöe, Alva, 133, 165–7, 180, 182, 187, 202
Nordström, Alison, 126, 131, 138

Ocasio-Cortez, Alexandra, 16, 98–110
Offenhuber, Dietmar, 18, 213–20, 224, 229
Owens, Craig, 130, 136, 138

Paglen, Trevor, 11, 18, 20, 188, 210, 213, 229, 232–8, 251
Panofsky, Erwin, 117
Pascal, Blaise, 50, 60
Patočka, Jan, 59–60
Phillips, John, 198, 209
Plato, 261
Playfair, William, 29, 40
Pollen, Annebella, 10, 16, 20, 89, 96, 137–8, 143

Rancière, Jacques, 261, 264
Ritter, Johann Wilhelm, 186

Sander, August, 77, 79–80, 92, 96, 233
Schmid, Joachim, 270, 272–3, 286–8
Schuppli, Susan, 18, 211, 213–14, 221, 226, 229
Sekula, Allan, 47, 58, 60, 79–80, 92, 96, 202
Semuels, Alana, 247, 251
Shaaf, Larry, 136
Sharma, Sarah, 103, 110
Shigetaka Kurita, 84, 95
Siegel, Steffen, 130–1, 139
Siegert, Bernhardt, 187, 210
Simmel, Georg, 47
Sombart, Werner, 47
Sontag, Susan, 48, 56, 60, 74, 76, 152, 157, 238, 279, 288
Sprenger, Florian, 202, 207, 210
Srnicek, Nick, 11, 21
Stallabrass, Julian, 11, 21, 61, 76
Stark, Luke, 68–9, 85–6, 93, 96, 160
Steichen, Edward, 15, 77–81, 90, 92, 96, 233
Steyerl, Hito, 16, 61, 66, 76, 97–100, 102, 110, 151, 157, 174, 182, 208
Szendy, Peter, 7, 21

Talbot, Henry Fox, 6, 28, 135–7, 139, 262
Theweleit, Klaus, 89, 96

Uexküll, Jacob von, 224, 230
Umbrico, Penelope, 17, 167–8, 170–2, 182, 270

Valéry, Paul, 254
Varga, Justine, 281–2, 287
Vilanova, Oriol, 16, 114, 116, 139
Virgil, 254, 261
Virilio, Paul, 186, 188, 197, 210, 226–7, 230
Vogl, Joseph, 50, 60

Wallace, David Foster, 261
Wark, McKenzie, 246
Weber, Max, 47, 272, 288
Weizman, Eyal, 18, 76, 220, 230

Wershler, Darren, 247–8, 252
Wright, Richard, 12, 22

Zylinska, Joanna, 18, 21, 61, 76, 89, 96, 153, 155, 186, 208, 210, 241

Subject index

aerial photography, 58, 202
aesthetics, 4, 6–7, 11, 15, 17, 18, 37, 46, 50, 63, 92–3, 96, 101, 123, 129, 142, 148–50, 158, 164–7, 170, 178–9, 188, 196, 198–9, 204–5, 207, 211, 217, 227, 246, 276
affect, 10, 16, 25, 32, 35–6, 65, 78–9, 85, 88, 99, 102, 104–7, 131–2, 239
affective images, 35, 65
Anthropocene, 29, 32, 34, 46, 97, 211, 213, 225
apparatus, 10, 34, 51, 66, 70, 91, 126, 128, 142–4, 147, 150–2, 180, 194, 212–13, 224, 227, 232, 237–8, 264
archaeology, 13, 15, 27, 187, 221, 254
archive, 4–5, 13, 25, 70–1, 80, 117, 123, 129, 143, 149, 220, 224, 228, 238, 254, 263
astronomy, 11, 15, 26, 49, 53
aura, 268–9, 271, 276, 286
autographic visualisation, 18, 213–21, 224–8

bubble vision, 97–100, 102, 104–7

calculation, 4, 17, 45, 52, 194, 225
camera, 6, 11, 26, 30–1, 47, 48–9, 56, 66–7, 80, 131, 135, 141–2, 145, 147, 149–51, 174, 185–7, 194–5, 203, 207, 211–12, 216, 231, 233, 235, 237–9, 242, 264, 268, 278, 283

capitalism, 7, 12, 17, 47–54, 79, 81, 100, 104, 147, 216, 218, 236, 247, 264, 271–2, 277, 283
computational culture, 3, 17, 186
contagion, 87, 90–1, 93
cyborg, 31, 103–4

daguerreotype, 6, 263, 267, 270
DARPA, 233–4
database, 4, 14, 25–9, 38, 88, 149, 233–4
diagram, 12, 26, 29, 36, 93, 211–12, 214–15, 217, 221, 224, 226–8
digital culture, 4–5, 12, 19, 105, 141, 144–6, 152
discourse, 1, 4–7, 10–11, 14–16, 18–19, 50, 63, 73, 79, 81, 89, 91, 113, 140–1, 143, 161, 186, 199, 204–5, 207, 225, 236, 238–9, 263–4
dismeasure, 63, 66, 68, 70, 72–3
disproportion, 49–50, 55, 57, 66, 72, 74, 104

ecology, 14, 18, 28–9, 31–3, 36, 152, 197, 282
emoji, 15, 78, 84–6, 89, 92–4
epistemology, 6, 11, 14, 46, 141, 189, 225, 235, 249, 276
ethics, 37, 46, 64, 66, 72, 74, 234, 250
extension, 29, 81, 129, 185, 238, 248

facial recognition, 11, 25, 93, 205, 233
feedback, 31, 34–6, 86, 88–9
Flickr, 116, 153

genealogy, 14–15, 17, 127, 186–7, 194, 203, 205, 207, 268
geology, 53, 194, 221, 224–5, 238

hardware, 98, 100, 170, 235

imagery, 56, 85, 91–2, 123, 128, 165, 170–1, 178, 186, 216, 224, 226–7
indexicality, 216
information overload, 6
Instagram, 11, 13, 16, 25, 85, 98–9, 102–3, 105, 153, 238, 250, 268
internet, 35, 42, 98, 101–2, 104, 153, 174, 232, 234, 247, 249, 276
invisible, 25–6, 46, 50, 56–7, 65, 170, 199, 205–6, 213, 215, 232, 244, 271–2, 282
iterability, 238

kitsch, 15, 81–2, 84–6, 92

literalism, 82
Lomography, 17, 140–1, 144–52
loop, 14, 31, 34, 87–8, 91, 232

machine, 5, 15, 18–19, 25–6, 28, 32, 34, 37, 66–7, 70, 78, 86, 91, 99–100, 103–5, 107, 136, 151, 160, 178, 180, 188–9, 196–7, 199, 203, 205–6, 212–13, 217, 224–7, 232, 234–5, 237–8, 242, 244–5, 264
machine vision, 10–11, 13, 18, 186, 188–9, 205–6, 232–3, 236
metaphotographers, 144
metaphysics, 45
metapictoriality, 141, 147, 151–2
metapicture, 16, 113, 129, 143, 144, 152
microscope, 49

modernity, 45, 74, 81, 160, 211, 221, 264, 268
montage, 27, 92
multiplicity, 64, 72, 113–14, 146, 149–50, 153, 273
multitude, 6, 13–14, 113, 206

observation, 50, 72, 102, 141, 186–7, 197–8, 212, 217–18, 226–7, 273
ontology, 18, 62, 66, 68, 185, 187, 198, 204, 232, 235, 238–9, 267
operational image, 212–13, 216–20, 227–8
ornament, 236–7

parergon, 10, 236–7
perception, 31, 50–1, 63, 108, 187, 189, 198, 202–5, 232, 237–8, 268
performance, 86–7, 98, 101–2, 169, 235, 245
phototheque, 62–3, 70
political economy, 47, 203, 206, 227, 266, 272
post-lenticular, 17–18, 186, 194–6, 199, 205–6
posthuman, 189
power, 6, 15, 33–4, 48, 65, 71, 90, 93, 97–100, 106, 142–4, 147, 187, 189, 216, 218, 232, 245, 248, 264, 267, 271–2, 286

quantification, 5, 7, 15, 41, 45, 48
quantity, 4–5, 10–14, 16–19, 43–4, 74, 98–9, 116, 126, 134, 141, 150, 217, 231, 270, 278

radar, 19, 185, 187, 198–9, 203, 207
representation, 1, 4, 15, 26, 29, 33, 42, 46, 48, 51, 56, 65, 75, 79, 90, 100, 106, 129–30, 134–5, 142, 175, 179–80, 205–6, 208, 212–14, 216–20, 226–8, 235, 254, 262, 264, 277, 282

reproducibility, 6–7, 136, 271
retromodernism, 280, 283

satellite imaging, 175, 224
ScanLab, 18, 186, 195–9, 202, 205
semiotics, 252, 276, 177
simulation, 1, 28, 26–37, 207, 212, 224
social networks, 100, 104, 107, 153
software, 11–12, 30, 36, 98, 150, 175, 188, 244, 248
stereoscope, 47
strobe photography, 9
subjectivity, 4, 15, 69–70, 264, 283
surveillance, 11, 64, 106, 205, 232–3, 238, 249

symbol, 12, 31, 79, 84–6, 91, 134, 146, 150, 169–70, 181, 214, 233, 278, 282

technical media, 4, 6–7, 29, 186
technology, 32, 34, 36–7, 46, 86, 88, 91, 97, 99–100, 102–3, 106–8, 116, 128, 131, 133, 145–6, 161, 165, 167, 175, 186–7, 194, 196, 198, 205–6, 232, 234, 237, 244
telescope, 49–50, 232
transmission, 185, 196, 207
transparency, 4, 91, 117, 165, 175, 232, 235

Umwelt, 224

visibility, 4, 11, 49–51, 57–8, 100, 108, 198, 206, 217, 236–7, 283

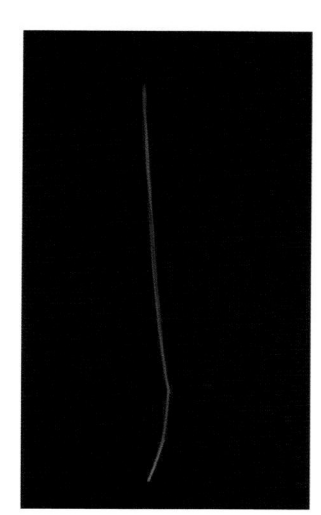

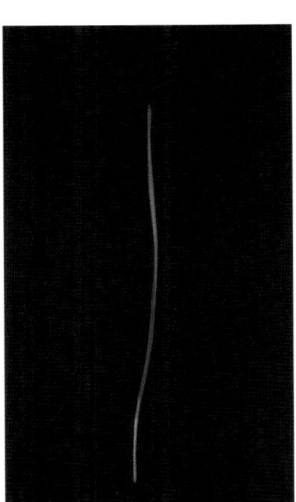

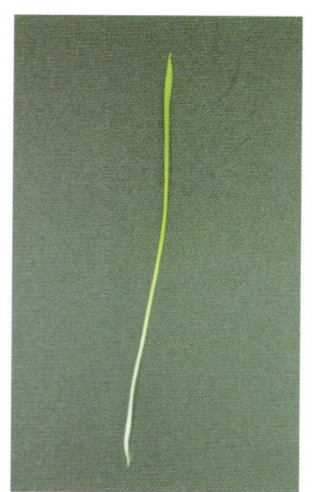